The Illusion
of
Statehood

Perceptions of Catalan Independence
up to the End of the Spanish Civil War

The Cañada Blanch / Sussex Academic Studies on Contemporary Spain

General Editor: Professor Paul Preston, London School of Economics

A list of all published titles in the series is available on the Press website. More recently published works are presented below.

Concha Alborg, *My Mother, That Stranger: Letters from the Spanish Civil War.*

Peter Anderson, *Friend or Foe?: Occupation, Collaboration and Selective Violence in the Spanish Civil War.*

Germà Bel, *Disdain, Distrust, and Dissolution: The Surge of Support for Independence in Catalonia.*

Carl-Henrik Bjerström, *Josep Renau and the Politics of Culture in Republican Spain, 1931–1939: Re-imagining the Nation.*

Claudio Hernández Burgos (ed.), *Ruptura: The Impact of Nationalism and Extremism on Daily Life in the Spanish Civil War (1936–1939).*

Darryl Burrowes, *Historians at War: Cold War Influences on Anglo-American Representations of the Spanish Civil War.*

Andrew Canessa (ed.), *Barrier and Bridge: Spanish and Gibraltarian Perspectives on Their Border.*

Kathryn Crameri, *'Goodbye, Spain?': The Question of Independence for Catalonia.*

Pol Dalmau, *Press, Politics and National Identities in Catalonia: The Transformation of* La Vanguardia, *1881–1931.*

Mark Derby, *Petals and Bullets: Dorothy Morris – A New Zealand Nurse in the Spanish Civil War.*

Francisco Espinosa-Maestre, S*hoot the Messenger?: Spanish Democracy and the Crimes of Francoism – From the Pact of Silence to the Trial of Baltasar Garzón.*

María Jesús González, *Raymond Carr: The Curiosity of the Fox.*

Helen Graham, *The War and its Shadow: Spain's Civil War in Europe's Long Twentieth Century.*

Arnau Gonzàlez i Vilalta (ed.), *The Illusion of Statehood: Perceptions of Catalan Independence up to the End of the Spanish Civil War.*

Xabier A. Irujo, GERNIKA: Genealogy of a Lie.

Mandie Iveson, *Language Attitudes, National Identity and Migration in Catalonia: 'What the Women Have to Say'*

Angela Jackson, *'For us it was Heaven': The Passion, Grief and Fortitude of Patience Darton – From the Spanish Civil War to Mao's China.*

Gabriel Jackson, *Juan Negrín: Physiologist, Socialist and Spanish Republican War Leader.*

Nathan Jones, *The Adoption of a Pro-US Foreign Policy by Spain and the United Kingdom: José María Aznar and Tony Blair's Personal Motivations and their Global Impact.*

Xavier Moreno Juliá, *The Blue Division: Spanish Blood in Russia, 1941–1945.*

David Lethbridge, *Norman Bethune in Spain: Commitment, Crisis, and Conspiracy.*

Antonio Miguez Macho, *The Genocidal Genealogy of Francoism: Violence, Memory and Impunity.*

Carles Manera, *The Great Recession: A Subversive View.*

Nicholas Manganas, *Las dos Españas: Terror and Crisis in Contemporary Spain.*

Jorge Marco, *Guerrilleros and Neighbours in Arms: Identities and Cultures of Antifascist Resistance in Spain.*

Emily Mason, *Democracy, Deeds and Dilemmas: Support for the Spanish Republic within British Civil Society, 1936–1939.*

Soledad Fox Maura, *Jorge Semprún: The Spaniard who Survived the Nazis and Conquered Paris.*

Martin Minchom, *Spain's Martyred Cities: From the Battle of Madrid to Picasso's* Guernica.

Olivia Muñoz-Rojas, *Ashes and Granite: Destruction and Reconstruction in the Spanish Civil War and Its Aftermath.*

Linda Palfreeman, *Spain Bleeds: The Development of Battlefield Blood Transfusion during the Civil War.*

Fernando Puell de la Villa and David García Hernán (eds.), *War and Population Displacement: Lessons of History.*

Rúben Serém, *Conspiracy, Coup d'état and Civil War in Seville, 1936–1939: History and Myth in Francoist Spain.*

Maggie Torres, *Anarchism and Political Change in Spain: Schism, Polarisation and Reconstruction of the* Confederación Nacional del Trabajo, *1939–1979.*

Dacia Viejo-Rose, *Reconstructing Spain: Reconstructing Spain: Cultural Heritage and Memory after Civil War.*

Antoni Vives, *SMART CITY Barcelona: The Catalan Quest to Improve Future Urban Living.*

The Illusion
of
Statehood

Perceptions of Catalan Independence
up to the End of the Spanish Civil War

Edited by **Arnau Gonzàlez i Vilalta**

Translated from the Catalan by **Enric Ucelay-Da Cal**

sussex
ACADEMIC
PRESS
Brighton • Chicago • Toronto

Generalitat de Catalunya
**Departament d'Acció Exterior,
Relacions Institucionals i Transparència**

2 4 6 8 10 9 7 5 3 1

First published 2020 in Great Britain by
SUSSEX ACADEMIC PRESS
PO Box 139
Eastbourne BN24 9BP

Distributed in North America by
Independent Publishers Group
814 N. Franklin Street
Chicago, IL 60610

Published in collaboration with the Cañada Blanch Centre for Contemporary Spanish Studies, and The Catalan Observatory, London School of Economics.

Publication of this work has been supported by Memorial Democràtic de la Generalitat de Catalunya, the Departament d'Acció Exterior de la Generalitat, whose respective logos appear on the title page and cover; and the research group Hispona of the Universidade de Santiago de Compostela.

British Library Cataloguing in Publication Data
A CIP catalogue record for this book is available from the British Library.

Library of Congress Cataloging-in-Publication Data
To be applied for.

Hardcover ISBN 978-1-78976-032-3
Paperback ISBN 978-1-78976-034-7

Typeset & designed by Sussex Academic Press, Brighton & Eastbourne.
Printed by TJ International, Padstow, Cornwall.

Contents

The Cañada Blanch Centre for Contemporary Spanish Studies

In the 1960s, the most important initiative in the cultural and academic relations between Spain and the United Kingdom was launched by a Valencian fruit importer in London. The creation by Vicente Cañada Blanch of the Anglo-Spanish Cultural Foundation has subsequently benefited large numbers of Spanish and British scholars at various levels. Thanks to the generosity of Vicente Cañada Blanch, thousands of Spanish schoolchildren have been educated at the secondary school in West London that bears his name. At the same time, many British and Spanish university students have benefited from the exchange scholarships which fostered cultural and scientific exchanges between the two countries. Some of the most important historical, artistic and literary work on Spanish topics to be produced in Great Britain was initially made possible by Cañada Blanch scholarships.

Vicente Cañada Blanch was, by inclination, a conservative. When his Foundation was created, the Franco regime was still in the plenitude of its power. Nevertheless, the keynote of the Foundation's activities was always a complete open-mindedness on political issues. This was reflected in the diversity of research projects supported by the Foundation, many of which, in Francoist Spain, would have been regarded as subversive. When the Dictator died, Don Vicente was in his seventy-fifth year. In the two decades following the death of the Dictator, although apparently indestructible, Don Vicente was obliged to husband his energies. Increasingly, the work of the Foundation was carried forward by Miguel Dols whose tireless and imaginative work in London was matched in Spain by that of José María Coll Comín. They were united in the Foundation's spirit of open-minded commitment to fostering research of high quality in pursuit of better Anglo-Spanish cultural relations. Throughout the 1990s, thanks to them, the role of the Foundation grew considerably.

In 1994, in collaboration with the London School of Economics, the Foundation established the Príncipe de Asturias Chair of Contemporary Spanish History and the Cañada Blanch Centre for Contemporary Spanish Studies. It is the particular task of the Cañada Blanch Centre for Contemporary Spanish Studies to promote the understanding of twentieth-century Spain through research and teaching of contemporary Spanish history, politics, economy, sociology and culture. The Centre possesses a valuable library and archival centre for specialists in contemporary Spain. This work is carried on through the publications of the doctoral and post-doctoral researchers at the Centre itself and through the many seminars and lectures held at the London School of Economics. While the seminars are the province of the researchers, the lecture cycles have been the forum in which Spanish politicians have been able to address audiences in the United Kingdom.

Since 1998, the Cañada Blanch Centre has published a substantial number of books in collaboration with several different publishers on the subject of contemporary Spanish history and politics. An extremely fruitful partnership with Sussex Academic Press began in 2004. Full details and descriptions of the published works can be found on the Press website.

An ongoing interest of the series has been the tension between Catalonia and the political establishment in Madrid over the last one hundred and forty years. The relationship in the late nineteenth century was dealt with in Pol Dalmau's analysis of the key political role of the principal Barcelona newspaper *La Vanguardia*. The recent resurgence of independence sentiment in Catalonia has given rise to several volumes. These have ranged from Ramon Tremosa on the Catalan economy; to Germà Bel both on the damage done to the Spanish economy by the country's dysfunctional transport and communications model and on the ever-intensifying scale of inter-regional distrust; and by Andrew Dowling and by Kathryn Crameri on the development of Catalan independence sentiment. Looking beyond the present, Antoni Vives' *SMART CITY Barcelona: The Catalan Quest to Improve Future Urban Living* was an investigation into ways in which life in our clogged and faceless cities can use digital technology to accommodate the needs of communities and individuals by improving all kinds of services ranging from public transport and recreational space, to waste collection and recycling; and most fundamentally acting positively and humanely toward the elderly and disadvantaged.

Oddly, in a series rich in works about Catalonia and also about the Spanish Civil War, with the exception of the studies by Olivia Muñoz-Rojas and Davia Viejo-Rose on reconstruction after the conflict, there has been a lacuna regarding the impact of the war on Catalonia. This is an issue not only in the Cañada Blanch series. In the historiography of Catalan nationalism, the period during which Catalonia enjoyed the highest level of autonomy, that of the Spanish Civil War, has received far less attention than the notorious issue of anarchist revolution. The essay collection edited by Arnau González now fills the gap with great distinction. Together, the component chapters constitute a hugely impressive contribution to the history of both Catalan nationalism and of the wider Spanish Civil War.

Series Editor's Preface by Paul Preston

In the long history of Catalan nationalism, it is curious that the period during which Catalonia enjoyed the highest level of autonomy, the years of the Spanish Civil War, is perhaps the least known. The present volume, with four major contributions from Catalan historians and a fifth from a Galician scholar, fills the gap with a remarkable combination of erudition and originality.

From the middle of the nineteenth century there was a revival of Catalan literature and of the language whose official use had been prohibited since the eighteenth century. Another factor driving resentment of Madrid was the lack of Catalan influence on the central government. Between 1833 and 1901, 902 men held ministerial office. Only 24 of them, 2.6 per cent of the total, were Catalan. Catalanist sentiment existed particularly in the rural areas where the language still flourished. However, perhaps more influentially, in Barcelona, it found enthusiastic adherents among the wealthy upper-middle classes. In 1892, a loose federation of middle- and upper-class Catalanist groups formed the Unió Catalanista. Its programme, known as the Bases de Manresa, called for the restoration of an autonomous government, a separate tax system, the protection of Catalan industry and the institution of Catalan as an official language. Spain's defeat at the hands of the United States in 1898 and the consequent loss of Cuba, a valuable market for Catalan goods, fostered further ill-will towards Madrid and fostered the growth of the conservative independence party, the Lliga Regionalista. Measures adopted by the central Government to pay off the war debt provoked a taxpayers strike in Catalonia, the so-called *tancament de caixes*, shop closures and riots. Tension would intensify as the Army assuaged the guilt of an ignominious defeat by concentrating its anger on Catalonia.

The officer corps became obsessed with the defence of national

unity and the existing social order and thus was increasingly hostile
both to the left and to the regional Nationalists. The military attitude
to Catalanism bordered on racism. Catalans were denounced as
cowardly traitors and misers. The anti-Semitic right frequently
described Catalans as 'the Jews of Spain'. In a similar vein, *La
Correspondencia Militar*, a newspaper that claimed to represent Army
officers, demanded that Catalan, and Basque, nationalists be forced
from the country: 'Let them wander the world, without a fatherland,
like the cursed race of the Jews. Let this be an eternal punishment.'
Regarding Cuba as simply an overseas part of the Patria, the right
saw its loss as a diminution of the nation. For many officers, the
burgeoning Catalan and Basque nationalist movements were intoler-
able threats comparable to the Cuban independence movement.
Moreover, military ambitions to rebuild the armed forces and
regenerate Spain would be fatally undermined if Catalonia's wealth
and its tax revenue were lost.

In revenge for a cartoon mocking military incompetence in the
satirical magazine *¡Cu-cut!*, on the night of 25 November 1905 three
hundred armed officers in uniform assaulted both the printing presses
and offices of *¡Cu-cut!* and the offices of Lliga's daily newspaper *La
Veu de Catalunya*. Forty-six people were seriously injured. This was
merely the most violent of attacks on newspapers and magazines that
had criticised the Army. The *¡Cu-Cut!* incident and the Barcelona
garrison's indiscipline were celebrated by both the high command
and the King himself. When parliamentary deputies debated their
response, the garrison of Madrid threatened to assault the Cortes.
Under the banner headline 'The Army in Defence of the Fatherland',
La Correspondencia Militar demanded that 'Catalan deputies and senators be immediately expelled from the Parliament'. Military pressure,
with the support of the King, saw the introduction of the so-called
'Law of Jurisdictions' making civilians subject to military justice in
all matters relating to the Armed Forces.

In response to the passing of the Law, a broad coalition of
Catalanist parties came together to create Solidaritat Catalana. Given
its internal right-left contradictions, Solidaritat Catalana would last
for barely four years. Nevertheless, its creation marked the beginning
of effective Catalan nationalism. In the elections of April 1907,
Catalanists won forty-one of the possible forty-four seats. However,

the central weakness of conservative nationalism was soon exposed. Fearful of the growing strength of the working class, the Lliga Regionalista subordinated its Catalanist aspirations to its need for military support. In 1923, when the would-be dictator, Miguel Primo de Rivera, set off for Madrid to take power, hundreds of industrialists were at the station to cheer him.

The principal organizations of Catalan industrialists and landowners made ecstatic declarations of support for the new regime. In a series of secret meetings with the top brass of the Lliga Regionalista and the industrialists' organization, the Foment de Treball, Primo had made explicit promises that, once in power, he would expand Catalan autonomy in return for their support for his coup. Primo's pro-Catalanism was merely a device to secure support for his plans. He could never have sold Catalan autonomy to the rest of the army. He moved against all regional nationalisms within days of taking power with a decree ordering that only the Spanish flag could be flown on public buildings and that, in public events and in schools, only Castilian Spanish could be used. The Basque Partido Nacionalista Vasco was banned and in Catalonia, the militant nationalist parties, Estat Català and Acció Catalana, were dissolved. The Catalan half of bilingual street signs removed. Primo declared that of the 'crimes' of syndicalism, communism and separatism, the latter was the worst.

The anti-Catalan measures of the regime saw the nationalist banner pass to more radical groups led by an ex-military engineer, Colonel Francesc Macià. A practising Catholic and by nature conservative, Macià had become a fervent nationalist in reaction to perceived betrayals by Madrid. With the Lliga Regionalista debilitated by the anti-Catalan policies of the regime, in mid-March 1931 the principal left Catalanist groups, Acció Catalana and Estat Català, united in Esquerra Republicana de Catalunya under Francesc Macià and Lluís Companys. In the municipal elections of 12 April 1931, in Barcelona, a wide coalition of the Catalan left, led by Macià and Companys, enjoyed an overwhelming triumph. The Lliga Regionalista was soundly defeated.

After the victory for the Esquerra Republicana de Catalunya on 14 April Lluís Companys proclaimed the Republic. Shortly after, Macià declared an independent Catalan republic under his Presidency. In previous, and indeed later, times, such situations led to bloody confrontation. Now, a peaceful resolution was negotiated by a deputation of three ministers from Madrid, Fernando de los Ríos (Justice) and two Catalans, Marcelino Domingo (Education) and Lluís Nicolau d'Olwer (Economy). Their suggestion that the Catalan administration be given the symbolic title of the old medieval government, the Generalitat, and the promise of a rapid statute of autonomy, persuaded Macià to make what he described as 'the greatest sacrifice of my life'. Macià was the President of the Generalitat until his death in December 1933. He was succeeded by Companys.

The very idea of a Statute of Autonomy was regarded by the Army and the conservative classes as an attack on national unity. In the Cortes, the Republican Prime Minister, Manuel Azaña, had to deal with the filibustering of around forty right-wing deputies and thirty Radicals who tabled two hundred amendments. A boycott of Catalan products was mounted in the Castilian provinces. In fact, the statute of Catalan autonomy finally approved in September 1932 was far from maximalist. Nevertheless, the right portrayed Azaña as determined to destroy Spanish unity.

On 6 October 1934, a perceived take-over of the Republic by the right saw miners in Asturias seize power and, in Barcelona, in an attempt to outflank extreme Catalan nationalists Companys proclaimed an independent state of Catalonia 'within the Federal Republic of Spain' in protest against what was perceived as the betrayal of the Republic. The rebellion of the Generalitat was doomed when Companys refused to arm the workers. Bloodshed was avoided by the moderation of both Companys and General Domingo Batet, commander of the Catalan military region. Batet employed great restraint in restoring the authority of the central government. He ordered his men to be 'deaf, dumb and blind' in the face of provocation. Nevertheless, Companys was arrested and remained in prison until after the Popular Front elections of February 1936.

The military coup of July 1936 led to the collapse of the apparatus of the Spanish state. This in turn led to the Generalitat being able to achieve unprecedented autonomy. Nevertheless, as president, Companys was severely constrained by the power of the anarchist movement, which had played a key role in defeating the military coup. That coup was motived by a desire to put an end to the social reforms of the Second Republic – agrarian reform, women's rights, education and regional autonomies. What happened subsequently in Barcelona overshadowed the determination of the military rebels to crush nationalism. The attention of historians has been monopolised by consideration of the impact on the war effort against Franco's military rebels of the revolutionary ambitions of the anarchist CNT-FAI and the more-or-less Trotskyist Partido Obrero Unificación Marxista (POUM). The achievement of the present volume is to rectify the consequent gaps in the historiography.

The book opens with a geographically and chronologically historical introduction by Enric Ucelay-Da Cal, impressively wide-ranging in its erudition. His chapter is followed by that of Xosé Manoel Nuñez Seixas, who provides a scholarly account of how Catalonia, its quest for political autonomy and the different currents of Catalan nationalism, fitted into a wider European context of the dissolution of the Russian, Austro-Hungarian, Ottoman multinational empires. In consequence, he makes fascinating comparisons of the Catalan experience with the cases of Ireland, Norway, Hungary, Alsace-Lorraine and Flanders.

The heart of the volume is Arnau Gonzàlez i Vilalta's 'A Most Uncomfortable Issue: The Independence of Catalonia as a European Geopolitical Concern (1936–1939)'. Itself of book-length at nearly 150 pages, it constitutes a profound account of the role of Catalonia in the Spanish Civil War seen through international reactions to Catalan nationalism. Both Fascist Italy and Nazi Germany were determined that Catalonia should not become independent and move into the orbit of France. Arnau Gonzàlez demonstrates how the widespread revolutionary violence that greeted the military coup, and what it meant in terms of the loss of state control, could have been a step towards Catalan independence.

In the vacuum created by the military coup, the Generalitat was able to occupy the space left by the Republic's administrative structures, and thus move towards its own statehood. Control of the borders, of its military and its finance all seemed to be key steps towards secession. However, the same dilemma that had dampened the nationalist fervour of the Lliga Regionallista now afflicted Companys. In attempting to control the revolution carried out by the anarchists of the CNT-FAI, the Generalitat seized many of the powers of the State within Catalonia but feared to go further because it needed the support of the Central government against the revolutionaries. The threat of the anarchists and the POUM put an end to Companys's ambitions of independence as, long before, it had those of the erstwhile strongman of Catalan nationalism, Francesc Cambó. Now, Cambó had no hesitation about putting economic factors before nationalist sentiment and actively supported Franco on many levels. On hearing news of the military coup, he stated: 'Those with money should give it and those of military age should fight.' Placed at the disposal of the rebels, his considerable fortune financed both a hugely influential pro-rebel propaganda operation in Paris and a rebel espionage service.

The transfer from Valencia to Barcelona of the Spanish Republican government under the Socialist Juan Negrín at the end of 1937 had the twofold purpose of removal from Franco's threat against Valencia and of re-establishing control over Catalonia. Well-founded rumours that the Generalitat was negotiating with representatives of Franco to prevent the war from reaching Catalonia were inevitably disturbing for Negrín. As early as February 1937, there was talk of the Generalitat seeking British and French mediation to end the war, establishing a federal Spain after the revolutionary forces were crushed by the forces of the

Generalitat along with a settlement with Franco. Just over one year later, more rumours surfaced that, in response to the anticipated invasion of Catalonia by Franco's forces, the Generalitat would try to "dissociate" itself from the governmental cause, proclaiming, in one form or another, its annexation to France. Arnau González disentangles these complex processes on the basis of painstaking research in the archives of several countries.

Equally fascinating is the analysis of the Soviet approach to Catalonia by Josep Puigsech Farràs. In October 1936, a sympathetic Russian gesture was seen in the appointment of Vladimir Antonov-Ovseyenko as consul general in Barcelona. Antonov-Ovseyenko was a legendary Bolshevik who had led the forces of the Revolutionary Military Committee that stormed the Winter Palace in Petrograd. Drawing on the Russian experience, he was sympathetic to Catalan aspirations, but was obliged to put forward the official Soviet defence of the Central government. Dr Puigsech shows how, despite his immense popularity, Antonov-Ovseyenko's was constrained by Soviet disquiet about the power of the anarcho-syndicalist movement in the Catalan rearguard. Soviet policy would never question the model of state unity of the Spanish Republic. Moreover, in September 1937, Antonov-Ovseyenko was replaced by Alexei Strakhov, a bureaucrat hostile to nationalism.

The study by Josep Sánchez Cervelló presents an even-handed analysis of the attitude to Catalonia of the Spanish Republican state. He evaluates the hostility generated by awareness of the desire of Catalan and Basque nationalists to achieve a separate peace behind the back of the Republic. He demonstrates the parallel diplomacy pursued by both the Partido Nacionalista Vasco and the Generalitat, and their endeavour to secure British mediation with Franco for a separate peace. The chapters make compelling reading of issues surrounding European statehood. Herewith an immensely important and original contribution to the history of both Catalan nationalism and of the Spanish Civil War.

Volume Editor's Preface by Arnau Gonzàlez i Vilalta

During the 1930s, as the complex context of postwar Europe disintegrated, Catalonia and its autonomy became the object of a truly remarkable level of outside attention. Autonomous Catalonia formed an integral part of the Second Spanish Republic. Spain had a historic reputation for disorder during the nineteenth century, but the easy change in 1931 from monarchy to republic, from military dictatorship to a parliamentary system based on universal suffrage (for both men and women), made the country seem stable, at least in appearance, by comparison to events elsewhere. The good impression did not last.

In particular, the Catalan capital, Barcelona, had a quite a long-standing repute for trouble. Foreign observers usually had a smattering of knowledge of Spanish affairs, but still less about Catalan matters. Without clear distinctions, everything that happened in Barcelona in the 1920s and 1930s would be seen as a translation of ongoing continental change: there was the looming contagion from the "red" East, from the Bolshevik Revolution begun in 1917, to which could be added lesser equivalencies regarding the collapse of the "central empires" and the rise of the "successor States" with their debated borders after 1918, as well as the impression made on Catalan nationalists by the creation of the Irish Free State in 1921. Similarly, the passing discharges of tense trends coming from French, German, Italian or even Belgian policies offered easy analogies. Inserted within the framework of the Second Spanish Republic, for foreign observers, whether they were diplomats or journalists, the political evolution of Catalonia – and responses from the rest of Spain – would not cease to be a true reflection of the European events and the increasingly dangerous local problems, moment by moment, crisis by crisis. Inversely, any analysis of a specifically Catalan socio-political evolution, when presented by itself, if seen as the main focus of instability in Spain, would lead to a series of mis-judgements between the generic European standard and the specific reality of that territory.

Admittedly, local politics in Catalonia was not easy to follow, even from Madrid. Non-State nationalisms were especially compli-cated to understand, with their multiple contradictions. Until after the German defeat in 1918, the dominant pattern for dissident or protest nationalisms was monarchist, like the State-system of the whole of Europe except France. The Paris Peace of 1919, with American input added to the French, changed all that: the "Successor States" established after the Great War were republics, except expanded Serbia, the so-called "Kingsom of Serbs, Croats and Slovenes", soon to become Yugoslavia. But the ideological confrontations of the postwar years, the struggle between "reds" and "whites", between communists and fascists, intoxicated the minorities, with varying impact. In Catalonia, especially in the mid-1930s, outsiders saw "Catalan fascism" all over the political scene, when such really never existed: there were numerous indi-vidual fascists – admirers of Mussolini, germanophiles – but these were all personalities with perhaps a small circle around them, but not political parties of clear significance and or forces which expressed their sympathies with no ambiguity.[1] Outsiders traced the easiest, simplest scheme: if nationalism was deeply-felt and lusty in making itself heard, then – in the 1930s – the logical outcome was fascism, or something very similar. Such was not the case. In general terms, Catalan secessionism was on the revolu-tionary left, not the radical right. In Catalonia, those deeply afraid of leftist upheaval looked to the Spanish army, strongly steeped in militarism. And those who wanted a stronger Catalonia needed a weak Spain, a feeble central State.

Nothing of all this was clear for outside onlookers. Foreign spec-tators wanted simple logic: if Catalan nationalism was robust and loud, and if the logical conclusion of nationalism was independ-ence, then there had to be a substantial – if not overwhelming – opinion in favor of separation from Spain. Seen in local terms, this was not the case. Autonomy, doubtlessly with well reinforced powers (it was hoped), was the absolute trend of Catalan politics.

The idea was sustained from the Esquerra Republicana (ERC, or Republican Left) in control of the self-government, the Generalitat consubstantial with the Republic, to the conservative *Lliga* (the "Regionalist League", converted in 1933 to the "Catalan League"). All the parties represented in the Catalan Parliament were autonomist, and thought out their policies in such terms. How such sentiment was understood in Madrid or elsewhere in Spain was a different matter.

But, after the late summer of 1932, Spanish politics became increasingly more unsettled, when the right attempted to overthrow the government. Then the left, having lost the elections in late 1933, rose up in revolt in the following year and failed. One center of the uprising was Barcelona, with the full implication of the Catalan government, which was tried, and sentenced to prison terms (except for one councillor of the Generalitat – Josep Dencàs – who managed to escape). The attempt at a Republic leaning rightward was unsuccessful. The February 1936 general elections brought the Popular Front to power in Spain (the *"Front d'Esquerres"* in Catalonia). President Lluís Companys and his government were released and returned to govern in Barcelona, with the exception of the ultra-nationalist councillor who bolted for exile, and was blamed for the 1934 revolt in Catalonia. In short, the republican years were marked by parallel politics, between Madrid, on the one hand, and, inferior in status, Barcelona, on the other. All of this was often hard to grasp from abroad.

In this sense, when the Spanish Civil War broke out in the summer of 1936, there was a ready-made and insistent analysis, in circulation since 1931. All international observers tended to express the absolute conviction that Catalonia soon would become an independent Republic. Diplomats said so, in a secret way in their reports. In public, journalists speculated about the probability. Both put the "Catalan question" in a European key, and transferred the realities of Central, Eastern and Balkan Europe after 1918 into a Catalan context. Because Catalonia had a language different from Castilian Spanish, a published culture of its own, with autonomous government institutions, a nationalist movement, and a powerful and modern economy centered on a large and growing metropolis, why should the Catalans not tread the path of

Finland, Poland, Czechoslovakia or Ireland? If Catalonia was small, so were each of the Baltic Republics.

Why not try to take advantage of the context of the Civil War to become independent? Why could it not play the card of its geostrategic position in the western Mediterranean in the context of a tense Europe? Would the Catalans do so in a democratic way? What would the Spanish Republic answer? And the military rebels of general Franco? Would Catalonia go behind the Soviet model, dragged by its proletariat? In any case, diplomats, from the Foreign Office to Quai d'Orsay, from the Palazzo Chigi or the Wilhelmstrasse, from the Vatican to lesser chancellories, all seemed to expect the same result. In sum, everyone thought that Catalan independence could be achieved, that it would be done, and that a new Catalan Republic would have immediate effects on the policies of the different powers, and on international relations in general.[2]

But where were the thousands of Catalan volunteers, presumably well-equipped and even trained, ready to take on general Franco's Spanish forces, his Italian allies and his German auxiliaries? In the summer of 1936, the Generalitat's amphibious assault on Mallorca was a miserable failure, but the government in Madrid could be blamed for the withdrawal. The attack from Barcelona on rebel Saragossa, also that summer, was quickly mired and stopped, until the Aragon front crumbled in the Spring of 1938. The republican counter-attack across the Ebro river in the summer of 1938 showed the limits of any serious offensive based on Catalan resources. During the succeeding autumn and winter, the Franco forces brushed aside any resistance. Barcelona fell without a fight in January 1939. By early February 1939, the French border was reached, as the Republican Popular Army was routed.

In the revolutionary heat of 1936, as churches set to the torch blazed and there was chaos in cities and towns, many Catalan nationalists – Lliga conservatives, but also militants of the ERC, and Catalan radical nationalists – were forced to flee, by sea in an international rescue operation, or, if they had no other solution, over the Pyrenees mountains. Burnt out by their experience, many refugees thought about the urgent need to stop the revolution, and condemned Catalan president Companys' method of manipulating the exaltation of the extremist labour movement, anarcho-syndicalist and socialist revolutionary. So there were individuals – with official credentials from the Catalan government, but perhaps not authorized to take the steps they took – who sought out political and diplomatic contacts among representatives of the major powers – France, Great Britain, Italy, but also the Vatican – to try and find a way out of what they considered to be the destruction of traditional Catalan society but also the evident and upcoming defeat of the Spanish Republic. Their hope was to exit the conflict with a proviso in favour of some sort of autonomy for Catalonia and the Basque Country, perhaps at the expense of the republican cause. The persistent hopes and sometimes the utter lack of realism of these initiatives was the Catalan reverse side of the mirror to the outside perception of a possible independence.

Because the proclamation of Catalan independence did not occur, either in 1936 or in 1938–1939, it is easy to summarize the contacts and the illusion of statehood for Catalonia as a misfire, as a non-performance: the exterior gaze did not go into the detail of Catalan politics. *Diplomats and newspaper correspondents on the scene took too many statements of bravado at face value and did not perceive that, in fact, there were almost no "independentists", but an abundance of Catalan nationalists lacking any vocation of separation with respect to Spain.*

Put briefly, there was a foreign misconception about Catalonia, a fallacy that perhaps could be coupled with some of the hopes bred among the ranks of Catalan nationalists. *The mirage of Catalonia – for the implicated in the 1936–1939 war, the envoys and the reporters, the "contacts" and the spies, as well as the ideological tourists, the indifferent sightseers, the chance onlookers – was not to attend to the contradictory details of a specific case, but, rather, to rely on creeds and alignments, or to ignore the complexity and leave the comprehension of Catalan specificity to vague generalities and continental guidelines.* Hence the surprise of foreign commentators that Catalan nationalists did not take advantage of the Spanish crisis to try to create their own State.

This "mirror game" between the outside and inside views of Catalan independence, and their interaction, is the subject of this book. The work presents articles that analyze the international context of the illusion of statehood that marked Catalan nationalism and its corresponding diplomacy. Prof. Enric Ucelay-Da Cal (Universitat Pompeu Fabra, Barcelona) reviews the processes and patterns of secession in Europe and America before 1931, focusing on the dilemma of the nationalist movements between monarchist or republican models. There follows an interpretative analysis regarding the different approaches applied to the management of national conflicts in the Europe of the 1930s by Prof. Xosé M. Núñez Seixas (formerly of the Ludwig-Maximilian Universität in Munich, now at Universidade de Santiago de Compostela). Thereafter, as editor of the volume (Prof. Arnau Gonzàlez i Vilalta, Universitat Autònoma de Barcelona), I provide the longest and most detailed text, around which the volume is built. *The Illusion of Statehood* was orginally written in Catalan, as the catalogue for a historical exhibition held in Barcelona between 2017 and 2018.[3] My own chapter is complemented, in an indispensable way, by the contribution of Prof. Josep Puigsech Farràs (Universitat Autònoma de Barcelona) on the perspectives of Soviet diplomacy regarding the Catalan national conflict. In the same way that, from the British context, Prof. Josep Sánchez Cervelló (Universitat Rovira i Virgili, Tarragona) presents a study on the attempts by delegates from the Catalan government in London to interest the British government in fostering peace negotiations in which Catalonia would eventually become some sort of "Free State" within a Federal Spain.

For the reader who does not know the Catalan language, a warning is necessary. In the translation of all the articles in this book, Catalan political terms – words like "catalanisme" and "catalanista", or "independentista" – with subtle gradations of meaning and which lack easy equivalents in English-language dictionaries, have been simplified in a generic usage: "Catalan nationalism". Both the editor and translator agree that it should be pointed out that current Catalan politics make this expression debatable in local parlance. Furthermore we note that surnames in Catalan are still often (but not always) separated by a conjunction ("i", meaning "and"), as formerly also used to be done at times in Castilian. This habit has been suppressed in the text to avoid misunderstanding, as sometimes such double and conjoined surnames can be misread as two separate persons.

Lastly, I cannot help but explicitly thank some of the persons who have made possible the appearance of the following work in English. First of all, my heartfelt thanks to to Plàcid Garcia-Planas for having promoted the initial project from which this volume is derived. In addition, I am deeply grateful to Prof. Paul Preston (London School of Economics) for his interest and help. No less important is my indebtedness to Prof. Enric Ucelay-Da Cal, for the translation into English of all the articles, and a general acknowledgement to Dorsey Boatwright for her assistance.

MONTORNÈS DEL VALLÈS, BARCELONA
May 5, 2019

Notes

1 Enric Ucelay-Da Cal, Arnau Gonzàlez Vilalta, Xosé Manoel Núñez Seixas (eds.), *El catalanisme davant del feixisme (1919–2018)*, Maçanet de la Selva, Gregal, 2018.

2 See the forthcoming work: A. Gonzàlez i Vilalta, *Cataluña y Barcelona en la crisis europea (1931–1939). ¿Irlanda española, peón francés o URSS mediterránea?*, Maçanet de la Selva, Gregal, pending publication.

3 This volume was published in Catalan as a complementary catalogue to the exhibition *Une Catalogne indépendante? European Geopolitics and the Spanish Civil War (1936–1939)*, curated by Prof. Arnau Gonzàlez i Vilalta at the Democratic Memorial of Barcelona (September 2017–June 2018).

List of Abbreviations

Archives

ASDN, Archives de la Société des Nations, Geneva.

CICR, Archives du Comité International Croix-Rouge, Geneva.

ACBB, Archives du Consulat de la Belgique à Barcelone, Barcelona.

ASPFAE, Archives du Service public fédéral des affaires étrangères, Brussels.

AFS, Archives Fédérales Suisses, Berne.

ACS, Archivio Centrale dello Stato, Rome.

ASG, Archivio di Stato di Genova, Genoa.

ASV, Archivio Segreto Vaticano, Ciudad del Vaticano.

ASMAE, Archivio Storico Ministero degli Affari Esteri, Rome.

AGMA, Archivo General Militar de Ávila, Ávila.

AMAE, Archivo del Ministerio de Asuntos Exteriores, Madrid.

ANV, Archivo del Nacionalismo Vasco, Bilbao.

AHMREA, Archivo Histórico Ministerio de Relaciones Exteriores y Culto de Argentina, Buenos Aires.

AHD, Arquivo Histórico Diplomático, Lisboa.

AGGV, Arxiu Arnau Gonzàlez i Vilalta, Montornès del Vallès.

AMTM, Arxiu Montserrat Tarradellas i Macià, Monestir de Poblet.

ANC, Arxiu Nacional de Catalunya, Sant Cugat del Vallès.

CADN, Centre des Archives Diplomatiques de Nantes, Nantes.

IA-AHDMRE, Instituto Artigas, Archivo Histórico Diplomático del Ministerio de Relaciones Exteriores del Uruguay, Montevideo.

IISH, International Institute of Social History, Amsterdam

NA, National Archives, Kew, London.

NARA, National Archives and Records Administration, Washington D.C.

PAAA, Politisches Archiv Auswaertiges Amt, Berlin.

USMMI, Ufficio Storico Marina Militare Italiana, Rome.

USSME, Uficcio Storico dello Stato Maggiore dell'Esercito, Rome.

Political Organizations

ACR, Acció Catalana Republicana (Catalan Republican Action, moderate nationalist party).

CGT, Confédération Générale du Travail (French national labour union center traditionally linked to the communists).

CNT, Confederación Nacional del Trabajo (Spanish anarcho-syndicalist labour union confederation).

EC, Estat Català (Catalan State, separatist organization led by Francesc Macià, 1922–1931; a separatist party founded in 1936).

ERC, Esquerra Republicana de Catalunya (lierally Republican Left of Catalonia, dominant Catalan political party under the Second Spanish Republic).

FAI, Federación Anarquista Ibérica (Iberian Anarchist federation, coordinating organization of anarchist groups in Spain and Portugal).

FE, Falange Española (Spanish fascist party, founded in 1933).

FET-JONS, Falange Española Tradicionalista y de las JONS (Franco's official "National Movement", Spain's single party under his regime).

FRF, Fédération Régionaliste Française (French Regionalist Federation, an umbrella organisation for French regionalist formations, founded in 1900)

IRA, Irish Republican Army

JEREC, Joventuts d'Esquerra Republicana-Estat Català (literally Youth of Republican Left-Catalan State, nationalist youth wing of ERC).

MI5 or Security Service (internal security intelligence service in Great Britain).

NKID, Narodnyi Komissariat Inostrannykh Del (People's Comissariat del Poble for Foreign Affairs of the Soviet Union, equivalent of foreign ministry).

NKVD, Narodnyy Komissariat Vnutrennikh Del (People's Commissariat for Internal Affairs of the Soviet Union, equivalent of interior ministry).

IMRO, Vnatrešna Makedonska Revolucionerna Organizacija (Internal Macedonian Revolutionary Organization, Organización).

PCA, Partitu Corsu Autonomista (Corsican Autonomist Party).

PCE, Partido Comunista de España (Spanish Communist party, Stalinist in the 1930s).

PCF, Parti Communiste Français (French Communist party, Stalinist in the 1930s).

PG, Partido Galeguista (Galician autonomist or nationalist party)

PNB, Partie National Breton (Breton National Party, on the extreme right).

PNV-EAJ, Partido Nacionalista Vasco (Basque Nationalist Party).

POUM, Partido Obrero de Unifcación Marxista (Workers' Party of Marxist Unification, dissident communist party in Spain, founded in 1935).

PSOE, Partido Socialista Obrero Español (Spanish Socialist Workers' Party, name of the Spanish Socialists).

PSUC, Partit Socialista Unificat de Catalunya (Unified Socialist Party of Catalonia, founded in 1936, "adhered to the Communist International", not admitted into the Third International until after the Civil War).

SDN, Société des Nations or League of Nations.

SFIO, Section Française de l'International Ouvrière (name of the French Socialists, 1905–1969).

SIFNE, Servicio de Información del Noroeste de España (literally "Information Service of the Border of the Northeast of Spain", Pro-Franco spy service paid for by conservative Catalan leader Francesc Cambó).

SIM, Servizio Informazione Militare (the military intelligence organization of the Italian army).

SNP, Scottish National Party.

UDC, Unió Democràtica Catalana (Democratic Union of Catalonia, christian-democrat nationalist party in Catalonia).

UNDO, Ukrayin'ske Natsional'no-Demokratichne Obyednannia (Ukrainian National Democratic Alliance, largest Ukrainian party in interwar Polish Republic, 1925–1939).

UNO, Organizatsiya Ukrayinskyj Natsionalistiv (Organization of Ukrainian Nationalists).

USSR, Union of Soviet Socialist Republics.

VNV, Vlaams National Verbond (Flemish National Union).

WNP, Plaid Genedlaethol Cymru/Welsh Nationalist Party.

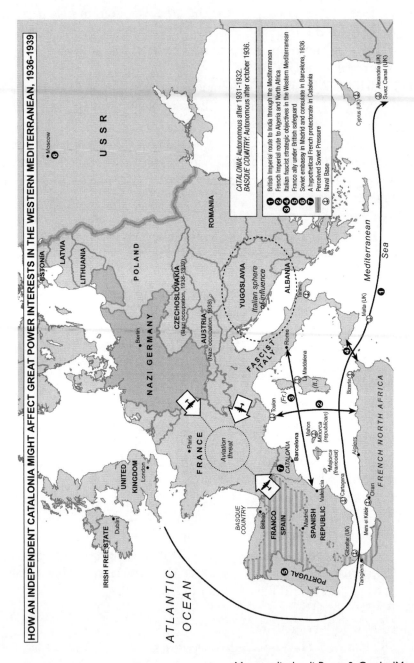

HOW AN INDEPENDENT CATALONIA MIGHT AFFECT GREAT POWER INTERESTS IN THE WESTERN MEDITERRANEAN, 1936-1939

CATALONIA: Autonomous after 1931-1932.
BASQUE COUNTRY: Autonomous after october 1936.

❶ British Imperial route to India through the Mediterranean
❷ French Imperial route to Algeria and North Africa
❸❹ Italian fascist strategic objectives in the Western Mediterranean
❺ Franco ally under British safeguard
❻ Soviet embassy in Madrid and consulate in Barcelona, 1936
❼ A hypothetical French protectorate in Catalonia
🅧 Perceived Soviet Pressure
🅧 Naval Base

Map credit: Jordi Barra & GradualMap

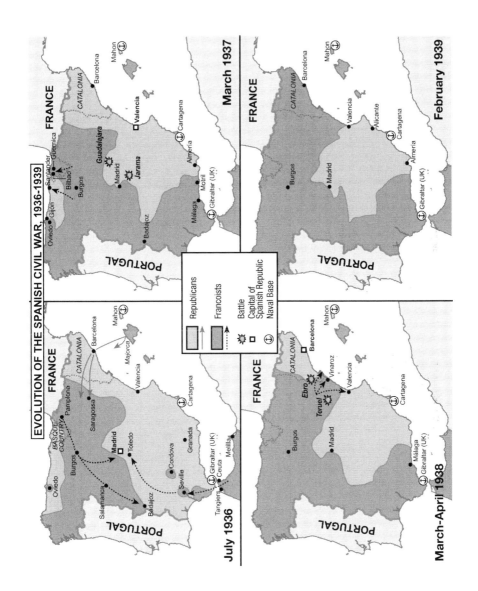

Map credit: Jordi Barra & GradualMap

Chapter I

How to Become Independent in Europe (and America) Before 1931: Upholding the Monarchy or Proclaiming a Republic?

Enric Ucelay-Da Cal

Today, almost in the third decade of the twenty-first century, monarchies seem like a rather exhausted political form. The dynasties – and the aristocratic families that surrounded their courts – now only appear in the glossy pages of *papier couché* society magazines, together with actors, actresses, multi-millionaires, and assorted lesser celebrities. Such decadence is, however, recent: it is less than a century old. We think today that almost everything everywhere is governed (or ought to be) by systems of "representative government" or "popular sovereignty" and that these open and participative State structures date somehow directly from the important revolutions of the end of the eighteenth century. It is a truism repeated often, but it is false. Democracy, insofar as it exists, is largely a creation of the twentieth century, built slowly on patterns developed in the nineteenth century, and then fragmented and put together anew after World War I, and again in the wake of World War II. It is – as should be remembered, with some caution, even fear – a reversible pattern.

What were the choices facing a "protest nationalism" that challenged the existing State system, and especially its territorial arrangement, in the second half of the nineteenth century? What practical options existed for the diverse strands of a movement like Catalan nationalism?

I

In Catalonia, today, it is assumed that the liberation of what used be called "small nations" is inherently a republican inheritance. The Catalan pro-independence movement revels in this identification. But such a focus in Europe, before 1918–1919, meant looking at the Americas. There were numerous ways to attain some sort of collective selfhood in a European format, a political space which was inherently monarchical until at least the end of the First World War. The key that opened the lock to "national freedom" then lay in the notion of "Crown" and its many useful ambiguities, rather than in the "Voice of the People", expressed allegedly through the vote and the ballot box.

It should be pointed out that, over the years and up to the present, Catalan nationalism, from its earliest beginnings as a political current in the 1880s, has maintained a marked interest in the fate of nationalisms of all types, but especially those of movements that fought to achieve autonomy or stable access to what, copying a British perspective, came to be called "Home Rule".[1] But often the interest in autonomy has been mixed and confused with the dream of national independence. This essay tries to situate this Catalan nationalist curiosity – and the consequent desire for sympathy and guidance – in a wider context.

Crowned Independence

Let us begin with the crux of the matter. The contrast of the "historical – or divine – right of sovereignty" (the foundation of monarchies) and the "doctrine of popular sovereignty" (the basis of republics) can be understood as a discrepancy easy to mix up or a contradiction impossible to resolve, depending to the observer's ideological point of view. Napoleon's monarchical step in 1804 – with a legitimating plebiscite – transformed the crowns of Europe while illustrating a reasonable encounter between the principles of the eighteenth-century revolutions – in North America, in France – and those of religious and political tradition dating back to the sixteenth and seventeenth centuries. As a result, after the Vienna Peace of 1815, the tendency of European statehood moved forward, slowly but surely, towards liberal forms of monarchy, with an inherited crown, with an official religion, but with an elected parliament balanced by a selected upper chamber, in some cases composed of peers of the realm. All nineteenth-century history in Europe can be easily summarized as a process of expanding the vote to more and more members of society, and, as a result, consolidating the greater power of the legislative branch over the royal authority of the State. In fact, nineteenth-century European political change is usually narrated in this fashion.

But the criterion of "Progress" must not be exaggerated. Manhood suffrage was slow in coming, and even slower in being made effective. In general terms, women did not get to vote unconditionally in most of the world until after the First World War. Even in a model republican regime like, for example, the United States, it should be remembered that not until 1913 was the American Federal Senate was elected by direct franchise (before, the senators were picked by state assemblies, these being elected by popular vote). In the idealized French Republic, so admired in the Latin world, women did not vote until their right was accepted by the provisional government in 1944. Voting on independence usually meant fighting, one way on another.

As can be seen, therefore, the way a territory might become independent depended on where the neighbors of a given community lived and how they managed their political affairs. Geography conditioned politics: Europe itself was not the same in the West as in the East, the Old Continent was different from the Americas, the Pacific was another matter from the Atlantic. Nevertheless, power politics (and therefore Europe), determined the formula for moving from being merely a "society" (or a "nationality") to credible power as a State. Statehood had to be seen and approved from the outside, and then be officially recognized, so as not to be perceived as merely a problem, to be avoided or dealt with by consular officials, rather than something stable, standing by itself, and therefore work for diplomats.

In the mid-nineteenth century, in Europe, two alternative patterns were set for the "correct" understanding of the political achievement of a independent status of a territory. The two main options arose throughout the process, coinciding with the experience of the 1860s around the globe, which stabilised the pattern of statehood from North America (the U.S. Civil War, 1861–1865, the British North America Act of 1867) to Asia, with the Meiji restoration (or sometimes "revolution") in Japan in 1868. After the turmoil of the European revolutions of 1848–1849, with their intense fever of a "Europe of nations", there was still overall feeling that large political entities – with considerable geographical extension – were the best for political and economic future.

One model of statehood was forged in a *unitary* fashion, in imitation of the long-term territorial pattern established in France, between 1790 and 1800, by the Great Revolution, and consolidated by Napoleon I. The prime example of new unitary statehood was the Italian *Risorgimento*, fraught with wars between 1859 and 1870, in which a lesser military power – the kingdom of Sardinia-Piedmont under the House of Savoy – annexed weaker independent kingdoms and duchies (the great Duchy of Tuscany and the Duchy of Modena in 1859, the kingdom of the Two Sicilies in 1860, together with the Papal States, all sealed with the capture of Rome in 1870). Together with the territories (Lombardy, Venice) "freed" from the Austrians to the north, in the brief but harsh conflicts of 1859 and 1866 in which Sardinia-Piedmont was backed first by Bonapartist France then by Bismarckian Prussia, these historical parts and portions were integrated into a highly centralized State, the new Kingdom of Italy, proclaimed in 1861. An anticlerical liberal monarchy vaguely compensated for the pressure of imposed territorial union.

The other option was federal, or confederative, based on historicism and "crown rights". The great example was the transformation of the Austrian Empire. After sixteen years of harsh political-administrative centralization in Vienna ("the Bach system") to compensate for the fears caused by the 1848–1849 revolutions, the Habsburg dynastic State then faced the consequences of a military defeat in 1866, at Prussian hands, that, to all effects, expelled Austria from German affairs. The Habsburgs responded to the misfortune with a radical internal reorganization of their regime, to recognize – in a "Compromise" or *Ausgleich* – the full equivalence between the Austrian Imperial Crown and the "Apostolic" Crown of the Kingdom of Hungary. The confederal state born in 1867 consisted of two parts and consequently was known as Austria-

Hungary; within each part, there were supposedly self-governing entities, like the kingdom of Croatia-Slavonia in Hungary – thus in itself an alleged double monarchy – or that of Galitzia-Lodomeria in Austria. In the political discourse of the nineteenth century, which did not clearly define statehood as freedom, and tended to confuse autonomy and "independency", *the achievement of independent status was most easily achieved through a crown, justified with elaborate historical legitimation.*

Both models – the unitary Italian State of the Savoys and the "dual monarchy" of the Habsburgs – marked the limits of options and strategies. Similarly to "Italian unification", the kingdom of Prussia under the Hohenzollerns "unified" Germany, between 1864 and 1871. Prussia, with the leadership of chancellor Bismarck, broke the Habsburg hold on the variety of German principalities, and, in the process, absorbed some (like the Kingdom of Hannover). But, in a sense similar to the Austrian "Compromise" of 1867, Prussia in 1870–1871 domesticated the rest of the German States. The dynasty of the Wittelsbachs in the Kingdom of Bavaria were granted special standing, but the particularity of the kingdoms of Saxony and Württenburg, the grand duchies of Baden and Mecklenberg-Strelitz, and a host of lesser entities remained unquestioned: they were all included within a unitary tariff zone, all brought together in a German Empire, which accepted the claimed ranks of the varied princes and princelings, with their rights and specificities, under a Prussian emperor, a united general staff for war matters, and the beginnings of a common navy. Less confederal than Habsburg dualism, rather a federal monarchy of sorts with a strong imperial presidency, the German Empire dominated continental politics until the conclusion of the Great War in 1918.

In other words, in the Europe of the 1800s, everything political or institutional was determined by the diverse crowns, with their ranking and their dynasties. In 1869, the general political form of the continent was monarchical. However, with the rapid defeat of the Empire of Napoleon III in the face of a German coalition during the month of August 1870, France became provisionally a republic. Nevertheless, even if republican institutions were permanently stabilized as such after 1879 (with the end of the presidency of

Marshal Patrice de MacMahon), it was because the various monarchisms or royalisms that were aspiring to the throne – Bourbon legitimists, Orleanists, Bonapartists – could never end up agreeing on anything. In 1890, the Grand Duchy of Luxembourg – ruled by the king of the Netherlands – became a recognized and independent country because the Salic law prohibited the Dutch heiress Wilhelmina from becoming the new ruler when William III died; by the Nassau Family Pact of 1783, the territory passed to the next available male, Adolphe, titular Duke of Nassau, a pretender really, since his duchy had been annexed by Prussia in 1866 and annuled.[2] *Thus, in Europe, the prevailing political system was the monarchy in all its forms – between parliamentary and absolutist according to the case – from Great Britain to Russia.*

By way of contrast, in a Europe composed of a few large States, until the turn of the nineteenth to the twentieth century, republics, in general, were either "small things" – the mountain of San Marino or senatorial cities such as Hamburg – or larger spaces, considered *exceptional*. Of these, there were two cases: one, old, was Switzerland; the other, repeatedly improvised, was France.

Long considered as a fact of life, Switzerland was indeed an exceptionally and unrepeatable case. Not even the great Napoleon, not timid about redrawing maps and redesigning institutions, was willing to do more than reinforce to historic Helvetian pattern with his "Mediation Act" of 1803. Nor, after Napoleon's downfall, did the Congress of Vienna in 1815 dare to alter the complicated and particularistic Swiss background. A civil war in 1847 between Protestant and Catholic cantons (the latter grouped together in a *Sonderbund* or "Special Alliance", with a ultramontane, secessionist air) gave rise to the "federal" Constitution of the Helvetian Confederation of 1848, and therefore to a more or less fixed pattern of peculiar statehood.[3]

The other exceptional republic was of course France, with strong and famous tensions of its own: the First Republic of the Great Revolution, from 1792 to 1804, was later transformed into the Bonapartist empire. The Second Republic, again revolutionary, from 1848 to 1851, was once again interrupted by a Bonapartist coup that brought about a "Second Empire" (under the nephew of the Napoleon I, Louis-Napoleon Bonaparte or Napoleon III). The

Third Republic came out of the spectacular defeat of French imperial arms by a German coalition led by Prussia. The new Republic
was announced but greatly debated in 1870–1871, under German
occupation, and not fully clarified for more than a decade. Even if
French Republican status was resolved by the 1880s, there
remained discussion and debate about the form of government best
for France – monarchy or republic – for many more years to come,
until the result of World War II and the failure of the peculiar "*État
français*" under the quite elderly Marshal Philippe Pétain (84 years
old in 1940).[4]

In short, at the beginning of the twentieth century, everyone in
Europe – including many Frenchmen – understood, without
discussion, that the monarchy meant political "civilisation".
When, in 1905, Norway – with its own specific constitution since
1814 – separated by referendum from Sweden, its population chose
by a second plebiscite to remain a monarchy. Before 1914, the only
change of political system on the continent was the overthrow of
the crown in Portugal in 1910, and the proclamation of a new
republic.

Spain was a unitary State and a constitutional monarchy in the
Italian mode (Amadeus of Savoy, the second son of the new Italian
king, Victor Emmanuel II, even reigned for two years, from the
beginning of 1871 to early 1873, when he abdicated, and was
replaced with the two-year hiatus of a First Republic, parliamentary in 1873, under military control in 1874). But against the
unitary pattern of France and Italy which dominated Spain, the rise
of Catholic and conservative Catalan nationalism tugged towards
some solution like the dual monarchy, seen with pro-Magyar eyes.
Catalan republicans looked to Cuba, then a part of Spain, and, by
extension to republicans in the Americas.

The Republican Pattern in the Americas

The Americas were the opposite of Europe. Seen globally, in the
Atlantic area, republics were a phenomenon typical of the
American hemisphere, both in the north and south. On the
American side of the ocean, monarchies were scarce, often regimes

(Mexico, Haiti) that were shown to be insufficient and soon inter-rupted as a form of rule. In 1822, Brazil proclaimed itself an empire under the same dynasty, the Braganzas, that ruled metropolitan Portugal, and lasted as such until 1889. Only the weight of British naval and military force sustained Canada against pressure from the "Americans" of the newly-born United States. The American revo-lution began in earnest in 1775 with a thrust to the north, an attack that was repeated in 1812, and there remained sometimes bitter border disputes in the west during first half of the nineteenth century. The U.S. disposition against foreign meddling was a republican statement, and meant as such, when it was articulated as a "Doctrine" by president James Monroe before Congress at the end of 1823. Nonetheless, it was largely ignored by the European powers, and depended on a paradoxical coincidence with British naval strength and policy to be effective, at least until the middle of the nineteeth century.

The successful independence of new, invented entities from the colonial empires of Spain and Portugal in the American continen-tal "*Terra Ferma*" in the 1820s was followed by an broad exchange of views surrounding the possibility of creating new crowns, but, as before, in the United States, republican institutions were chosen. Following on the path trod by George Washington, the South American "liberators", Simón Bolivar or José de San Martín, chose heroic leadership and a foundational role, rather than an imperial mantle. In both North and South America, the republican inspiration came from the separation of the Dutch Protestants from Catholic Habsburg within the Spanish crown: the Seven United Provinces, proclaimed as a confederation in 1581, incipiently recognized by Spain and the powers in 1609, and which lasted, sometimes bumpily, until 1795. Especially for Spanish American revolt against Spain, the Dutch Republic was a major inspiration: there were "United Provinces" in Argentina in 1810, in Venezuela in 1811, and in Central America in 1823. Once established, the new republics all underwent a sour political debate between the supporters of confederal, federal, or unitary systems of government. Such often bitter disputes remained very much alive during the rest of the century. Needless to say, dis-agreement and dissension caused numerous civil wars in the several "unions" or "united states" (like Mexico, Venezuela, Brazil) that were established in La Plata (afterwards Argentina), Mexico, Central America, Great Colombia, and, eventually, Brazil.[5] The United Provinces of Central America blew apart in 1841 with the secession and unilateral declaration of independence of El Salvador, and, despite successive attempts at reunification over the next eighty or so years, remained a host of small, independent republics, all unstable in the extreme.

With the unionist triumph in the U.S. Civil War in 1865, there would be no more secession anywhere in the American Hemisphere, except when and where it was ordered by "The Big Brother of the North": Cuba and Puerto Rico were taken from Spain after a war in 1898, and Panama was separated from Colombia in 1903 so that "*los ianquis*" ("the Yankees", a epithet not merely reserved for New Englanders) could create a sea channel in the Isthmus of Darien, and a U.S. "Canal Zone". In that same 1903, the military occupation of Cuba ended and the island became an independent republic, juridically subject (in its constitution) to the explicit right of intervention by the United States. It did not matter much: the implicit right to step in was generously exercised By U.S. Presidents from William McKinley to Herbert Hoover throughout the Caribbean area. American foreign policy in principle wanted to avoid European conflicts, so as to better concentrate itself on "Pan-American" questions and, by extension, on China, always of commercial interest. Thus, in the Pacific, after the overthrow of the Hawaiian monarchy in 1893 by local American interests, the new Hawaiian Republic, which applied for admission to the Union, was rejected by President Grover Cleveland as the product of an illegal overthrow. Hawaii was only annexed as a "Territory" in the wartime excitement of 1898, at roughly the same time as the Spanish colony of the Philippines was seized, although a long, bitter war of "pacification" was necessary to assure control on the more distant archipelago.

The republican nature of U.S. expansionism was always subtly emphasized, in opposition to the last monarchies that were present in the Americas. Established in 1890 at the First Pan-American Conference, the Union of American Republics acted as a republican front of the "New World" against the monarchies of the "Old

Continent". At the foundation, in 1890, April 14 was proclaimed as the "Day of the Americas". The set-up had of course mercantile implications (Commercial Office of the American Republics), under a Superior Council created in 1897, with functions expanded in 1902; the union became in 1910 an International Office of the American Republics. Excluded were the colonial monarchies: Great Britain (numerous continental possessions – most notably Canada – and a large variety of islands); Denmark (Greenland and the Virgin Islands – the latter purchased by the U.S. in 1916), The Netherlands (Suriname and Caribbean islands).

What about Catalan self-awareness in all of this historical dynamic between monarchies and republics? Catalan nationalism was born oriented towards republican ideals, at the beginning of the 1880s, with antecedents going back to the 1830s. The initial preoccupation of any incipient sense of Catalan nationhood, in its most primary sense, was historicist: the desire to return to the "Old Constitution" of the Hapsburg multi-crown system that ended in Spain with the victory of the Bourbons in the War of Spanish Succession, a European conflict fought as a civil war in 1705–1715.[6] The return to a lost past meant the recovery in some way of the old, abolished form of local parliament and executive, without necessarily questioning the crown at the top of the political system. As the Bourbons won the struggle against the Hapsburg pretender, administrative and political reorganization was put in place, especially after 1716, with the abolition of older institutions, much centralization, and the dominance of Castilian Spanish as a tool of easier bureaucratic and judicial work. Language was still a given, and the message was that the elite wrote in Spanish and the illiterate spoke in Catalan. Romanticism questioned such diglossia, but the existence of Catalan usage was not socially questioned in a fundamental way until urban density pushed and finally overwhelmed the countryside, and, although the agrarian economy and rural areas pushed back – the dream of Carlist dynastic legitimism – under an alternative Bourbon branch, identified with traditional religion – became a monarchical solution for the recovery of "historic Catalan rights". This idea – almost an invocation of the "Old Constitution" before defeat in 1714 – started dimly in the 1820s, and developed into something more cohesive during the long "Carlist War" of the 1830s. Precisely, in the 1830s, the old word *provincia* or "province" – like the difficult term *"patria"* ("fatherland" or "motherland", meaning anyone's place of origin) – had seemed to reproduce that sense of the better olden days, until liberal administrative reform in 1833, creating a new pattern of "provinces" equivalent to French departments born in the Revolution, slowly wiped out the older meaning, and brought the notion of "region", initially as an evocative, literary or sentimental remembrance of a territory, an idea increasingly politicised as the nineteenth century wore on.

Then, by the mid-nineteenth century, as the the political vocabulary of the Spanish left evolved, and "progressives" (*progresistas*, in Castilian) turned into "democrats", and then into "republicans", the Catalan native impulse followed, since the indigenous dynasty had disappeared by the beginning of the fifteenth century. In a world of growing industrialization and urbanization, tendencies that existed for Spain as a whole, Catalan nationalism either looked to Hungary and its pact with the Hapsburgs – the dominant trend – or to the endless Cuban civil war, snuffed out by U.S. intervention in 1898, with the island turned into a Republic in 1903, under the protection and patronage of "American" power. Dreamers among the Catalan emigrants in the Caribbean, then numerous, confirmed the Catalan idea of reforming and modernising Spain through federalism or a confederal solution – shared with the self-styled "regionalists" who thought in terms of a dual monarchy under the Spanish crown – rather than with independence as such.

The Hidden (Protestant) Modernity of Post-Religious Political Language

Before we go any further, let us deal with the hidden evolution of political jargon and its meanings over time. To begin with, to give one eloquent example, "republic" and "commonwealth" are essentially the same word, a translation of the Latin *res publica*, or "public affairs". In the mid-seventeenth century, Oliver Cromwell might well have preferred one sense for the designation for his rule as "Lord Protector", but, at roughly the same time and even before, Spanish *arbitristas* (mercantilist writers on economic, social, and political problems) had no problem writing about the realms of the Spanish crown as *"nuestra república"* (literally "our republic"). Disambiguation came later, with the eighteenth-century revolutions.

The terms "separatist" and "self-determination" both came out of dissident Protestant opinion in the English Revolution of the seventeenth century. "Separatists" were those who broke away from the episcopal Anglican established Church – and, by extension, those who refused the tutelage of the similarly official Presbyterian Scot Kirk, or those who organized themselves in autonomous or breakaway chapels, and thereby moved towards what in British North American colonies, with the religious "Great Awakening" of the 1730s and 1740s, would come be called "congregationalist" attitudes, under which each community of believers would decide its own course. Such were the spiritual origins of the American Revolution of 1774–1783.

The "separation" of a territory from its previous rightful ruler was a simple enough perception to be already applied the Catalan revolt of 1640–1653, against the Spanish crown. It should be noted that the suffix "-ism" – as in "separatism" – tends to be a nine-teenth-century neologism; older words referred to people, groups or institutions with an "-ist". So, in English, "nationalism" is from the eighteen-hundreds (interestingly enough, first used in the United States as a religious term in the 1830s), while "national*ist*" appeared around 1715, coincidental with the English debate about "the deplorable case of the Catalans", former allies abandoned to their fate under the victorious Spanish Bourbons after the War of Spanish Succession.

But the big Enlightenment term through the eighteenth century was "patriot", a political word put into circulation by the Corsican struggle against Genoese domination, from the 1729 to 1769, when Louis XV bought the island from Genoa and French forces put down the islanders' revolt. The initial uprising was led, among others, by Giacinto Paoli, and his son Pasquale proclaimed a free Republic in 1755, which lasted until the French conquest. From the end of the Corsican fighting to the beginning of the

American Revolution there was, roughly speaking, a scant five years. Lest anyone think that this was a minor contest in an out-of-the-way place, the Corsican conflict directly implicated minds as diverse as Jean-Jacques Rousseau, James Boswell, and Catherine the Great. Furthermore, a son – born precisely in 1769 – of the secretary of the last great Corsican leader, Pasquale Paoli, was one Napoleone Bonaparte, who was an island "patriot" before his break with Paoli and local politics, who frenchified his name and personality, and went on to a stellar military and political career.

"Patriot" thus became a defining term for the "Thirteen Continental Colonies" in their battle against British domination, and also in the Netherlands and then Poland, and in the French Revolution, and finally in the Spanish battle against Napoleonic invasion after 1808. The Peninsular War popularised the expression "liberal", found before in revolutionary France. The imposition of French order in German lands and Austria brought the response of Romanticism and the term "nationalists" and "nationalism" to the fore, as a reply to "patriots", and what seemed the discourses of the soon out-of-date recent past.[7]

The word "secession" offers a good example of the evolution of language and therefore ideas over time. Until the mid-sixteenth century, it was an erudite historiographic term that referred to a repeated and highly significant succession of events in the early Roman Republic: on repeated occasions between the fifth and third centuries BCE, the Roman plebs fought the patricians using as their weapon a *secessio plebis*, with which the city's plebian citizens simply abandoned their work and left for a nearby hill, where they encamped, leaving the wealthy to their own devices. On the last circumstance, in 287 BCE, during the final *secessio*, there was established the *lex Hortensia*, named after the dictator Quintus Hortensius, who approved the law, a measure which made binding all measures passed by the Plebian Council or *Plebiscita*, hence the modern word "plebiscite", also a historiographic term until the mid-sixteenth century. Both words, accordingly, had a social rather than territorial sense, and, after about 1530 to 1550, were applied to religious separations.

The first political use in of "plebiscite" English is dated by some around 1776 with allusion to Swiss habits (the term "referendum" is supposed to have been originated in Switzerland in the sixteenth century, but is clearly a late Latinism, that really appears commonly in English in the mid-nineteenth century, with the Swiss *Sonderbund* conflict and the expansions of Napoleon III); significantly, in Spanish, the *Diccionario de Autoridades*, the first etymological dictionary compiled in 1726–1739, still does not recognize "*secesión*" but, for reasons of Roman civil law, accepts the term "*plebiscito*". Certainly, by the time of French Revolution, plebiscites had become a method for republican change, as in the constitutional referendums of 1793 and 1795, as well as a legalistic way of approving the justifying forcible republican annexations, for example French in the mosaic of the (mostly) Hapsburg Lowlands. Under Napoleon Bonaparte, plebiscites took place next to elections, notably in 1800, 1802, 1804, and even 1815, as usual happily producing nearly unanimous results.[8] This was the secret of Bonapartism, the integral mixture of republican and monarchical forms, as was shown almost a half century by Louis-Napoleon Bonaparte in 1852, when, with the slogan *Vox populi, vox Dei*, the republican ex-president become dictator promoted once again the Empire; in 1860 the incorporation of Savoy and Nice as the French price for helping Sardinia-Piedmont against Austria in 1859 was again sealed by the habitual mechanism of a popular plebiscite in both areas.

In other words, we cannot be careless with the sense of "modernity", as even the most ancient-looking political institutions are often merely an antiquarian exercise of the more Romantic period of the nineteenth century, and, all their regalia aside, are in fact comparatively recent.[9] Thus, as an example, monarchical dual confederation, as in Austria-Hungary in 1867, postdates not only federalism in the United States or in Latin America, but even the Confederacy of the South proclaimed in 1861. Religious authority of the crown dates from the Peace of Augsburg in 1555, when the emperor Charles V gave up trying to dominate the Protestant princes of Germany, and "sovereignty" may have resulted from the Spanish recognition of Dutch republic, the Seven United Provinces, after an "Eighty Years' War", in the treaty of Munster as part of the Peace of Westphalia in 1648, but statehood in the fullness of the principle of outside recognition is very much a product of the Vienna Peace of 1815. Behind the monarchs gathered at the Austrian capital, the foreign ministers convoked by Klemens von Metternich (Prince only since 1813) established the full system of diplomacy and consular service that served basically untouched until the very end of the twentieth century: diplomats were the mechanism for mutually recognized official communication between fully accepted States, and the consular service was used for everything else, especially helpful for dealing with unrecognized political entities.

Evidently, the sense of modernity was (and still is) a class issue, in which, since 1815 to today, informality in social interaction and dress has consistently subverted hierarchies which ever have sought to justify themselves by reference to History and rules of etiquette. Literally, titled landlords were *politically entitled*: the fact was that, in Europe (including Great Britain), persons of explicit rank and landed wealth dominated political and social life until the debâcle of World War I.[10] By way of reply, early on, rising democrats invoked "ancient basic rights"; in Europe by reference to an "Old Constitution", while in the Americas response was made with allusion to Humanity as a whole. Even France, with its Great Revolution and successive Republics, in name of the "rights of Man", was a place where aristocrats and titled nobility still fondly chatted about genealogies at the end of the nineteenth century; such a social scene was light years away from the American crucible, where proudly "self-made men" made ostentation of their inherent vulgarity (a subject that fascinated English novelists of the time). Titles of rank implied that public life was a service determined by *noblesse oblige*, while American businessmen acted out the ideal of "do-it-yourself" rather than the "*laissez-faire, laissez passer*" of the European bourgeois. This makes sense according to the old American advice of "Mind your business" but "We are One", a paired idea that was already expressed as a double motto on the "Fugio Cent", the first U.S. federal currency coined in 1787, with a design already used in 1776.

In sum, the Americas as a whole erected political institutions in terms transformed from the Protestant Reformation and its ongoing inheritance, in increasing individualist terms that facilitated moves either to secularism (transcendentalism, for example) or mysticism, or, strangely enough, both at the same time. In the meantime, Northern Europe remained linked to either official State Churches in Protestant countries (Great Britain famously, but also Sweden, Denmark, and Prussia), which slowly gave a shift to the idea of an "Establishment" (in English, from the early eighteenth century sense of an "established Church", to the nineteenth century idea of a place of business), from the religious to the commercial, and then to the sense of representative citizenship without full participation (in England, the notion of a ruling elite in twentieth century, a term fully recognized only in the mid 1950s). The alternative for Catholic Europe, from Belgium and Luxembourg, through Southern Germany and Austria (including, before 1918, Bohemia and Galitzia, i.e., southern Poland and western Ukraine), through to Portugal, Spain, and newly forged Italy, was to live with the institutional salvation offered by the Roman Church, and its implications for power and society, or to challenge it frontally with anticlericalism, which meant assuming in some sense Protestant values. As was demonstrated by the persistent instability of all Latin American political and social experience, grafting Protestant civic and individualistic values onto the trunk of a Catholic society has proved extremely difficult. Certainly the left in Spain in general, and Catalan politics in particular, faced this problem with largely unconscious militancy.

The Successful British Formula of Commitment to Crown Autonomy and "Independency"

Thus, in Europe, secession, whether by pact or from rebellion, was resolved monarchically, through the institution of the crown. A very influential British political thinker, such as Walter Bagehot, reflecting in the 1860s on this subject in the book on *The English Constitution* (1867), spoke of little else.[11]

The British started the route with their overseas territories by converting, in 1867, Canada into a *dominion* or autonomous "domain", independent in practice, with its own parliamentary system, at least regarding local matters, under the English crown. The major part of the British colonies of the continental North

American area that did not participate in the initial confederal agreement covered by the foundational British North America Act were added on during the following years.

This invention created an interesting semantic problem: what was the difference between a *suzerainty* and a *dominion*? According to a dictionary, a *suzerainty* is "any relationship in which one region or nation controls the foreign policy and international relations of a tributary state". Put differently, a suzerainty cannot act in international relations, despite having internal sovereignty. This was standard operating procedure, to take an obvious example, for the Ottoman Empire. But for the British, so ruddy pink and superior? The "dominion" formula was designed for settlements dominated by white settlers, and, as such, was opposed to the notion of "empire" proclaimed by Disraeli for India in 1875, and put into practice the following year. Insofar as it was advisable, in 1907, as part of the agreements of the Colonial Conference (hereafter "Imperial Conference") the newly merged Commonwealth of Australia, as well as New Zealand, were proclaimed "dominions", and the South African Union, an area of long-standing conflict between Anglophones and Afro-Dutch speakers or *Afrikaners*, and an active and angry battlefield in 1899–1902, also reached the same title in 1910.

The dominions, starting with Canada, depended on the Colonial Office, which had a Dominions Division, while their external difficulties depended on the Foreign Office. Needless to say, this generated considerable paperwork, often of a very local nature. In 1909, the Canadian prime minister Wilfred Laurier submitted to the pressure – through the governor-general Lord Grey, who represented the crown – of the British ambassador in Washington D.C., James Bryce (in office, 1907–1913), who roughly calculated that two-thirds of his ambassadorial duties as representative of the Court of St. James were absorbed by Canadian details. The solution, very English, was to find a term that meant nothing and implied everything: after 1909, Canada would have a "high commissioner" in the U.S. capital to deal with problems like borderlines and tariffs, while the British ambassador could deal with major diplomatic questions. As they achieved "dominion status", other territories of the crown demanded equal rights.

After the Great War, two events changed the nature of the dominions. First came the Anglo-Irish Treaty of December 1921: note the concept of "treaty", not pact. For the British side, Ireland became a dominion under king George V, but for the Irish nationalists, the result was a Irish Free State (a term borrowed from the Afrikaners, and the Orange Free State, already in the system). The Free State flag was of necessity the Irish tricolour of the nationalist cause. The Irish, however, were divided between pragmatic "freestaters" and purist "republicans", and immediately fought their own particular civil war about the distinction (June 1922 to May 1923), more bitter and nasty than the just-ended "War of Independence" against their British overlords. Needless to say, the Irish "high commissioners" took maximum advantage of their direct access – like Canada – to the League of Nations and the International Labour Organisation.[12]

The other decisive event was the so-called "Chanak crisis", a war scare in September of 1922, that faced off British troops and the Turkish nationalists near Istambul. Prime minister David Lloyd George called for Imperial defense, and Canadian premier Mackenzie King frontally refused. The upending was the fall, for evermore, of Lloyd George, and the establishment of a relative independence on the part of the dominions.[13] In 1925, Dominion Affairs became a separate British ministry of its own. At the Imperial Conference of November 1926, Lord Balfour dictated policy: the dominions were "autonomous Communities within the British Empire, equal in status, in no way subordinate one to another in any aspect of the domestic or internal affairs, though united by a common allegiance to the Crown, and freely associated as members of the British Commonwealth of Nations." As time passed, between 1926 and 1929, it looked as if it should be understood that the domains – depending on their internal pressures – were entitled to their own embassies and consulates, a sign of their independence *de jure*. By 1927, the Union of South Africa had a Department of External Affairs (and the following year its own Afrikaner-style flag, with but a slight nod to the Union Jack), while, in sharp contrast, Australia did not begin to do deal with its own foreign affairs until the outbreak of the Second World War (and New Zealand still later). In 1931, the Statute of Westminster recognized the power of dominions to declare war (or not) as they saw fit.[14] Ireland achieved full independence in 1937, in many ways a by-product of the British abdication crisis during the previous year.

The Suzerainty or the Princely Autonomy of the Ottoman Empire

In the strict European framework, the dynamics of secession – first autonomy and then an independent kingdom – were made by the monarchies, thanks to suzerainty, or sovereignty, limited to the domestic policy inherent in a territory. The Ottoman Empire worked, for a long time, with the North African "regencies" of Egypt, Tripoli, Tunisia and Algeria, tributaries of the Sultan who paid regular contributions to the Sublime Porte, said that they ruled in his name, but locally they did more or less whatever their vice-regal appetites suggested. The *Oxford English Dictionary* summed up the whole business quite neatly in the 1930s: a suzerain was a "feudal overlord", or, "in recent use, a sovereign or a state having supremacy over another state which possess its own ruler but cannot act as an independent power". As can be seen, this was not suitable to British tastes, but rather something appropriate for foreigners or, worse still, for the distant and dusky.

There was a perfect example that to a large extent defined the "Oriental Question" of the nineteenth century. Between 1805 and 1848, the improvised strong man of Egypt, Mohammed Ali Pasha, forced the situation towards an internal monarchy, formalized in 1867 as *Khevdivat* (a seemingly original term of Persian origin, although the term had already been used before), a viceroy that was on the edge between reign and recognized independence (but always with consuls from the powers, not ambassadors). So fluid was this situation that after 1882 Britain established a protectorate in fact on the Ottoman suzerainty of Egypt (until 1914 the Egyptian independence to the Ottomans was not proclaimed, with the announcement of a sultanate of its own).[15]

A year before the British occupation of Egypt, in 1881, the French imposed their version of full suzerainty and effective sovereignty in Tunis, despite maintaining the dynastic figure of the bey, a prince who reigned but did not rule.[16] Once the Turkish defeat against Italy in the war from 1911 to 1912 took place, the Ottoman Sultan – with his Eastern cynicism – yielded to the Italian king his suzerainty on Cirenaica and Tripoli, after recognizing the "independence" of the territories.[17]

In the Turkish Europe, that space conquered between the battles of Kosovo (1389) and of Mohács (1526), called by the Turks as *al-Rûm*, "Rumelia" or Ottoman "Roman land", where there lived Christians, the peoples of the Eastern Orthodox Churches, suzerainty ruled. The Serbians, the Moldavians and Vlachs from the "Danubian principalities" (Moldavia and Wallachia), and the Bulgarians, followed down a well-trodden path: fiercely crushed rebellions, a peace with an autonomous Christian Slav *knaz* or prince, a *hospodar* (a lord or ruler) and then a *domnitor* in the Danubian case (Serbia from 1817 to 1878; Moldavia and Wallachia united after 1859; Bulgaria in 1878) to reach their own kingly crowns, with full independence (Serbia in 1882, Romania in 1881, Bulgaria in 1908).[18]

The Ottoman government preferred this system rather than repeating the open struggles it had with the Greeks, until they first achieved a *politeia* (or republic) and finally a monarchy fully recognized in 1833, with a Bavarian king, replaced by another, a Danish-German, in 1862. In fact, all the new "Balkan States" that arose in the nineteenth century suffered problems of stability and harsh dynastic rivalries until the abolition of the monarchies in the second half of the twentieth. However, while the Ottoman Empire existed, the use of the crown – or crowns, in plural – in state or national construction was essential. Thus, for example, the Greek–Turkish War for the control of the island of Crete in 1896–1897 resulted in a "republican" autonomy under the "presidency" of the Greek prince (until he got bored) and the direct administration by the powers. This complex set-up was erased by Greek *enosis* or "Hellenic union" on the island in 1908, but which could not be made effective – externally recognized – until 1913.[19]

When finally, after the Turkish revolution of 1908 and the Italo-Turkish war of 1911–12 (which left Italy in possession of the Dodecanese islands, around the Greek-speaking Rhodes), all the

Balkan countries that had emerged throughout the eighteen-hundreds – including Montenegro in 1910 and Albania in 1912 – despite beginning as a principalities were internationally recognized kingdoms. They immediately rallied to enlarge themselves in the first Balkan war of 1912, to fight each other in a second war in 1913.[20] The next step – pending, but coming – was a direct Serbian conflict with Austria-Hungary for Bosnia. As a result of the negotiations in the Congress of Berlin between the great powers in 1878, this puzzle of a land, Bosnia-Herzegovina, became in 1878 an Ottoman suzerainty, administered by Vienna (in the same way that, from the same date, the island of Cyprus was run by the British).[21] With the the Turkish Revolution of 1908, however, Bosnia was completely annexed by Austria-Hungary.[22] As is well-known, Bosnian pan-Serb nationalists killed the Habsburg heir in the capital of the territory, Sarajevo, on June 29, 1914.[23] This unexpected, uncontrolled fact generated a chain of problems that began the Great War of 1914–1918. The new general conflict now would change everything, from top to bottom.

The Difficult Republicanism of Europe and Catalan Nationalism

Thus, in Europe, at the end of the nineteenth century or the beginning of the twentieth, to be Republican and secessionist was somewhat complicated. In the British Isles and on the Continent, there was no division like that of "democrats" and "republicans" in the United States. In general terms, the anti-dynastic left was for free labour, against slavery, for unrestricted manhood suffrage. Abraham Lincoln was regarded as "The Great Emancipator", an assassinated martyr, even a saintly figure, not considered really comparable to the Russian tsar Alexander II who abolished serfdom in 1861. If the American track was followed, the signs pointed directly to Lincoln's 1865 victory against the Southern Confederacy. The term *unionism* was consolidated as a politically friendly word. Second, there was the prejudice that it was better to favour territorially big States, both in Europe and in the Americas. Nobody praised the collapse of the Central American Union in the late 1830s. And no one wanted to be a small, poor and deprived independent State with internal political chaos and economic control from New York, which, using a sufficiently well-known expression, would be called "a banana republic".[24] But such sympathy did not exclude misunderstandings about secession as such, and even about the failed and tainted Southern Confederacy.

Such predilections – and confusions – are reflected in the two major contributions of Catalan political thinking in the Spanish repertoire: *iberisme* (literally "iberanism"), a scheme for Peninsular union originated by the inventive Sinibaldo de Mas, in the years after 1851, and, more or less on the same dates, the federalism of Francisco Pi i Margall. Both were born Catalans, but spent most of their lives in Spanish contexts of one kind or another. The scheme of Mas, a professional diplomat who spent much of his life as Spanish consul in Macao, was monarchical, but could be applied in a republican key.[25] The scheme of Pi – a publicist and politician – was, of course, clearly republican. But if the doctrinal foundation (the "synallagmatic pact", equal to equal, person to person, on the basis of the sovereignty of the individual, and therefore of relatively participatory institutions like a municipality, and then moving higher to forms of more distant representation) was eliminated and was reduced to a rather more practical scheme. It could also be applied to a modern monarchy as a reinvention of the past of a multiple crown: more than one Carlist writer scribbled away to make it all fit. To summarize, a Spanish solution was needed, better still a peninsular one, but with an assured Catalan specificity. The problem: these options did not really please anyone. Neither *iberisme* seduced the Portuguese, nor federalism the central Castilians, in contrast to some Galician or Andalusian individuals.

In the 1880s, a younger rival of Pi Margall, a well-to-do Catalan named Valentí Almirall, faced the problem, but, despite his writings on the United States and Switzerland, deep down he knew that neither Spaniards nor Catalans were akin to the Americans, much less to the Swiss (who were the ones whom he liked the most, with their cantons and their Helvetian Confederation).[26] To become a republican meant to enthrone the city, the district, the "county" as expression of "The People" as did the Fenians (the Irish Republicans), with solid support from Hibernian emigration to the

United States.[27] Dealing in depth with the town was to play the card of the Paris Commune, raised against the French provisional government installed in Versailles in a destructive civil war, a source of endless leftist ideologies but an entity that only endured from mid-March to the end of May 1871.[28] In Spain, just over two years later, a belated reflection of the revolt in the French capital, cantonalism, exploded everywhere along the Mediterranean (like in France) to concentrate in Cartagena, a naval base with a fleet. The memory of the war between the provisional government of the Spanish Republic and the Canton of Cartagena, which lasted from mid-July 1873 to mid-January 1874, was not a glorious evocation to recall, except for the most delusional.[29]

Despite the defeat of the Confederacy and of "states' rights" in North America, Almirall was interested in the implications of "nullification", like the doctrine proposed by John C. Calhoun and South Carolina, in defense of the rights of a territory to govern with less interference from a central government, federal or otherwise. He called his proposal "particularism", and defended it in his newspaper (the first published in the Catalan language), and in various books, the most important of which was called *Lo catalanisme* (1886). Like the earlier U.S. idea of "Americanism", which took a philological term for dialectal forms of American English and made into a long-lasting and more acceptable alternative for "nationalism" in U.S. usage, Almirall took the expression for Catalan turns of phrase in Castilian Spanish, and turned it into the name of an ideology of selfhood. Unlike his Confederate models – which he did not recognize – Almirall placed himself firmly on the left, indicated his preference for an ultimate republican solution to Spain's problems and for Catalonia, all of which made him fail in his political initiatives. The Catholic conservatives won out, and Almirall retired, embittered.

What conservative remedy was possible, if one wanted to be a monarchist and, therefore, think of real solutions to one's own nationalistic demands in a European context? The effect – by design or unexpected, is not clear – of Napoleon III's predominance over international politics in the 1850s and 1860s, with its consolidation of a system of large States, and the suppression of the mosaic of large powers and smaller entities that came out of the Vienna

Congress of 1815.[30] But the reserved, even inscrutable "Little Napoleon" was not able to foresee the manoeuvres of Prussian Chancellor Otto von Bismarck. The Prussian chancellor pushed a series of rapid, tough conflicts: the War of the Austro-Prussian allies against Denmark, which lasted nine months in 1864; the Austro-Prussian War, settled in seven weeks in 1866; and finally the Franco-German War, 1870–71, with a French imperial defeat in scarcely a summer month, followed by sieges and combats, from September to January of the following year until an armistice was signed with the provisional republican government of France. As a result, Bismarck unified the German Empire, erased French predominance, and redesigned the map of Europe. Bismarck masterfully dominated continental politics and international relations from 1870 until he was obliged to resign by the young German emperor Wilhelm II in 1890, but his inheritance was ominous. Lacking any criteria other than the Machiavellianism of *Realpolitik* (practical policy, without further calculation than that of immediate benefit) and the exaltation of the *Staatsrecht* (understood as the Law of National Interests and not Constitutional Law), the Bismarckian was a manipulative style, a long balancing act by a superb tactician rather than via authentic statesmanship. In the new German politics, he merged Historical Law with the Law of Popular Sovereignty, so that the second could be effectively destroyed.[31]

Catalans and Irish Look to the "Hungarian Model"

In this crucible of the turn of the century, in Barcelona a young Enric Prat de la Riba emerged, for example, as a nationalist thinker, an activist who defended "political interventionism" and desired to overcome the apoliticism of the Unió Catalanista (Catalanist Union) founded in 1891.[32] Like others in Europe at that time – in Ireland, Arthur Griffith, the founder of Sinn Féin (1905), to give a striking parallel – Prat de la Riba considered that the successful path towards independence was the broad way established by the Hungarian politicians and their ability to force the proud Habsburgs to accept their demands and requirements after the brutal defeat of the dynasty in the Austro-Prussian war of 1866. The "imperialist" end of *La nacionalitat catalana* (1906) of Prat, therefore, must be understood in the key of *The Resurrection of Hungary* (1904) of Griffith, subtitled very explicitly *A Parallel for Ireland*, although, in any case, neither was likely to have ever read the other.[33] A more extreme step, such as the Norwegian separation in 1905 from the Swedish–Norwegian joint Crown, was still "acceptable" in the Swedish and Scandinavian framework because of the ease of accepting a new independent monarchy with a young Danish prince as a king.

The change was announced indirectly. The "dual monarchy" of Sweden–Norway had been in place since 1814, but at the cost of a foundational war. Before, since at least the fourteenth century, Norway formed part of the Danish crown. In the so-called Scandinavian "United Kingdoms", Norway had a different constitution from that Sweden (from 1809), which dated back to the resistance against the Swedish takeover in 1814, as well as its own language (or, in fact, several, the most cultured being closest to the Danish). The Norwegian social tone was marked by an accentuated egalitarianism, which included the abolition of noble or aristocratic titles. Sweden, on the contrary, was a much more hierarchical society, with a powerful absolutist tradition ingrained in the Crown and a strong link between the king and the armed forces, especially the Army. The Swedish military looked down with a certain superiority at the Norwegians, who, nevertheless, had a comparatively vast merchant navy, the third in the world in tonnage in 1880. The fact was that the Crown and the Administration were in Stockholm and the Norwegian capital, Christiania (Oslo, after 1924), would endure a viceroy or governor-general until the office was abolished in 1873. The general opinion was that the Swedish administration had a strongly-felt inability to work in easy relation to the *Storting*, or Norwegian parliament.

A conflict over the nature of the Norwegian consulates (necessary for all the sailors of the mercantile fleet) poisoned political life during the final decades of the nineteenth century, until, amidst threats of war, the Norwegian Parliament forced a plebiscite on the separation of the two kingdoms, a right that was included in the

1814 constitution. The referendum was held in the middle of August 1905 and won absolutely, with 368,208 votes in favor of the secession and a most minimal 184 votes against.

The disgusted king Oscar II rejected the compromise of a Swedish prince for the throne, but, nevertheless, on October 26 his cabinet recognized Norway as an independent constitutional monarchy. Then, that same year, a new question was asked about whether Norway should be a monarchy or a republic. Held on November 12–13, the second plebiscite chose the option of monarchy with almost 80 percent of the votes. With a practical sense for the language, a Danish prince was chosen, Charles, who, crowned on November 22, took the royal and patriotic name of Haakon VII.[34] Events, as can be seen, went quickly, but all flowed due to the fact of monarchical agreements.

In Catalonia, the separation of Norway excited Catalan nationalist opinion intensely. The impact was strongest especially amongst those that were situated politically between republican nationalism and the regionalist *Lliga*. The influential intellectual Eugeni D'Ors invented an entire theory about the "imperialist" function due to self-conscious Catalans in the light of the Norwegian events. Having said that, it was still another step in the path already set in the Hungarian monarchical pattern, established since 1867.

However, the substantive indication of the great political change to come in European state forms took place in October 1910, with the dethronment of the King of Portugal and the proclamation of the Republic of Portugal. In the country there remained a sympathy for Brazilian republicanism, which in 1889 overthrew the American empire of the Bragança, since the same Portuguese dynasty also reigned in the vast Latin American country. The fall of the Brazilian monarchy, due to the Crown's push for the abolition of Black slavery, paradoxically radicalized anti-monarchy opinion in Portugal. This was ironical, since the king, Charles I, was blamed for his good relationship with the Prince of Wales, just as Great Britain had prevented the Portuguese transcontinental ambitions in Africa, a territorial push which implied the expectation of heavy use of forced African labour. The republicans had already declared their intentions with a great revolt in Porto in January 1891, having gained some military support. Years later, on February 1, 1908, given the blatant stagnation of the parliamentary system, self-styled "Carbonari" conspirators assassinated – in the very heart of Lisbon – the king and his successor, the prince royal, Louis Philip. The unexpected heir, Manuel II, did not know how to create himself a role in the face of the subversion and fell after revolt in the capital, beginning in the Navy from the Tagus estuary. During the same 1910 revolution, attacks began on religious orders: the new regime stood out due to the "masonic" and aggressively anticlerical tone of Portuguese republicanism, which soon generated equally assertive responses from the aggrieved right. The Catalan and Spanish republicans were greatly excited by the events in the neighboring country, but there was no real tactical analogy.[35]

Nevertheless, anticlericalism was a lively spiritual presence on the European horizon at the beginning of the twentieth century, especially in the Latin countries of Roman cult. In France, the secularism identified with republican leader Émile Combes was imposed in 1905, dictating the predominance of the democratic regime even on the facades of church buildings. The intensity of municipal actions in areas close to Catalonia, starting with the border department of the French Pyrénées Orientales, coincided with an angry agrarian agitation that indicated the death of Occitania as a traditional cultural sphere, the so-called "*Révolte des vignerons*" in 1907 (literally, the "revolt of the wine-growers").[36] Two years later, in Barcelona and other places in Catalonia, the warm summer of 1909 saw an explosive uprising, with barricades and calls for a republic, which was soon converted into a host of iconoclastic fires of Catholic buildings. Accordingly, seen from a distance, from places such as the very Catholic Ireland or Papist Poland, the link with the "Catalan cause" became incomprehensible: the Irish nationalists fought against the Protestant English predominance, just as the nationalist Poles sought to end Russian Orthodox abuse. Religious conflict was an important element of the nationalist protest elsewhere, but not in a way in which Catalan nationalism – neither left nor right – could take advantage.

It is clear that in the summer of 1914, after late July and early August, the explosion of the European war was enthusiastically received everywhere, so that it contrasted very quickly with the hardness, brutality and general misery that came with the war, soon lived as interminable carnage.[37] In the summer of 1914, the image of combat was still largely a Napoleonic cliché: elegant, even enchanting in a male key, with often colorful uniforms and the supposition of a short campaign that would end "before Christmas", as had occurred with most wars from 1859 to 1871 in Europe. For leaders and citizens, the shock came when the conflict stagnated and remained stuck in an ugly stalemate, with trenches that went from the English Channel to the Swiss border, ugly ditches cut across a landscape quickly stripped bare down to the mud and clay, dug out in "the race to the sea" from September to October, a pattern of frontline warfare that, more loosely, also took place on the vast Russian front.

Why did the governments launch themselves, one after another, into the crazy bet of a short war? Perhaps, as in the 1930s as was suggested in a brilliant essay by historian George Dangerfield about the British decision to enter into combat, the decision to go to battle was about getting out of a political impasse on the domestic stage. The British government of the liberal H. H. Asquith encountered a grave disruption in Ireland, with a royal army threatened by the lack of discipline of the officers, favorable to unionists in Ulster, whilst, in addition to the Irish mess, British society as a whole seemed to come apart between the challenge of labour unions and that of women suffragettes. King George V tried, using his personal prestige, to convene party leaders in an informal conference to at least point to a pact on Ireland, in the face of the absolute confrontation between autonomists and hard-core unionists. Meeting between July 21 and 24, 1914, there was no agreement.[38] The British cabinet declared war on August 4.

The underlying pattern serves perhaps to explain the accelerated actions of the Imperial-Royal Chancellery of the Danubian dual monarchy and the head of the Austro-Hungarian armed forces, the risky action of the German Kaiser and his minister or the risk assumed by the Russian czar and his ministers. All these absolutist regimes, although autocratic in varying degrees, feared the results of a "radical" understanding of liberals and socialists, against what was in essence the decisive structure and power of the Crown. A small adventure, especially if it went well and lasted little time, could be useful for collecting supports for neo-absolutism, for "modernising" the existing system; maybe perhaps it could work even with a defeat (as had happened with Austria in 1867), if altogether, fight and failure, were not too expensive.

The Germans, at the center of the coalition of the "Central Empires" with Austria-Hungary, the Ottoman Empire and later Bulgaria, tried to forge a customs zone or *Zollverein* on an European scale, hypothetically well founded on *Mitteleuropa*, and formed by monarchical entities, kingdoms, grand duchies and mere duchies in the best Germanic style.[39] Had not all the new dynasties of the new kingdoms of the nineteenth century – Italy and Serbia as cases apart – come from the principalities of the mosaic of German states within the *Reich*?

But the Germans and their partners lost their struggle in their last offensives in the spring of 1918. By then, the vast Russian Empire had already overthrown their tsar and even destroyed the "bourgeois" Republic in a bold blow of the Bolsheviks led by Lenin in early November 1917 (a force that paradoxically grew with German help). Indeed, the change really came in 1917, which was the decisive year of the vast world conflict. Until then, the German war plans, seconded by Austro-Hungarians and Ottoman Turks, foresaw the rebuilding of defeated Russian space with a multitude of new kingdoms and great duchies – constitutional in appearance but expected to be very strong crowns. In April, the United States entered the war against the "Central Empires", followed by a long list of major and minor republics of the American hemisphere. In August, the Russian provisional government, formed with the fall of autocracy in March, proclaimed the republic. The success of the Bolshevik coup against the new regime in November only confirmed the trend. In 1918, the clumsy peace attempts of the new Austro-Hungarian emperor-king Charles I (the eternal Franz Joseph finally had died at the end of 1915), who tried to negotiate a separate exit for the Habsburg monarchy from the Great War, definitively turned the French towards a position favorable to the destruction of the dual crown: the only alternative, for the Allies (and especially from the perspective of French ambitions), was, then, to create new independent republics. The question was how many and on what a national-cultural basis?

The change took place abruptly, in Berlin and Vienna, when the inevitable armistice of November 11 became reality. Emperor Wilhelm II was ushered into Dutch exile by the army, and throughout Germany, the kings and princes fell. Republics were proclaimed in Germany and "German-Austria". The Peace of Paris, which was formulated in many treaties between 1919 and 1920, confirmed the tendency towards the primacy of republican government: by 1923, a few (although still influential) monarchies remained in Europe in a sea of republics. How did the such a "suicide of Europe" take place? The end of the monarchies took place in dream-like confusion, in struggles between revolutionaries and counter-revolutionaries. It was what a recent historian, Christopher Clarke, has called the world of the sleepwalkers, borrowing the title of a series of novels by the Austrian author Hermann Broch (*Die Schlafwandler*, published between 1931 and 1933).[40]

The New Twentieth-century Separatist Model: Ireland, not Hungary

The great European model of national freedom achieved in the nineteenth century had been Hungary. From 1867 on, the Apostolic Kingdom was part of a great power, but free to manage its affairs (or those of the great Magyar magnates and their political friends, allies, and supporters), without male universal suffrage, which was rejected until 1918. The *Ausgleich* had even a ten-year limit, which obliged further Austrian concessions in renegotiations every decade. The defeat of 1918 led to the destruction of the dual monarchy of the Habsburgs. Both parts of the joint empire – Cisleithania and Transleithania – were chopped down to stumps. The philo-Bolshevik Magyar revolution of 1919 – which lasted from March to August – could not stop the partition of "historic Hungary", which yielded territories to Romania, the new republic of Czechoslovakia, to the new South Slav Kingdom (soon to be called Yugoslavia), and even a tiny portion to Austria.

The Western European alternative to the failed, ninteenth-century "independence" of Hungary appeared in the United Kingdom. Although Britain was the largest of the allied powers, it emerged from the global struggle to face a painful secession. It had seemed that Home Rule would be possible for Ireland rather than for Catalonia, but this was not the case. In 1914, a project of the Mancomunitat (or "Commonwealth") of Catalonia was recognized by the Spanish government thereafter presented by Catalan nationalists as an interprovincial government, while the third Irish law was approved, but postponed, by the beginning of the European war. The deferral, perhaps unavoidable given the vehemence of Protestant opposition, would be very costly. The religious division of the Kingdom of Ireland would confront rabidly Protestant and unionist Belfast, to the Catholics and committed nationalists, from Dublin and Cork to the south, perhaps willing to settle for autonomy for the entire island. The north was industrial, the south agrarian. Soon, there was a nationalist uprising in Dublin on Easter Monday of April 1916, with a week of bitter fighting in the capital. Tension ensued after the repression of the revolt. When the Great War was over, the triumph of the Sinn Féin in the British elections of December 1918 (73 out of 101 Irish seats in the House of Commons) determined the future. Instead of going to Westminster, an Irish National Parliament or Dáil was proclaimed, together with an Irish Republic. A long armed struggle for control of the island began, lasting until the end of 1921. The British resolved the confrontation in negotiation, with the separation of the north, the six counties of Ulster, with an autonomy of their own, while they granted dominion status to the south, that is, the rest of Ireland. The "Anglo-Irish Treaty" was accepted by the moderate part of Sinn Féin, even though they said they were establishing a "Free State", acted in a republican manner, and ignored, as best they could, the restrictions of still being a part of the British empire. Their opponents, republican nationalists of all-or-nothing mindset, launched a fight in June 1922 against their former colleagues. They would lose, as they acknowledged in June 1923, but they did not abandon the battle.[41]

Viewed from Catalonia, the Irish model was too extreme. Independence by popular sovereignty, achieved through armed combat and terrorism, as in Ireland, had never been attractive to conservative Catalan nationalists, given to stirring speeches but moderate in habit. However, the example of the Irish struggle blew on the still warm embers of Cuban memories of resistance and a flame flared up: the cause of free Ireland inspired the appearance of the first organized separatist movement, paradoxically under the leadership a former Spanish army colonel, Francesc Macià, in the winter of 1918–19. But fighting in ambush, assassinating ideological enemies, destroying the property and resources of the country, was only a pattern then hailed – on an urban basis – by excited anarchist and anarcho-syndicalist revolutionary workers, militant sectors that had become a real presence in Barcelona and the industrial towns of Catalonia.[42]

The New Republics in Eastern Europe

The republican change of 1918–1923 did not take place in Western Europe, which – with France a victorious great power, Portugal already transformed – remained monarchist until the proclamation of the Spanish Republic in 1931. Ireland – as a British dominion – was technically a monarchy, fought against by the most fanatical Republicans of the IRA (Irish Republican Army).

Not counting the Bolshevik Russia (itself a Republic composed of smaller republics), in Eastern Europe the new republics covered a wide arch from north to south, which began with Finland and the three Baltic states, continued with Poland and Czechoslovakia, and then jumped to Turkey and, for a time, Greece.

The republican change stopped with Hungary as a transitional entity (an idiosyncratic "regency without a king" in charge of an admiral – Miklós Horthy – without a navy, after a communist republic in 1919). Then, following the map, there appeared the Balkan monarchies consolidated in the wars of 1912–13 and reinforced by the allied victory of 1918: Serbia would absorb Montenegro at the same time as it would incorporate Croatia and Slovenia at the expense of defeated Austria-Hungary, confirming its territories to the east, in rivalry with the routed and demoralised Bulgarians (Macedonia) and the south (Kosovo), with the

Albanians. The entire area was set up a new federal monarchy that, in 1929 and, after serious tension between Croats and Serbs, was converted into a centralist State, under authoritarian control of the crown, under the name of Yugoslavia or "South-Slavia".

Similarly to the creation of a Serbian-led South Slav Monarchy, as a result of the Allied victory permitted the kingdom of Romania to expand by winning the vast territory of Transylvania, formerly Hungarian, and Russian Bessarabia or Moldova, which some two decades later was taken over by Soviet Russia. The Romanian inheriting prince – Carol II – soon showed signs both of his instability and his ambition to lead politically. Finally, monarchical Bulgaria – defeated completely by its neighbors Serbia, Romania and Greece – had to yield up bits of territory, a strongly-felt loss, which converted the country into a permanent back-and-forth between Macedonian terrorists and militaristic sectors that looked towards the young king, Boris III, with the peasants in between, once, in 1923, the Agarians of Stamboliyski were set aside with their leader's murder.

Meanwhile, Greece was a mess all to itself. To the south, in front of the monarchies in the midst of a strong authoritarian drift, which would be more visible in the 1930s, Greece was present, with a "national schism", an endless bad split that had started in 1917, and which, despite agreement on the annexation of much of Asia Minor (which proved a disaster), by the military, had no real solution. The military proclaimed the Republic in 1925, and a restoration of the dynasty would come about in 1935, with an evolution towards dictatorship.

All of these were called "successor States" that replaced the perished Russian, Ottoman, Austro-Hungarian and German empires. The "successors" were not the product of secessions strictly speaking, but rather the result of the implosion of the various empires upon being vanquished. The new States were also the result of the redesign by the Western European great powers of Central, Balkan and Eastern Europe after the gigantic changes of 1918–1919. The small and reduced "Republic of German Austria" tried to merge with Germany, a first intent of *Anschluss* that was vetoed by the Allies. Germany assumed its own diminished situation with dissatisfaction and open struggle between the red forces, contrary to the new "bourgeois" republic, and the private armies or *Freikorps* of the nationalist extreme right, who in principle defended the institutions of an "imperial republic".

Within the German federal scheme, many of the heretofore semi-independent dynastic states that formed part of the new republic looked for forms of territorial self-definition, on the extreme left or on the radical right, by means more or less of their own design, sometimes more or less separatist. Bavaria was a revolutionary social republic in 1919 and the object of a confused German-Bavarian right-wing *Putsch* in 1923, which made Adolf Hitler famous; Saxony was briefly an autonomous socialist regime between 1919 and 1923; the city-state of Hamburg was the object of a communist revolution in 1923.[43] It is necessary to understand that, given Russian propaganda, the year 1918 entailed the fashion of Soviets or "workers' and soldiers' councils" everywhere: even Luxembourg and Alsace, after the Germans pulled out, had brief "Soviet" episodes before the French troops imposed order and a certain common sense.

The "succession" could hide a lot of falsehood. In Germany, it was the self-same Imperial Army that dismissed the Kaiser and forced the hand of Social Democrats and Catholics to proclaim the Republic. Soon, however, Marshal Paul von Hindenburg would explain that he and his team had nothing to do with it, abetting the myth of the civilians and their "stab in the back" of Germany's fighting forces in 1918. But the militarists, those whom the left and the radicals blamed exclusively for starting the Great War to begin with, formed the "factual power", "the state within the State" from 1918 to 1933, until the arrival of Hitler to power. When Hindenburg, ardent monarchist turned stalwart republican president, finally died, perhaps already senile, Hitler took the *Reichwehr*'s oath of loyalty to his person, perverting the monarchist tradition.

The Self-determination of Wilson and Lenin

During most of 1918 and until the beginning of 1919, the stiff and not very sympathetic U S. president T. Woodrow Wilson was a world hero, a figure with a completely disproportionate projection of world justice and mutual understanding, on whom even his German enemies could pin their final hopes. Wilson spoke, in a foggy fashion, of a global parliament that would eliminate wars and give voice to the "small countries", and not only to the great powers. He was an obvious counterweight to Lenin, another leader who promised a new post-war world. Soon, however, the illusions surrounding Wilson vanished, and the man was reduced to his real dimensions. Even worse, due to his arrogance by not opening bi-partisan participation in foreign policy, the Republican Party formed a strong resistance to the Wilsonian internationalist project in the U.S. Senate (the chamber with the responsibility for approving foreign affairs). When campaigning against the Senate, he suffered a cerebral embolism, and was in bed until the end of his term. His second wife accordingly controlled everything, decided who came in his bedroom and who did not, so established the loud and persistent rumour that she was the authentic president at the end of Wilson's term, a supposition not to be discounted.

Wilson, the son of a Protestant Presbyterian Reverend (therefore formed with "congregationalist" discourse), was a native of the South of the United States (who therefore knew a tradition of secessionism, with the Confederacy) and a man of firm belief in white supremacy (he liked the new Ku Klux Klan). But his career took him to a teaching post in the North, in New Jersey, where – active in academic politics – he invented Princeton University where there had once been a rather modest Presbyterian educational center. From being a university constitutional scholar (what later came to known as a political scientist), he was the author of a highly admired book about the political system of the United States. Whatever his roots, he was a unionist, not a defender of states' rights, but he was an ardent segregationalist (who, as president, minimized Black fighting regiments in the U.S. Army, and reduced African-Americans to the area of mere logistics, to being drivers and cooks). As he eventually faced emnity from sectors within the university, he jumped to politics as the conservative governor (but a Democrat) of the state of New Jersey. In summary, Wilson offered a perfect mind with which to convey ideas from the

powerful American Protestant tradition to the English, and especially to the French diplomatic and institutional culture. He placed
the concept of Presbyterian dissidence ("self-determination" of the
believers, the "separatism" of chapels and congregations, an idea of
the Puritan revolution of the seventeenth century, which allowed
"congregationalism") in a broad vocabulary of international
relations. Each individual and, by extension, each group, had to be
able to "say their own" and in their place in a "representative
government" and configure their own space within the "popular
vote". It was understood that Wilson rather liked "civilized",
white, Protestant people, of "his" kind, more than exotic peoples,
such as the Indian national movement of British India, who
pretended to have him to pressure the English so as to obtain
dominion status for the subcontinent. The Indians were to be
disillusioned by him, like many others.[44] Although often invoked
by those who have no power, the notion of self-determination has
never been accepted more than nominally in international law, due
to its slippery nature, when confronted with the interests of the
great powers.

In fact, Wilson confessed his limitations to a delegation of
Americans of Irish descent, then fundamental clients of the
Democratic Party. When beginning to redraw the map of Europe,
Wilson had no idea of the complexities that he faced. To his interlocutors, the U.S. president indicated that he had "touched the
great metaphysical tragedy of our time". Wilson added: "When I
mentioned these words [he was refering to the famous "Fourteen
Points"] I spoke them without the knowledge that there were
nationalities that now come to see us day after day."[45]

Facing the overblown figure of Wilson was the magic aura of
Lenin. The Bolshevik government in Russia encouraged the contagion of red revolution everywhere, while proclaiming in March
1919 the Communist International as a genuine successor of the
previous false workers' internationalism of the social-democrats.
The "reds" fought against the "whites" in violent civil wars that
would end up with some consolidated secessions and other frustrated ones. In Finland (from January to May 1918), in Estonia,
Latvia and Lithuania (from 1918 to 1920), as well as in an open war
between Russia and Poland (from February 1919 to March 1921),

while fighting in Belarus and Ukraine comprised many-sided conflicts, with the ports of the Black Sea in the hands of Allied war fleets.[46] Communist Hungary lasted from March to August 1919 and was overwhelmed by the Czechoslovakian and Romanian armies.[47] In Bulgaria, in June 1923, the right crushed the political "peasantry" of the Bulgarian Agrarian People's Union, led by Aleksandr Stamboliyski, in power since 1919, and then faced an aggressive communist revolt in September, a dynamic that in a sense was closed some two years later by a spectacular terrorist act, when the Cathedral of Sofia was subject to a bomb outrage while full of governmental authorities in mid-April 1925.

On the other hand, Greece, animated by the British, set out to conquer western Asia Minor, Turkey, while, to the east, the Armenian Republic – established in the Dashnak, nationalist tradition – was built upon the living memory of the genocide of 1915, attempted to win the other half of the historic peninsula. The surge of a new Turkish nationalism, with a direct appeal to the peasantry of Anatolia, once again quashed the Armenians with massive killings and turned around to literally expel the Greeks into the sea, with the conquest and burning of the city of Smyrna (now Izmir) on the Asian coast of the Aegean Sea. Turkish neo-nationalism – anti-Ottoman in spirit – abolished the Sultanate and proclaimed the republic, then went on to eliminate the Caliphate the following year (1924). It was, in broad strokes, "Kemalism", a revolutionary, often brutal, transforming movement, led by Mustafa Kemal Pasha, the hero of Gallipoli and the most beloved propaganda protagonist of the Turkish fight in the World War that had just ended.[48] The Armenian diaspora faced a century of pain when the Bolsheviks invaded Transcaucasia, took over Armenia in the Fall of 1920, then invaded and annexed Menshevik Georgia in the Winter of 1921.

In other words, the five-year post-war period from 1919 to 1923 was a chaos for Europe and the Middle East. Depending on where, the times of disorder could be easily extended for a couple of more years. Whoever lived the prolonged hangover after the Great War very often did not quite understand exactly what was going on. In practice, it was not until the middle of the 1920s that the dust and smoke settled and the dominant political forms, the new adaptations and the changes became perceptible. In Catalonia, the great turn towards republican forms of government in the center and east of Europe had immediate consequences.

On November 11, 1918, the singular Catalan nationalist Francesc Macià led demonstrations in front of the Barcelona consulates of Serbia and Belgium, the "small nations" first crushed by the great and abusive empires but finally victorious. So excited by the response as he saw it, Macià dreamed of founding a new Catalan left at the same time of working-class and nationalist attribution, a "Nationalist Workers' Party". Macià had enjoyed a long parliamentary career, along with much experience as a military engineer. His idea of a well-controlled "Nationalist Workers' Party" was not possible and he had to remain content with a National Democratic Federation made up of existing Barcelona neighborhood entities, formally established at the beginning of March 1919. Worse, his new Federation failed abysmally in the municipal elections of February, 1920.[49] So, in the summer of 1922, Macià went paramilitary and founded "Estat Català" ("Catalan State"), with a privately-organized "Army of Catalonia", which purported to imitate the IRA, but in fact had no forward policy.

Nevertheless, given his long army background, Macià had thought – deeply if perhaps not wisely – about paramilitary political action. "Private armies" were a common innovation of the postwar years, notably in Germany and Eastern Europe, but also in the west of the continent, after 1918 visible in Ireland and recovered in Italy beginning in 1919 (in March, in Milan, Mussolini led the renovated *Fasci di Combattimento*). At the time, much was said about "national socialism", from the right (as in Germany) or from the Bolshevik or the Social Democratic left. It was a confusing time, where right and left exchanged the platitudes and convictions of the past two decades, during the prewar and the burning crucible of the war years.

Insofar as the political and ideological environment in Barcelona was clarified, Macià, perhaps surprisingly, stood on the extreme left. Why? Perhaps because of the fact that Benito Mussolini, from the most revolutionary and pro-syndicalist wing of Italian socialism, found that, once the Great War was over, all the families of the left united against him and he only found friends and hosts among demobbed ex-military personnel, *arditi*, and other enthusiastic fans of the adventurer-poet Gabriele D'Annunzio who occupied the Dalmatian city of Fiume (now Rijeka, in Croatia) from 1919 to 1921. That is, Mussolini, expelled from the left, attached himself to the nationalist neo-right. Heretofore a republican, Mussolini established himself in October 1922 (or, rather, began to) as a parallel power to the crown and the House of Savoy. On the contrary, Macià who had been a professional officer and grew up in an old Spanish liberal tradition, with many friendships to other officers and even access at the court of king Alfonso XIII, now saw himself cut of all conservative ties (it was well-known, for example, that he and Francesc Cambó, the leader of conservative Catalan nationalism, had a very poor relationship). Conversely, Macià saw the open, waiting arms of the rising working-class organizations, even among the anarchists, all of whom who were dedicated to unionising gun in hand, and shooting it out with right-wing and Catholic syndicalists, with backing from the manufacturers' associations, as well as with the police. During the period between 1919 and 1923, several hundred activists from both sides were killed, largely murders attributed to *pistoleros* (in Castilian Spanish, literally "gunmen").

The Monarchical-Republican Synthesis: From "The Republic Within The Monarchy" to "The Monarchy Within the Republic"

The year 1923 marked a clear indication of the change both in the forms of government in Europe, from liberal to post-liberal or even socialist, now with communist presence, and of popular responses to the shift. At that time, in the English-speaking world, there was an outpouring of studies on the "New Governments of Europe", which sought to assess the representative, parliamentary, character of the new "successor states".[50] In France, always more "cartesian", more theoretical than what the French called the "Anglo-Saxons", there was talk of innovations of constitutional law, of the new "*Magna Cartas*" being written with the aid of the new "political science". A little of all this academic discourse came to Madrid or Barcelona, in general (but not always) in translation.

But by 1923 an alteration was perceived of what, in the war years, has been the anticipated pattern of liberal continuity. In a Belgium invaded by the Germans in 1914, the socialists were immediately brought into the cabinet by king Albert I, with corresponding political changes over the next years. Similar effects were wrought in the Netherlands. There had been numerous "crisis of 1917", from Spain to Russia. Where such events worked positively, as in Sweden (unlike in Spain or Russia), they led to the culmination of the "new liberalism" that was born with the twentieth century and the criterion of a *lib–lab* alliance, of liberals and Labour. In Sweden, the liberal leader Nils Edén called on the socialist leader Hjalmar Branting to participate as a finance minister in a coalition government, Branting meditated all night (perhaps with some sober Lutheran prayer). He accepted, thanks to a formula that he discovered in the darkness: within the existing government structure, there could be established the "republic within the monarchy", so as to empty the crown's political content, to strengthen Parliament and to finally "civilize" the armed forces, which thereafter should obey the politicians and not a king disguised as general-in-chief. When the Edén government died, Branting governed from March to October 1920, and again in 1921–23 and 1924–25. Afterwards, the Socialists, despite conservative resistance, came to play an increasingly important role: they dominated the government from September 1932 onwards, for five decades (with a brief interruption).[51] Similar processes, without the exact chronological alignment: in late 1918, Denmark granted formal autonomy or independence within the crown to Iceland, after the obligatory plebiscite, and, two years later, the king accepted finally the institutional predominance of parliament over crown rights. In 1919–1922, Branting's formula seemed to provide a model for the future, with Aleksandar Stamboliyski in Bulgaria, with Eleftherios Venizelos in Greece, among other liberal leaders leaning gently to the left. It began to be thought that in Eastern Europe, rural smallholders could play the social role of a middle class.[52] It would not be so.

Instead, the dark pattern of the immediate future came from the situation in Germany, which was exactly the opposite: instead of "the republic within the monarchy", Germany became an "imperial republic" in which monarchism – or the hint of monocracy, single-man-rule (in the oldest sense of the word "monarchy") – revived inside the institutions. Increasingly, the *Reichswehr*, now defined as "imperial defense", commanded republican politics.[53]

But, often enough, the figure of the strongman or "guide" came from new forms of authority. In Bolshevik Russia, "the Party" replaced not only the "service aristocracy" of tsarism but all the leftist competition: the SRs (or militants of the Socialist Revolutionary Party) or the "Mensheviks", not to include the libertarians or anarchists as well. In 1918, the Russian Democratic Federative Republic was created as the dominant entity within the Russian Soviet Federative Socialist Republic. But, starting in 1922, following the conquest of the Menshevik Socialists in Georgia and the Armenian and Azerbaijani nationalists in the rest of Transcaucasia, the hypocrisy of a system of "Republics of Councils" (which were not such) was revamped with a foundation in nationalities, through Soviet republics, autonomous republics, and lesser institutions – such as *oblasts, okrugs, krays* – varied terms all meaning autonomous districts or territories. The complexity of the system was relative, as the real power lay in "the Party", rather than in the State hierarchy. The constitutional reform called for the formation of a great socialist "Union", as a path to the creation of the "Soviet human being" endowed with a new human nature and the consequent liberation of the world. Such a successful political hallucination was consolidated largely by the Commissioner of Nationalities Josif Stalin, secretary general of "the Party" after 1922, and definitively after 1925 the *Vozhd* or "guide" (but better understood colloquially as the "boss"), but the underlying conception was in fact purely Leninist, despite the vast rhetorical literature of justificatory apologetics after destalinization in the mid-1950s. The flagship Union of Soviet Socialist Republics or the USSR began with initiatives that seemed to appear in the periphery, in Transcaucasia or Central Asia. Everything was reflected in the Soviet Constitution of 1924. With this base, entities that had emerged temporarily, such as the Republic of the

Far East, with a capital in Chita, from 1920 to 1922, were easily absorbed. Better yet, it was possible to literally invent national states of a "socialist type" in Central Asia and suppress Islam with energy.[54] Seen from afar, all the rigmarole of apparently decentralized government, of autonomous republics and autonomous regions, was exciting for Catalan Marxists, and represented perhaps the one component shared by Stalinists, Trotskyites and Bukharinists in Barcelona in the 1930s.

If the creation of the USSR offered new models of revolutionary self-determination and of territorial organization, it should be noted that parallel alternatives arose at the same time on the left in Western Europe. Within the "radical" scheme and the Liberal Party in decline, in Britain, the Labour party managed to rule briefly in 1924, between January and November, while in France, a *Cartel des gauches*, a left-wing coalition with no participation but with socialist support (and in a space where the first Communist deputies were elected), occupied the government between June 1924 and April 1925. For the British and for the French left it was just a start, that pointed in the French case (as in Spain) towards the Popular Front in 1936.

But "the republic within the monarchy" could be considered as an option in other even more original, even shocking, ways, especially as an ex-socialist key. The arrival to power – in a concentration government – of "fascism" ("unitarism", of *fascio*, the Italian term that invited making an active union in politics), in October of 1922, as a result of a "March on Rome" tolerated by the crown and, therefore, by the armed forces. The movement, conceived in 1919 by Mussolini, was a nationalist one, unionist but also republican. Now, however, Mussolini could accomplish Branting's dream of institutional synthesis, but with the friends on the right.[55] Mussolini's movement began to fully master the situation, domesticating the legislative chambers and eliminating all political opposition, thanks to enactments that broke the liberal State. Such legislation, based on the so-called "Extreme Fascist Laws" *(leggi fascistissime)* of 1926, completed in 1928, consolidated the image of Italian fascism as an innovation at the same time both modernizing and conservative. It was a mixture that impacted immediately throughout Europe, especially outside of Italy, wherever appearances counted for more than political substance. The test was the consecration of the improvised and self-defined "Dictatorship" in Spain of general Miguel Primo de Rivera, a product of a coup d'état in the middle of September 1923, with the approval of king Alfonso XIII.

Indeed, the following November, on an official visit to Rome, the Spanish monarch presented the brand new dictator to the Italian king Victor Emmanuel III with the joke that Primo de Rivera was "my Mussolini".[56] Indeed, imitations abounded in 1926; for example, at the end of May, with the "March on Lisbon" of the Portuguese militarists, which closed but did not abolish the republic (to begin with, there was no viable candidate to the throne).[57] A few months later, in September, the Polish national strongman, Marshal Józef Piłsudski, carried out his own "March on Warsaw" and closed the experience of the initial period of post-war Polish Republic.[58]

In short, within the change to the ideological vanguard of post-liberal patterns of statehood that took place around 1922–1923, there were three models which suddenly bloomed, with resulting fascination. First, there was Soviet state federalism marked by a treaty system and a constitutional process that took place from December 1922 to January 1924. Much could be said about self-determination, as unity was sustained indirectly by the dictatorship of the Bolshevik Party; within the newly established USSR there remained a core of the Russian Republic, together with numerous other soviet socialist republics that composed the Union, and, within them, especially in the major Russian entity, there were all manner of autonomous republics of lesser status, as well as autonomous regions. As the system congealed into the 1930s, many Catalan Marxists – both stalinists and trotskyites – were fascinated by the system, and took its appearance seriously. Against the Communist State, there was a clear response to Italian Fascism: a system inside a system, the intervention of a monarchy of nineteenth-century liberalism that, within its crowned and constitutional shell, retained a kind of dictatorial anti-government, which was the fascist regime.

At roughly the same time, in 1923 an alternative emerged that consolidated aspects of both, at least according to the opinion of many contemporary observers: the Kemalist Turkish Republic. This was a way towards Westernization, diverse from both the communist and the fascist patterns of development – which forced a poor and backward Muslim society that believed that it had won a traditional struggle (they called Kemal the "Ghazi", the destroyer of infidels), when the system represented as a triumph was in fact a war of national liberation typical of the twentieth century, with a resulting predominance of militarists, and with the establishment in 1928 of a "one-party democracy," the People's Republic Party.

Kemalism was sufficiently revolutionary to make agreements when deemed convenient with the Bolsheviks, and to establish a regime of rigid control that was admired in the West by those (like the Nazis) who considered liberalism, parliamentarism, and freedom of expression as futile. Kemal never doubted – literally – about hanging an annoying reporter from a street lamp when appropriate.[59]

In the interwar years, a restless nationalism such as the Catalan movement, taken as a whole, found itself subject to the crossed attractions of the three new models, all of them aimed at the Mediterranean basin. Barcelona, then, was the largest growing port and industrial city in the entire Mediterranean area, as well as an obvious challenge to the Spanish capital, Madrid, which risked falling behind the Spanish urban system's "second city".

To summarize. In practice and seen as a whole, World War I would last more than a decade, from the Balkan Wars to the relative postwar pacifications (1911–23). With the success in Russia of Leninism (the completion of the constitution of the Soviet Union of 1924), the progressive constituent process of the Fascist dictatorship under the monarchy in Italy (1922–26) and the consolidation of Kemalist dynamics in Turkey (notably with the establishment of the Turkish Republic in 1923), the liberal-democratic idea of statehood in Europe was subject to violent challenge, as well as new and sudden contrasts. Increasingly, freely-voted parliaments were out, strongmen of different sorts were in. After the mid-1920s, the innovations of State-controlled political power, would continue to dominate political thought and intellectual specualation during the remainder of the interwar period. But this most visible aspect of executive power, apparently omnipotent, "totalitarian" according to the neologism in fashion (to refer to the right rather than the left), covered truly deep, even more important, changes.

At this stage, the presence of women in civic and social life (in more than a domestic sense) was confirmed for the first time in world history. The most obvious progress was the concession of female suffrage, which, country by country, finally became a fact and eventually made voting "universal". However, nothing was for sure between the wars. No matter how much France was established and consolidated as a general model of republican statehood throughout Europe, with a centralized political game, based on the notion of generic citizenship, the "original" French Third Republic was much slower than its imitators throughout Eastern Europe. Even Spain assumed the vote for women in 1931, and put it into effect in the 1933 general elections. But France only granted females the right to vote in 1944, with general Charles De Gaulle and the Fourth Republic, once the worst part of the Second World War was over.

The Ambiguous Solution of the Republican Autonomic Sub-state

However, in view of these strict options of centralized control in the French fashion, which left behind the federal or suzerain ambiguities of the old empires, a new quasi-state alternative arose to quiet the complaints of some "protest nationalisms", such as the Catalan case, which again offered the useful ambiguity of forms of transition between full sovereignty and more forceful subjection.

The postwar solutions centered on German frontiers, as a model for hypothetical European problem-solving, rather than on the complexities of the Soviet Union. The Germanic borders had historically been equivocal, both West and South, facing the Latin Catholic world, as in the East, against the Slavs. Because Wilsonian vigour explicited national borders, with plebiscite and high transparency, to establish the limits of the "Republic of the German Empire" (still *Deutsches Reich*, given that the first article of the

Weimar Constitution ruled textually that "The German Empire is a Republic") was complicated, especially in Poznań (Posen in German) and Silesia, between Germans and Poles, in addition to other ethnic subgroups. It must be added, all said, that there were doubts with Belgium, Luxemburg and French-recovered Alsace. And there were even equivocations with Switzerland (a part of the Austrian Tyrol wanted to be added without success to the Confederation). And also beteen former Austrian German-speakers or the Czechs in the former Bohemia (including Moravia), before part of the Habsburg monarchy, and now a fused republic of Czechs and Slovaks, called Czechoslovakia.

The solution to many such problems – seen especially from a French perspective – was the mini-State, halfway between the micro-principalities of the type of Liechtenstein, Monaco or even (more complex) Andorra and a more respected sense of statehood. On German frontiers and using as a template the pattern of sena-torial city-states within the Reich, like Hamburg – there arose the Free City of Danzig facing Poland, the Lithuanian autonomy of Memel/Klaipedia on its border with East Prussia, as well as the French pompously called the *"Haut-Commissariat de la République Française dans les Provinces du Rhin"* (certainly not the same as what the British termed the "Inter-Allied Rhineland High Commission"), not to mention the hazy French dream of a Rhenish Republic under the influence of Paris rather than Berlin. With the practical experience of the Free State in Ireland as well as that of Canada, there was no longer any need to speak of "Home Rule" and monarchical forms of political delegation and services, though Irish authorities were cautious until the Anglo-Irish Treaty of 1937, together with the Eire Constitution of that year, which brought about a tangible disconnection (the Republic was not formally and effectively proclaimed until 1949). It was necessary to be up-to-date regarding borderlines and think of the masses and systemic voting, as an expression of popular sovereignty.

Another face of novelty of reinventing boundaries was the alleged "science" of geopolitics. It was accordingly easy to situate such difficulties with perimeters or partial territories in an inter-ested perspective, and therefore pleasing to speak of small and possible "buffer States" that, before or after a plebiscite, sealed a hole in a border, which covered up difficulties on the edges of discontented powers, which represented a procedural "solution", pending future events. The more sarcastic spoke of "rump States". Republican statehood did not necessarily imply foreign respect.

The fact was that with the Paris Peace, and very particularly the Versailles Treaty of 1919, the Belgians in 1919–20 – after the obligatory plebiscite, demanded by the U.S. – recovered the German-speaking territory of Eupen-Malmedy (Prussian since 1815), and France, needless to say, regained Alsace-Lorraine. But the military Generalissimo of the Allies, French Marshal Ferdinand Foch, argued for the creation of a Republican Rhineland separate from Germany but dependent on France, much more so than the areas occupied by Allied troops (especially Franco-Belgian forces) throughout the river basin, according to the Treaty of Versailles of 1919.

In eastern Germany, where the mutual hostility of Germans and Poles abounded, the Free City of Danzig was established, independent and under the auspices of the League of Nations to defend a German town within a Polish hinterland. Lithuania lost its historic capital, Vilnius, to the Poles (a maneuver, under orders of Marshal Piłsudski, of general Lucjan Żeligowski, in an operation that looked very similar to the action of Gabriele D'Annunzio in Fiume). The pseudo-republic of Central Lithuania of 1920 passed the city, converted to Wilno, to Poland in 1923. But the Lithuanians did not hesitate to do the same thing when they considered it convenient. The port city and area of Memel had a Germanic population in the town but not in the hinterland, as so often used to happen (a diplomatic solution similar to Danzig was proposed). Despite recognised international management, the area was formally annexed by Lithuania in 1924 with resigned approval to the *fait accompli* from the "Conference of Ambassadors of the Principal Allied and Associated Powers", responsible for cleaning the messes left over from the peace treaties after 1920: the year before, thanks to an act of pressure – Lithuanian nationalist militia took the town, and French supervisors of the autonomy ignored the action, their eyes on the Ruhr and the Rhine – Memel was converted into the Lithuanian city of Klaipeda, with an autonomy proclaimed, recognized as valid in 1928 by the Weimar Republic (but, in 1939, the territory was hurriedly "returned" to Hitler and East Prussia).

There was then problem-solving in the postwar, a new exceptional formula: the autonomic or mediatized State, really a "sub-state" pending future developments. When the recognition system was ruled by the historical rights and the sovereignty of crowns, such ambiguity was easy – the Ottomans did so comfortably in a "feudal past" increasingly seen as long ago – and operate through suzerainty. But when the only possible legitimization – determined in the United States' perspective (and similar to the Soviet criteria) – was based on the idea of *popular sovereignty* and some kind of *representative government*, then unexpected problems arose. As noted above, Wilson's abysmal ignorance must be taken into account in relation to ethnic and/or European language problems. He was a politician, but an American, WASP – white-Anglo-Saxon-Protestant. From a Southern family, he understood, sympathetically, both racism and the defense of local rights (to explain it in some sense), but he could not ever imagine the complications that his Presbyterian idealism would generate with the notion of religious root, of self-determination.

The new republics that appeared under the aegis of the Paris Peace largely rose up on the shoulders of national movements, which, like good nationalisms, did not accept those who did not speak the authentic language of "the People", and who did not share their values nor perhaps their religion. Creating, then, a "civic culture" in the middle of Europe meant, paradoxically, suppressing any new multicultural "civil society", made up of linguistic, ethnic, and even racial "rebirths" across the continent. This was a problem that eventually, as of 1939–42, German Nazism tried to "solve" drastically and simplistically.[60]

Out these contradictions, the ideal of autonomy – or of the incipient realisation of national selfhood, somehow to be obtained from a revolution or major change in Spain – was established and consolidated in Catalonia and in the Basque Country in the 1920s. Thus, on April 14, 1931, the proclamation of the Spanish Republic in Barcelona and then in Madrid, together with the announcement of a "Catalan Republic", gave left-wing Catalan nationalists their opportunity. Called the "Generalitat" after the executive council that, under the "Old Constitution", had governed before the Bourbon victory in 1714, the new institution was negotiated with the Provisional republican government in Madrid, and was converted into an autonomous minipower. Barcelona was the second capital of the Republic, but also a counter-capital, a kind of living urban reply to centralisation. The new Generalitat collected both the most ideological viewpoints of the previous century regarding the idea of popular sovereignty, as well as the principles of Historical Law with regard to borders. During his trial in Paris, in January 1927, arraigned before a French tribunal for the attempted invasion of Catalonia from France, the so-called "events of Prats de Molló" that hoped to start a leftist and nationalist uprising against the militarist and Spanish nationalist dictatorship under the monarchy in Spain, Francesc Macià offered the French the creation of a future and allied "Pyrenean Belgium". Obviously, he retained the French dream of the frustrated "Rhenish Republic" but directed more towards the South.[61] But, not quite four-and-a-half years after his trial, in his varied proclamations of April 14, 1931, Macià produced the Spanish Republic, and an effective Catalan autonomy. Although a self-proclaimed separatist, he assumed in part the federal dream of a Spain as territorially-representative State.

Macià the separatist had merged his symbolism to the variety of Catalan republicanism, led by Lluís Companys, among others, to create a broad-scale party, Esquerra Republicana de Catalunya (ERC, or Catalan Republican Left). On the 14th of April, both spoke successively from the two official balconies on Barcelona's central political square. Companys, faithful to his federalist republican formation, recovered the regional meaning of Pi Margall of Catalonia and Spain. Shortly thereafter, Macià insinuated the Calhounian sense of an "Iberian confederation", with the sovereignty of the parts of a historical union, adding memories of Sinibaldo de Mas and nineteenth-century "iberianism" by including in his proclamation Portugal (then involved in a revolt against military rule). The only thing, however, Macià most explicitly did not contemplate was to propose a monarchical solution for Catalonia. And the proposal of autonomy for Catalonia within a royal Spain presided over by king Alfonso XIII was precisely what

– within the tradition of the *Lliga* – the conservative Cambó offered, together with his minister Joan Ventosa in His Majesty's government, overthrown that same day by the "republican revolution". Republicanism – always linked to the idea of nullification – would become the basis of any future idea of Catalan autonomy, even with the return to democracy in the 1970s, under king Juan Carlos I. The republican dream for an independent State would reappear in its fullest expression with the surge of pro-independence sympathies after 2012.

Macià acted in the terms of Wilsonian self-determination as lived during the winter fever of 1918–19 in Europe. That the Spanish Republic lived its constituent process during 1931 as an "integral", unitary State which was willing, in Article 8 of the new Constitution, to tolerate autonomous exceptions was a harbinger of imminent contradictions to be seen in 1934 (by which time Macià was dead) and during the Civil War of 1936–39.

To conclude, in spite of the simple narrative that has longed for History (with a capital "H") to be no more than a lineal "progress" towards greater "democracy", Historical Law – the legal legitimation in terms of the past, rather than of immediate populations and their opinions at the polls – has tended to determine aspects of statehood such as the justification of borders or existence of territories with simultaneously varied forms of administration. At the same time, however, demographic pressure itself and the strength of market participation seemed to render unsustainable the oldest forms of symbolic leadership. Increasingly, monarchs have yielded place to the charismatic leaders and "guides" that seemed to arise from "the People" themselves, as a suitable collective abstraction, instead of being born in a niche of a socially remote aristocracy or some special "blue-blooded" nobility. Although, at the end of the twentieth century it seemed that all the forms of personalization of power – old or new – would definitely be transferred to representative institutions, the second decade of the twenty-first century has rediscovered charismatic heads of state, and has even generated new "dynasties" (the Kim succession to so-called "Supreme Leadership" in North Korea, since 1946, for example, or the al-Assad succession in Syria), that are supposedly legitimized by their presumed "revolutionary" basis.

Notes

1 This essay is an expanded version of the article originally published in Catalan. Expansions in the text are intentionally not matched by a further footnotes, which could become a multitude, quite unnecessarily, and so clog and overload the text. I am keeping therefore the original notes, with some very few additions. In general terms, for the foreign influences on Catalan nationalism in the early twentieth century, see: E. Ucelay-Da Cal, "'El Mirall de Catalunya': models internacionals en el desenvolupament del nacionalisme i del separatisme català, 1875–1923". *Estudios de Historia Social,* num. 28–29, January–June 1984, pp. 213–219; J. Llorens i Vila, *Catalanisme i moviments nacionalistes contemporanis, 1885–1901: missatges a Irlanda, Creta i Finlàndia,* Barcelona: Dalmau, 1988; G. Cattini and C. Santacana, "International models of Catalan nationalism: 1882–1914" in A. Biagini and G. Motta (eds), *Empires and Nations from the Eighteenth to the Twentieth Century*, Newcastle-upon-Tyne (UK): Cambridge Scholars Publishing, 2014, pp. 327–336.

2 J.-M. Kreins, *Histoire du Luxembourg*, Paris, PUF, 1996, pp. 58–59.

3 C. H. Church and R. C. Head, *A Concise History of Switzerland,* Cambridge (UK): Cambridge University Press, 2013, chaps. 5 and 6.

4 As a clear sample of the conflict with Canada, can be cited the first book of a very young T. Roosevelt, *The Naval War of 1812*, New York, G. P. Putnam & Sons, 1900, Part II, which dedicates a good part of the text to the fights in the Great Lakes.

5 J. Lynch, *Las revoluciones hispanoamericanas, 1808–1826,* Barcelona: Editorial Ariel, 2008; also, by the same author: J. Lynch, *Caudillos en Hispanoamérica 1800–1850*, Madrid: Editorial Mapfre, 1994.

6 I'm taking the idea of J. G. A. Pocock and adapting it to another context: J. G. A. Pocock, *The Ancient Constitution and the Feudal Law: a study of English Historical Thought in the Seventeenth Century*, Cambridge: Cambridge University Press, 1987 (2nd ed.).

7 E. Ucelay-Da Cal, *Breve historia del separatismo catalán: del apego a lo catalán al anhelo de la secesion*, Barcelona Ediciones B-Penguin Random House, 2018, pp. 21–48.

8 M. Crook, "The Uses of Democracy. Elections and Plebiscites in Napoleonic France", in M. F. Cross and D. Williams (eds.), *The French Experience from Republic to Monarchy, 1792–1814: New Dawns in Politics, Knowledge and Culture*, Basingstoke (UK), Palgrave-Macmillan, 2000, pp. 58–71. Also P. Dyer, *Citizen Emperor: Napoleon in Power, 1799–1815*, London, Bloomsbury, 2014.

9 The classic statement in: E. J. Hobsbawm and T. Ranger (eds), *The Invention of Tradition*, Cambridge (UK), Cambridge University Press, 1983.

10 See yet another classic: A. J. Mayer, *The Persistence of the Old Regime: Europe to the Great War*, New York, Pantheon, 1981.

11 W. Bagehot, *The English Constitution* (originally published 1867), republished with an index and student guide to further reading by Sussex Academic Press, Brighton/Chicago/Toronto, in 1997; introduced by Gavin Phillipson and reviewed by Lord Lester of Herne Hill QC.

12 D. Keogh, *Ireland and Europe, 1919–1948*, Dublin, Gill & Macmillan Ltd, 1988.

13 D. Walder,*The Chanak Affair,* London, Hutchinson, 1969.

14 Very useful for its nature as a theoretical work of transition: Lord Elton, *Imperial Commonwealth*, London: Collins, 1945; for the Balfour quote, p. 491.

15 P. J. Vatikiotis, *The History of Modern Egypt: From Muhammad Ali to Mubarak*, London: Weidenfeld & Nicolson, 1991.

16 K. Perkins, *A History of Modern Tunisia,* Cambridge (UK): Cambridge University Press, 2004.

17 F. Cardini, and S. Valzania, *La scintilla: Quando l'Italia, con la guerra di Libia, fece scoppiare il primo conflitto mondiale,* Milan: Mondadori, 2014.

18 M. Glenny, *The Balkans: Nationalism, War, and the Great Powers, 1804–2011,* New York: Penguin, 2012.

19 L. Kallivretakis, "A Century of Revolutions: The Cretan Question between European and Near East Politics", P. M. Kitromilides (ed.), *Eleftherios Venizelos: The Trials of Statesmanship,* Edinburgh (UK): Edinburgh University Press (2008), pp. 11–35 (pdf).

20 J. Brissa, *La guerra de los Balcanes*, Barcelona, Maucci, 1913.

21 W. Mallinson, *Cyprus: A Modern History,* London: I. B. Tauris, 2009.

22 N. Malcolm, *Bosnia: A Short History,* London: Pan, 1994.

23 V. Dedijer, *The Road to Sarajevo,* New York: Simon & Schuster, 1966.

24 L. Bethell (ed.), *Central America since Independence*, New York: Cambridge University Press, 1992.

25 M. C. M. Pereira, «Sinibaldo de Más: el diplomático español partidario del Iberismo», *Anuario de derecho internacional*, num. 17 (2001), pp. 351–370.

26 V. Almirall and J. Pich i Mitjana (ed.), *Antologia de textos*, Barcelona, Generalitat de Catalunya, Institut d'Estudis Autonòmics, 2011.

27 R. Kee, *The Bold Fenian Men: The Green Flag*, vol. 2. Northhampton (MA): Interlink Publishing, 1983.

28 J. Rougerie, J., *La Commune de 1871*, Paris: PUF, 2014.

29 A. Puig Campillo, A., *El Cantón Murciano*, Murcia: Editora Regional de Murcia, 1986; M-A. Médioni, *El Cantón de Cartagena*, Madrid: Siglo XXI, 1979; J. Alvarez Junco, *La Comuna en España*, Madrid: Siglo XXI, 1971.

30 A. J. P. Taylor, *The Struggle for Mastery in Europe 1848–1918*. Oxford (UK): Oxford University Press, 1971.

31 E. Crankshaw, *Bismarck*, London, Macmillan (1981), pp. 181–183.

32 E. Ucelay-Da Cal, *El imperialismo catalán. Prat de la Riba, Cambó, D'Ors y la conquista moral de España*, Barcelona, Edhasa, 2003.

33 A. Griffith, *The Resurrection of Hungary* [1904], Dublin, UCD Press, 2003; E. Prat de la Riba, *La nacionalitat catalana*, Barcelona, Tip. L'Anuari de l'Exportació, 1906.

34 T. K. Derry, *A Short History of Norway*. London: Allen & Unwin, 1968, cap. X; J.-F. Batail, *Les destinées de la Norvège moderne (1814–2005)*. Paris: Michel de Maule, 2005.

35 A. De La Villa and A. Vivero (prologue of Rodrigo Soriano), *Cómo cae un trono (la revolución en Portugal)*, Madrid: Renacimiento, 1910; see E. Ucelay-Da Cal, «European state-building as a "European state-building as a function of Iberian staterhood: An interpretative and narrative essay", in S. Campos Matos and L. Bogotte Chorão (coords.), *Península Ibérica. Nações e transnacionalidade entre dois séculos (XIX e XX)*, Vila Nova de Famalicão, Edições Humus, 2017, pp. 15–75.

36 F. Napo, *1907, la révolte des vignerons*, Tolouse: Privat, 1971.

37 B. Tuchman, *Los cañones de agosto*, Barcelona: Península, 2004.

38 A. T. Q. Stewart, *The Ulster Crisis: Resistance to Home Rule, 1912–14*, London: Faber & Faber, 1967.

39 F. Fischer, *Germany's Aims in the First World War*, New York: W. W. Norton, 1961.

40 C. Clarke, *The Sleepwalkers: How Europe Went to War in 1914*, New York: Harper Perennial, 2012.

41 According to a map of J. F. Horrabin, *Atlas of Current Affairs*, London: Gollancz (1934), pp. 56–57. In general, see: M. Hopkinson, *The War of Independence*, Dublin, McGill–Queen's University Press, 2004; M. Hopkinson, *Green Against Green: The Irish Civil War*, Dublin, Gill, 2004.

42 See, as an indication: T. Ryle Dwyer, *The Squad and the Intelligence Operations of Michael Collins*, Douglas Village (Cork), Mercier Press, 2005.

43 P. Broué, *Révolution en Allemagne (1917–1923)*, Paris: Éditions de Minuit, 1971; J. Paschen, *«Wenn Hamburg brennt, brent die Welt». Der kommunistische Griff nach der Macht mi October 1923,* Frankfurt am Main: Peter Lang, 2010.

44 E. Manela, *The Wilsonian Moment: Self-Determination and the International Origins of Anticolonial Nationalism*, Oxford (UK): Oxford University Press, 2007.

45 E. Holt, *Protest in Arms. The Irish Troubles, 1916–1923,* New York: Coward-McCann, 1961, pp. 181–182.

46 A. F. Upton, *The Finnish Revolution 1917–1918,* Minneapolis (MI): University of Minnesota Press, 1980; Davies, N., *White Eagle, Red Star: The Polish–Soviet War, 1919–20,* London: Pimlico, 2003; A. Zamoyski, *Warsaw 1920: Lenin's Failed Conquest of Europe,* London: HarperCollins, 2008; S. W. Page, *The Formation of the Baltic States: A Study of the Effects of Great Power Politics upon the Emergence of Lithuania, Latvia, and Estonia,* Cambridge (MA): Harvard University Press, 1959.

47 R. L. Tökés, *Béla Kun and the Hungarian Soviet Republic: The Origins and Role of the Communist Party of Hungary in the Revolutions of 1918–1919,* New York: Praeger, 1967.

48 H. C. Armstrong, *Grey Wolf. Mustafa Kemal: An Intimate Study of a Dictator*, Harmondsworth (UK): Penguin, 1940; P. Kinross, *Ataturk: A Biography of Mustafa Kemal, Father of Modern Turkey,* New York, William Morrow, 1964; A. Mango, *Ataturk: The Biography of the Founder of Modern Turkey,* New York: The Overlook Press, 2002.

49 I. Molas, «La Federació Democràtica Nacionalista», *Recerques*, num. 4, 1974, pp. 137–153.

50 M. T. Graham, Jr., *New Governments of Central Europe,* New York: Holt, 1924, and again by M. T. Graham, Jr., *New Governments of Eastern Europe,* New York: Holt, 1927.

51 B. J. Nordstrom, *The History of Sweden*, Westport (CT): Greenwood 2002, pp. 93–113.

52 H. Seton-Watson, *Eastern Europe between the Wars, 1918–1941*, New York: Harper & Brothers, 1948.

53 See the classic work of J. Wheeler-Bennett, *The Nemesis of Power: German Army in Politics, 1918–1945*, New York: Palgrave-Macmillan, 2005.

54 H. Carrère d'Encausse, *Réforme et Révolution chez les musulmans de l'empire russe,* Paris: Presses de la Fondation nationale des sciences politiques, 1966, and, by the same author: H. Carrère d'Encausse, *Le Grand Défi: bolcheviks et nations, 1917–1930*, Paris: Flammarion, 1987.

55 A. Lyttelton, *The Seizure of Power: Fascism in Italy 1919–1929*, London: Weidenfeld & Nicolson, 1973.

56 E. González Calleja, *La España de Primo de Rivera: La modernización autoritaria, 1923–1930*, Madrid: Alianza, 2005.

57 D. Wheeler, *A Ditadura Militar Portuguesa (1926–1933)*, Lisboa: Europa-América, 1986.

58 J. Rothschild, *Pilsudski's Coup d'Etat*, New York: Columbia University Press, 1966.

59 From an approving point of view: J. Benoist-Méchin, *Mustapha Kemal ou la mort d'un empire*, Paris, Albin, 1954.

60 M. Roseman, *The Villa, The Lake, The Meeting: Wannsee and the Final Solution*, London: Allen Lane, 2002.

61 Estat Català, *La Catalogne rebelle,* Paris: Agence Mondiale de Librairie, 1927, p. 25.

Chapter 2

Nationalities, Nations, States: Models of the National Question in Europe in the 1930s

Xosé M. Nuñez Seixas

The complexity of European identities during the interwar period and the various solutions presented at that time would suggest a series of questions of essential response so as to best situate Catalan nationalism and social trends in its continental context. In the 1930s, it must be said that Catalonia, its political autonomy and the different currents of Catalan nationalism, were by no means an exceptional case. Based on this premise, in this brief study there is no intent to offer an exhaustive history of the diverse trends of ethno-national litigation in the "Old Continent" that shaped the European context of the situation of Catalonia during the Second Republic and the Spanish Civil War. Here will simply be developed an integrated perspective that should help to better understand how exceptional, or not, were the Catalan nationalist approaches to autonomy, self-government, sovereignty or independence in Europe of its time.

Before 1914, Five Paths to Organized National Selfhood

One has to go back to the years before the First World War. When in 1913 the French historian Charles Seignobos published *Les aspirations autonomistes en Europe* as an indication of his interest into what was called the "nationalities question"; he placed on a similar level, among others, the issues of Alsace-Lorraine (then still within the German Empire), Catalonia, Poland, Ireland or Lithuania.[1] In February of that year, the transnationalist magazine *Les Annales des Nationalités* published a report on the revindications of European *autonomous* movements, namely: Catalonia, Bohemia (in Austria), Lithuania, Latvia and the Ukraine (in Russia). According to French public opinion – then representative of European standpoints in general – the project of autonomy for Catalonia already presented in 1907 and the initiatives of the *Lliga Regionalista* (Regionalist League) of Enric Prat de la Riba and Francesc Cambó were easily comparable to the aspirations of John Redmond and his Irish Parliamentary Party, the activist fraction of the Young Czechs' party, or the Lithuanian nationalists in exile. Both Seignobos and *Les Annales des Nationalités* distinguished between nationalities in the proper sense of the term (those of the multinational empires of Central Eastern Europe) and the "annexes of old states in which the desire for autonomy has been stimulated: Ireland and Catalonia".[2] But there was not a common program that fit all these aspirations.

Before the Great War, there coexisted in Europe five models of what could be termed ethno-national diversity management.[3] First, there subsisted a premodern autonomy in a compound monarchy in the style of the Ancien Regime, in which a given national community aspired to become a formally admitted and defined territory, a body within a multinational and multi-ethnic monarchy, such as been realized in a paradigmatic manner the case of Hungary after the Compromise or *Ausgleich* of 1867. A second possible aspiration consisted of transforming such a community into a body (organic or not) or federated state forming part of a multinational federation. Here the influence of the federalist theories was often noted, from classics such as the American Alexander Hamilton or French Pierre-Joseph Proudhon to lesser-known thinkers like the Spanish (and Catalan) Francisco Pi Margall. It was easy to propose several combinations of the ideas of such authors, mixtures which can be found from the theories of Catalan journalist Antoni Rovira i Virgili down to several of the formulations coming out of left Occitanism. Third, a given State could proffer decentralization (or be encouraged to do so) in the form of autonomy and/or regional self-government, with several variants, which could go from the granting of a statute of administrative autonomy to territories where there were cultural, institutional or geographical peculiarities of some kind or other, to the French model of "decentralization from above" advocated by the *Fédération Régionaliste Française* (FRF) of Jean Charles-Brun, based on criteria of administrative rationalization. In fourth place, there could appear local autonomy, neither territorial nor corporate, which was characteristic of ethnic Hungarian or Germanic communities in Transylvania or on the Russian Baltic. Finally, in fifth place, a given community, with enough leadership, backing and determination, could convert itself into a new national State.

However, there were in fact few examples of secession in Europe between 1878 and 1914. There was one that exercised some fascination in Catalan nationalism: the independence of Norway in 1905, which took place by means of a plebiscite, but – by means of another second referendum – the country was constituted as a kingdom. There were several parties in western Europe which went on to defend independence *tout court*, but with several variants, that went from the first Basque Nationalist Party (PNV, from the name in Castilian Spanish, founded in 1895), until the National Breton Party (with the initials PNB, which lasted from 1911 to 1914). Nevertheless, such options all oscillated in their goals. In the case of the Basque PNV after 1903–1905, for example, the party updated the model of a premodern pact: it began to defend the formula of "foral reintegration" (from the Spanish *fuero*, privilege or legal exception), as the manner of returning to the status previous to 1839, interpreted as an independence *avant le lettre*. Others aspired to confederalism, or even full independence obtained by insurrection, as preached by Macedonian nationalism.

It should be stressed, therefore, that nationalist claims previous to the First World War were not only a question of Central Eastern Europe. There were also the cases of Catalonia, of the Basque Country, of Ireland, and of Flanders, as well as the regionalist/nationalist demands within the French State. If World War I had not suddenly exploded on the scene, probably there would have prospered a model of territorial self-government for Ireland, which perhaps could have been extended to Scotland. Doubtless, Europe would have been very different.

The Impact of the Great War of 1914–1918

The First World War supposed the irruption on the international scene of the geostrategic use of the "principle of nationalities" on the part of the two contending sides, especially by the Entente powers. During the conflict, the theoretical elaboration of the "principle of nationalities" was renewed and expanded with new meanings.[4] It was still not fully equipped with the affirmation of the right of self-determination, which was incorporated into the European political vocabulary in a more generalized way as of 1917. The principle of nationalities expressed that the communities that could be defined as being a nation based on organic objectives and/or voluntaristic criteria within plurinational States could aspire to a full self-government, but not necessarily to the free decision to handle themselves alone, i.e., as an independent State with full foreign recognition. The principle of the consent of those governed and that of self-determination were incorporated progressively to that of the nationalities, thanks above all to the North American president Woodrow Wilson and the Russia Bolsheviks as of 1917. In addition, a pacifist reading was acquired: if the world was to be reformed in a natural manner so as to be composed of different and authentic nations, the underlying causes of conflict would disappear only if all were free. This was a principle in sympathy with the tenets of pacifists, Christian and Socialist humanitarians; this contributed to the international legitimacy of what had been considered nationalities. But that did not eliminate the basic problem: what was a nation? There coexisted a variety of schemes, dreams or interpretations: an organic-historicist principle of the nationalities, and another of a liberal-voluntary nature, as well as various intermediate positions, that drank from the doctrinal legacy of the nineteenth century. And although the colonial peripheries were often left out of any discussion, or debate, many activists in the colonies took good note of the nationalist irredentism of Europe, and, after 1918, frequently communists were seen as the authentic anti-imperialists.[5]

The great geo-strategic convulsion that came at the end of the war, with the dissolution of the Russian, Austro-Hungarian, Ottoman multinational empires, gave rise to a new map of "nationalizing states", as well as a new distribution on the continent of national minorities, nations without a State, and nationalities. The success of the new States, from Czechoslovakia to Estonia, had to do with the mobilization of their nationalist elites, but also with the reformulation of the geostrategic interests of the victorious Entente, and greater or lesser proximity to the new Soviet power. Lenin and the Bolsheviks used pragmatically the principle of nationalities, always in a way subordinated to their fundamental interests (the expansion of the revolution and, later, the consolidation of "socialism in one country"). If the Soviets recognized the independence of Finland in 1917, hoping that the Finnish Socialists would take power in a civil war during 1918, the short Ukrainian republic of 1918 was crushed by the new Bolshevik Red Army, whilst the Baltic States survived thanks to Western military aid.

The new "successor States" in Central and Eastern Europe wanted to follow the example of the national State by definition: France. Their goal was to apply a homogenizing policy: a State had to correspond to a single nation, a single language, a homogeneous national culture, and a unique vision of the past and the present. But the pursuit of such a policy was now badly timed, because nationalism or, at least, the consciousness of belonging to an ethnic minority, had rooted in several populations of those new States which did not speak the new "national language". Besides, the capricious distribution of several diverse national minorities – similar to a leopard skin of ethno-linguistic groups – on both sides of the new borders turned their claims into an international policy question. Several ethnic groups, which at one time in the past had been dominant, now, after 1918, saw themselves in an inverted position: the Hungarians became a minority in Slovakia and Romania; the Germans in Pomerania and parts of Silesia, and so on, but they continued counting on the protection of their "maternal" states.[6] Identification with these irredentist minorities became, after 1918–19, a fundamental element of the internal political debate and a revindication associated with radical State nationalism, both in the Weimar Republic in Germany, as well as in Hungary, Poland or the Soviet Ukraine. But it could also have imitators in new pan-nationalisms, such as pan-dutchness of the Flemish nationalists.

National minorities as such were never recognized as collective subjects by the new international jurisprudence regarding national minorities created under the protection system of the League of Nations. The philosophy that inspired the treaties of minorities under the sponsorship of the League, imposed on the new Eastern European States, was the obliged recognition of individual rights of those belonging to minorities "of race, language and religion". The hope was that in the long term the "successor States" would assimilate ethnic majorities, just as had allegedly happened with the Welsh in England or the Bretons in France. Likewise, and despite its limitations, the structure under the umbrella of an international organization of a system of protection of minorities was a clear precedent and a stimulus for the theoretical debate and the exploration of legal channels and international alternatives. During the 1920s, a significant part of political Catalan nationalism also considered that the recognition of Catalonia as a "national minority" protected by the international treaties could be a step forward in the achievement of national freedom. But Spain was a neutral power in Great War, and therefore not included in the treaty system of the Paris Peace. Catalan nationalist pressures were thus to be frustrated.

The Interwar Years: The Six Claims for Decentralization

During the interwar period, the same models of decentralization and nationalist revindication survived with few modifications. Such models now were not restricted to the geographic sphere of Central Eastern Europe, nor to Spain. In the face of those who insisted on the supposed "Spanish exceptionality" in this regard, it should be remembered that in the Western European area there were, with diverse political and social force and influence, various movements of ethno-territorial claims. One can most prominently point to the "Irish question", resolved only provisionally with the Anglo-Irish Treaty of 1921 and the division of the island. Other signs of political change in postwar Britain were the birth of Welsh nationalism, and the political re-articulation of Scots identity. But there were other instances within the victorious Allied powers. In Belgium, there was the development of a new and more exalted Flemish nationalism after the demobilization of the soldiers in 1918. France saw the emergence of a new Alsatian question, more important after 1924–1926 than Breton or Corsican nationalisms, much smaller minorities famous later for their drift towards collaborationism with the German and Italian occupiers in World War Two. Similarly, after the effort of the Great War, Italy had to face the rapid growth of Sardinian autonomy between 1919 and 1924, in addition to the demands of the newly annexed border minorities, such as the Slovenes or the South-Tiroleans, from the Adriatic to the Alps.[7]

Six major groups of claims to achieve self-determination can be distinguished. They were not an exclusive characteristic of each and every nationalism or ethno-territorial movement, but rather were often were inter-crossed and recombined in the diverse political fractions in which each of these movements were divided.[8]

In the first place, there remained the still functional model of pre-modern autonomy: becoming a part of a "composite" empire, which was made up of different sovereignties and suzerainties under a Crown. This is what was imposed as a negotiated solution for a time in the Irish Free State, between 1922 and 1937; Ireland was a dominion of the British Empire, part of the realm of king George V. In practice, it was a de facto independence. This solution seduced broad sectors of Scottish or Welsh nationalism, a fact that was only comprehensible from the assumption of the peculiarity and flexibility of the British imperial model, which, within a single Crown, could control dominions with their own representation in the League of Nations at Geneva. A similar model also subsisted within the Danish "composite monarchy" in the relationship between the metropolis (Denmark) and Iceland, analogous to a confederation agreement.[9]

Secondly, after the Great War, there appeared the ideal of a road to independence through insurrection. This is a tradition set up by Sinn Féin and other Irish nationalist groups in the wake of the 1916 Easter rebellion in Dublin, whereby three years later the image of a sacrifical revolt had ended up promoting the triumph of radical nationalists as the majority of Ireland in the United Kingdom parliamentary elections of December 1918. The failed Dublin uprising generated a mirage, appropriate for the fantasies of minority pro-independence sectors: the sacrifice of a a few valiant fighters provoked a spiral of repression, which made a growing part of the population feel solidarity with the victims, until the cause of the martyrs became the majority opinion. This suggestion, more or less deformed through various mirrors, could be found behind the first organized ambition of Francesc Macià in the creation of Catalan nationalism, as well as in the tendency of the *aberrians* within Basque nationalism at the same time, and also among the militants of the *Parti National Bréton* and the dream State proposed by some of its leaders, and indeed even among some Galician or Flemish nationalists.[10] "Independentism", i.e., pro-independence sentiment, however, was often more rhetorical than real, and usually was translated into medium-term confederal approaches.

Thirdly, one could point to federalism, a tradition that is especially influential in Western Europe, but also present in Central Eastern Europe, for example, among Polish nationalist thinkers like the pianist and politician Ignacy J. Paderewski, or in the projects for the creation of a Danubian confederation as an alternative to a *Mitteleuropa* of German influence drawn up, for example, by Ószkar Jászi. The models oscillated between broad confederal designs, those inspired by asymmetrical federalism – federal units out of which had to come the "authentic" nations. It was thus expressed in the various models of the federal statehood for Republican Spain that came out of Esquerra Republicana of Catalonia (ERC) or, in France, the ideas of the Parisian federalist group of Eugene Poitevin. In the case of Belgium, in addition, successive steps towards the federalization of the State were made, beginning with the territorialization of linguistic rights of Dutch speakers, and their rights to use their language in courts, schools and within the Administration.

In the fourth case, interwar nationalisms were nagged by the more or less idealized model of Soviet federalism and its nationality engineering prepared by ethnographers and ethnologists. The Soviets combined symmetry and asymmetry, autonomous republics and federated republics. It was not just a model advocated by the communists, who acted in multinational political communities as a possible solution for the definitive structuring of the State – for example, the Polish or Czechoslovakian communists – but also, for example, by the conservative Catalan regionalist Joan Estelrich in 1929, when he stated that the new Hispanic federalism should "take into account the new doctrines of minority rights and especially the new experiences, without forgetting those of the Soviets", since the formula of the moment no longer consisted of "each nation a State", but in the coexistence of "free nationalities within the complex State". The development of culture should be the work of "autonomous cultural entities", and here the state was reduced to an arbitrational role. Still, Estelrich also advocated a structuring of the State that would also have parallels with that which existed in the USSR and Fascist Italy: a constitution "according to nationalities", which would allow a gradation in "free states, allied republics, autonomous territories", and that in addition could adopt corporate criteria for what could refer to its formulas of internal representation and its external articulation.[11] This was not very distant from the eclectic position of the Galician leader Alfonso R. Castelao in his work *Sempre en Galiza* (written in exile in 1944).[12]

In fifth place, there were proposals for territorial autonomy or decentralization from above, a model suggested in Spain by the Catalans of the Lliga Regionalista, among others. As a solution, State decentralization was revindicated in Italy with variations, from the idealization of the South of the Peninsula by Umberto Zanetti-Bianco, to the Sardinian regionalism/autonomy or the *Partito Molissano d'Azione* until 1922. Similar ideas of institutional regionalism also existed in Central Europe. Examples included the Transylvanian regionalism advocated by the *Partidul National-Taranesc* (National Peasants' Party) and its supra-ethnic concept of a multicultural region for Transylvania (supported by former Rumanian activists who prior had acted in the Hungarian parliament and now had become regionalists within the Rumanian State). The same sort of schemes came out of the organic federal tradition represented by the Bavarian autonomists of the *Bayerische Volkspartei* or some Rhenish organizations, which arose between 1919 and 1922 with an anti-Prussian surge that wanted more than federalism and resentment against the discipline and militarism of "Prussianism". This was the case of the then young Rhinelander "separatist" Konrad Adenauer, to cite a representative figure with a long-term trajectory.[13]

The territorial model – based on autonomy *à la carte*, of a political and administrative nature, without federalization – that was offered during the brief existence the Second Spanish Republic was considered, in fact, by several theoreticians of the question of nationalities, ws a good example to imitate in other parts of Europe. Such was, for example, the evaluation made by Theodor Veiter, the Austrian jurist, national conservative, and specialist in the subject of nationalities.[14] But there were also other designs with some success in attracting attention, if more restricted to isolated communities, that were very ethnically homogeneous and of little demographic significance: the major success story was the 1921 agreement of the League of Nations with Finland regarding the Swedish linguistic minority on the Åland islands in the Gulf of Bothnia in the Baltic Sea; but there were other cases, such as some special clauses in the minority treaties of Czechoslovakia, Greece and Rumania which respectively recognized the territorial autonomy of the Subcarpathian Ruthenians and the monastic communities of Mount Athos and the Vlachs of the Pindus mountains of Northern Greece; the religious and educational autonomy of the Germans of Transylvania; and some provisions regarding the Jewish communities in Poland, Greece and Romania. Finally, in sixth place, there were many plans or projects regarding a non-territorial collective autonomy, based on the principle of the individual adscription of each person to a national and cultural identity. This principle was reformulated in the period between the wars as a panacea to solve the dilemma that was posed in many geographical areas of the continent between national identity and State affiliation, between linguistic and cultural rights and political citizenship, and between maintenance of peace and satisfaction of feelings of national selfhood of millions of Europeans. This was particularly problematic in the areas of ethnically mixed populations of Central Eastern Europe, where a solution based on territorial self-government was not always feasible. The doctrine of non-territorial autonomy had at least three theoretical sources. First, one can point to the legacy of Zionist thought concerning the self-government of Jewish communities in Europe. Faced with the alternative options of the Jewish national State and, where it was possible, a territorial autonomy of the Jewish communities or *shtetlekh* (in Yiddish, a *shtetl* was a single small village with a large concentration of Jews) in the Russian Pale of Settlement, in Austrian Galitzia, or in Romania, from the end of the nineteenth century on, various theorists conceived the idea of a non-territorial autonomy for Jews. Such an arrangement would guarantee the religious freedom of Jews, with their own schools in Yiddish or (for Zionists) in Hebrew. This idea was presented in Central Eastern Europe as an alternative to the option of cultural assimilation.[15] In the second instance, one can look at the corporate tradition of the Baltic-German elites under Russian tsarism, which conceived of minorities as a sort of corporation within an organic State. And, finally, in third place, of the ideological left there was the rich legacy produced by the main theorists of the Austrian Social Democracy on the "national question", Karl Renner and Otto Bauer, relatively complemented by the relatively similar views of Social Christian chancellor, monsignor Ignaz Seipel.

The European nationalities movement defined in its program on a personal model, the cultural autonomy of nationalities, based on the personal principle, that is to say, in the free adscription of each citizen to a national identity. This was particularly true of the Congress of European Nationalities between 1925 and 1939, an organization that aspired to represent the entirety of all the more moderate political organizations representative of the national minorities of Central Eastern Europe and some of the sub-state nationalisms of Western Europe.[16] That should have made possible a separation between citizenship and ethno-national identity and thus rise above of the formula of the nation State, which should be transformed into an *anational* State, as defined by the Baltic-German politician Paul Schiemann. However, within the European national movement there were very significant differences over how to interpret cultural autonomy. For sectors more inclined to the liberal left, like Schiemann, the denationalization of the State and the extension of the model of cultural autonomy would be a key safeguard of continental peace, as well as allow for a lasting co-existence between nation(s) and State. For sectors which leaned to the anti-parliamentary right and later were close to German National Socialism, the future was seen in an altogether different manner. A spokesman like Werner Hasselblatt, also a Baltic-German who theorized about the matter, stated there was no need to renounce a future reordering of the continent in homogenous zones where nationality and State would correspond perfectly, although he was not explicit how this new reordering could be attained. While the first sector lost importance after the rise of Nazism to power in Berlin, especially in its base among the German minorities in the "Successor States", the anti-liberal and authoritarian current progressively took over the reins of the European nationalities movement.[17]

Cultural autonomy also presented several problems in practice. In the interwar period it even was applied in some places. The cultural autonomy of Jews had already been a precedent in the ephemeral Ukrainian Republic of 1918. But cultural autonomy was tested, above all, in one country, Estonia, as of 1925. The agreement was made easier by the influence of the Baltic-German parties and the looming Soviet threat. The beneficiaries of the law were the citizens belonging to the German, Swedish, Jewish, and Russian minorities. The criterion of belonging to a minority was the voluntary inscription in a census of nationalities. Autonomous cultural councils were formed where the majority of the members of an ethnic group wanted to manage their own cultural and educational affairs. The Estonian State offered resources for their operation, but the cultural councils in large part also were self-financed. Their operations were satisfactory, above all, for the Germans and the Jews, but not so clearly for the Swedes, who were concentrated in geographical areas and who opted for a model of territorial autonomy, or for the Russians – poor peasants, left without resources and lacking autonomous elites. The authoritarian drift installed itself in the country after January 1934, when the president Konstantin

Päts assumed full State powers; this provoked a restriction of minority rights, in part due to the growing fear within the Estonian leadership circles about the possible construction of micro-states within the State. Both the Estonian law, as well as the more limited law of scholastic autonomy in Latvia, promulgated already in 1919, were surprisingly idealized throughout Europe. But these measures also showed their limits. Because they treated all minorities in a similar manner, Estonian and Latvian laws underlined the contrast between the "weak" minorities (for reasons demographical, economic, cultural and political, even remainders cut by new borders) against the "strong", the latter with more advantages (especially if they could count on powerful patron States such as Germany, Hungary, or other local powers). Thus, in 1928, the Prussian Land, a German sub-state, approved a law of cultural autonomy for Lithuanians and Poles in its territory. But how many Poles, Lithuanians, or Lusatian Sorbs or Wends were willing to renounce the advantages of the German language? And, on the other hand, how many Sudeten Germans would renounce their imperial *Muttersprache* and would opt for acculturation in Czech?

European Autonomies in the Interwar Years

The dialectic between strong and weak minorities was superimposed on another matter: the dialectic that contrasted national minorities in Central and Eastern Europe, on the one hand, and the state-less nationalists of Western Europe, on the other. It was not possible to treat different realities with identical legislations. In Central Eastern Europe, in addition, the question of minorities was intertwined with international politics, and in particular with concepts of internal security, especially in the "successor States": any concessions made to the co-national minorities of a neighbor could be converted into a cession of sovereignty in favor of another rival nation State and, therefore, into an irredentist border conflict.[18] Furthermore, probably one of the main differences between the national question to the east and the west of Europe was probably the stronger underpinning of State nationalisms in Western Europe, which had enjoyed several decades more of implementation and administration than the improvised "successor States", together with the difference in the unequal nature of the distribution of ethnic populations. But this difference could also be conveniently relativized. For the influential Catalan nationalist writer Antoni Rovira i Virgili, for example, in 1931, autonomous Catalonia should learn from the European experience of protection of minorities, but treat Castillian-speaking immigrants with generosity.[19] Truthfully, the most influential model were the triumphant nationalisms, those that had established a nation State. These were the ones, accordingly, that entered history as successful nations.

A good example of this evolution are the views of the Catalan nationalist conservative jurist Francesc P. Maspons i Anglasell, vice-president since 1926 of the Congress of the European Nationalities.[20] In the years 1927–1929, Maspons opposed the "nefarious" consequences that would be entailed by a cycle of oppressive politics (such as that of the Primo de Rivera military dictatorship in Spain) and the consequent reaction of violent resistance to the State (the failed revolts of the anarcho-syndicalists and their ally, Macià), which negated any pacific solutions. He favored answers that would avoid separatist excesses, and pointed out that the revindication of cultural autonomy would be essentially similar to the foundational theories of Prat de la Riba. According to Maspons, Catalonia should follow this road.[21]

In 1931, however, the Catalan nationalists of the Lliga and the republicans, and Maspons himself, changed their discourse. Maspons serves as a good example of the shift. After being recovered by the rising administration of the Generalitat after April 1931, as a member of its Legal Commission, Maspons embarked on an active personal political campaign to defend the integrity of the Catalan-written Statute of Núria of August of 1931, which posited a confederal model of a bilateral nature for the relations between the "Catalan State" and the Spanish Republic. These relationships would be based on a recognition of the right to self-determination of Catalonia, acknowledged, according to Maspons, by the International Permanent Court of Justice of The Hague. In Maspons view, such steps would lead to the annulment of the eighteenth-century abolition of Catalan "statehood" by the decrees of Nova Planta (the result of Bourbon centralization after victory in the War of Spanish Succession, in 1714–16), with which, in practice, the country regained a lost sovereignty. In his perspective, Catalan–Spanish relations would be of an international character, and subject therefore to the arbitration of the League of Nations and the Hague Court, in line with contemporary models such as the Irish Free State and the revised "pacted union" between Iceland and Denmark, or even Subcarpathian Ruthenia (in Czechoslovakia) and the territory of Memel (in Lithuania), cases in which the chosen route had been a reform of the Constitution of the State to which they belonged, backed by a referendum.[22]

Evolution of the 1930s

Throughout the 1930s, the situation of nationalities and ethnic minorities in Europe underwent diverse changes, conditioned by the international geopolitical context. At the beginning of the decade, there still remained internationalist optimism and the faith of a part of the nationalist elites in the good offices of the League of Nations and its minority protection system, which nevertheless was becoming less effective when it came to providing solutions to minorities' petitions arriving in Geneva. The paralysis of the procedure was seen aggravated by the unilateral abandonment of League by Nazi Germany in 1933, and, in the following year, the unilateral revocation of the Minorities Treaty by Poland (allied to Germany by a pact in January 1934), which thereafter refused to apply the agreement's clauses.

Contrary to what, in its origins, had been predicted optimistically by the inspirers of the League of Nations, ethno-nationalist mobilization among various minorities of Central Eastern Europe continued to increase, whether it was among the Germans and Ukrainians in Poland, the Magyars in Romania, or the Germans in Czechoslovakia.[23] From the late 1920s on, the authoritarian regimes that were established in Eastern Europe could not stop with repressive measures the aggravation of nationalist conflicts. This happened in Poland, in eastern Galicia, where the Ukrainian nationalists, organized largely in the National Democratic

Ukranian Union (UNDO), had broad electoral support. Nevertheless, the growing frustration produced by the immobility of the Warsaw Government on the Ukrainian issue led to the founding of new organizations that advocated armed struggle, in particular the Organization of the Ukrainian Nationalists (OUN), formed in Vienna exile in 1929.

In Rumania there was also a radicalization of ethnic rivalries between the most extreme and pro-fascist variants of Rumanian nationalism and the German, Jewish and Hungarian minority organizations. Similarly, the aggressive nationalization policy of the Yugoslav government in Macedonia and the establishment of an authoritarian regime by King Alexander I of Yugoslavia in January 1929 also provoked a radicalization of the insurrectionary tendencies of Croatian nationalism, on the one hand, and of Macedonian nationalism, on the other. In any case, a taste for violence was present from their first steps, in the Macedonian case dating back to before the turn of the century. The Internal Macedonian Revolutionary Organization (IMRO) was character-ized during the 1920s and 1930s by the promotion of terrorist activity. The IMRO had a strong base in the Macedonian refugee community in Bulgaria, and benefitted from increasing connec-tions in the political elites and the Bulgarian army. In fact, in October 1934, it was a Croatian–Macedonian joint commando team that assassinated King Alexander I in Marseille.

Even in the liberal and republican Czechoslovakia, the refusal of the Prague government to grant Slovakia a statute of territorial autonomy, as requested by the various nationalist Slovakian parties (which reached 30.1% of the votes in 1930), embittered Slovakian nationalist opinion. Worse still, rejection of autonomy was added to the attempts promoted from Bohemia, the domi-nant sector of the Republic, to reform Slovakian grammar, in order to bring its standard closer to Czech and thus to favor the merger of the two languages in some near future. All these measures generated a radicalization of younger generations of the Slovak movement.[24]

However, nationalist demands also grew in Western Europe, and flourished in conditions of full parliamentary democracy.[25] This was the case of Flemish nationalism in the 1930s. After a decade overwhelmed by the division between the old *activistes*, who had collaborated with the Germans in 1914–1918 to achieve cultural and political goals, and *passivistes*, supporters of loyal collaboration with the monarchy and parties of the Belgian sphere, the *Frontpartij* (Front Party) arose. The Front Party was formed in good measure by Flemish ex-combatants of the Belgian army, who, like the Sardinians, expressed their dissatisfaction with an ethno-linguistic key. Numerous activist leaders joined, and in 1936 guided the Flemish movement to achieve 13 percent of votes in Flanders. Three years later, the influence of a new generation of nationalist students imbued with corporate and authoritarian ideas brought about the hegemony within the movement of an authoritarian and paramilitary party, the National Flemish Federation (*Vlaams National Verbond*, VNV). With other groups, the VNV won 15 percent of Flemish votes in 1939. These were modest figures, but deceptive: there were supporters of the Flemish revindications in other Belgian parties, especially in the Catholic Party, the majority in Flanders. As a result, the linguistic demands of the Flemish movement were accepted progressively by the Government of Brussels, from the Law of Bilingualism of 1921 to the institution of "cultural communities" (Flemish and Walloon) within the state in 1938.[26]

There was also a strong growth – with reorganization – of Alsatian autonomism. In general, as of the second half of the 1920s, "regional nationalism" in France divided into several tendencies, from the Catholics to the Liberals and Communists, all of which radicalized their demands in face of the "Jacobin intransigence" of the Third French Republic. The internal diversification and the transversal character of the Alsatian movement, which attracted activists from across the political spectrum, along with the *border minority* character of Alsace, converted the region into a major headache for the authorities in Paris, partly because of the intrusion of the German government – and of the Alsatian nationalist refugees on the other side of the Rhine – especially from 1933 onwards. In other ethnic outskirts of the Hexagon, ethno-nationalist groups arose over the 1930s, driven partly by the example of their *brothers* on the other side of the border, and partly as a renewed radicalization of the regionalist outbreaks before 1914; often the protagonists were members of the local clergy who still saw in their subnational identities a possible brake to Republican seculariza-tion. This is how new nationalist groups emerged in the French Basque Country, in particular the *euskalerrista* movement founded by Father Pierre Lafitte in 1933. Lafitte was a Social-Catholic and personalist Christian, without any influence of the doctrines of PNV (or Basque Nationalist Party) of the peninsular Basque side of the Pyrenees. Similar dynamics occurred also in French Catalonia, French Flanders and in Corsica (the *Partitu Corsu Autonomista*, Autonomous Corsian Party or PCA). Clearly organ-ized nationalist groups were also created in meridional Frisia, or Dutch Friesland (the *Young Frisians* as of 1916, in favor of a polit-ical self-government of a federal nature for Frisia, and the culturalist *Kristlik Selskip*).[27]

In the British Isles, the Irish example, but also that of the domin-ions integrated in the British empire together with the ongoing nationalist agitation in India, generated sequels of sympathetic responses in Wales and Scotland, where, until 1914, the move-ments in favor of autonomy had adopted the form of transversal pressure groups that attempted to have influence in British parties so that these might promote decentralizing projects in the Parliament of Westminster. As for the new Welsh nationalism, it was the result of the radicalization of the cultural demands induced by the Wilsonian demands after 1918, as well as Irish nationalism, together with the surprising influence of both integral French nationalism of Charles Maurras. Its best expression was the *Plaid Genedlaethol Cymru* or Welsh Nationalist Party (WNP, formed in 1925), tendentially conservative, a partisan of the rural and labor cooperativism, which led campaigns for the preservation of the Welsh language and, in later years, the intended achievement of a Dominion status for Wales within the Commonwealth. Also born at the end of the 1920s were the first Scottish political parties of nationalist orientation, which abandoned the transversal mobiliza-tion model of the Scottish Home-Rule Association and opted for a more radical political agenda, including pro-independence claims, now as ever influenced by the examples of Ireland and India. Thus were born the National Party of Scotland in 1928 and the Scottish Party in 1932, and, with the merger of these in 1934, the Scottish

National Party (SNP) arose, characterized by coexistence within the party of autonomists, independentists, conservatives and socialists. The electoral results of the new SNP were modest until 1939, but not insignificant.

In addition to France and Great Britain, within Spain the Galician nationalist movement was consolidated in the 1930s with the foundation of the Galicianist Party (*Partido Galeguista*) and underwent a considerable increase of its political support that allowed it to have a great political influence in Galicia and to obtain the plebiscite of the Statute of Autonomy in June 1936, a month before the Spanish Civil War erupted. Similarly, political Valencianism – regional-nationalism in the area in the historic region of Valencia on the Mediterranean – also experienced significant social growth between 1932 and 1936. Even Andalusian and Aragonese groups lived a certain expansion and political influence in their respective areas during the years of the Second Republic, from 1931 to the Civil War.[28]

In most of these movements in western Europe, what predominated were liberal-democratic and social reformist tendencies, with more or less important differences: liberal and republican left in some cases, socialist tendencies in others. That too was characteristic of the political articulation of some "strong" national minorities in Central and Eastern Europe, as in the case of the Germans of the Sudetenland in historic Bohemia (*Sudety* in Czech): during the early 1930s, even the tendencies of the radical and para-fascist nationalist right, represented by *Sudetendeutsche Partei* of Konrad Henlein, coexisted with an influential "German Social-Democratic Workers Party in the Czechoslovak Republic", led among others by Wenzel Jacksch, who went into exile in London during the Second World War and was in favor during the postwar period of the recognition of the right to self-determination of the Sudeten Germans.[29]

However, most nationalist movements in Western Europe were also characterized by internal political plurality. There were socialist and conservative Bretons, as there were left-wing and right-wing Alsatianists, as also happened in the case of political Catalan nationalism. However, in other cases it was always a party that was designed like the majority representation or "beacon" of the nationalist movement, as an authentic "ethnic party" that, in general, tried to balance between a conservative wing and another aimed at social reform, or in between a radical pro-independence tendency and an autonomist/federalist one. This was the case of Plaid Cymru in Wales, but also of the Basque Nationalist Party (PNV) in Euskadi, of the Partido Galeguista in Spanish Galicia and of the SNP in Scotland. In several cases, a native synthesis, allegedly based on tradition, combined cooperativism, agrarianism or reformist socialism in a manner that was considered the best expression of a program that had to combine national emancipation and social advancement, against the "exotic" nature of Marxism and the devastation of old-style social life due to the effects of capitalism; in Scotland, this was the theory of "social credit" celebrated by the SNP, in the Spanish Basque Country, it was the interpretation of social Catholicism as a "third way", properly Basque and linked to the PNV. One can compare the appeal to the Galician agrarian program proposed by the Partido Galeguista as the best way to solve social problems of the Galician peasants, as something not very different from the solutions proposed at the same time by the Croatian Peasant Party of Stjepan Radić, the main exponent of Croatian nationalism, or by the Slovene Peoples' Party, also then strongly hegemonic in its territory.

A Retrospective Assessment

As the interwar years advanced, stateless nationalist movements could not escape from the influence of the two great worldviews that had determined the evolution of the political situation in continental Europe. On the one hand, Soviet communism was sometimes seen as a strategic ally for the overthrow of the existing oppressor states: Catalan separatist leader Francesc Macià interpreted his option this way in 1925, when he traveled to Moscow to try to get Soviet aid for the independence of Catalonia. In a comparable manner, in 1924, the radical Macedonian nationalists, specifically a "leftist" wing of IMRO, reached an agreement with the Komintern to achieve an independent Macedonia within a Balkan federation of Communist states. In the 1930s, different organizations were born that advocated the compatibility of national liberation for nationalities without a state and a Soviet-style social revolution. Until 1934–35, European Communist parties sustained the theme of the freedom of the oppressed nationalities of their territories. Breaking the principle of a one party/one State on which the Communist International was based, proved much more difficult. For example, there were Breton and Alsatian groups of communist tendencies. It was the Communist Party of Spain (PCE) that first permitted the creation of a Basque autonomous section (PC de Euskadi, 1935) and, in July 1936, of a Unified Socialist Party of Catalonia (PSUC), that was constituted as the first political laboratory of the popular front and of an anti-fascist union of socialists, communists and other tendencies (in this case, catalanist socialists and communists, as well as left nationalists). The doctrine that was to be applied everywhere was based on a balance between defense of State patriotism and the freedoms of nationalities (very clear in the Spanish case), waiting to apply the idealized federal territorial model of the USSR, as expressed in the Soviet constitutions of 1924 and 1936.[30]

A second transnational influence was fascism, both projected from Italy in the 1920s and, above all, as of 1933, with German inspiration. The image of fascism, of its proclamation of the resurrection of the nation as the most important principle of political action, the unitary mobilization of youth, and the militarization of their mass organizations were elements that also created a certain fascination among minority nationalist politicians, from the Welsh Saunders Lewis to the Galician Vicente Risco, passing through the Breton Olier Mordrel or the Corsicians of the PCA. The fascist powers were masters when using a double measuring rod. On the one hand, they ruled through centralization and tendential homogenization of the populations under their mandate, with concessions (above all in the German case) to federalism, to the decentralization of the *Gau* (*Gaue* in plural, a Medieval term used as the basis of administrative reform by the Nazis after 1934) and to regionalism, but also to the minorities considered suitably "Germanic".[31] On the other hand, they offered strategic support to some nationalist movements outside their borders so as to weaken neighboring states or opposing powers.

Thus, Italian fascism gave support to Croatian, Macedonian and other nationalisms. In a much more modest way and in part as a personal obsession of Count Ciano and his paternal family, who were fascists from Livorno, the Mussolini regime showed some sympathy for Corsican nationalism (seen as an Italian irredentism). Italian consular agents abroad had no difficulty to cultivating contacts with "separatists" – for example, in Barcelona – as a reserve option.[32] The fascist influence extended to other parties, from the Ukrainian OUN to the Macedonian IMRO.

The Nazis, on the other hand, showed select sympathies of an ethnographic nature with other peoples that excited the curiosity of their academic intellectuals. This was the case of the interest in the *Keltologen* of the University of Munich for part of French Brittany, or the efforts to approach the Basque question at the beginning of the 1940s. However, they were far more reluctant to offer decided political support to nationalisms without a State, both in Eastern and Western Europe. With all, the German influence was decisive for the consolidation of radical right and pro-Nazi tendencies within Flemish nationalism (like the Verdinaso party, *Verbond van Dietse Nationaal-Solidaristen*, founded in 1931), within Frisian trends (the *Frysk Faksiste Front*, 1933), or within the Alsacian or Breton movements – exemplified in the second half of the 1930s by the pro-Nazi drift, from the National Breton Party, adorned with pan-Celtic mysticism.[33]

In sum, were there major tensions of a pro-independence nature in Europe in the 1930s? Certainly, in Western Europe, in Britain or in France, there was little discussion of autonomies in public and political debate. The exceptional case was Irish Free State, which during the 1930s – especially after the electoral victory of the party of Éamon de Valera, *Fianna Fáil*, in February 1932 – developed a pragmatic viewpoint aimed at the consolidation of their own Irish power within the flexible structure of the British Empire. To the East, the Ukranian nationalists from the OUN, the Croatians and Macedonians (IMRO) were distinguished by their armed and sometimes violent opposition to authoritarian or dictatorial regimes, and, as a consequence, they suffered exile and persecution so that, as has been seen, they became closer and closer to the fascist powers. In any case, as has been seen, the model of territorial autonomy put into practice by the Spanish Second Republic, and above all by the Statute of Catalonia, was subject to a certain curiosity among the specialists of administrative and minority law of several European countries, from Italy to Austria and Germany or Poland, since the Spanish model was a territorial autonomy not inspired by the models of corporate autonomy or protection of minorities.

The achievement of new political independences in Europe of the 1930s only took place in exceptional geopolitical circumstances, and always under the tutelage of a great power, such as, after 1938, Nazi Germany, and also the USSR after 1939. This was the case of the puppet state of "independent" Slovakia, together with the establishment of the colonial regime of the Protectorate of Bohemia-Moravia, after the German intervention in Czechoslovakia that followed the Munich agreements (March 1939). There were other similar examples, like the incorporation of Subcarpathian Ruthenia into Hungary, after an ephemeral declaration of independence, in 1939; or the annexation of a part of Transylvania, also by Hungary in 1940, and of a part of Dobrogea by Bulgaria in the same year, under Nazi hegemony. Apart from the seizure of eastern Poland at the start of the new European War in September 1939, the USSR incorporated Bessarabia and Northern Bucovina, at the expense of Rumania in 1940. In addition, the Soviet Union absorbed the three Baltic Republics, along with the entire Karelian Isthmus, taken from Finland in the "Winter War" of 1939–1940.[34]

The Catalan case during the Civil War in Spain (1936–1939) was, in the end, a peculiar circumstance, without many known or close political or juridical precedents to which to refer. In fact, those who proposed parallels and analogies with the past recalled the Russian civil war of 1917–1923, when the White Russians were uncompromising about the demands of Caucasian or Ukrainian nationalities, and who, as a result, were not capable of forging a great alliance of anti-Soviet forces. In 1936–1937, some Germans, such as Werner Hasselblatt, would attempt vainly to lobby pro-Franco authorities in favour of some recognition of Catalan and Basque home rule so as to win the sympathy of anti-communist nationalists in both areas.[35] But, on the other hand, the same model of the Russian civil war allowed the Spanish Communists to invoke similar principles: virtual independence from Spain, under the principle of freedom for nationalities. The absence of clear precedents allowed each side to imagine the fate of Catalonia and Spain in a totally new and different way.

Notes

1 The text published here differs from the original in Catalan in some small respects: revisions and minor additions for the English-language reader. Ch. Seignobos, *Les aspirations autonomistes en Europe. Albanie, Alsace-Lorraine, Catalogne, Finlande, Iles Grecques, Irlande, Macedoine, Pologne, Serbo-Croatie*, Paris: Librairie Félix Alcan, 1913.

2 See: *Annales des Nationalités*, II: 7-10-1913.

3 Related to a good part of the information that follows, see: X. M. Núñez Seixas, *Movimientos nacionalistas en Europa. Siglo XX*, Madrid: Síntesis, 2004 [2nd ed.]. Also, for integrated visions: M. Hroch, *On the National Interest. Demands and Goals of European National Movements of the Nineteenth Century: A Comparative Perspective*, Prague: Art Faculty, Charles University, 2000, and by the same, M. Hroch, *Das Europa der Nationen. Die moderne Nationsbildung im europäischen Vergleich*, Göttingen: Vandenhoeck & Ruprecht, 2005.

4 See: X. M. Núñez Seixas (ed.), *From Empires to Nations: Nationality Questions during the First World War and its Aftermath*, Leiden: Brill (pending publication).

5 See: E. Manela, *The Wilsonian Moment: Self-determination and the International Origins of Anticolonial Nationalism*, Oxford: Oxford UP, 2007.

6 R. Brubaker, *Nationalism Reframed. Nationhood and the National Question in the New Europe*, Cambridge: Cambridge UP, 1996.

7 S. Fontana, S. (ed.), *Il fascismo e le autonomie locali*, Bologna: Il Mulino, 1973.

8 See: B. Trencsényi, B. and M. Kopecek (eds.), *Discourses of collective identity in Central and Southeast Europe (1770–1945): texts and commentaries*, Budapest: CEU Press, 2010, vol. 3.

9 See: B. Hermannsson, *Understanding Nationalism: Studies in Icelandic Nationalism, 1800–2000*, Stockholm: University of Stockholm, 2005.

10 D. Leach, *Fugitive Ireland: European Minority Nationalists and Irish Political Asylum, 1937–2008*, Dublin: Four Courts Press, 2009; S. Carney, *Breiz Atao! Mordrel, Delaporte, Lainé, Fouéré: Une mystique natio-nale (1901–1948)*, Rennes: Presses Universitaires de Rennes, 2015.

11 See: J. Estelrich, *La qüestió de les minories nacionals i les vies del Dret*, Barcelona: Catalònia, 1929.

12 A. R. Castelao, *Sempre en Galiza*, Buenos Aires: Ed. As Burgas, 1944.

13 See: H. Ortmann, *Rheinischer Separatismus und Westdeutsche Republik: zu den politischen Zielen im Rheinland in den Jahren von 1918 bis 1923*, Hildesheim: Universitätsverlag Hildesheim, 2016.

14 See, for example: T. Veiter, *Nationale Autonomie. Rechtstheorie und Verwirklichung mi positiven Recht*, Viena/Leipzig: Braumüller, 1938. Also: K. Braunias, "Die nationale Autonomie in Spanien", *Nation und Staat*, May 1931, pp. 515–24.

15 C. Fink, *Defending the Rights of Others: The Great Powers, the Jews, and International Minority Protection, 1878–1938*, Cambridge: Cambridge UP, 2004.

16 For more details: X. M. Núñez Seixas, *Entre Ginebra y Berlín. La cuestión de las minorías nacionales y la política internacional en Europa, 1914–1939*, Madrid: Akal, 2001.

17 J. Hiden, *Defender of Minorities. Paul Schiemann, 1876–1944*, London: Hurst, 2004; X.M. Núñez Seixas, "Unholy Alliances: Nationalist Exiles, Minorities and Anti-Fascism in Interwar Europe", *Contemporary European History*, 25:4 (2016), pp. 597–617.

18 W. Kymlicka, "Federalism and Secession At Home and Abroad", in R. Máiz and F. Requejo (eds.), *Democracy, Nationalism and Multiculturalism*, London: Frank Cass, 2005, pp. 108–26.

19 A. Rovira i Virgili, *Catalunya i la República*, Barcelona: Undarius, 1977 [1931], pp. 11–12.

20 X. M. Núñez Seixas, *Internacionalitzant el nacionalisme. El catalanisme polític i la qüestió de les minories nacionals a Europa (1914–1936)*, Catarroja/Valencia: Afers/ Universitat de València, 2010. Also: F. Armengol Ferrer, "Francesc Maspons i Anglasell. Reivindicació jurídica i projecció europea de Catalunya", various authors, *República catalana, Generalitat de Catalunya i República espanyola. A l'entorn de "La Generalitat de Catalunya i la República Espanyola", de Francesc Maspons i Anglasell*, Barcelona: Generalitat de Catalunya, 2006, pp. 39–58.

21 F. Maspons i Anglasell, *Els Drets de ciutadania i la Societat de Nacions*, Reus: Gràfics Navas, 1927.

22 "El plebiscit", *Clarís*, 7-V-1932 and 21-VI-1932.

23 See, for a general perspective: H. Timmermann (ed.), *Nationalismus und Nationalbewegung in Europa, 1914–1945*, Berlín: Duncker & Humblot, 1999; U. Corsini, and D. Zaffi (ed.), *Die Minderheiten zwischen den beiden Weltkriegen*, Berlin: Duncker & Humblot, 1997, and also M. Beer and

S. Dyroff (ed.), *Politische Strategien nationaler Minderheiten in der Zwischenkriegszeit*, Munich: Oldenbourg, 2014. Equally: P. Ther and H. Sundhaussen (eds.), *Regionale Bewegungen und Regionalismen in europäischen Zwischenräumen seit der Mitte des 19 Jahrhunderts*, Marburg: Herder-Institut, 2003.

24 See: X. M. Núñez Seixas, *Movimientos nacionalistas*, *op. cit.*, pp. 137–54; J. Rothschild, *East-Central Europe between the Two World Wars*, Seattle/London: Univ. of Washington Press, 1992.

25 For the following information, see: X. M. Núñez Seixas, *Movimientos nacionalistas*, *op. cit.*, pp. 153–243. Equally: J. W. Friend, *Stateless Nations: Western European Regional Nationalisms and the Old Nations*, Basingstok: Palgrave-Macmillan, 2012.

26 See a good collection of documents in: T. Hermans, L. Vos and L. Wils (eds.), *The Flemish Movement. A Documentary History, 1780–1990*, London: Bloomsbury, 2015, pp. 225–304.

27 See a good synthesis of the Alsacian case in: J. Fuchs, "La jeunesse alsacienne et la question régionale (1918–1939)", Histoire@Politique, I:4, 2008 (https://www.cairn.info/revue-histoire-politique-2008-1-page-8.htm) [consulted 26-VI-2017]. For the Corsians, the following is still useful: Y. Yvia-Croce, *Vingt années de corsisme, 1920–1939. Chronique corse de l'entre-deux guerres*, Ajaccio: Editions Cyrnos et Méditerranée, 1979. On the Basques of Iparralde, see: J. E. Jacob, *Hills of Conflict. Basque Nationalism in France*, Reno: Univ. of Nevada Press, 1994. On the Frisons, see: A. Zondergeld, *De Friese beweging in het tijdvak der beide Wereldoorlogen*, Leeuwarden, De Tille, 1978.

28 For the Scottish case in this period, see: J. Brand, *The National Movement in Scotland*, London: Routledge & Kegan Paul, 1978. For Wales: H. D. Davies, *The Welsh Nationalist Party 1925–1945: A Call to Nationhood*, Cardiff: University of Wales Press, 1983. For an integrated perspective of the national question in the Spanish Second Republic, the following still is useful: J. G. Beramendi and R. Máiz (ed.), *Los nacionalismos en la España de la II República*, Madrid: Siglo XXI/Consello da Cultura Galega, 1991.

29 See: M. K. Bachstein, *Wenzel Jacksch und die sudetendeutsche Sozialdemokratie,* Munich/Viena: Oldenbourg, 1974.

30 See: M. Mevius (ed.), *The Communist Quest for National Legitimacy in Europe, 1918–1989*, London: Routledge, 2010.

31 See: X. M. Núñez Seixas, "Fascism and Regionalism", en X. M. Núñez Seixas & Eric Storm (eds.), *Regionalism and Modern Europe. Identity Construction and Movements from 1890 to the Present Day*, London: Bloomsbury, 2019, pp. 119–134.

32   See: A. Gonzàlez i Vilalta, *Cataluña bajo vigilancia. El Consulado italiano y el Fascio de Barcelona (1930–1943)*, Valencia: PUV, 2008.

33   See a still useful synthesis in: R. Arzalier, *Les perdants. La dérive fasciste des mouvements autonomistes et indépendantistes au XXe siècle*, Paris: La Découverte, 1990, as well as X. M. Núñez Seixas, *Movimientos nacionalistas*, *op. cit.*, pp. 246–69.

34   See: M. Cataruzza, S. Dyroff, and D. Langewiesche (eds.), *Territorial Revisionism and the Allies of Germany in the Second World War: Goals, Expectations, Practices*, Oxford/New York: Berghahn, 2012.

35   Politisches Archiv des Auswärtigen Amtes, Berlin, R 60533, Letter from Werner Hasselblatt to general Wilhelm Faupel, Berlin, 15-1-1937.

Chapter 3

A Most Uncomfortable Issue: The Independence of Catalonia as a European Geopolitical Concern (1936–1939)

Arnau Gonzàlez i Vilalta

Let us compare two statements. One is from a letter by the Archbishop of Tarragona, Cardinal Francesc Vidal i Barraquer, to the Secretary of State of the Vatican, Cardinal Eugenio Pacelli (who would be Pope Pius XII as of March 2, 1939). Cardinal Vidal's letter is dated the 6th of November of 1936:

> I have had a providential opportunity to speak with a Frenchman who has passed through this Holy House and I have been able to know with all reservation: [...] b) that those of the Government of Catalonia are in relation with Geneva and with Mr. Blum; c) that they find the terrain ill-disposed as a result of the horrible crimes committed [by the CNT-FAI and the extreme left].

We know that Cardinal Vidal was not an enthusiast of the Franco cause. But the anticlerical destruction and mass murder of ecclesiastics during the summer and fall of 1936 in Catalonia made his position equivocal. He was not alone. Most conservatives agreed with the distrust or horror, as did many liberals. Only the left that idealized working-class revolution and the struggle against fascism had no qualms. This made someone like the Cardinal-Archbishop – who barely had escaped his own death – have his doubts. Cardinal

Pacelli, who remembered with much bitterness and personal emotion the Bavarian revolution of 1918–1919, for he had been nuncio in Munich then, had no such qualms: he was opposed, under whatever circumstances.

The second text is from a report, undated, probably written at the end of 1937 or the beginning of 1938, by the British consul general in Barcelona, Norman King, which arrived at the French legation regarding the possible evolution of Catalonia towards independence. How it got to the French is not clear: a little spying on a friend? A friendly gesture from one ally to another? A clever manoeuvre, a paper dropped where it could be found and copied? In any case, Sir Norman (who had the title by 1938) loathed the Catalan revolution of 1936 probably as much, if not more, than the future Pope. But he felt that there was a distinct possibility of an independent Catalan Republic, and he insistently warned his superiors as to that danger as much in the hot summer of 1936 as in the following years of the Spanish conflict.

> An independent Catalan State can be established, which probably would adopt the form of a Soviet State. The Catalan separatists are not in favor of this, their ideal is a Catalonia separate from Madrid under some form of democratic government, but it is unlikely that their views prevail against the strong communist influences in vogue. [...] The French Consulate General regards it as possible that, if a Soviet or Anarchist State is set up in Catalonia, attempts will be made to induce French 'comrades' on the other side of the Pyrenees to join them. This would create a very difficult problem for France, which would not be averse, despite their uneasiness at Italian interference, to foreseeing a landing at Roses to cut the railway line to Portbou and the motorway to La Jonquera, both of which pass through Figueres, in the immediate hinterland of Roses.

So we have two texts with two themes, which are interrelated.[1] In one, there is expressed the disgust at revolutionary violence, especially in Catalonia, as a discredit to any possible republican future for Catalonia or Spain as a whole. In the other, the possibility of independent Catalan statehood is taken with complete seriousness, a real likelihood, which, paradoxically the bulk of Catalan politics, as much nationalists as their revolutionary opponents, never considered that probable. On the whole, Catalan nationalism was federally-minded, and wholly into autonomy. Independence was only a minority opinion, not seen as an option by the great majority. Only when things got really bad with the progress of the Civil War did some actors dabble in clandestine diplomacy among the great powers.

A point to be made before starting: in the interwar years, all the embassies, legations or representations of powers great and small were in Madrid, to handle high politics on a State-to-State basis. But everything else, all matters that dealt with particular or individual interests – of businesses or persons – were run from consulates general located in Barcelona. This reflected economic practice: the foreign chambers of commerce in Spain were initiated in Barcelona, and then had a delegation in Madrid, and not vice versa. For example, the German entity was founded in 1917 in the Catalan port and industrial city, and that would not have a section in Madrid until 1933. Similarly, the Círculo Comercial Suizo was established in 1924, and Barcelona was the reference for all Spanish–Swiss commerce. In the Latin American case it was even more obvious. In short, Barcelona was a diplomatic reference point, below Madrid as capital of Spanish statehood, but with an autonomous rank of its own in diplomatic terms. For diplomats, the fact that Catalonia had an autonomous status of some kind – in 1914–1924 or in the 1930s – seemed a normal reflection of their own day-to-day work. The same can be said of journalists. Really major newspapers – like, say, *The New York Times* – had correspondents in both Madrid and Barcelona; at worst, the Catalan metropolis had a "stringer", a reporter who was paid not a regular income, but only by his articles published. (In those days, there were almost no women in such activity.)

So the jump from "autonomy" to "independency" (said in oldtime terms) was not so marked as it might seem today. For many outside observers, Catalan independence seemed like a clear option, an almost tangible reality, waiting to happen. But such a jump was not so clear for most Catalans, however nationalist they might be. So this study is about the contrast between two kinds of illusion surrounding statehood for Catalonia.

Introduction: It Was a Real Debate

On November 4, 1936, the French weekly magazine *Vu* published an article by the politician, diplomat, and journalist Bertrand de Jouvenel on the "New Spain" that would be built by general Francisco Franco after the hypothetical conquest of Madrid. Jouvenel was a well-known essayist, who by then had evolved from being a militant of the Radical Socialist Party to touting the extreme right. Between lauding the establishment of "order" and the creation of a totalitarian State to be administered by a single party, the journalist reserved space to comment briefly on the thoughts of the generalissimo about the future of Catalonia. According to Jouvenel, the reaction shown by Franco seemed to reduce the importance of the subject: "We should not be surprised" – wrote Jouvenel – "if the General welcomes with a contemptuous smile the questions about the possibility of independence of Catalonia."[2] This smile will figure, again and again, throughout this text.

At that moment, in the Fall of 1936, everything pointed to the success of the future dictator. It seemed unquestionable that, in a few weeks time, the fighting should end with a Franco victory and the conquest of the capital of Spain. Two days after the interview appeared, the Republican government presided by the socialist Francisco Largo Caballero moved its headquarters to Valencia just before what was presumed to be fall of Madrid. If Franco's forces entered Madrid as was expected, the international ambient forecast was a series of consequences with Catalonia as protagonist.

In spite of such predictions, the reality was different. The spirit of resistance of the people of Madrid and arrival of the first Soviet arms avoided what seemed the unavoidable. Despite what was repeated in the controlled Italian press, openly pro-Franco, the beseiged Spanish capital did not yield.[3] In defiance of the comments and declarations that, during those weeks in November, gave no possibility of doubt to Franco's imminent triumph, in the columns of newspapers throughout the world, Madrid was not vanquished until the end of March 1939.

Leaving aside the heroic resistance of Madrid, ten days after Jouvenel's text, the London magazine *The Sphere* published a report by war correspondent Ferdinand Tuohy – then a best-selling author on espionage in Britain – exclusively dedicated to Catalonia. Tuohy claimed that if the conquest of Madrid by Franco was almost a fact, something to be expected shortly, "it can be assured that the attention of world" would be focused on Catalonia and its probable secession. With a strong title, "All Eyes on Catalonia", Tuohy placed the future Catalan situation as the touchstone of the European international scene. Through Italian, German and Soviet interests, what might happen in Catalonia could cause the outbreak of the war in Europe: "You look at whatever you see, Catalonia is all set to become the moral terrain, the starting point, that most of us have feared so long." After the Italian war in Ethiopia began in October 1935 by the Italian *Duce* Benito Mussolini against the wishes of the international community, and the German remilitarization of the Rhineland decided unilaterally by German *Führer* Adolf Hitler in March 1936, ignoring the treaty of Versailles, the stage was set. In a territory of extraordinary political contradictions, Tuohy placed the significance of geography – Mediterranean coast and French frontier in the Pyrenees – above any other element when he wrote: "Its strategic importance for other powers eclipses its industrial and commercial importance with respect to the rest of Spain [...]".[4] In short, before the crises of Austria or Czechoslovakia in 1938, Catalonia – in the context of the Spanish war that began in July 1936 – took the role as "the" hot spot. It was deemed a fuse of a grenade that could provoke a continental fire.

It is true that the maps gave Catalonia an unexpected protagonism. Geopolitics was then at its most important, as was stated in the theories of strategy by the French admiral Raoul Castex or his German colleague Otto Groos. In a small sea like the Mediterranean – and even more, when compared to oceans – the key, as explained by another Italian admiral, Giuseppe Fioravanzo, was geography and the possibility to use the best situated naval bases.[5] The Catalan ports, especially Barcelona, would become points to control by any naval power with ambitions in the Western Mediterranean.

Thus the Catalan geographic situation, set in a Europe in full boil at the end of 1936, would provoke more than one author to request a cool study in favor of the maintaining European peace. Certain press, for example in Belgium, argued for this, requesting a gesture from Franco in his own benefit, but also in that of Europe in general: "If he can be victorious in Madrid, he cannot let his country fall under a foreign dominion, nor can he reduce it into ashes with the risk of provoking a European conflict; he would act sagely by not threatening Barcelona but recognizing, on the contrary, Catalan independence".[6] Initial German Nazi analysis indicated the same in a report, without date but probably from these same days. What would Franco do in the face of the "Catalan problem"? Responding to the question, the German text was totally pessimistic in relation to a positive handling of the situation that might permit the eventual stabilization of Spain: "neither the old constitutional monarchy [1876–1923] nor the military dictatorship of Primo de Rivera [1923–1930], nor the Republic [1931–1936] have found a satisfactory solution for the Catalan problem; the result is the question, anguishing, if the future regime in Spain [Franco] will have the necessary comprehension and the necessary generosity and necessary love to give this problem a good and lasting solution. It is not likely nor probable that the new regime could feel inclined to attempt old methods of the monarchy".[7] Certainly, the German analysis was not mistaken, as the response of Franco would be the classic Spanish centralist reply: repression, an attempt at cultural genocide, and the negation of all administrative, autonomic or federal specificity. Evidently, any type of secession applying the principle of Wilsonian self-determination was to be clearly rejected out of hand.

In sum, questions, appreciations, doubts and anguished views on the possible independence of Catalonia and its international effects explain the reality of an authentic political hypothesis, apparently plausible and believable even though uncomfortable in the international scene of the second half of the 1930s. This is a sign of a interest which was a product of previous knowledge, especially of the Catalan reality during the 1931–36 period, and not just circumstantial response, an immediate consequence of the Spanish war.[8]

An Anticipated Independence?

Let us look at the context with the perspective of the time, when political actors did not know how things would end up. Franco, "Generalissimo" of the rebel armies from 21 September 1936 onwards, denounced the reference to Catalonia in the French press five months after the Spanish Civil War had started. The closing of the Spanish conflict almost three years later would end the short life of the Second Republic (1931–1939). The republican regime was the first serious attempt to install a democratic system in Spain. It did not even last a decade. This regime was the unsteady product of different internal socio-economic and political dynamics, but with evident international implications.

To the policies of reformist and moderate left-wing forces of democracy, the most conservative sectors headed by the army and the Catholic Church responded with two unsuccessful coup attempts: one in August of 1932, and another which, in failing, would lead to the outbreak of civil warfare in mid-July 1936. On the other side, the reformist forces were no less active, and the left was raised in arms in October 1934 in defense of the main laws passed between 1931 and 1933, such as the Agrarian Reform, the Statute of Autonomy of Catalonia, the Constitution itself or the secular conception of the State. Both the right and the left had revolted after losing the respective elections of June 1931 and November 1933.

The truth is that here there were few democrats ready to accept ideological plurality and so permit the consolidation of a new regime. Still more to the left, other forces, openly revolutionaries – anarchists, socialists and some communists – bet on totally over-coming the reformist policies that advanced too slowly for any improvements to have perceived effects of the conditions of life of the peasantry and the working class.

The parliamentary period of the Second Republic had been six years of brutal political and social intensity, under the shadow of the global economic crisis of 1929, and the ideological struggles that were moving through Europe at that time. In the political storm which Spain would become in the 1930s, one of the main elements at stake would be the role to be played by the new Catalan autonomy. Catalan autonomous institutions were provisionally created in April of 1931, together with the Republic itself, and constitutional recognition was consolidated between December 1931 and the same month of 1932. The resolution of the Catalan national dispute originated in the late nineteenth century in Spain would be one of the elements of continuity of those years. With ups and downs, with confrontations or complicities with the left-wing central governments of Madrid (1931–1933) or with the confrontations with those of the right (1933–1936), the new Catalan government, called the Generalitat of Catalonia, became a main actor in the Spanish drama. The successive presidents of the Generalitat, Francesc Macià (1931–1933) and Lluís Companys (1934–40), both from the same party, Esquerra Republicana de Catalunya (ERC, familiarly called the "Esquerra"), would be important figures of the Spanish political system. And even more, considering that Catalonia would be the only autonomous territory until October 1936, with the Civil War several months on, when the Basque Country acceded to autonomy for a short time before being occupied by Franco's forces in the summer of 1937.[9] This was a Spanish model of administrating identity diversification praised in Europe at the beginning of the 1930s. The system constituted a certain exception by proposing a simultaneous territorial and political autonomy, as compared to most solutions established to solve the problems of national minorities in the center and east of the continent.

Therefore, when, a few days before November 4, 1936, *Vu*'s correspondent Bertrand de Jouvenel asked Franco about the fate of Catalonia, he did nothing but present a familiar reply in a long-term debate regarding the territorial and national identity of Spain. No longer considered a significant power after the loss of its last American and Asian colonies in 1898, which was the end of a world empire started in the fifteenth century, Spain would focus its identity concerns on dissident Catalonia. Therefore, far from the lightness with which Franco seemingly smiled, the facts were different: he was worried. This meant repetition: according to the British press, the same Franco authorities that had focused the issue, already indicated: "frequently it was announced that they will not allow for any formation of a separate government in Catalonia or the Basque provinces [...]".[10]

An Apparently Logical Assumption: Catalan Nationalism Wants Independence

However things may appear in retrospect, what becomes clear, reading the international press and the diplomatic reports of the time, is it that was evident that there existed a vision of Catalonia as a geopolitical reality. The country was described as pertaining to a people with a different identity – language, culture, traditions – as well as a unique system of political parties, and its own economic model within the Spanish Republic, all more than consolidated decades before. Although it now may appear surprising, it was a vision of a country clearly in transition towards full independence. Such analyses and speculations, in great measure, came from the awareness of an unquestionable reality in the cultural and political terms, but, equally important, also from a mistaken interpretation of the 1931–36 period, and from the difference or comparative singularity of Catalan nationalism in the general framework of European nationalisms. During the years from 1931 to 1936, with striking unanimity, all the commentators in diplomatic circles and in the international press insisted on an assumed endgame: Catalan national evolution had to culminate in secession, a separation that well might prove successful, according to outside observers. In this interpretative dynamic, the de facto autonomy achieved in April 1931, in a parallel manner to the instauration of the Second Spanish Republic, would be qualified as semi-independency; the Autonomous Statute approved by the Spanish Constitutional Parliament in September 1932 would be perceived as a confederal treatment on the part of Spain, and the revolutionary movement of the sixth of October 1934 in Catalonia would be understood as an attempt to certify the definitive break, seemingly so clearly pending.[11]

Italian Fascist watchers of Catalonia were keenly attentive. The presumed Catalan dynamic was analysed, for example, from different Fascist viewpoints in the 1930s. As summarized by historian Ismael Saz: "Of the three possible alternatives or solutions for the 'Catalan problem', the Italians did not wish an independent Catalonia, and preferred, with all confidence, a 'conquest of Spain by Catalonia'. Or, explained in a different fashion, they wanted to see Catalonia industrious and prosperous, developed and modern and, even better, Fascist or 'Fascistized', be put at the head of Spain. The other possibility is only that [which has always been], the conquest of Catalonia by Spain, the break of all autonomical veils and, precisely, in the charge of the least modern and more reactionary sectors of the traditional Spain. Also here, the Italy of Mussolini will end up backing strongly, ignoring all the 'modernizing' pretensions, this last solution".[12] Certainly, as Saz has argued, during the Civil War the Italian position would be the extremely pragmatic from the military point of view: a united and allied Spain would be much better, in spite of possible ideological or geo-strategic disagreements, than an independent but unstable Catalonia with an imprecise regime. This decision was taken, although both Mussolini as his diplomats had made clear repeatedly – and so stated for the record – that only Barcelona and Catalonia could truthfully understand the meaning of Italian Fascism. The industrial development, the working-class conflicts, the social tensions and the contact with Europe situated the country on the road to modernity. Madrid and Castilian Spain were seen as still pointed in another, more agrarian, direction, a dynamic that aimed to somehow preserve the nineteenth century.[13]

There was a positive Italian perspective that in these years would follow with special interest the Catalan question. In 1933, Nicola Pascazio, a journalist especially close to the Fascist regime (he had directed the party organ *Il Popolo d'Italia*, and after 1927 ran the Sicilian daily *L'Ora* in Palermo) wrote a book on the "Spanish Revolution". Pascazio dedicated a central place to the Catalan question in his book of analysis of the politics of the first two years of the new Spanish Republic. As he wrote, the identity conflict between Catalonia and Castillan Spain was in its definitive concretion phase in which: "The intransigence of the 'assimilists' (Madrid) stimulates the claims of the separatists (Barcelona). The formula already is inadequate: We do not assimilate, no separatism. The other formula is also outdated: no despotism, no separatism".[14] In a Catalonia that he believed to be in a fast process of "dehispanization", Pascazio echoed the Catalan Mediterranean view in contrast to the Spanish Atlantic one: "In the Catalans dominates the will to be and remain Catalan. They repeat: our culture is much closer to the Italian and French ones, not the Castilian. In Catalonia the Roman influence has left more traces than in other lands of the Peninsula".[15] To sum up: Pascazio offered a geocultural vision presented with a view to geopolitics.

Pascazio's observation on the evolution of the Catalan question would be enhanced by other Italian works published later, well into the Civil War: for example, in the book of analysis of the first year and half of battle, written by the military man and member of the Italian intelligence services Emilio Faldella. Destined to the Italian consulate in Barcelona in the years before 1936, Faldella set the origins of the conflict in the proclamation in April 1931 of the "Catalan Republic" by the Catalan nationalist leader and founder of the ERC, Francesc Macià, although the newly-proclaimed entity was converted a few days later into an autonomous government: "Thus did separatism cause the first wound to the unitary essence of Spain".[16] From that moment on, and until the war, the different stages of the successive years would be analyzed as blows by Catalan independentism against the Spanish unity: the Autonomy Statute of 1932, the revolution of October 1934, the beginning of a new and more extreme revolution in 1936. At this point, and taking into account that any possible collaboration between Italian Fascists and Catalan nationalists had been abandoned by then, the intervention of Rome in the territory had to assure the defeat of Catalan nationalism and of its possible variations, not help or encourage them.

Other Italian observers said much the same thing. General Francesco Belforte wrote in 1938: "The beginning fundamental principle of Italian politics, of not tolerating the intervention of Russia in the Mediterranean, has been reinforced by the words of the Duce in the speech of Palermo on August 20, 1937: he has said most categorically that, in the Mediterranean, we will not tolerate Bolshevism or anything similar." And he added, in a direct reference to Catalonia: "The current war will mark the appearance of a Spanish totalitarian state. One by one the region-alisms will be removed. [...] The war has shown to all the separatist forces that Spain constitutes a geographic, economic, and political unit, absolutely undivisible. The Government of Barcelona has found, from harsh experience, that a Catalonia, separated from the rest of Spain, does not even have the most basic resources to live."[17]

Nello Quilici – a friend of well-known Fascist leaders as Dino Grandi and previously director of influential Bologna newspaper *Il Resto del Carlino* – insisted on this same conclusion in his study on Spain, also published in 1938. From his point of view, the Catalan exit from the war and towards independence was clearly to be excluded from any Italian scenario. In the first place, this had to be so for purely economic reasons. As he argued, the Catalan bourgeoisie would be the first to oppose a break with Spain from practical economic pragmatism: the need for the Spanish market to sell its products. In addition, Franco could not allow it, since a Spain without Catalonia would be destined to fragmentation and disaster, while the new Catalan state "would gravitate by force, towards France [...]".[18]

In fact, this hypothetical dependency on France was perhaps the key to all Italian worries. As had been written years before by intellectuals close to the ERC, like the brothers Marià and Nicolau Maria Rubió Tudurí: an independent Catalonia, as was the case of the rest of the smaller countries of Europe, would develop an instinct of a "satellite State". In this case, as Quilici argued, the Catalan attraction would be towards France.[19] In this same direction of speculation, there were more than just a few justifying articles in the international press – not merely Italian newspapers – on the supposed historical ties, from the High Middle Ages right up to Napoleon, between Catalonia and France and their possible union in one or another sense.[20]

Consequently, from the Italian Fascist point of view, there was no real space for a collaboration with any brand of Catalan nationalism. The Catalan movement had to be extirpated without further contemplations. And even more so, if its tendency was to end up in or with France. In fact, from Rome, there was active and absolute distrust of the role played by conservative Catalan sectors around Francesc Cambó who were collaborating with Franco, putting the recovery of the bourgeoisie order ahead of their nationalist sympathies.[21] Money could be given for the buying of arms, press space in British press bought for articles favorable to Franco, or all possible financial contacts could be offered up – but it made no difference: they were still Catalan nationalists at heart.

The fact is that all observers – Italian or not – seemed to forecast, although without any real proof, that Catalan nationalism was attempting to achieve full self-determination because of an assumed dissatisfaction with the 1931 autonomy achieved within Spain. With what had happened in Europe between 1917 and 1919 – the creation of a dozen new States, successors of now collapsed empires – seemed to be the interpretative step necessary for the presumption of large-scale Catalan pro-independence sentiment. In reality, to complete the general framework of this view, which accepted the assumed logic of the goal of Catalan independence, it would be necessary to say that it was not only a possibility seen by international observers, but that also alarmed the more radical sectors of Spanish nationalism. In this line of analysis, one example alone, with two major protagonists, permits us to visualize the consternation. These were not marginal figures: José Antonio Primo de Rivera, head of the leading Spanish fascist formation, minority but influential, Falange Española (FE), and son of the previous Spanish dictator who governed between 1923 and 1930, and, in second place, the then loyal republican general Franciso Franco. In a letter of September 24, 1934, with the outbreak of the Civil War still far away, Primo de Rivera seemed to be able to foresee the reality of 1936. Whatever the case, the conflict would convert Franco into a dictator and Primo into a martyr and icon of the single party of Franco's regime.

A few weeks before the October 1934 revolution – in which Franco would be placed in charge by the republican government to end the uprising in of the miners in Asturias – the Falange leader warned the general of the international implications that could be created by a mixture of the factor of the Catalan independence movement with the socialism represented by the *Partido Socialista Obrero Español* (Socialist Workers' Party or PSOE): "In the imminent danger there is a decisive element that equates it to an external war; it's this: the socialist uprising will be accompanied by the probably irretrievable separation of Catalonia." And he added, remembering the transfer of the responsibility for public order to the Catalan Autonomous Government through the Statute of

Autonomy: "The Spanish State has handed over to the Generalitat almost all the defense instruments and has given the left a free hand to prepare the attack. The concomitancies between socialism and the Generalitat are well known. Thus, in Catalonia, the revolution would not have to take over power: it already has it. And it is planned to use it, in the first place, to proclaim the independence of Catalonia." But this was a possibility that Primo de Rivera supposed worked on an international scale, especially with France: "But here comes the important question: it is certain that the Generalitat, cautious, has not embarked on the revolutionary projects without previous international explorations. Their allies are known with a certain near-by power [France]. Well, yes, if the independent new Republic of Catalonia is proclaimed, which is not beyond belief, but on the contrary plausible, will the new Republic be recognized by an established power? After that, how do you recover it? Invading Catalonia would be presented before Europe as an aggression against a people that, by self-determination, had been declared free. Spain would face not only Catalonia, but the whole anti-Spain of the European powers."[22]

At the end of his missive, José Antonio Primo de Rivera only increased his expression of the worries that since 1931 had been transmitted by all the members of the Barcelona consular corp and the ambassadors in Madrid: the possible alliance of the interests of the extreme right with the Catalan nationalism. If, in 1931–1932, there was fear of a consolidation of an agreement between left Catalan nationalism and revolutionary mass anarcho-syndicalism in Catalonia, by 1934 trepidation has moved to a Catalan alliance with the Spanish left, the Socialists, to end up arriving, after the summer of 1936, during the Civil War, to the dread of the influence of Soviet communism among the Catalans. There was fear – real belief but also much propaganda – that Spain would explode in Catalonia because of two classic dangers: the national question and the social divide.

This analysis was not proved correct in 1934, but it reflected concerns that would become common as of 1936. The problem was formulated in a perverse sort of way just after the end of the Second World War by the Catalan pro-independence activist, Ramon Arrufat i Arrufat – using the ironical pseudonym Pelayo Meléndez y Solá – in his interesting essay, *La unidad hispánica. España y Cataluña (1892–1939).*[23] Put out in 1946 in a semi-clandestine way, without any visible publisher, probably this was the first work to deal with the issue of Catalan geopolitics in a direct frontal manner.[24] Arrufat, writing as a fake pro-Franco Meléndez, reversed his arguments to avoid censorship. He wrote about Primo de Rivera's letter: "Fortunately, the Catalan politicians did not have that vision of high political sense like the [Spanish] nationalists [...]."[25] But, he added, if 1934 was not the moment of a real secessionist manoeuvre, two years later the scene again arose: "Catalonia was presented with another opportunity to play the pawn in the board of the European nations, if it had meditated on its future in politics."[26] Planning in retrospect the various fronts on which the rebel military led by Franco should fight, and in particular the danger of a possible Catalan secession, Arrufat affirmed: "The nationals, we, did not have enough force to cope with all the fronts at one time."[27] However, events did not take place as Arrufat wanted, and he wrote: "The mission of Catalan politics in the months from September to November [1936] was, with deep and patriotic reasoning, to take a look at Europe, without neglecting the Spain of the nationals and the weakness of the Republic. The time had arrived to study the geographical situation of the triangular cosmos of the Catalan territory, and the ambitions and needs of the future and possible partners, to offer collaboration and support, as an independent people to countries interested in the reconstitution of the new Europe."[28]

Studying the geography of European conflicts and taking advantage of the world conflict to look for outside partners that could protect a new Catalan State that, in exchange, would offer its strategic position in the Western Mediterranean and the Pyrenees, seemed a rational geopolitical option. Clearly, all sides questioned the historical position of Catalan nationalism in the European sphere, especially regarding the left. But such Catalan objectives and, in addition, their supposed international vision, all never really existed.

The International Implications of a Catalan Secession

As can be seen, insisting on situating the period of 1931–1936 in a special way is not just a manner of gaining a certain perspective on the "Catalan question" in debate during the Spanish Civil War. It is a useful perspective because, according to certain Spanish and international political literature prior and contemporary to the conflict, this period was the point of origin for the Catalan part of the struggle.[29]

This line of interpretation, not just Italian, would give important weight to the Catalan question that had to coexist with another, completely diverse perspective. If for Pascazio, Quilici, Belforte or the commentator of *L'Osservatore Romano*, Guido Gonella, the debate concerning the Catalan status was one of the repeated themes of the Spanish Republic in peace or war, for other observers, the discussion that stage was already left behind. As was affirmed by the Polish press correspondent in Madrid and later a diplomat for Free Poland in World War Two, Ksawery Pruszyński, "The Catalan question [...] has been closed down" or, as he put it, more concretely: "Today the Catalan question no longer exists, because the modern bourgeoisie who raised it and struggled to solve it did not manage to do so when liberalism and the bourgeoisie were in their strong position." Furthermore, he added, with emphasis: "The Catalan question now does not exist, because it is something alien for the new working class".[30] This argument would be repeated years later after a very close analysis by the Catalan pro-independence advocate Ramon Arrufat, already cited above. According to Arrufat, the problem of Catalan nationalism during the Civil War was, definitively, the role of a part of the Catalan working class: "Catalonia could not count on the Catalanism of the Communist workers, nor with the support of the C.N.T., directed by Castilians, although it was an organization born in Catalonia, with its headquarters in Barcelona." And he added, in the same interpretative line as Pruszyński: "The road followed by Catalonia with the simple ideal of 'antifascism' was the worst of all, since, if ignored, it would take it to the place called *Finis Catalonia*."[31]

Was this really so? Did the incomplete revolution led by the anarchists of the CNT-FAI and unleashed immediately after the

failure of the coup d'état of 19 July 1936, permanently halt the
seemingly undying Catalan question? The long controversy, apparently impossible to solve, between the two principal movements of
contemporary Catalan society, nationalism and labour, had opted
for definitive non-understanding? Obviously, the answer was
pending on the result of the Civil War, but there seemed to be no
basis for an accord. At least this was believed by the majority of the
foreign observers. Although, on the other hand, Pruszyński was
correct in one aspect: this new revolutionary reality and the ideological violence that accompanied it would perhaps be the the
political perspective that most influenced in a determining sense
on the Catalan political evolution towards the option of non-seces-
sion from Spain. The anarchist revolution in 1936–37, and then
the communist control afterwards, through the Partit Socialista
Unificat de Catalunya (the Unified Socialist Party of Catalonia,
universally alluded to by its acronym PSUC), faithful to Moscow,
reinforced political significance of the transfer from Valencia to
Barcelona of the Spanish Republican government presided by the
socialist Juan Negrín at the end of 1937. Negrín had already
requested the move in August of 1936[32] as a way of assuring
centralizing control by the republican cabinet. – The shift of the
locus of republican power to Barcelona conditioned the solutions
of questions of sovereignty and predominance in one or another
sense, but the relocation did not eliminate in any way the underlying nationalist debate.

Therefore in the middle of the revolutionary debate begun in the
summer of 1936, the key territorial question of this scenario seems
evident. Why should pro-independence opinion not be accepted,
if, seen from outside, from abroad, it appeared as so obvious?
Speaking clearly: on one side, the foreign observers believed they
were applying an apparently unquestionable logic and they were
mistaken. And, on the other, the nationalist sectors of the
Republican side, the ERC, Acció Catalana Republicana, Estat
Català, the Generalitat and the liberal democratic sectors and the
nationalist lefts, did not accept the bet nor did they take up the
challenge. Perhaps they did not want to, they could not or already
they had lost their chance, as Pruszyński asserted. Or, perhaps,
reality was different and as the Soviet journalist Ilya Ehrenburg had

written at the end of 1931: "The Catalan nationalists are content with little."[33] In any case, in 1936, Ehrenburg was back, extremely active in Barcelona before and after the beginning of the Spanish war. Be it because of cowardice, or of solidarity with the Spanish republicans, or due to the lack of political ability that Arrufat would cite as a major factor, in all events the Catalan option did not happen. Independence did not take place. But to insist, what is being discussed here is an opportunity, not looked for in Barcelona but nevertheless real. How did the puzzle of European politics in the mid-1930s redetermine the Spanish and Catalan political ecosystem, however weak and unstable? Was such a change – a Catalan breakaway – possible? Perhaps. Were there true "independentists"? Yes, but few. And Catalan nationalists? Yes, many. This complication was the key, however difficult to explain in a European framework. All claimed to be "Catalanists" (an untranslatable term), nationalists, perhaps more autonomists and federalists that anything else, but the important question was the context. A scenario developed that appeared to oblige the Catalan nationalists to take serious and unexpected decisions in a context as that of the Civil War in which everything could be modified, especially by their extreme foreign implications.

This reality was discussed in the Catalan Governmental Council, concretely, in the session of 11 November 1936, when the then First Councillor – in practical terms, the Prime Minister – Josep Tarradellas (ERC) proposed the study of the viability of an independent Catalonia in case that Madrid fell into rebel hands, a serious danger at that time. However, the simple idea of evaluating such a possibility was rejected in the face of the very strong opposition put forward by the leader of the PSUC, Joan Comorera, who was frontally against any "measure that could be interpreted as separatist".[34] In contradiction of the fear of all the European and Spanish sectors that Catalonia was a seething den of separatists, the Catalan communists would follow the orders of Moscow contrary to the Catalan secession, even though pro-Franco propaganda stated the opposite. In spite of the fact that the PSUC eventually would become the only non-national communist party that in 1939 would be accepted – against the rules – as a full member of the Third International and the fact that the Catalan Unified

Socialist Party was loaded with extreme left separatists – the militants of the Partit Català Proletari – integrated in its creation in July 1936, its devotion to the Komintern and the Partido Comunista de España (PCE) pitted it against any possible secessionist move.[35]

In popular front terms, it was necessary to defend a democratic Spain as a part of Western Europe that could block the enemies of the Soviet Union. If, at this juncture, the extension of the Soviet revolution in Spain was not the object of Stalin, less was any Catalan secession, no matter what was said. The PSUC did not play a game only on a Catalan or Spanish chessboard, but it formed part of the movements on a continental scale decided by the Kremlin. Moscow and its assumed but unreal foreign policy in favor of the expansion of communism would be placed at the center of the Catalan debate. And this was done in a basically contradictory fashion. In 1932, Catalan nationalism was dominated by the Esquerra, by the petit bourgeoisie. The autonomy had been described critically by the Soviet journalist Ehrenburg as: "a Catalan State that only exists as a dream project".[36] Would now everything be different? To substitute the ERC with the PSUC, would it be possible to re-play the social revolution, absolutely necessary for Ehrenburg, with the national one? The answer was again, no.

Thus, at the margin of the position of Esquerra or the PSUC, what results is that this was not a debate merely conditioned by the local actions of the Catalan or Spanish parties and syndicates, but rather that it was an ongoing process of interaction with the international scenario. Inside events bounced off what was happening outside, rather than the other way around. This was a context of which Catalan nationalism took no advantage of, nor were there any serious connections or alliances looked for during the 1930s, before the failed coup and the revolution in 1936. Until the very end of the Civil War, there was no international policy for Catalan nationalists because the autonomy reached in 1931 seemed to solve all the expectations and demands that were most immediate to the movement. In addition, those who had played a role in favour of internationalizing the Catalan position during the years of the Primo de Rivera dictatorship (1923–1930), that is, the sectors of conservative Catalan nationalism around the Lliga Regionalista –

the prime leader Francesc Cambó and his right-hand man, Joan Estelrich – totally sided with the Franco rebels probably as of August 1936, a position made absolutely clear in October.[37] It is certain that some members of Acció Catalana Republicana, on the loyalist, pro-republican side, also had assumed this same attitude before and would recover it during the Civil War, but it cannot in any way be sustained that this signified a resolute will to create a coherent foreign policy by the leading sectors within and around the ERC, until the end loomed as the Civil War wound down, and desperation grew.

In fact, the debate regarding a hypothetical Catalan independence itself came from the international diplomatic and geopolitical game, and not from the internal dynamics of Catalan nationalism. Each power with ambitions of playing a relevant role in Europe proposed a future for Spain favorable to its own interests. On the chessboard which was Europe at that time, the piece that represented Catalonia within or outside Spain could be important in moves or strategies that were being acted out at the continental level. A "Catalan pawn" which, from Rome and Berlin, never would be seen as a solitary piece, but always would be represented with powerful figures on its sides. But at the same time, such knights or rooks – France, or the Soviet Union and, in a broader manner, Great Britain – were uncomfortable with the question of the pawn's supposed presumptions to move by itself, at its own bidding.

From the point of view of the Axis or the Nazi–Fascist alliance in construction, it was important to avoid the creation of an ally of France, however small, or, even more dangerous, to circumvent any advance into Western Europe by the feared Soviet revolutionaries. This common position seemed to leave aside the more than tense relations between Hitler and Mussolini, between their diplomatic services and public opinions since 1933.[38] Without doubt, Spain showed certain coordination, although not willingness. There was agreement about the advantage of a desired Franco victory to assure and close the fascist encirclement of France. This Italian geostrategic analysis had a historical basis, that was explained decades ago by John Coverdale and Ismael Saz in their studies of Italian implications in the attempt to bring down the Second

Spanish Republic.[39] This initiative did not happen at the start of the Civil War, but rather had been going since April 14, 1931, with the inauguration of the Spanish Republican regime. Similar motives, although not identical, were argued by Hitler in matters such as German investment in the Spanish economy , the need for an anti-communist position regarding Spain, the desire to carry out a military test of the capabilities of the German army, as well as an anti-French geostrategic vision.[40] At the same time, there was a consensus in the sharing of zones of influence by both revisionist powers at the European level: the Mediterranean for Italy, whereas Central and Eastern Europe were for Germany. The break and disagreement in respect to Austria or other locations seemed to quiet down as the Spanish Civil War developed. Close objectives between Rome and Berlin would go hand in hand in the Spanish theatre, and in which a Catalan secession could lead to failure.

Such evolving Nazi-Fascist plans were in partial contradiction with those of Paris or London. To be emphasized: partial. And it is true that in the first case, there was an absolute and common consensus among the majority of the European powers in blocking any Soviet intervention on the Iberian Peninsula in general, though it would not be that easy to define the real strategies of Paris – and London – in relation to Catalonia (and Spain). In this aspect, the most important position would be that of France. The argument of the "Catalan pawn" in French hands was a preoccupation in Rome and Berlin, always taking into account France's scant reliability, as well as the unlikelihood of statehood recognition. If, at first, at the outbreak of the Spanish conflict, the French prime minister, the socialist León Blum, had accepted the legal request for the sale of armaments expressed by the Spanish republican authorities presided by José Giral, only a few days later, on August 8, 1936, he contradicted himself in a decree prohibiting the export of arms to Spain. This line was broadened a week later when, starting from a French initiative, the first steps were taken for a "Committee of Non-Intervention" to be organized in London, which would become a block for any official help to the Spanish republican authorities – and also to the Catalan ones. Another matter would be underhand French actions from the different ministeries, security services or transport border structures. Some of these, in radical contradiction with the decision of the government itself (though not of certain ministers), did not stop collaborating with the movement of arms to the Republic throughout the war in Spain. This was no less contradictory than the official openings and closings of the Catalan–French Pyrenees border for the shipping of weapons. With these ambiguities, France showed its weaknesses, its evident defensive position in the European pre-war context, as well as its lack of leadership capacity in the face of overt and aggressive German and Italian initiatives.

The fact was that the French Third Republic was debilitated by the instability of the decade of the 1930s, its policy-making marked by constant governmental changes and shifts, with an extreme right visibly active on the streets: there were the "incidents" of February 1934 in Paris, the ostentation of Croix de Feux and the Parti Social Français, with a right-wing terrorist plot – la Cagoule – feared close to becoming a coup d'état. In short, *La République* was a feeble giant. It was a victorious power in 1918 but its over-sized demands, its imperial overreach, was out of relation to its real economic, military and diplomatic capacities. In addition, in the second half of the 1930s the euphoria generated in a substantial part by the French society by the election wins of the Popular Front in May and June of 1936 would be the counter-image of the fear of the bourgeoisie and conservative sectors in the face of the immediate wave of strikes. To many observers (and not least to a part of the French press), France also appeared to coming close to a civil war. In this context, the diplomatic gestures carried out between 1931 and 1936 in favor of incorporating Spain into a block that would guarantee the stability of the Mediterranean under French protection would be totally changed by 1936.[41]

Furthermore, France, apparently so consolidated in the previous decade, had lost its way in the game of multiple alliances by the mid-1930s. Although Pierre Laval (of all figures) signed a mutual assistance pact with the Soviet Union in 1935, Paris clearly found itself in a defensive position in the complicated continental scenario.[42] This was a position that until 1935 harbored that hope of an agreement with Italy that would maintain Mussolini outside of the German sphere, but which in 1936 had already failed definitively. And this in spite of the promising approach certified after

three years of negotiations in the Laval-Mussolini pact signed
between Paris and Rome at the beginning of 1935. In this document it was agreed to create a common front together with Great
Britain against Germany, as well as certain agreements in colonial
questions that could lower the tension provoked by Italian
demands in Africa. Nevertheless, the document did not survive the
secret diplomacy of its signers nor even the negative response of the
French parliament, which never ratified it.[43] A failed agreement
that would belittle the hope of the French naval sector to avoid the
inclination of the Italian Fascist regime towards an alliance with
Hitler that would complicate, in particular, French strategy in the
Mediterranean.[44] This was the position that the French army
which, in addition and without alternatives, had to coordinate with
the British Royal Navy.[45]

With a panorama like this, the outbreak of the Spanish Civil
War south of the Pyrenees provoked a new headache to the French
authorities that now, suddenly, needed to worry about protecting
a border practically forgotten about since the Napoleonic wars of
the early nineteenth century.[46] From Paris, Nazi diplomacy,
starting at the beginning of August, analyzed the French defensive
situation in this way, assuring that French perception contemplated no other circumstance than that of being "encircled" and
"beseiged", if the Third Republic was faced with a rebel victory in
Spain. It would be Germany on the Rhine, Italy on the Alpine
border, and Spain on the Pyrenees. But it has to be taken into
account that Paris already had scant doubts regarding a possible
Franco neutrality in the case of an European war.[47]

That said, if France could derive some positive result from the
Spanish conflict, it would not be easy to determine exactly what
such benefit could be. And even less, if it found itself obliged to
work with Great Britain, given that it would be only with great
difficulty that the United Kingdom would accept implicating
itself militarily on the continent. In this sense, British politics
would not suffer such accentuated tensions as those that rocked
France, especially if the permanence of the Conservative Party as
the major governmental force since 1929 (with the Labour leader
James Ramsay McDonald, as prime minister, being expelled from
his party) is taken into account. From then until 1935, McDonald

would carry out a successful foreign policy concentrated on economic recovery, strengthening ties with the British dominions, as well as attempting to block German aggression. While Great Britain re-armed in face of the information of increased German military capacity coming from Berlin, the public discourse of the new prime minister Stanley Baldwin (1935–1937) continued speaking of peace, negotiations, and the League of Nations. This line was maintained as the policy of the British government by Baldwin's successor, the also conservative Neville Chamberlain (1937–1940). The attitude in the face of Hitler was radically different from that held towards Stalin. Although the USSR had entered the League of Nations in 1934, London was much more fearful of communism than of a German threat. This is scarcely surprising if one considers the fascination for fascism and nazism of major figures of government such as Lord Halifax or members of the well-known "Cliveden Set", a Germanophile aristocratic and press group. Things would not change, basically, until 1940, once the European War began. Even by then, there would be strong pressure in the cabinet of national unity presided by the unpredictable Winston Churchill in favor of a deal with Hitler, once France was lost.

Therefore, in 1936, the positions in Europe were defined alternately: either a growing Rome–Berlin pact, or, less clearly, the alliance between London, Paris and potentially Moscow. Thus ideological polarization on an international scale was the confrontational reality before which the possible secession of Catalonia, desired or not, was placed on the chess table of European governments, as well as in the ongoing press debates. This background was evidenced clearly in contemporary journalistic commentary.

The spreading contradiction between the thrust and mutual attraction of the "revisionist powers" and the confused attitudes of the historical defenders of "collective security", together with the possibility of a a breakaway Catalan option, was evident only one day before the publication of Franco's comment of November 4, 1936, in a lead article that appeared in the Swiss *Journal de Genève* with an explicit title that asked: "Catalogne contre Espagne?". The editorial, in what was the main newspaper of Geneva, headquarters of the League of Nations, warned Swiss public opinion that the "eventuality of an independent Catalonia, separated from Spain, deserves to be considered".[48] After a long explanation of the supposed cultural and character differences between Catalans and Spaniards, the example of Portugal was mentioned so as to argue that a sovereign Catalonia could perfectly survive next to the remainder of Spain. Who would carry out the protective role of the British towards Lisbon was not specified. But this opinion was opposed by other observers. For example, Charles Graves in *The Sphere* of London, defended that in such eventuality, Franco would not militarily attack Catalonia but would rather drown it economically, evidencing the need of the Spanish market for the survival of Catalan industry.[49] Something similar was also stated by the Portuguese dictator António de Oliveira Salazar. As he expressed in an interview with the Swedish ambassador to Spain and Portugal – Ivan Danielsson – Salazar affirmed the need to help the rebels so as to avoid the "bolshevization" of Spain and its possible contagion in Portugal. And, in reference to Catalonia, after the conquest of the rest of Spain, *"O Chefe"* Salazar insisted on the necessity of attacking and suffocating the Catalan economy until it surrendered.[50]

In any case, as we have seen, in late 1936 the conventional international view sustained that, if indeed Franco conquered Madrid at any time soon, the war would then become a contest of Spain against Catalonia. Proof of this, to take one example, was the point of view of certain British academic circles that revived a recurrent comparison between Ireland and Catalonia, prevalent in the nineteenth century and often reiterated up to the December 1921 formal Treaty that created the Irish Free State. From this perspective, Anglo-Irish and Catalan–Spanish comparisons were a standard cliché. Catalan dynamics – Spain's "Irish Problem" – meant that any force opposed to the Spanish Republic could only win and consolidate their power taking into account the Catalan factor: "there seems to be no hope of a peaceful solution until Catalonia receives full independence [...]", it was said.[51] This is an observation to which should be added similar opinions in the British and European press and the criteria of French authorities.

If one follows the bulk of the commentaries, a remarkable obsession is found: many sources expected or presumed the fierce resistance of Catalan society to the advance of Franco's troops. As a French source emphasized: "The big problem of tomorrow is that of Catalonia: this has caused great concern in the Foreign Affairs Committee of the Chamber [of the National Assembly] in their last session." A note added dramatic references to the First World War: "There, one can say that there is not a single Catalan favorable to Franco. If he [Franco] becomes the head of the rest of Spain, he intends to place Catalonia again under the dogma of the unity of Spain, and it will be necessary to pass over the corpses of hundreds of thousands of Catalans killed in war or shot afterwards. [...] The world will meet a new Georgia or a new Armenia."[52] There were numerous comments in this sense. In fact, some correspondents met with Catalans who actively desired to make declarations in the same direction. One such statement would be reproduced on a cover article by the Canadian correspondent M. H. Halton at the end of November 1936: in an interview with an anonymous Catalan – who refused to be identified as a Spaniard – the respondent would add Franco to the pile of supposed historical victims of Catalan anger in an act of flagrant anachronism: Hannibal, Pompey, Charlemagne, Napoleon, and so forth.[53] Doubtlessly, this was an unusual view. If there existed Catalans who assured they would die before being conquered by Franco, there also were – and not just a few – among the soldiers of the rebel armies commanded by the future dictator.

A Secure Independence?

Such was the abundance of rumours about the eventuality of Catalan secession that the diplomatic documentation and the press released quantities of information that seemed to confirm the split during the first months of the Spanish war. For example, on 31 July 1936 one could read in the Belgian press – making reference to the *Manchester Guardian* – that observers "forecast, in the case of a victory by General Franco, the end of the Spanish unity [would be produced], and that Catalonia would be separated from a central government controlled by fascist troops".[54] A few days later, on 3 August 1936, Radio Club Português broadcast a note, picked up immediately by the Spanish rebel press, in which it was said: "They say by telephone from Ciudad Rodrigo that the government of Catalonia has proclaimed independence, and that Burgos [seat of the rebel authorities] answered that the Catalans should enjoy this situation for a few days, since, in a few days, later accounts would be settled".[55] This was an absolutely false statement that would be denied thereafter, doubtlessly the product of the understandable confusion of interpreting the different decisions of the Catalan government, while it assumed absolute control of the State administration in Catalonia.[56] In fact, the denials during these early days of the conflict were constant. We may take as an example the item published by the Austrian correspondent R. G. W.: "The news in the foreign press, according to which the Catalan government led by Joan Casanovas has already proclaimed the independence of Catalonia, is not correct. Nevertheless, it is possible that sooner or later, Catalonia will attempt this [...]".[57] This possibility was connected to the expected taking of Madrid by Franco and led the correspondent to a long explanation of the previous years with the frequently repeated interpretation of events in a separatist manner. The diverse stages of the Republican pre-war period were often poorly interpreted abroad. But some observers were justified discerning the fragmentation of power in Spain at the beginning of the struggle: "There is the government of Madrid and that of Barcelona. There is the provisional government of the south under the control of General Franco and that of Burgos led by the General Cabanellas. Nothing permits affirming that these divisions will not continue. Barcelona and Catalonia have always aspired more or less exclusively to a total independence."[58]

At this point, in Barcelona, some of the more outstanding diplomats in Barcelona went even further. For example, British diplomacy assured that deployment of Alpine troops of the Generalitat throughout the Pyrenees was underway, as well as the presence of soldiers in Barcelona, "would seem to serve to mark the limits of the new Catalan State".[59] Facts and more facts, sometimes real, even if incorrectly interpreted, would be completed with comments like those of the Vice Consul of His Britannic Majesty in Barcelona, Edgar Vaughan, who would write to London affirming the almost absolute independence with which the

Generalitat acted in respect to Madrid.[60] This was a plausible analysis but it did not completely describe the weakness of the Catalan government and the importance of the revolutionary groups, especially the anarchist CNT-FAI, which forced a pact to share power immediately after the defeat of the military uprising in Barcelona in late July 1936. A first step was the creation of the Central Committee of Antifascist Militias (CCMA), parallel to the Catalan government; but already in late September, and after having dissolved the CCMA, the anarchists entered into the Catalan government. It was true that the Generalitat often acted as if it enjoyed recognized statehood, but the anarchists were – in their own inimitable way, pro-autonomy – and in no manner inclined to "independentist" adventures.

This important aspect was valued by some of the few that studied the real situation of the war and not the geopolitical map of Europe. Among these, British diplomats asked about the role of the anarchists. Didn't they have anything to say? In truth, the majority of the diplomatic observers were characterized by an analysis of the Catalan and Spanish reality in which the CNT-FAI, despite of being an actor of great importance, seemed not to be the determining force at any time.[61] Nevertheless, if the anarchists had almost all the power in Catalonia, but were not characterized by any sympathy for Catalan nationalism, the only option left was some sort of French/Soviet action that would permit a effective coup by nationalist backers.[62] But there were other possibilities: an internal coup d'état could be carried out against the anarcho-syndicalists with outside support or, conversely, any attempt at independence would be annulled by anarcho-syndicalist action; in practice, this double game is what was tried unsuccessfully by both factions in November 1936. It was not out of the question that the CNT leadership could imagine a map of Spain and understand that the only territory they controlled was Catalonia and the area of the Aragonese front; consequently, they might decide to act exclusively in Catalonia. This prospect was summarized by the British consul general in Barcelona, Sir Norman King, when he said that "the national independence of Catalonia" and the anarchists – but also the communists – could "with difficulty form part of the program".[63] Another British report at the end of November put aside pro-independence options given the attitude of the different revolutionary sectors, and dismissed the utterly unlikely union of interests between the Catalan nationalists, the Soviets, the anarchists, and Franco.[64]

The practical difficulty of any scenario was well described in an interesting article at the beginning of September by the correspondent in Barcelona of *The Times* of London. As he reflected concerning "The Future of the Catalans", the three principal elements that made difficult the creation of a Catalan State were the confrontation with the Franco rebels, the necessary French protection of the new political subject, as well as the future social structure of the country. In relation to the French factor he stated: "There has been much speculation about the possibility of a political alliance with France, for which France would guarantee the Catalan security in the case of a rebel victory in Spain. It is known that the Catalan leaders are studying this question. But any attempt to 'break apart' Spain in this fashion would provoke almost inevitably a new civil war between Catalonia and the victorious rebels, one of whose characteristics is a pronounced unitarism." And he added: "The future complexity of the new State without doubt will be an important factor for France, which would doubtfully take under its protection a new 'State' defined as 'red' [then a revolutionary colour]. The international complexities that would accompany any movement would signify the virtual extension of the French Mediterranean coast are evident".[65]

Nevertheless, the principal argument concerning Catalonia would be made from an overall European perspective. Thus, following this dynamic, at the end of the month of August 1936, the Italian diplomatic services also came to confirm the "fantastic" proclamation of independence that would be created by the imminent fall of Madrid into the hands of the Franco forces.[66] In this line some Italian military speculation would recommend that Franco ought not to occupy the Spanish capital so as to not propitiate a Catalan secession. An alleged proclamation of independence that would be led by the moderate sectors of the Catalan left, that is, the Esquerra or ERC (together with Acció Catalana Republicana). But, in fact, these parties, as fighting forces, were incapable of battling on the double front in which the conflict had situated them: they were incapable of struggling against the military rebels, and, at the same time, against the local leftist extremists, notably the anarchists of the CNT. This was a situation that supposedly would have driven them to opt for the separation of Spain under the protection of France.[67] This possibility would be analyzed in a contradictory manner and taken as fact as early as August 21 by the Italian embassy to Spain, which by then – like some other embassies in Madrid – had withdrawn to French territory: "The news of the partial proclamation of the independence of the Catalan State has produced a remarkable impression between the numerous Spanish and foreign diplomats living in this area. It is generally considered that the demonstration of willpower of the government of Barcelona to now separate its fate from that of the government of Madrid, and, thereby confirming the difficult situation, also in military terms, in which it is the latter [that] continues [...]".[68] The same could read on the other side of the world by the readers of the Australian *The Daily Advertiser*, in a brief note that appeared on the cover page, on September 10, which left no doubts about the oncoming split.[69]

This mix of information, rumours, and news would be summarized by the Belgian consulate in Barcelona in late October of 1936. In those days, the consul, Jules Simon, sent another letter, generically addressed to the First Councillor of the Generalitat, regarding the seizure, by a workers' committee, of the potash mines of Súria operated by the influential Solvay S.A. company, based in Brussels. As Simon argued, the action of occupying the mines had occurred in an absolutely illegal manner. But not just because of the appropriation and subsequent legalization of the seizure of these mines by the Collectivization Decree of the Generalitat of October 24, but, as he argued at the end of his letter, for an action that exceeded the legal Catalan and Spanish frameworks: "Understanding that the Decrees and orders of the Generalitat of Catalonia that have permitted to occur the Acts which have been explained [above], have not only been dictated with a manifest extralimitation of powers granted to the same by the Statute of Catalonia, but also violating precepts contained in the Constitution of the Spanish Republic, I do, in addition to the protest, make an express reservation on behalf of the Government of His Belgian Majesty, of rights and actions that are part of Belgian interests [...]."[70] This Belgian opinion was not shared by certain correspondents, who only saw in the agreement a wish to organize Catalan reality, but leaving apart both a separatist project, as well as a communist one.[71] Depending on the point of view, there was no doubt that the collectivizations decreed by the Generalitat, although they wished to legalize a situation existing in fact, were an act of sovereignty by the Catalan authorities. And this is the way they were regarded, not just by Belgian representatives, but by the British diplomats, for example, as well.

Interestingly enough, actions taken, appreciations, and forecasts that, despite being circulated among diplomats, and occupying newspaper covers like that of *La Stampa* of Turin in Italy, tended to be lacking in precision. That is to say, were all the news, reports and rumours a prelude to independence? Not really. *The New York Times* could speak of a "Catalonia [that] establishes a virtually independent State" or "moves towards secession" but the details were pending greater specification.[72] Someone had to put the separation into actual practice. And that did not happen even in spite of the fact that the President of the Catalan autonomous Parlament and, during August and September of 1936, also Head of Government, Joan Casanovas, was presumed to be an ardent separatist by much of the French press.[73] There were evident samples, of course, of the concerns generated by the simple possibility, the hint of a break.[74] These were examples of an event that seemed to some observers, perhaps many, inevitable and in line with what had been the European evolution after the Paris Peace and during the following years.

Nevertheless, if it was not clear if the road taken by Catalan nationalism coincided with the diplomatic and press analyses, what was without doubt was the question from Jouvenel to Franco cited previously; this was not a simple anecdote. It was not just the whim of a more or less informed journalist fond of geopolitics. Rather, it was a symptom of the atmosphere existing at the time in public opinion and European, American and worldwide diplomatic sectors. Another matter was to discern what was true in the whole situation.

What connection existed between the outside view and the interior perceptions? A basis existed on the plausibility of a Catalan secession that would remain a permanent part of the background during the entire conflict but it would have active points during the initial months of the war (July–December 1936), as well as during its last stage of 1938 to 1939. Views of consuls, ambassadors, military figures, and journalists would seem to see Catalan pro-independence nationalism, perhaps more or less pragmatic, just about everywhere. This included even – perhaps surprisingly – in the anarcho-syndicalist sectors of the CNT or the anarchist FAI, that in some diplomatic-journalist illusions seemed to be in line with pro-independence positions. This was remembered at the end of the war by the former Commissar or Commissioner of Propaganda of the Generalitat of Catalonia, Jaume Miravitlles, in reflections published posthumously, some eighty years later: "Since the beginning of the conflict, Italy, more interested than anyone else in the Spanish question, denounced 'Catalan separatism', to which were attributed different political and social meanings, but before which an attitude of opposition was always fixed." According to Miravitlles, in the first phase of Italian intervention in the Peninsula, 'Catalan separatism' was sustained over the anarchist movement in the Fascist-controlled press. "The anarchists wanted to create, according to the Italian newspapers, a red and black Catalan republic [the colors of the anarchist flag] destined to be a focus of rebellion and disorder in the Mediterranean."[75]

As Miravitlles indicated, the Italians were certainly attempting to discredit any sort of pro-independence movement at the same time as it was doing the same with the idea of anarchist revolution. However, there is no doubt that such criticism formed part of political reality: the insubordinate posture of the Catalan anarchists and the fight with the republican central Government, on the part of both the anarchists and the Generalitat. Given the declarations of some of the most outstanding Catalan anarchist leaders of the moment, such as Diego Abad de Santillán, one can certify that at least a certain anarchist viewpoint could be understood as indulgent with regards to many aspects of Catalan nationalism.[76]

Without a doubt, the animosity created between the republican authorities and the sum total of Catalan political sectors, anarchists included, would be one of the persistently sour themes of the Civil

War. But it is not less certain that the connecting points between anarchists and Catalan nationalists – circumstantial allies in dispute during wartime – were below minimums after the period 1931–36. During the years prior to the outbreak of the Spanish conflict, the action groups of the dominant nationalism, in the youth wing of the ERC, had fought anarchist militants for control of the streets of Barcelona and the lesser industrial towns of Catalonia. In addition, the management of public order and the use of the police in the hands of Esquerra were converted into an aggressive element of mutual loathing.

Geopolitics is All: A Maginot line on the Catalan Ebro?

The general concern regarding the geopolitical importance of the Catalan situation formed part of the international context in which the Spanish war was included. A demonstration of this is that in the press of a place like Australia, so far from Spain, but so politically close to Europe through London, there was speculation on the siren songs of Catalonia towards France, remembering the historical connections between both countries.[77] Until the opening of the Soviet consulate in Barcelona in October 1936, speculations about a hypothetical independence could only be linked to a democratic solution, that was understood, in practical terms, as receiving Frnch backing. Between July and December 1936, diplomatic-journalistic speculation inevitably linked Catalan independence to the expected fall of Madrid into the hands of the rebels, every day imminent according to both secret official documents and newspaper headlines.[78]

This anticipated relationship between an expected Franco entry into Madrid and a fierce Catalan response somehow dependent on France, generated intense French worries – clearly expressed by the both the Parisian and leading provincial press in a long list of preoccupations starting from the first moments of the struggle. French forecasts offered approaches to Peninsular difficulties that, in some respects, would be shared by the bulk of the most conservative or centrist British and Italian press. This was a scenario that had already been described at the beginning of August 1936 by Georges Rotvand, correspondent of the conservative Paris daily *Le Figaro*.[79] Thus, within a month of the outbreak of war, Rotvand wondered about the international performance in the Catalan case if everything happened as he presumed (in a way that was not unlike the speculations of José Antonio Primo de Rivera in 1934): "If Madrid was taken by the whites and if, immediately afterwards, Catalonia declared itself independent, claiming the right of the peoples to dispose of themselves, and at once entered into the League of Nations, what would the League do when the whites sent a military expedition against Barcelona? Could the Catalans not request an intervention of the League of Nations against the whites [i.e., the Spanish rebel right]? We believe that this project, in appearance full of fantasy, is taken seriously currently in Barcelona."[80] What would the League do? And what would France do, worried about the effects caused by the appearance of a new State that could affect its internal territorial structure?[81] In fact, it was feared that a Catalan secession would lead to a domino effect that could affect several French territories such as the neighboring Catalan Roussillon, Brittany or the island of Corsica, as well as shifting identity balances in Belgium and Switzerland. Such a fear was made explicit in the French National Assembly by the rightist deputy Henri de Kerillis, who was also director of the newspaper *L'Écho de Paris.* In his speech to the Chamber, he would criticize alleged Soviet involvement in Spain and the danger that it supposed for the integrity of France. Specifically, de Kerillis argued: "A Catalan Soviet Republic, [which] will be a danger to French national unity [...], since there is a solidarity of blood, language and culture between French and Spanish Catalonia."[82]

In this way, at that moment, what France would do would be to seriously fret with fearfulness. The anxiety was expressed by another editorial of *Le Figaro*, signed by Lucien Romer on August 20, 1936, entitled "Spanish Unity".[83] In an interpretative line widespread at that time, the article called artificial a Spanish unity that believed itself in danger. Similarly dark visions of the instability of Iberian politics, and of the complications supposed that an independent Catalonia would represent for France and Portugal, could be read in the majority of the western press from the summer to the end of the year.[84]

As has been seen, this alarm – the cause-effect link of the fall of Madrid and the independence of Catalonia – would be lived, both in the press and among the diplomatic services, according to contemporary tensions. Among diplomats, each country would express itself according to its geopolitical interests. Some, geographically remote, would simply inform about the secessionist possibility to their superiors without adding more connotations. For example, when in early August 1936, the Argentinian consul in the Catalan capital, Jorge Blanco Villalta, commented on the maintenance and reinforcement of the barricades throughout Barcelona, derived from the failed coup d'état in mid-July, through three possible interpretations: (a) Defense of the city in the face of an attack by the rebels in Zaragoza; the (b) the FAI's defensive position in the face of an eventual action of forced disarmament promoted by the Generalitat; and (c) "and some [defenses] are based on to strengthening the combative resources of Catalonia so that, if the military wins, it can rise the flag of freedom and declare itself independent of Spain".[85]

Significantly, other foreign representatives, with interests closer to Spain, insisted on a similar analysis. Thus, while dedicated to the work of protection and evacuation of Portuguese and Brazilian citizens, the Portuguese consul in Barcelona, Alfredo Casanova, did not stop reporting on the political map resulting from the outbreak of the war in Catalonia. Writing in August, he claimed the country was awaiting "very tragic days" in a war of uncertain duration but of extreme ideological violence, in a city dominated "virtually" by anarchists. But he also foresaw the proclamation of Catalan independence before the possible fall of Madrid into the hands of the military rebels: "The Government of the Generalitat, anticipating the possibility of a defeat of the [Republican] Government, works actively, if that day arrives, for the proclamation of independence, converting this region into an independent republic".[86] He would insist on the same point weeks later, in October: "In the measure that the rebels advance victoriously, the Government of the Generalitat prepares to proclaim in Catalonia the independent Republic".[87] This commentary would be received in Lisbon, like all news that came from the Spanish war, with great concern. If the democratic republicans won, the end of the dictatorship of António de Oliveira Salazar was feared; if the more left-wing sectors triumphed, the communist contagion seemed impossible to avoid; if the Franco forces won, they perhaps could possibly try to complete the unity of the Iberian Peninsula at Portuguese expense. In the case of an independent Catalonia, the situation was not so clear. On the one hand, it could be positive insofar as it weakened Spain. But such a benefit was plausible only so long as there was not a new communist-type State or any entity that might promote any type of Iberian unity movement, as was common in traditional Catalan nationalist rhetoric.

Like the Portuguese, also the Italians – as has already been pointed out – believed that any option towards Catalan independence would have effects on their foreign policy. Accordingly, at the end of August 1936, the commander of the Italian naval deployment in the Mediterranean based in the waters of Barcelona, Admiral Ildebrando Goiran, warned about the possible precipitation of events in Catalan politics. While the Italian residents of Barcelona were being evacuated, with their consulate protected, Goiran was busy introducing spies into the city and pointing out possible bombing objectives for his aviation forces stationed in Mallorca. Thanks to his readings of the Barcelona press, consular contacts, and various informants, Goiran believed that, after the first moments of revolutionary chaos, there would be a recovery of public order and an administrative reorganization in Catalonia. At the same time, the admiral was aware of a struggle to win the support of the petty bourgeoisie on the part of the CNT-FAI. This phenomenon was graphically identified – in his language – as a fertilizer for independence. So, despite the strong and obvious ideological contradictions between the Catalan parties and the labour unions, the admiral believed it was possible to see a viable Catalan State that, in turn, could determine the general fate of the Civil War and cause certain effects on a European scale.[88]

After all, the geostrategic vision of the officers in charge of the naval war fleets on display in the port of Barcelona would be a conditioning element, since – in the context of the long summer of 1936 – they expected to be the first to most actively respond to a possible Catalan secession. It was only a question of looking carefully at the maps of the western Mediterranean and assessing who would benefit most from each hypothetical scenario. Bordering with France and continuing its coastline to the south, a small but independent Catalonia would be undoubtedly useful to the French fleet. The general staffs of every major power knew this. Since the beginning of the 1930s, the German consulate – before and after the rise of Nazi power – was alert to see in whose hands could fall all or part of the Spanish Mediterranean coast, from Gibraltar to Portbou.

Thus, the suitability of Catalan independence would be an option considered by certain high-ranking members of the Marine Nationale, the French navy. This was openly explained by the French *contre-amiral* Emmanuel Ollive in a conversation with his Italian colleague, Goiran, on September 11, 1936: Ollive advocated the international occupation of Catalonia and its segregation from Spain. This move would, as he believed (in the version of his Italian counterpart), facilitate the pacification of Spain and mark the end of the conflict.[89] There was a strong French viewpoint in naval questions if one follows what was explained in his memoirs by Goiran's substitute, Italian admiral Vittorio Tur, confirming the insistence of that perception, in the words of his French equivalent Marcel Gensoul.[90] With careful insistence, Tur transcribed Gensoul's opinion that the loss of the Catalan autonomy that would be a victory for Franco, and "would displease" a France that always thought in terms of an "independent Catalonia".[91] And Gensoul would say even more, indicating that what was needed was a Catalan Republic with the Balearic Islands included within its borders.[92]

The possibility that this was indeed the position of the high command of the French navy was information that immediately spread through the warships in Barcelona's harbour. And that, in addition, had to be explained with a surprising frankness and/or an intentional or deliberate lightness, as was pointed out by the ex-governor general of Catalonia and the ex-prime minister of the Spanish Republic, Manuel Portela Valladares. In several press articles that appeared in 1937 as well as in his memoirs written years later, the Galician politician recalled the different rumours he listened to in his passage through different French ships anchored in the port of Barcelona, before being successful in sailing to France in the summer of 1936. After being unpleasantly surprised because all the ships under a foreign flag interpreted the Catalan hymn – *Els Segadors* – as a mark to hoist their own ensign every morning, Portela recalled the analysis that French diplomats and the officers of the Marine Nationale made of the conflict in Catalonia in conversation.[93] According to Portela, the global French impression was that Catalonia was controlled by an autonomous government that could treat its political status with whom it wanted and with sufficient capacity to decide on its own future. This opinion was reflected by the French consul in the city, the catalanophile Jean Trémoulet. According to Portela, Trémoulet supposedly treated as deserving respect and attention the offer of the Catalan president Companys of "annexing Catalonia, the Balearic Islands, Valencia and Murcia to the French Republic" a matter which "seemed to be in serious negotiations".[94]

Undoubtedly, statements such as these could respond to a simple projections of certain officials or senior naval officers on the scene without regard to the political connotations of the matter, as seen from highest spheres of Parisian politics. The reality, nevertheless, was that control of the Catalan coast could be evidently useful (or dangerous) to any Mediterranean naval power (including the British). The nautical charts of the Mediterranean placed Catalonia in an excellent position to help ensure the safety of the French naval routes between the metropolitan base of Toulon – close to Marseille – and that of Bizerte in colonial Tunisia. In addition, Barcelona was in close proximity to the rest of the ports of French North Africa. From the early 1930s, these bases were prime targets for their hypothetical air attacks that were being studied by the staff of the Italian naval air arm.[95] Launched into a policy of adventurism, and in the context of the Spanish conflict, Mussolini would come to believe that, with the support of Germany, he could break the predominance of the French and British in his "*Mare Nostrum*". In this panorama, the narrow waters between Catalonia and the Balearics assured French naval ascendancy. Menorca concretely, traditionally the Spanish navy's major Mediterranean base after Cartagena, was still loyalist, and would remain in republican hands until the end of the conflict. Occupation of Menorca would be planned, by both Italian and French strategists, given that, thanks to Spanish rebels, the Italians had access to Mallorca, and Ibiza, after a brief Catalan conquest in the Mallorcan expedition of the summer of 1936, was also back in pro-Franco hands.[96] Furthermore, together with the Balearic Islands, the Catalan coast could be an important strategic asset for the action of the French armed forces expanding much further south down the coastline in terms of Allied defense.[97]

In addition, two political-military elements increased the geostrategic importance of Catalonia. On the one hand, German occupation had been at the doors of Paris in 1870 and 1914; in a few short years it would fall, although the French defeat of 1940 had not yet taken place in 1936–1939, there were anticipatory fears. Therefore, Algiers, Oran and other main cities of the French African Mediterranean coast could be a key governmental and military rearguard, points of retreat in the face of an overwhelming German invasion. Added to this possibility, with a third of its men quartered in North Africa, the French Army urgently needed full operational capacity to transfer troops to metropolitan territory in the case of a European war. This was explained in a memorandum of November 20, 1936, by vice-admiral Georges Durand-Viel, when he stated that if the circumstances were favorable to the French navy, which he thought unlikely in the case of war, possibly transfers of African troops could be considered through the Spanish republican government ports.[98] And all this in the face of the real fear of the French naval commanders in relation to the power of the Italian armed forces. In fact, Rome would demand of Franco that, in exchange for sending more Italian troops to the Iberian Peninsula, the rebels should become naval allies and close their borders to the passing of French soldiers in the event of a European armed conflict.[99] Consequently, the difficulties of moving troops to the Hexagon would be more complicated if later events consolidated the Italian bases on the island of Mallorca, facilitated by the Franco side in the war.

French strategic needs were clear to everyone in those days. One example of this, among others, was the opinion of one of the correspondents of *The New York Times*, Frank L. Kluckhohn, who, in an extensive analysis on the possible future scenarios for Catalonia, emphasized French doubts. Thus, explaining that Italy needed a Catalan coast in the hands of its Spanish allies, at the same time he wrote that "only an independent Catalonia can guarantee security in the French communication lines with its Empire of North Africa".[100] In fact, weeks before, the same newspaper had already published a similar analysis from another point of view, when it wrote about the victory of Franco: "The French left hopes to compensate for the [Spanish] dictatorship by helping the Catalans to become independent."[101] The Catholic daily of Toulouse, *L'Express du Midi*, expressed itself totally critical of such a result in a surprising context. On May 8, 1937, in the heat of the battle between Catalan republican and revolutionary sectors in the crisis known as the "Events of May of Barcelona", Charles Capus defined the position of the ERC and Lluís Companys in the following way: "The ambition [of Companys] is to be, someday, [leader] of an independent Catalonia, leaving the anarchist elements (F.A.I.) [sic], fulfilling their work of destruction 'Neither God, nor boss', thinking, that with the subsequent disorder, he could more easily reach his ends." This initial comment was followed with an attack on Catalan society – as well as on the Basques – and their supposed nationalist obsession against Spain, helped, allegedly, by the leaders of the Third Republic: "Meanwhile, our government sustains in Spain this separatism favoring Companys in Catalonia and Aguirre in Vizcaya. That is anti-Republican and anti-European. Would we French see with pleasure that a foreign power favored the separatism of one of our regions, like Brittany, Alsace or Algeria?"[102]

Valued with a certain long-term historical perspective, these considerations regarding French–Catalan collaborations were in no way strange: from the Hispanic Mark of the Carolingian Empire, through the appointment of Louis XIII of France as Count of Barcelona in 1641, and until the incorporation of Catalonia into the Napoleonic Empire in 1812, a French monarchy would try several times to push itself into the Iberian Peninsula. These were trans-pyrenean disputes that finally would end in 1827 and that did not re-awaken again until 1936.[103]

At the end of the Spanish war, some authors offered retrospective musings, as for example the medical captain of the Spanish army, Juan Vázquez Sans, in his book, *España y Francia, Meditaciones de actualidad*, published in Barcelona in July 1939. The work was a clear demonstration of exalted francophobia.[104] Specifically, in one chapter, "France and Catalonia", Vázquez analyzed most sharply the Catalan separatist attempts to break with Spain under French protection as a senseless act that showed the lack of human maturity of these political actors. What was worse, Vázquez Sans qualified the whole business as a selfish French manipulation in its meddling in internal disputes with Spain: "The idea of the dismemberment of Spain has lingered several times in the minds of French statesmen, being warmly welcomed by them; but it is true that the initiative has come in the majority of times from Catalan separatist nuclei that have believed to find in France the protective nation for their nationalist ambitions."[105] Through a systematic criticism of the French action to help the Spanish Republic and given the attitude of the Catalan nationalists, the author reviewed the French attempts to take advantage of the supposed naivety of the Catalan pro-independence "traitors". The same argument was clearly stated in some statements repeated from the famous speeches of the rebel general Gonzalo Queipo de Llano sent through the airwaves by the Radio Sevilla: "That the French, this degenerate race, have no dreams! When I have conquered Catalonia and when I am at the Pyrenees, you will see what I reserve for you!".[106]

In spite of whether or not the profusion of rumors or dreams about Catalan independence was a French attempt to take advantage of the Catalans, the French spokesmen, not only the from the *Marine Nationale*, speculated about the more than probable action on three fronts – Rhine, Alps, and Pyrenees – that would pounce on the Hexagon in case of a Franco victory. Indeed, for Nazi Germany and Fascist Italy the victory of the pro-Franco rebels could be better achieved with France isolated within a circle of totalitarian countries, whatever strategic divergences between fascist allies might exist on the sidelines. This circumstance was referred to constantly in the political literature of the Spanish or French left with titles as explicit as that of Philippe Lamour and

André Cayatte, *Sauvons la France en Espagne* (1938). They were an odd combination, as Cayatte was a literary figure on the left, while Lamour, a lawyer, was so ultra-right (he had militated in the French fascist *ligues*) that he feared the pacificism of right-wing conventional wisdom in the late 1930s. Their alliance was due to the conviction that the defense of France did not start where its borders did, but necessarily had to go beyond them.

This was an idea with which some spokesmen for Catalan governmental nationalism tried to flirt. Specifically it appeared in one of the usual newspaper press releases addressed to the international community (October 14, 1937) by the Commissariat of Propaganda of the Generalitat. In an evident synthesis of the geopolitical arguments more favorable to Catalan independence under French protection, the Commissariat proposed a confusing synthesis when stating: "Catalonia plays a very important role in this fight of Iberia [i.e., the Peninsula] against conquering international fascism. Not only because of its participation in men, matériel and sacrifices to the cause that is common to all brother peoples, if not also for their geographical and strategic situation, in what refers to the possible expansion of the war and the security of other European countries, France in particular." Recalling the importance of the Pyrenees border and the territorial extension allegedly controlled by the Generalitat, as well as the kilometers of the Mediterranean coastline in Catalan hands, press bulletins added the implied control of the Valencian coast and the Balearic Islands, that is, to the whole of the territories that spoke the Catalan language. This veiled proposal for the construction of a pan-Catalan Republic was summarized, again, in the potential Catalan role: "Catalonia, then, for its condition and its geographical and strategic situation, constitutes the southernmost advanced position of the French border, and France knows, moreover, that our people, committed to peace, who fight the war to ensure peace, has always been and will be a friendly neighbor, faithful to the ideas of democracy and of progress to which France is firmly committed." This affirmation, reiterative, was repeated using Churchill as a reference: "And, regarding the situation in Catalonia, we remember that at the end of the European War [of 1914–18], Winston Churchill said that the eastern border of England was the Rhine. It is necessary, now, to consolidate the idea that the Ebro can be the southern Rhine and thus become one of the frontiers of France and, therefore, of England."[107]

These were Catalan siren calls to Paris between threats to Barcelona that were all the more disturbing because they came neither from the sea nor the land. At a time when air warfare was already an established fact, the areas of action and limits of range of military aviations would be an increasingly determining factor in any conflict. If Franco won, only a part of French Brittany would be out of reach of enemy air-raids. From Barcelona to Toulon and Marseille there were less than 400 kilometers, and of course even less from Genoa. Nazi or fascist bomber squadrons certainly could attack French urban centres. Therefore, as on sea or land, Catalonia could also be an ally in the air or, at least, an interesting and useful territory that might offer support to the French aerial perimeter. All this, undoubtedly, was established according to the defensive – and never offensive – doctrine of the General Staff of the French armies.

This same potential geopolitical scenario would not go unnoticed by German specialists on international relations and military strategies. With this same geopolitical perspective, towards the end of the Civil War there appeared some works like that of the German publicist Franz Pauser. His book – *Spaniens Tor Zum Mittelmeer Und Die Katalanische Frage* ("Spain's Door to the Mediterranean and the Catalan Question", 1938) – warned of the importance of the political status of Catalonia in a future European or Mediterranean conflict.[108] These were points of view that would be picked up shortly after by the British in titles such as *Axis Plans in the Mediterranean: An analysis of German geopolitical ideas concerning Italy, France, Balearic Islands, Gibraltar, Catalonia and Spain* (1939).[109]

In short, both Mussolini and Hitler surrounded the hated and weakened France, with which one and the other kept alive various tensions or confrontations in Europe and Africa. The growing collusion of Germans and Italians made difficult the connections between Paris and its colonies or territories in the Magreb, and eliminated Spain as a possible French ally. The increasing collaboration between Berlin and Rome created a western Mediterranean theatre certainly favorable to their objectives, directly threatening to France, and which, in addition, even could disturb the British presence in Gibraltar and its maritime corridor through the Suez Canal to India. To this it should be added the control of the Sicilian channel with the threat of the Italian Libya to the control of the British possession of Malta. In fact, the Italians were preparing since 1935 – another thing was their real potential – for a war against the British in this perspective.[110] That is to say, an attempt was made to take advantage of the main Franco-British imperial weaknesses and contradictions in the Mediterranean: the excessive extension of its communications lines both vertically, North–South, and, horizontally, West–East. Not accidentally was the alliance of Rome and Berlin, established tentatively in October 1936, treated as an "Axis".[111] It was true that both French and British could live outside the Mediterranean by sailing much longer Atlantic routes to their colonial interests, but that would be a serious drawback in any war effort. In fact, the British fear was not so much the beginning of a direct confrontation with Italy (which eventually would break out in 1940, after the fall of France), but rather a maritime clash between Rome and Paris in the Mediterranean that would in time involve the Royal Navy, and its string of bases from Gibraltar and Malta to Cyprus and Alexandria.[112]

In this way, it would be understood by the French government, which, shortly after the Spanish Civil War began, sent Admiral François Darlan to London to advise the British Admiralty of the risk posed by the conflict for both countries. In spite of this, the First Sea Lord, Admiral Ernle Chatfield of the Royal Navy, would not give credit to such an analysis. He argued that both the Balearic Islands and the Canary Islands could be left in nazi or fascist hands without much danger. In London, Franco's victory was not as feared nearly as much as a strong Soviet appearance on the Mediterranean scene.[113] The idea was clear: Franco before Stalin. It was synthesized by the reaction of the commander of the Mediterranean British Fleet, Roger Backhouse, who proposed an alliance with Germany and Italy in the face of certain information on the supposed "Bolshevization" of Spain and Catalonia that had arrived in London, written personally by His Britannic Majesty's Consul General in Barcelona, Sir Norman King.[114]

Consequently, any attempt to help create a new strong and united New Spain or, from another point of view, an entity subdued and dominated by an ideology that approached fascism and nazism with its own peculiarities, i.e., the possibility that Catalonia would develop a process of emancipation, of whatever type, was not seen as a positive element by either Rome nor Berlin. But, if such a secession were to actually happen, the new small State, with or without the coveted Balearic Islands, Valencia (and even with the port of Cartagena) could become the exception that could break the plans of the Hitler–Mussolini Axis. Who was therefore interested?

With the Help of France or the USSR? A Strategic Republican retreat or Catalan Independence?

If the paper trail on the subject is closely followed, two key questions can be raised: what objective was independence looking for? And no less important (as has already been seen), with the help of what foreign ally – what major power – could independence take place? If one starts with the first question, one can see how possible scenarios were extremely open in more than one direction. On the one hand, there were those who would speculate on the creation of a Catalan Republic under the control of the Spanish Republican government as the last space of a loyal Spain. While others, the majority, simply presented a clear secession led by left Catalan nationalism. Another thing was, whatever the final purpose, who would support that manoeuvre, if France or the Soviet Union.

For example, Italian fears of a Catalan independence scenario – only one month after the beginning of the war – regarded the emergence of French protection more or less in tandem with the Spanish Republican government. In a report from the air attache of the Italian embassy (still in Madrid), commander Ferrari, it was stated that the rebel general Emilio Mola was aware of the advanced development of a French plan together with the Spanish Republican government. According to a trusted informant of Mola, the French Popular Front authorities would have started the operation with the trip to Madrid of a leading French labour unionist, no less than the Secretary General of the Confédération Générale du Travail, or CGT, Léon Jouhaux. According to Ferrari, Mola told him: "He [Jouhaux] had advised [the Republican government] to abandon Madrid and withdraw, with the rest of the army and the militias, to Valencia to resist if it were possible and, if not, to Catalonia, making this region and the Balearic Islands the inflexible point of the red resistance." Ferrari added: "In this case Jouhaux has promised the unconditional help of the 'French popular front' in men, weapons, aircraft and technicians. The plan would therefore consist in organizing a Catalonia that would be separated from the nationalist Spain, which would own the Balearic Islands and that would be a French pawn in the Mediterranean".[115] This plan, according to the Italian report, would explain the Catalan attempts to occupy Mallorca during August 1936. Everything seemed to fit. However, the Italian information ignored the fact that the operation in Mallorca was not Spanish republican as was explained by some journalists, but a strictly Catalan initiative. In the ERC Barcelona daily, *La humanitat*, the party press organ, articles of the Catalanist historian and politician, Antoni Rovira i Virgili, would give the amphibious attack an epic nationalist tone that harkened back to Medieval history.[116] In fact, the Mallorcan expedition received neither the approval nor the backing of the central government of the socialist Francisco Largo Caballero (opposed notoriously by Indalecio Prieto, minister of Naval and Air affairs), despite the great geostrategic importance of Mallorca for the control of the Spanish Mediterranean coast. The withdrawal of Catalan forces was seen as a typical Madrid-style betrayal by many in Barcelona.

The Mallorcan expedition was reviewed from another direction by the British Consul in Barcelona, Norman King, who thought he saw in the steps undertaken by the Generalitat during those weeks the beginning movements of independence. According to King, the raising of the Catalan flag in the military fortress of Montjuïc in Barcelona, despite the theoretic control of the Republican government, was understood by Catalan society as "a step forward towards independence [...]." And he added: "There is no doubt that the Catalans also hope to include the Balearic Islands in their independent State if they can achieve the conquest of Mallorca [...]."[117] These are relatively aseptic observations by

King, which contrasted with his absolute conviction that any Catalan secession would be harmful to the interests of his own country. In fact, this would be King's reply to all and any questions about the British attitude towards secession put forth by certain sectors close to the Catalan government, like the Councillor of Culture, Ventura Gassol.[118] Consequently, there were two different visions, the British, who thought they perceived steps by the Generalitat towards secession in any Catalan action, as against the Italians, who deduced a Catalan redout led by Spanish Republican authorities.

If we consider first the Italian perception, this could consist of a Catalan Republic, backed by the Spanish Republicans, and, when it was proclaimed, that would be recognized by France, and, by extension, by the League of Nations. This idea, as is evident in the text, was also shared by other diplomatic sectors and journalistic opinion-makers. For example, the Italian delegate to the League of Nations, Renato Bova Scoppa, claimed that France intended to create an ally to confront a Spain subject to intrusion by Rome and Berlin.[119]

This idea would be repeated in the interpretation that different diplomats would make regarding the transfer to Barcelona of the president of the Spanish Republic, Manuel Azaña, in October of 1936. Belgian representatives interpreted Azaña's move as a clear demonstration of the absolute defeatism of the government side. According to the Belgian embassy in Spain, Azaña's relocation responded to a plan to create a Catalan bastion from which, with the help of the Soviet Union, there could be created an independent communist Catalonia where the Generalitat and a Spanish Republican government would collaborate, having "realized the impossibility of continuing the fight, and would have decided to retreat to Valencia and Catalonia where they hoped, thanks to the support that Russia has promised them, to oppose with victorious resistance and establish an independent Soviet State".[120] In the meantime, according to other diplomats like the U.S. consul, Mahlon F. Perkins, in direct conversation with Azaña – after the intermediation of Companys – the President of the Republic was not negotiating a Catalan–Soviet alliance but was rather a prisoner of the Catalan nationalists.[121] These were not particularly strange perceptions if one accounted for the views of family members of the republican president. His brother-in-law and close friend, Cipriano Rivas Cherif, wrote that Azaña would be received by Companys as a foreign head of State who was going to make an alliance against a common enemy.[122]

From a similar perspective, the Belgian ambassador Robert Everts, like many others in the diplomatic corps, would continue to analyze the hypothetical realization of plans or projects for republican retreats to Catalonia. When, at the beginning of November 1936, the Republican government led by Francisco Largo Caballero decided to move to Valencia from the besieged capital of Madrid, the Belgian representative saw a new manoeuvre, this time a sort of contradictory trick, tending to deny the construction of that Catalan-Valencian stronghold: "One can ask why the government has moved to Valencia and not to Barcelona where the President of the Republic has [been] installed for some time. Most of my colleagues attribute this decision to the desire not to give the impression that the government would be willing to follow the advice given by the Russian ambassador to settle in Barcelona and proclaim the Catalan Soviet republic."[123] Accordingly, Everts seemed to explain a certain division between the Presidency of the Republic and the Republican government with respect to two new and special protagonists, who were none other than the new Soviet ambassador, Marcel Rosenberg, appointed in August, and his second in command in loyalist Spain, the consul general in Barcelona, Vladimir Antonov-Ovseyenko.[124] After several years and diverse vicissitudes, finally diplomatic relations between Spain and the Soviet Union, established in theory years before, were made concrete. The connection had been paralyzed by the death in France in December 1933 of the "Old Bolshevik" who should have been the first Soviet ambassador in Madrid, Anatoly Lunacharsky, along with the conservative electoral victory in Spain a few weeks before. As a result, formal diplomatic links would have to wait until the Spanish Civil War had started. In fact, once the Soviet diplomats were established in Spain between September and October, the European press was abuzz with conspiracy theories: some papers even published the conditions allegedly proposed by Manuel Azaña to proceed to a surrender of the Republic, among which were: "The independence of Catalonia was a condition for the suspension of hostilities".[125]

This was an apparently solid vision but which at no time mentioned the real desires of the Spanish Republicans to control the de facto Catalan independence and the widespread revolutionary violence, and resulting lack of effective control, that was developing in Catalonia during the summer of 1936. This last factor would compromise in an absolute manner the Spanish Republic's "media campaign" towards European and world public opinion. There was a Catalan revolution, in the hands, mainly, of the anarchists of the CNT-FAI, but which was also the responsibility of a Generalitat that had seized almost all the powers of the State within the territory, in a decision halfway between an imperious and immediate necessity, and an insufficient political will to overstep the Spanish constitutional framework of 1931. By dismantling Republican state structures, the Generalitat would occupy the space left by the Republic, and so becoming, in practice, a State. Controlling the borders, assuming the direction of military defense, seizing the delegations of the Bank of Spain, the Generalitat would seem to be carrying out precisely the steps previous to a secession that had been indicated by different consuls and journalists. Symbolic events such as the issue of paper currency by the Generalitat seemed to confirm this, as commented by the British and Italian press.[126] In fact, this was one of the explanations justifying the conviction held by so many foreign diplomats regarding the upcoming Catalan secession. If they were already almost independent, why didn't they take the next and definitive step? This question should be placed with a certain impression that took for granted that there was a Catalan policy capable of conditioning the whole of the Republican zone. This theme was heard throughout the Spanish war. In this sense, there were individuals, such as the Swiss chargé d'affaires in Madrid, who, writing in late October, who placed the socializing pressure of the labour unions in Catalonia in collaboration with the Generalitat as a decisive element for the evolution towards the extreme left of the whole of the Republic: "As can be seen, the influence of the radicalization of Catalonia that now houses the Presidency [of the Spanish Republic] continues to grow."[127]

This view of a Catalan revolutionary hegemony would increase with the entry of three Catalan ministers of the CNT in the Republican executive after the governmental crisis of early November, significantly after the entry of the CNT into the Catalan cabinet. This Catalan element, as has been indicated at the beginning of this essay, would unleash a certain nervousness in the international sphere. With Azaña in Barcelona and Franco closing in on Madrid, the insistence on the danger that a Catalan secession would mean at a continental level was evident and persistent in the press. For example, in the eyes of some analysts of the newspaper *Le Temps*, the daily closest to the French Ministry of Foreign Affairs: "What the government of Mr. Largo Caballero is forced to foresee, under the pressure of the circumstances, such a possibility, is without doubt; but nobody knows exactly the existing situation in Madrid, especially now that the President of the Republic, Mr. Azaña, is in Barcelona [...]. The misfortune is that, whatever the fate of Madrid in the next few days, the atrocious civil war that has bloodied Spain, with all the risks involved for the general peace [...] will not end with the eventual occupation of the capital by the forces of General Franco. This event will have the effect of placing a series of questions of major importance, such as the recognition of a new Spanish government and the solution to contribute to the problem of the Catalan state, a problem that threatens to make new implications appear in particularly dangerous conditions to disputes concerning the policy of non-intervention." And it was not entirely reasonable – though the British press insisted on negotiations in that direction[128] – to hope that Franco and his backers would accept the segregation of Catalonia without further ado. But *le Temps* persisted: "It is difficult to conceive that the nationals [Franco represented the self-styled "national cause"] of General Franco, who have a very strong conception of the unity of Spain, and its intransigence with regards to the claims of the Basque autonomists proves this, would want to abandon Catalonia to itself, on the pretext that it is economically less indispensable for Spain than Spain is for Catalan prosperity." This Catalan problem, therefore, would make it inevitable that, once Franco conquered Madrid, he would launch an offensive to occupy Catalonia in a campaign that was expected to be long and complex. However, despite the lack of viability of the plan, the article still asked: what would Catalonia do? And what would be its effects on European international relations? *Le Temps* insisted: "The fact that the president of the Republic, Mr. Azaña, is currently in Barcelona leads to think that the Spanish Republican government would expect, after the fall of Madrid, to take refuge and stay in Catalonia in its current form, becoming one more reason for the nationals to continue the war. Would the Catalans, very linked to the cause of autonomy, lend themselves to such a combination? It is very doubtful. The idea of the creation of an independent Catalan state is already old, and the intention of Soviet Russia is to favour and facilitate with all its power and its help the establishment of a first proletarian State in Western Europe."[129]

The same theme but in a slightly different sense could be read in the Belgian press: "According to information not confirmed received from Salamanca [the headquarters of general Franco], the government of Madrid would have contacted the nationalist general Franco to inform him that the government would put an immediate end to hostilities if the independence of Catalonia were recognized. General Franco would have rejected this offer."[130] This possibility again led the writer to venture the continental complications that an option like this could trigger. These were opinions that in large part responded to reality. On one hand, it had to take into account that Azaña was in Barcelona, in contradiction to the Republican government of Largo Caballero, that had decided to move to Valencia. On the other hand, although with a certain irony, the same President Azaña would privately write in exile about a plan of the Republican central staff that would assume a retreat in Catalonia as a base for a reconquest of the remaining territories in rebel hands.[131] Thus, this was an operation with two protagonists insistently cited, Azaña and the Soviet Union. A Soviet role was one that would never completely supplant the French one but that would quickly take almost all the visibility and protagonism.

In addition, the rumours collected by the French press stated clearly: "According to news arriving from London, Moscow would be taking steps to help politically and militarily the Marxists [sic] of Barcelona to make Catalonia a communist state."[132] In this

sense, Paris would be the point of international journalistic diffu-
sion of this alternative – an independent Soviet Catalonia – half
way between fear and demagoguery. This is shown, among others,
by a note signed in the French capital that appeared in the Austrian
Salzburger Volksblatt of October 22, 1936, where the simple and
direct question was: "A Soviet state in Catalonia?".[133] In short, an
approach born of the intoxication of the rebel allies and of Franco's
own side became successful *fake news*, which would last throughout
the war.[134]

This Soviet Catalan Republic was an alleged decision of Moscow
that was bound inevitably to the supposition that believed in an
immediate Franco occupation of Madrid. Subsequently, it was
presumed, there would take place an open attack by Italy and
Germany against Catalonia. These powers then would occupy the
Mediterranean strip and avoid Soviet control.[135] In fact, at the end
of October 1936 it was claimed that the Soviet Union would have
decided to use its diplomatic representative in the Catalan capital,
the new consul Vladimir Antonov-Ovseyenko, to force the creation
of a Catalan Soviet republican State. As a clear objective, this new
regime would aim at the installation of a Soviet "imperialist" base
in a "hot" sea: the spearhead of the entry of Moscow into the
Mediterranean.[136] It was even said that it was the consul who
actually directed the Generalitat.[137] Given such logic, this Catalan
Republic, as an assumed counter-offer to the economic and military
aid arriving from the socialist giant, would require a pact with the
Spanish Republican authorities. Much fanciful information was
added about the pacts between the Generalitat, Catalan political
parties and the Spanish Republican government: "The announced
exit from Madrid to Barcelona of the President Azaña [...] is really
considered as a proof that Azaña moved to Catalonia to negotiate
with the autonomous authorities [...] the transfer to Barcelona of
the Government of Madrid."[138] In fact, the Italian press claimed
that as soon as Madrid fell, the troops of Franco would head towards
Catalonia to crush and "sweep away the Bolshevik terror".[139] This
was an argument later described as a campaign of intoxication of
international public opinion by the Italian press. According to
Jaume Miravitlles, despite intense Soviet attempts to dilute
Catalan political capacity, Italian newspapers were "perfectly aware

of the weakness of the communists in Catalonia and the Russian intentions regarding the Catalan country". But, said Miravitlles, the fascist-controlled press "presented it differently and soon Antonov-Ovseyenko, who, as we have explained, came with a concrete objective, was presented by the Italians as the catalyst agent destined to precipitate the birth of a Bolshevik Catalan republic that would represent for Russia the point of support against Italy".[140]

This was an option quite distant from the plans of the Kremlin, but one that was understandable if one follows the public attitude of the consul Antonov-Ovseyenko. Thus, as Josep Puigsech explains in his analysis of the Soviet documentation, the representative of Stalin in Barcelona would be totally opposed to any Catalan secession. This would not be incompatible with the understanding that he would develop about Catalonia, with all the component elements – language, culture, history and the right to be considered as a full standing "nation". But Catalonia would be a nation within a State, the Spanish Republic, that supposedly mistreated her. This consideration would lead the Barcelona representative of the USSR, against changing borders, to propose a mutual recognition between the Republic and the Generalitat in favor of a military collaboration. Antonov-Ovseyenko would express his idea in various meetings with Azaña – like Ilya Ehrenburg had done weeks before – citing Catalan complaints, together their absolute justification in his opinion.[141] This position derived from the strength of the Catalan arguments, but it basically pursued another objective derived from the Bolshevik experience during the Russian Civil War (1917–22) after the "October revolution". From his point of view it was necessary to have the peripheral nations in favor in order to win in a common struggle. The Republic needed the participation of Catalonia and Euskadi. To achieve this goal, Antonov-Ovseyenko would propose some visible and viable measures already requested by the Generalitat some time before, such as, for example, the accreditation of Catalan – and Basque – diplomatic attachés in the Republican embassies and consulates.[142] With other proposals more in depth, he attempted to draft modifications in the notion of Spain itself. Such was the conviction of the Soviet consul, that in a meeting at the end of November with Azaña and the president of the Republican government, Francisco Largo Caballero, he came to demand public recognition of the pluri-nationality of Spain. This was a change of the historical discourse. It was necessary to make a qualitative leap and turn Spain into a Federal Republic to silence Catalan separatism towards which the consulate showed itself sympathetic.[143] Antonov-Ovseyenko rejected separation, as did all the Soviet world, besides not believing it to be viable without powerful allies, but was understanding of the feelings it generated. In the Catalan case, he was sure, what was required was recognition, loyalty and collaboration with the Spanish Republic.

Such alleged Soviet influence in Barcelona, without knowing much real detail, would greatly concern not only the authorities of the European dictatorships, but also the liberal democracies led by France and Great Britain.[144] Eliminated was the aim of creating a Soviet Catalonia as a Spanish republican stronghold or as a new Catalan nation-State. In this situation, the option of a Republican refuge could be understood as suicide in such an initial moment of conflict, a demonstration of absolute defeatism and even more when Madrid was successfully resisting its besiegers. Therefore, the "Spanish" secessionist option for Catalonia with French or Russian help was highly unlikely in its realization and very much in the minority in respect to the second: the French or Soviet help to a secessionist project of strictly Catalan nationalist style. For example, at the beginning of September 1936, the Belgian Legation in Berne communicated a conversation maintained with the Italian ambassador to Switzerland. Mussolini's representative in the Swiss capital stated that Catalonia would proclaim its annexation to France if Franco occupied Madrid: "According to information coming from Rome, Catalonia would plan to declare, in the event that the insurgents win, their annexation to France, forcing France to take over its military defense against General Mola. Is this possible?"[145] In fact, what was commented in Switzerland was simply the same speculation that Portela Valladares and many others had stated weeks before.

But, if the Catalan nationalist scenario that some foresaw was actually fulfilled, it would leave the French authorities in a most complicated situation. That is, if Franco won the Spanish conflict and, at the same time, the Generalitat proclaimed independence or incorporated itself into France, would the rebels and their Nazi and Fascist allies declare war on Paris? If Italy and Germany decided to officially enter the conflict by blockading the entire Spanish coast and declaring war on the USSR, what would happen?[146] The response, given the failure of the hypothesis to come true, was not carried out in any direction. No one in Barcelona forced Paris to position itself. No one seemed to want to bother the Blum government or its successors. But the stubborn facts would not avoid a series of debates and changes of opinion in respect to the French attitude.

At the end of August 1936 the Italian and German representatives in Paris, Vittorio Cerruti and the Count Johannes von Welczeck, gave credibility to the notion of a French rescue: "The eventuality is foreseeable that the Catalans, practically separated from the rest of Spain, do not hesitate to proclaim a separate state, resorting to French aid, which Count Welczeck thinks would not be denied either in men, nor weapons, nor in money. The consequences of such an eventuality would be very serious, also in relation to the Balearic Islands, which, as is well known, are already partially dominated by the popular front militias."[147] This German analysis was, in theory at least, based on the direct knowledge of Welczeck regarding Spain; the Count had represented Germany in Madrid from the end of the Weimar Republic to the consolidation of Nazism (1926–1936). This thinking was confirmed by a second contact, now directly in the German capital at the beginning of October, and in which was added the possibility of a common reckoning with the British given the attentive posture of the Intelligence Service regarding moves in Barcelona.[148] German points of view – shared by the Italians – would be progressively modified over the following weeks. While the Italian Embassy in Paris insisted on the attention that the French press devoted to Catalonia and to various Catalan nationalist figures, such as the Councillor of Culture, Ventura Gassol, now resident in the Hexagon, nevertheless the matter quieted down. Little by little the opinions would be inclined to deny or to question the option to a French alliance with Barcelona. This was written in the report of an Italian representative dividing the French position:

"Regarding France's position towards Catalonia, Count Welczeck did not doubt that the Quai d'Orsay will always assert its position contrary to the constitution of an autonomous State, but fears that the extremist part of the [French] government, that the Popular Front, can pressure to obtain the recognition of the Catalan government on behalf of France." At this point, there was no doubt that Soviet influence caused much more alarm than a French takeover: "The ambassador of Germany is also worried about Catalonia fearing that the government of the USSR will manage to send considerable arms."[149]

In this sense, in an interview maintained by Ambassador Cerruti with the Secretary General of the French Foreign Ministry, Alexis Léger, the latter assured the French conviction regarding a Franco victory, at the same time that he would categorically deny any option of intervention by his country in Catalonia: "Speaking about Catalonia, Léger says he can offer assurances that France does not consider in any way to help the authorities of Barcelona, nor to enter in any case in such a delicate problem."[150] The clear position of Léger would be reinforced two months later: "Essential for France is that the civil war of Spain ends soon while it does not matter which side wins. I had nevertheless a serious concern for a further evolution of the war, since the resistance of Catalonia will be tireless."[151] It was necessary, therefore, to get the conflict to end quickly, and, in that matter, Léger was insistent with the Italian ambassador. It was essential to avoid Soviet intervention. There was no similar conviction regarding the French position in the Nazi embassy in Paris. Confirming partially Léger's arguments but contradicting his conclusion, Welczeck insisted on the French social and political division: if "a Catalan state is proclaimed, the French Popular Front will lean heavily, for psychological and political reasons, to sustain this government", and he added, "although career diplomats of the Quai d'Orsay feel apprehension".[152] Politicians, to a large extent, bothered professional diplomats who wanted to mark the foreign policy of their respective States. In fact, according to Welczeck, the Catalan secessionist proclamation would be a serious problem for France, since it would force the country to take a concrete position and to intervene, breaking with its policy of neutrality. In the same way this would happen with the diplomatic recognition of Franco by the Italians and Germans. If finally Catalonia separated from Spain and France did not manifest itself clearly, this space – many worried – would be seized by the Soviets.

In the face of all this, what should France do? At this point, and into the first weeks of the Spanish war, as the conservative press advocated abstention, political positions began to be more and more antagonistic. For the French Communist spokesman, Gabriel Péri, the scenario that was being drawn was none other than the demonstration of the failure of the Blum government's position. Péri, journalist, party deputy and vice-president of the commission of foreign affairs in the National Assembly, stated in November 1936: "The no intervention [policy], under the false pretext of exorcising a risk of imaginary war, has provoked a very real risk of war, born of the siege and isolation of France, which arises from the triumph of the black shirts and brown shirts on the Mediterranean and its shores."[153] This call for French help to Catalonia and the Republic was obviously not shared by all.

From the conservative *Le Figaro*, journalist and future diplomat Wladimir d'Ormesson stated that the Blum government's only option remained the strict observance of total neutrality. There was no way to recognize an independent revolutionary Catalonia under Soviet influence across the border from French territory, however much it was openly attacked by Italy and Germany: "It is still possible that the independence of Catalonia be declared and that the leaders of this revolutionary pseudo-state direct their petitions [for help] to France where they are sure to find support and echo within the majority of the Chamber." This was a demand that should receive a clear negative reply, a response that was related to the position of Léger: "France will never recognize the creation of this State, it will never lend itself either closely or remotely to its establishment [...]."[154] If instead what happened was the outbreak of an open war in Catalonia between the nascent Berlin–Rome alliance and Moscow, France ought to remain silent and look the other way. Not surprisingly in someone born into an aristocratic family with a tradition of producing diplomats, d'Ormesson seemed to be in agreement with the position of the Quai d'Orsay. Better a victory for Franco than the triumph of Stalin's allies at a time when French internal tensions were bubbling on the surface. This position was very close to the one maintained by the French ambassador to Spain, Jean Herbette, after having made a 180-degree turn in his attitude towards the Civil War: from pro-Republican to pro-Franco.[155]

Such pro-Franco evaluations were encompassed in a broader discourse that, according to the communist *L'Humanité*, blurred reality. The PCF daily denounced that such a perception confused real actions on the ground with imagined future dangers: "Today guns, airplanes, tanks and fully formed regiments have been dis-embarked" while others "meditate the constitution in Barcelona of a Soviet Catalan republic that would constitute a grave danger to French unity". This was an allegedly manipulated vision that tried to make the French public believe that Republican Spain and Catalonia were already a Soviet regime, when, in reality, they were still democratic territories. The right-wing argument was that such democracy was only nominal, in practice dominated by anarchists, socialists and diverse communist currents: "Always the same not very subtle 'trick' that consists, in order to scare away the middle classes of France, by presenting Spain, and especially Catalonia, as a Sovietized country", wrote the Communist daily.[156] In fact, this was the question under debate: why was Catalonia at war and why did the Catalans fight? Was Catalonia an advanced democracy or a country in a revolutionary process that was moving away from the French democratic and republican model? Or perhaps such a change was precisely that what the French Socialists (the SFIO or Section Française del International Ouvrière) and the Communists (the PCF or Parti Communiste Français) wanted for their country?

Be that as it may, the views of the Soviet role in Catalonia mani-fested in France contrasted with the testimony of one of the key security service officers – Walter Krivitsky, NKVD *rezident* in The Hague – in charge of much of Soviet operations in Western Europe who wrote: "At this point, I received more strict indications from Moscow to not allow the ship to deliver super cargo [sic] in Barcelona. Under no circumstances should these airplanes pass through Catalonia, because Catalonia had then an autonomous Government, very similar to that of a sovereign State. This Catalan government was dominated by anti-Stalinist revolutionaries. Moscow did not have confidence in them [...]."[157] A disclaimer of Soviet–Catalan collaboration to which should be added those that the consul Antonov-Ovseyenko did not tire of repeating whenever he had his chance before the Western press.[158] The USSR was not attempting to create a Soviet Catalonia even if everyone said the opposite about Moscow's consular presence in Barcelona.[159] It was taken for granted that the Soviet diplomatic structure would facilitate propaganda, ideological influence, and the shipment of military aid from Russian and Ukrainian ports on the Black Sea towards Barcelona.[160]

All this was realized through an Antonov-Ovseyenko who easily introduced himself into the Catalan government circles through his predisposition to learn Catalan.[161] This was remembered by a then young Catalan communist, Teresa Pàmies: "I remember, yes, – I will never forget it – the sympathy of that man who represented the interests of the USSR in Barcelona. He spoke a picturesque Catalan, with bits of French and Castilian. Being Ukrainian of origin and feelings, he considered that every foreign consul in Catalonia had the obligation to learn Catalan, even as any consul in France should learn French."[162] Ideology, the conventional wisdom of the moment, and the Soviet consul's evident personal charm, would make him appear in the eyes of the Italian consul general in the Catalan capital Carlo Bossi, as the "Effective Governor of Catalonia".[163]

In this way, from the Italian point of view – although there was official insistence on French aid for the Catalan nationalist sectors of what would be the new Catalan State – everything began to focus on the actions of the USSR. In a similar fashion, the change in attention was indicated by the British vice-consul in Barcelona, Edgar Vaughan, in a memorandum of August 22, 1936 just before the arrival of Antonov-Ovseyenko. According to him, in Catalonia two processes were converging. On the one hand, while, from the Catalan government everything was being done to separate from Madrid, on the other, the workers were doing everything in their power to collectivize the economy. The result of the sum of the two elements, said Vaughan: Catalonia was set to become the Second Soviet Republic of the world.[164]

Perhaps the individual who expressed concern most forcefully was Pope Pius XI in an audience granted to the Italian ambassador to the Holy See. In that reception there was reference to the possibility of the creation of a Soviet Catalonia as a general danger: "The Pontiff expressed himself with less security about Catalonia. It seems, he added, that the Moscow government intends to establish, in Catalonia, a model Bolshevik state, which, if fulfilled, this is the Pope who speaks, would constitute for a long time a danger beyond that for Spain, for France and, in general, for the whole of Western Europe."[165]

The constituent process of a Catalan Republic was an action by Moscow which was by all accounts, according to all observers, not merely a simple manoeuvre to hinder fascist expansion in Europe, but a decisive involvement in a Spanish conflict that could lead to an open continental conflagration. Thus, an Italian report signed in Salamanca on October 31, 1936, and sent to the Servizio de Informazione Militare (SIM), stated that Moscow would not be willing to lose a war that could be interpreted as the beginning of the Soviet decline, propitiating a broad anti-USSR front. Therefore, if it was necessary to provoke the beginning of a new, *second* World War, which would be unleashed with Catalonia as one of its main theatres: "At the end of the day, Russia has always thought that from a great war would emerge a general revolution, which, it is understood, would occur all to its advantage. That is why Russia would be willing to act thoroughly, even at the cost of provoking, acting like this, a great conflict."[166] The anti-communist point of view was disseminated by the all the European press that was worried about the possible collision between the budding Rome–Berlin "Axis" and Moscow: in the words of *The Scotsman* of Edinburgh: "Especially if the Italian and German warships try to intercept the Soviet ships with supplies from the Soviet government consigned for Catalonia".[167] The whole matter would even be more complicated with the possible implications of an official Soviet intervention in Spain in general or limited to Catalonia in relation to the Franco-Soviet Pact of 1935. In this sense, the French foreign minister, Yvon Delbos, categorically denied that such an eventuality would force France to provide assistance to the Soviets in the Iberian Peninsula.[168]

This kind of demurral was the opposite attitude to that of the bloc increasingly led by Nazi Germany. Precisely, after the signing of the Antikomintern Pact by Japan with Germany at the end of that same year 1936, the press picked up the statements of the Japanese foreign minister, Hachiro Arita, who said that the co-signers would act where the communist emergency was relevant, both outside as well as inside Asia, in "China as in Catalonia".[169] This strong statement forced the recently appointed minister, a well-known a Japanese politician and diplomat, to make precise the intention that the Empire of the Rising Sun would not send troops to Catalonia while its ally in Europe, Germany, already intervened there.[170]

However, not everyone thought of the Soviets as the only Catalan allies. In fact, some editorials in the British press believed that sympathy for Catalonia extended beyond Moscow if what was being discussed was a defensive war against a Spain completely controlled by Franco.[171] The press of French Algeria put it differently; a local daily said that "at this point, it is not only the Spain of the Popular Front, it is an independent Catalonia with a radical tendency that combats against the Führer and the Duce [...]".[172]

Whether it was only with Soviet support or with that of some other country, an antifascist stance was a strategic option that would trigger different international implications and complications that would become evident from the end of November when Rome and Berlin would diplomatically recognize the government of the general Franco. This recognition was interpreted as dangerous by the conservative French Catholic newspaper, *La Croix*, since it could serve as an excuse for a massive intervention of the USSR in Spain, promoting a semi-independent Catalonia.[173] In this sense, *Le Temps* picked up the anti-French threat assumed by Italy in its desire to achieve control of the western Mediterranean.[174] This could derive in an Italian–German frontal attack against a Catalonia under Moscow protection.[175]

Thus, while French opinion-makers were alarmed almost exclusively in reference to the intervention of Moscow, among Italian observers there would still persist a Franco-British protagonism in relation to Catalonia. In fact, there were rumours that indicated out the possible creation of a State that was perhaps not Catalan nationalist but with clear pan-Catalan connotations under British protection: "They point [...] to a well-informed source, according to which if Madrid fell into national [i.e., Franco] hands, the provinces of Catalonia, Valencia, Alicante and the Balearic Islands, would become an independent social-democratic Republic and would request British protection."[176] Even in Berlin there were discussions between the Nazi foreign ministry and the Italian ambassador, Bernardo Attolico, around the position to be adopted by Franco if Catalonia became independent or, at least, if it remained as a territory with some undefined degree of autonomy. This was a discussion in which, again, Great Britain appeared as a possible protector of a Catalonia that Franco and his army should put aside for a later stage of the war.

Obviously, there were Italian and German press and propaganda agencies linked to the project of diplomatic recognition of Frenco's rebel Junta, the aim of which was to lose its illegitimate "rebel" status. But the eventual consequences easily could extend to Catalonia, as explained in an Italian report of mid-October: "The opportunity to extend the consultations between the Italian and German governments in the face of an eventual 'Catalan culture' that could arise, has appeared in the course of a conversation maintained by me and this Ministry of Foreign Affairs and in which it has been acknowledged that it does not exclude that [to mitigate the backlash of an Italian-German recognition of the Spanish national government], it may be opportunely suggested to the latter not to show itself, at least at first, to be absolutely contrary to any form of Catalan autonomy. English liberalism could, in relative condescension to us, and with regards to Franco's government, find 'a lesser pretext' for action and reaction than, having the air of being in favour of Catalonia, would be directed in fact against us."[177]

Another option would imply that, in the face of a proclamation of Catalan independence, Germany and Italy would immediately recognize the Franco government and would facilitate – even more – arms so as to occupy Catalonia as quickly as possible. This idea was launched by General Queipo de Llano through the airwaves of Radio Sevilla, and picked up by the French press: making "allusion to a rumour according to which the Spanish [Republican] government would take refuge in Barcelona. 'If Catalonia, declared

General Queipo de Llano, is proclaimed independent, the three countries that make up the Fascist front will recognize the new government of Madrid and proclaim the integrity of the Spanish territory. Thus the Catalan independence movement will take the character of an insurrection and the three countries in question will reserve the right to supply the necessary arms to the new Spanish State so as to prevent all aid to the Catalans'".[178] In the same sense, a few days later the German press gathered up another radio warning from General Queipo de Llano, who stated that "a Catalan Marxist delegation, which aims to achieve the recognition of Catalonia as an independent State, has arrived in Geneva". In the face of this alleged fact, the loud-mouthed general claimed that Catalonia, like the rest of Spanish territories, soon would be "liberated".[179]

Diluted Fears or Preventive Action? The Ciano–Neurath Pact (October 1936)

Whether or not like a highly complex multi-sided game, the question of a Catalan secession circulated with such facility through the diplomatic offices that the pressure would force the subject to be made public and put in writing by the joint positioning of Rome and Berlin. Thus, the circumstance of the new "Axis" was fully settled by the end of October 1936, as a step prior to the recognition of the Francisco Franco regime. The talks held in Berlin on October 21, 1936 between the German and Italian foreign ministers, Konstantin Baron von Neurath and Count Galeazzo Ciano, already made it publicly clear that they would oppose a sovereign Catalonia and even more so, logically enough, if it were Soviet. Among the different points that would subscribe tendencies to ensure the Spanish territorial integrity in the Italo-German meeting was one that explicitly proposed "a common action, which will be defined, in due time, to prevent that a Catalan state from being created and consolidated".[180] Significantly, this point would be advanced to the world press, from Lithuania to Uruguay, before the rest of the agreement was made public.[181] The message on Catalonia in the Berlin accord was already conventional wisdom, the way the majority of sagacious observers of the Old Continent by now argued; the war in Spain – it was repeated – was being played out (in the words of a Belgian daily) "between the Russian Soviet influence and the Italo-German one. Moscow, if one wants, the Third International, understands to favor the establishment of a proletarian state in Spain, at least in Catalonia, while Germany and Italy, above all the second, want to oppose this [...]".[182] The Catholic journalist Guido Gonella insisted on this notion in *L'Osservatore Romano*, the Vatican newspaper, affirming that a Soviet Catalonia would alter the Mediterranean equilibrium just at the time of applying the agreements of the Montreux conference of the preceding July. This agreement, which went into effect on 9 November, opened the way for the straits – Bosphorus and Dardanelles – to Soviet ships of the Black Sea fleet.[183] At last, Moscow could get its fleet to sail towards warm waters, if it so desired.

The Montreux agreement and the Italo-German pact were realities that the *Frankfurter Zeitung* – the only newspaper in Germany intentionally not under Goebbels' full control – made explicit when it stated that: "Neither France, nor England, nor Germany, nor Italy will not be able to eventually reduce spectators of the evolution of Catalonia [...]."[184] These were the days when the front pages everywhere also speculated about an immediate attack by the Nazi *Kriegsmarine* against Barcelona.[185] Be that as it may, Montreux and the Berlin talks gave a second kick-off to the propaganda campaign of fear in the face of the "Moscow Preparations for the Soviet Republic in Catalonia". The article of the Nazi mouthpiece, the *Völkischer Beobachter*, was titled with large print and was the main cover headline only two days after the Neurath–Ciano accord.[186] It was followed by the main German newspapers, already subject to the Nazi regime, or in the British dailies that also reproduced in Berlin news items.[187] And this would take place in the full debate about the false Soviet neutrality – as deceptive as that of the rest of the interested powers – in the Non-Intervention Committee of London. In that sense, criticizing the shipment of food and some weaponry to Republican Spain, the German press stressed the importance of Ciano's trip. In fact the question was: What was Moscow going to do now after the joint Nazi-Fascist declaration of intentions?[188]

For Mussolini and Hitler there was no other option other than a mutual understanding. This convergence was exemplified unequivocally by a series of reports from United States' diplomacy after a round of contacts in the European capitals on this and other issues. First, a few days after the Berlin agreement, Mussolini himself, in a meeting with the American ambassador in Rome, William Phillips, ratified the Ciano–Neurath pact. According to the representative of Washington, the Italian dictator would have said that he did not aspire to obtain any Spanish territory ... adding a "but Catalonia".[189] As was communicated to the Secretary of State, Cordell Hull, that "but Catalonia" could justify any intensification of Italian intervention.[190] This was a position identical to that of Minister Ciano[191] and to the statements making the diplomatic rounds in Berlin.[192] Meanwhile, the United States ambassador in the British capital, Robert W. Bingham, explained to Hull that the British believed a proclamation of Catalan independence was possible in order to achieve a position of strength of the Generalitat before the best of the options: the negotiation of a confederal Spain that could satisfy Catalan nationalism.[193] This analysis implied bargaining chips, achieving of a strong position for a later negotiation. This same assessment also was believed by the British Consul in Barcelona a few weeks later, when he reported a talk given by Josep Tarradellas in the following terms: "Catalonia had reached a degree of independence" which would not be renounced. Stating that there would "never be a surrender", he concluded that "Catalonia was going to take Spain towards a federation of the Iberian peoples".[194]

In the end, some British reports of a legal nature such as the one prepared by the second legal counselor of the Foreign Office, Sir William Erich Beckett, were not reluctant to recognize Catalan sovereignty. Considering that Beckett could be described as pro-Republican, his cold juridical gaze made him write: "The main condition for recognizing a new State that was previously part of another and separates is that independence seems to have established itself rather firmly. In general, when the government of the country from which it separates agrees and accepts the separation, this condition is automatically fulfilled, and little more can be said of the question." Evidently this was not the scenario at hand: "In this case, the situation is perhaps a bit more complicated. It is true that, if the government of Madrid recognizes the total independence of Catalonia while this government is still recognized as the government of Spain and General Franco merely as the chief of the insurgents, looking at the question from a strictly legal point of view, I believe that there would be no obstacle for the United Kingdom to recognize a Catalan State. But, even so, it would not be advisable to consider unimportant the existence of General Franco, and his performance. If he not only were opposed to the separation, but also it seems likely that this would be done by force and there would be reasonable doubts about the possibilities of success, it would be prudent to adopt delaying tactics and [?] Limiting [sic] the maintenance of de facto relations, but as friendly as possible with the Catalan authorities, on a basis not very different from the current [British] relations with General Franco."

In the event of an eventual recognition of Franco by London, Beckett said: "Anyway, if at the time of separation the step has already been taken of granting greater recognition to General Franco and of recognizing the status of a belligerent government, it would not be fair, in our opinion, to grant the Catalan government a recognition greater than that of another belligerent government that has de facto authority over the territory which in fact it controls. According to this recognition measure, I think it would be convenient to obtain the promise of the government of Barcelona to respect the treaties currently in force between the United Kingdom and Spain; but, before taking this step, it would be good to study the question a bit more and check which treaties would be of practical importance from this point of view".[195]

Therefore, the Foreign Office acted with extreme caution. British diplomacy was not opposed frontally to the recognition of a Catalan secession as was Alexis Léger at the Quai d'Orsay (who considered it a threat to French unity), but such a step required a guarantee of survival of the newly independent State. This was reaffirmed by Beckett's superior, Sir William Malkin, in his assessment of the previous report: "I agree. It would not be appropriate to recognize Catalonia as an independent State until it was clear that General Franco will not destroy its independence. Regarding this, I can think of the precedents of Georgia, etc.

I think it would be better to study the question of treaties. We must weigh the exact moment in which we will invite the government of Barcelona to respect the current ones, and perhaps we have to make a distinction between different kinds of treaties."[196] In sum, further reports were requested, and archival inquiries were undertaken to settle a position that, to a large extent, would be more concerned with the continuity of the treaties and commercial matters than with any opposition or aid to the possible independence of Catalonia. In short, London was flexible in principle. Another option would be to ignore the approaches of the delegates of the Generalitat in later times (something in fact not done).

Therefore, facing off against a pragmatic and hypothetical British position, the Rome–Berlin axis was transparently clear. So much so that the Italian press would transmit it in terms of a defense of Spanish territorial unity in all its extremes: "The integrity of Spain is valid not only for the Balearics and Riff, but also for Catalonia, Cartagena and for Malaga."[197] This reaction was also cited with special emphasis by different French and British leaders, even before the points of the agreement were made public.[198] On one hand, the correspondent of *Le Figaro*, Georges Rotvand,[199] emphasized the negative Italo-German posture against the French communist daily *L'Humanité*, which summed up the situation in these terms: "The German government and the Italian government declare by common agreement that they will not be willing to admit or recognize the existence of a Soviet republic in Spain, either in the entire Iberian Peninsula or in Catalonia by itself."[200]

The prestigious diplomatic columnist Geneviève Tabouis, then at the height of her influence as a voice for the left in the Parisian daily *L'Oeuvre*, insisted recovering the option of a Spanish republican withdrawal in Catalonia but with the alternative of a Catalan government as a successor to that of Madrid. This could be a republican redoubt or defensive barrier, but in Catalan hands.[201] In fact, this last option would provoke certain reflections in French conservative sectors, even speaking of a duel between Companys and Azaña to know who would govern from Barcelona the remains of Republican Spain or a sovereign Catalonia. The fact was that, in the increasingly polarized and rambunctous French press, some believed that left Catalan nationalism would not miss the opportunity: "Nobody can believe that Mr. Companys will not try to take advantage of the fall of Madrid to proclaim the independence of Catalonia vis a vis Spain, which will be the Spain of General Franco. And Mr. Azaña will be able to accept to appear as the head of this Catalan State, which would mean that there would only be one government in Spain, that of the general Franco."[202]

Doubts or determination, beyond those of the Axis allies, were shared by the Spanish rebels themselves in the words of their maximum leader: "'We are not going to allow the formation in Catalonia of a Soviet Republic', declared General Franco".[203] Did the smile expressed by the Generalissimo in *Vu* reflect a real fact a certitude that flew in in the face of some of the international support for the Catalan cause? In fact, in those days interesting reflections on the nature and future of Catalan nationalism were published in the French press. For example, in the Catholic press of the French Midi an unidentified J. L., surely an exiled conservative Catalan, dedicated two half covers and something more than another page to study in detail why Catalan independence could not happen. Primarily, independence was impossible because, as he believed, neither the bourgeoisie or the majority of the people were in favor of that possibility. This was because the Catalan wealth came from the Spanish market and, ultimately, because the anarcho-syndicalist CNT was radically against this possibility. Conclusion: the efforts of the Catalan nationalists, in spite of recognizing the Catalan cultural and linguistic personality, had not been sufficient to get majority support.[204]

Actually, the news of the Ciano–Neurath agreement was sufficiently important to extend to talks between foreign representatives in Barcelona. In an interview held at the beginning of November 1936 by the consuls general of Italy and the USSR, Carlo Bossi and Antonov-Ovseyenko, the second would ask the representative of Rome for the veracity of the pact between Italy and Germany to avoid the creation of an independent Catalonia. In fact, what Antonov-Ovseyenko would say, according to the testimony of his Italian counterpart, was if Rome and Berlin sought to liquidate Catalan autonomy: "He has asked insistently to know if the news appeared in the foreign press around the Italian–German secret agreement tending towards the suppression of autonomy in Catalonia was true, adding that if such news were not true it would be timely to try to deny it in the local press, which could calm the most excited spirits here."[205] The question, apparently, would disconcert Bossi who did not answer for lack of an official opinion that, immediately, he requested from Rome. Perhaps he was not used to such a direct dialogue in a context such as this, and, as a diplomat, was accustomed to measuring his words.

This beginning of joint action between Rome and Berlin would reappear in different conversations being held in late 1936. For example, one maintained on December 29, 1936 by the Italian ambassador in Salamanca, Filippo Anfuso, with his German colleague, General Wilhelm Faupel, the first representative of Nazi Germany to the newly recognized Franco. In this meeting, Mussolini's representative confirmed how he already had declared in the act of his appointment as the person in charge of affairs in the "National" area, that neither a communist Spain nor a Catalan communist republic would be tolerated.[206]

The German position was reiterated three days later in another context by Werner Hasselblatt, the Baltic-German leader and advisor to the official Nazi agency for ethnic Germans residing in other States. So, after an interview with the Catalan nationalist activist Josep Maria Batista Roca, of extreme pro-independence views and later delegate of the Generalitat in London, Hasselblatt would try a personal mediation before the Franco government through Faupel, with negative results. German diplomacy made it clear that it was not favorable "in the current state of the situation, to activate the Catalan question in any direction".[207] As adds the historian Xosé M. Núñez Seixas, a specialist on German policy to national minorities: "Hasselblatt presented the promises of Batista i Roca about a possible development of a Catalan fascism, and remembered that the intransigence of the white Russian general Anton Denikin towards the national claims of non-Russian peoples had been the motive of his defeat facing the Bolsheviks. That is why he suggested – recalling the 'faithful' and anti-Marxist trajectory of the 'Catalanists' in their participation in the Congress of European Nationalities – that General Franco promise to respect the 'ethnic specificity and the corresponding individual rights' of the Catalans, in order to win the support of broad Catalanist anti-marxist sectors."[208] The proposal could sound promising, but had no real possibility of coming to fruition.

If the position of Hitler and Mussolini seemed clear and without apparent fissure (although there were existing cracks regarding Austria or the Balkans), everything that resembled the Berlin agreement would also be picked up with enthusiasm by the Franco side. In this way, from the Ciano-Neurath summit of the end of October onwards, press notices affirming the dominant Axis consensus would be constant.[209] The press of the rebel zone recon-firmed its sympathy by explaining the *Gentlemen's Agreement* of January 2, 1937 between Italy and Great Britain as the alleged extension of the opposition to the Catalan secession, although London would have liked to leave the Spanish affairs out of the accord.[210] Specifically, the principle consensus reached between Minister Galeazzo Ciano and the British ambassador in Rome, Sir Eric Drummond (a diplomatic with long experience in the League of Nations, who became Lorth Perth on the death of his brother in 1937), established a mutual interest in the freedom of navigation in the Mediterranean as well as the commitment to avoid any territorial modification in the countries of the so-called *Mare Nostrum*. London tried to de-escalate the internationalization of the Spanish conflict and to approach Rome with such an initia-tive, so as to better distance it from Berlin. At the same time Drummond was trying to assure the safety of the communications channel between London and the dominions of Australia and New Zealand, as well as the connections with India, the Asian colonies and the British imperial metropolis.[211] In a similar fashion to the *Gentlemen's Agreement* that began the year 1937, both the Italian and the American press, but also the Spanish rebel leaders, referred explicitly in different degrees to Catalonia.[212] The Italian reader could perceive a veiled Catalan reference in the middle of a consid-eration on a continental and even world scale that incorporated the African colonial empires: "The two governments exclude at the same time any purpose to modify or to see modified the status quo in relation to national sovereignty in the continents that surround the Mediterranean [...]. This is important to point out, in reference to assumptions and not at all implausible plans of partition or secession of Spain as a response to alleged autonomist whims, which on the contrary would be the vehicle of the Sovietization of this or that part of the Iberian Peninsula."[213] A Roman reader could follow a direct mention also in the daily *La Tribuna* when it claimed that the Soviets were trying to "exploit the separatist phenomenon in Catalonia".[214] These were interpretations completely correct by Fascist standards, that Mussolini himself would confirm in an interview granted to the journalist of the German newspaper *Völkischer Beobachter*, Roland Strunk, in which he declared: "We have no territorial claim of any kind in relation to the situation created in Spain by the intervention of the Soviet Union." And the Italian leader emphasized his point: "Asked if the proclamation of a Soviet republic in Spain or in a part of Spain could have the importance of a threat to the status quo, the Duce replied: Obviously!".[215] This strong comment of the Italian dictator forced the Foreign Office in the figure of the minister, Anthony Eden, to publicly remind everyone that the agreement of January 1937 did not contemplate the right of any foreign power with respect to any territory – specifically Catalonia.[216] That was not the focus of concurrence for the British, but it was for the Franco side. But not just for Franco. Even the Spanish Republican government shared in the immediate harmony, as was certified by a visit by ambassador Pablo de Azcárate to Eden a day after the agreement. According to the memoirs of the British foreign minister, Azcárate, in the name of his government, "welcomed" the pact "for the references made to the Spanish territorial integrity".[217]

In addition to the more or less explicit references of the Italian press, the Franco newspapers, for example the *Lucha* of Teruel, proposed a totally frontal approach in line with Mussolini: "This point is that which refers to the agreement of these two powers not to consent that in Catalonia an independent Republic is established of a Bolshevik character."[218] This was even more explicit in *Labor* of Soria: "Official circles interpret the Anglo-Italian agreement to respect Spanish territorial integrity, as a true joint opposition to the establishment of Catalonia as an independent nation. [...] Certainly Russia will do the impossible to help Catalonia, but they will stumble with Italy and England, which under the Pact of Rome will not tolerate an independent Catalonia and even less one protected by Russia."[219] In similar terms, Arnaldo Cortesi, the Italian correspondent in Rome of *The New York Times*, agreed. In his chronicle, the pact had as its central point the Italo-British opposition to any suggestion of a Soviet Catalonia, since although it was true that it could be seen as a "purely Spanish internal matter", it also could become a fact of international character if "Soviet Russia tried to establish itself on the shores of the Mediterranean [...]".[220] The fear of the Soviet presence in the Mediterranean, the control of the Dardanelles and of the Bosphorus and beyond, would last for decades. This was a dread that would cover the true origin of the reference to the Spanish territorial integrity: it incorporated from a British demand, not referring to Catalonia, but to the Italian presence in Mallorca and the whole of the Balearic Islands.[221] This was a real element, but it should not hide that the Italo-British agreement was not just focused on the Spanish war.[222]

Undoubtedly, the Franco press, as well as Nazi and Fascist propaganda together with the foreign press in general, was paranoid on the subject of Soviet power. With great frequency, plans were attributed to Moscow that were very far from Russian reality. However, it was evident that the ghost of Soviet Catalonia was extremely useful to scare conservatives in general throughout the continent.[223]

The Italian–German Recognition of Franco and the End of Certain Contacts

If the future sovereignty of Catalonia was seen as of necessity linked to France or the USSR, the explorations and connections made by Catalan nationalists with Italy cannot be ignored. The first of these failed contacts would be a product of the evacuation to Italy of the pro-independence leader and former councillor of the Generalitat, Josep Dencàs, already known in Italian diplomatic files because of previous conversations between 1933 and 1934 in which he – in private – declared himself as a fascist. In June 1936, Dencàs had just established a party called Estat Català (Catalan State, a split-off a portion of the nationalist youth wing, the JEREC) from the

Esquerra and had joined together with other smaller, like-minded organizations. In the chaos of July 1936, his life was explicitly threatened, and he fled on an Italian ship. Thus, although his biographer Jordi Rabassa denies any political intentions to his desperate trip to Italy, the documents seem to indicate the opposite.[224] It was August 2, 1936 when the Italian Royal Navy informed Rome of the evacuation of Dencàs together with the geographer Francesc Glanadell Torras.

Certainly, Dencàs was fleeing from real anarchist warnings generated by his actions at the head of the JEREC and as Councillor of the Interior of the Generalitat between 1933 and 1934. This was a period in which police clashes with the anarchists would be constant, and nationalist youth actively backed law-enforcement agencies with strike-breaking and assaults on activists. During April–May 1936, Dencàs, blamed for the failure of the 6 October revolt in 1934, confronted Companys: a newly reunited radical nationalist Estat Català under Dencàs split off from ERC. Thus, despite having fought the military uprising in Barcelona on July 19 with the few forces of Estat Català, the new revolutionary situation, after the fighting in Barcelona was more or less over by Monday, July 20, 1936, was clearly unfavorable to the radical nationalists, left out by a consensus between the ERC and the anarcho-syndicalists with which the revolutionary socialist POUM (Unified Marxist Party) and the pro-Soviet PSUC (or Unified Socialist Party, forged by a fusion of smaller groups on July 23) concurred. Dencàs and his Estat Català would leave him politically suspended, without allies on the scene. The ERC was not helpful, and considered him an enemy.

Menaced with death by the anarchists action squads, Dencàs decided to leave, with the intention of delivering a message to Mussolini. This objective he himself, hidden at Catalan police headquarters, would explain to the Italian Consul Carlo Bossi in July 1936 in terms that were close to what he had already expressed to the Italians in 1934. According to his intentions stated to Bossi, Dencàs went to Italy "with the aim of negotiating with the Italian government to obtain its intervention in the questions of the state of Catalonia, with Republican intention, but with a Fascist regime".[225] These plans sought Italian aid for the attainment of a fascist Catalonia. Dencas' plan had to be assessed through two premises that he made clear to Bossi: he would not accept leaving the Catalan people in the hands of leftist extremists, while at the same time it had to be understood that he spoke on behalf of Catalonia and not of Spain. Days after this contact, which served to get Dencàs on ship and out of Barcelona, Bossi was interested to know from his superiors if the rumours published by the Catalan press which alleged the arrest of Dencàs upon his arrival in Genoa aboard the Italian hospital vessel *Tevere* were true.[226] Bossi remembered the objectives pursued by Dencàs, and the possible interest that they could offer Italy's strategic ends.[227]

Nevertheless, no documentation – perhaps once existing but now missing from the files – allows knowing if there indeed was a meeting, perhaps not directly with the Duce, but with some Italian authority to whom Dencàs could explain his political plans for the future Catalonia.[228] In fact, his arrival in Genoa under the protection of a false Uruguayan passport with the name of "José Bustamante Durán" would awake some attention from the Fascist authorities. While the Prefect of Genoa, Belle, asked Rome what had to be done: to simply watch over him, to protect him from the wrath of the Spanish Falangists in the city, or to jail him, Dencàs seemed to be torn between a temporary stay in Italy or a move to France. The decision he finally took was to move to France, a resolution taken with the approval of the head of the Italian police, Arturo Bocchini.[229] Therefore, any possibility of direct relationship between Catalan separatism and Fascist Italy was frustrated, only a few weeks after the outbreak of the Civil War in Spain. Rome was betting on the likely winners, and therefore only conceived of any serious collaboration with the Spanish military. There was no room for any kind of "fascist catalan nationalism", that never existed in formal, organized terms.[230] Practical politics, the preference of highly statist Italian Fascism for a pro-State Spanish nationalism, dynastic circles who urged a monarchical restoration in Spain, even a determined vision of geopolitics, overruled any other choices. Although in 1933 the Italian ambassador in Madrid, Raffaele Guariglia, had said that, unlike Madrid, only in Catalonia could Fascism be understood, his appreciation had no chance to materialize in anything that was concrete.

In spite of the fact that this was the case, was this the only invocation that pretended to place Catalonia outside of the conflict in collaboration with Italy? The answer is simply no. In the context of what would be known as the "Rebertés case", in the Autumn–Winter of 1936, there was a plot against the President of the Generalitat, Lluís Companys: certain sectors of dissident Catalan nationalism would seek a pact with Franco through Italian diplomacy that would assure the survival of autonomy and facilitate the end of the conflict.[231] This failed initiative was silenced, never really clarified. To the cover-up, some press – outside Catalonia – would add the secessionist intention of a coup – the same business? Something else? – that would end with the concealed death in late November of Generalitat police chief Andreu Rebertés.[232]

A few days after the closing of the Italian consular legation in Barcelona, following the path of the rest of the Italian and German representations in the republican zone after the official recognition of Franco, consul Bossi informed of what, subsequently, would seem the preparations for the conspiracy against Companys. As reported in a telegram of November 16 sent to Rome via France, the Catalan nationalist lawyer Francesc Maspons i Anglasell, a well considered jurist, on behalf of several Catalan political personalities, would have requested Italian intermediation to contact Franco.[233] This attempt to establish a communication route and an eventual negotiation contained the seeds of a part of the plot against Companys. In this way, always according to the Italian documentation, Maspons would offer Franco Catalan nationalist collaboration to break the overall Catalan resistance, in exchange for a firm assurance that Catalan autonomy would be maintained and the move to a system that would approximate the traditional "Basque Rights" or *fueros*, recognized by Franco for Alava and Navarre, provinces which had sided with the July uprising. This was an offer that, according to Maspons, would benefit both parties: for Franco, military victory was facilitated, while Catalonia was spared the devastation of the conflict while being freed from the anarchist "dictatorship".[234] The possibility of an agreement was apparently non-existent, but that more or less in those terms would be disseminated by the small news reports worldwide, as exemplified in a note that appeared in the faraway Estonian press.[235]

On the other hand, the Catalan nationalist offer would mean that all the forces in the hands of the Generalitat, of the Catalan-minded parties and organizations at that time involved in fighting against the rebels, would devote their efforts to defeat and crush the anarcho-syndicalist CNT-FAI. But what were the points involved in this start of negotiations? According to the Italian document, the initiative involved those that would later appear implicated in the Rebertés case, cited messily: "The afore-mentioned [Maspons] has stated that he is in charge of fulfilling this step on the part of the following parties: Estat Català; the Separatist *La Falç*; the left party organization of the Catalan republican party [ACR?]; the Unió Democràtica Catalana [UDC]; the Catholic Democratic Party [the same as the UDC?] and of a part of an important faction of the Republican Catalan party [ERC] currently in the Government of the Generalitat that, to my interlocutor, would constitute a majority of great importance in the communist party led by Companys [does this refer to the radicalization of the Esquerra?], in which is now becoming harshly criticitized against its excessive proximity to the anarchist organizations that virtually control [everything]."[236]

Therefore, it seems that a broad representation of Catalan nationalism was involved in something more than a simple criticism towards the behavior of the president of the Generalitat. There was a desire to make a pact with Franco, since it was considered that the anarchist predominance was worse than a deal with Burgos. But, in all this plotting who would exercise the leadership of the movement? According to the Italian telegram, Maspons anounced to his interlocutor, as a measure of pressure, that the "President of the Catalan Parliament, [Joan] Casanovas, is currently in Paris with the objective that in the case of nationalist victory [of Franco] in the rest of the country, France would recognize an independent Catalan State that eventually would be proclaimed".[237] The pressure around the French connection seemed credible. Everything seemed well thought out, even it had little chance of success before a Military Junta that made "Spanishism" ("*españolismo*") or "Spanish collective identity" one of its essential arguments: at least, as well as other efforts made at those same time before Nazi instances. In fact, the response of

Franco to the Catalan nationalist proposals did not do more than confirm the utopian nature of these approaches. Once again, we turn to Franco's smile expressed in *Vu* a few days before this initiative was attempted. The leader of the rebels did not accept any kind of autonomy; the budgetary systems of Navarre and Alava, loyal to the uprsing, could be a relative exception. In any case, someone in Franco's name could inform Maspons that, from the first moments of the war, thousands of Catalans had gone over to the rebel side without claiming at any moment neither autonomy nor Catalan national rights, but rather the opposite. Franco was right, the dilemma between nation and social position had pushed a part of the Catalan bourgeoisie toward saving their money, and, needless to say, saving their lives as well. The more than 8,000 people killed by revolutionary violence during the summer and autumn of 1936 were there, as a grim reminder, along with at least another 8,000, who were evacuated by the Italian rescue operation.

In short, there was an absolutely negative response, a one hundred percent no, in which it was stated that the survival of a political actor of any Catalan party was not accepted. From this point of view, Franco's "National" movement only aimed at Spanish unity and the creation of a strong State. In short: "to make disappear the feelings of hatred and resentment among Spaniards [...]".[238] Even so, whether it was viable or not, all contact was cut short with the departure of the Consul Bossi from Barcelona and the disappearance of the Italian consulate in the Catalan capital immediately after the recognition of the Government of Burgos by Rome.[239] Even this withdrawal was seen by certain observers as a diplomatic manoeuvre that was nothing more than a gesture towards Catalonia: "It is above all against Catalan autonomy that the Franco recogitition is directed."[240]

Nonetheless, things need not have happened in this fashion. Apart from the diplomatic structures and institutions themselves, the Italian authorities had an information service in Barcelona with police functions to classify all Italian anarchists, communists or opponents in general established in Catalonia during the Civil War or before its outbreak. The Italian foreign ministry could have decided that consular services could be maintained, even unofficially, and only diplomatic relations broken. But this was impractical, unrealistic. The subject was raised and discussed. Apparently there was sufficient conviction in the future of an independent Catalonia that the Italians and Germans for a time asked themselves if it were better to leave an open consulate in Barcelona so as to obtain first-hand information.

The end of the contacts did not erase their trace in the memory of the Italian dictator Mussolini, who, a few months after closing the consular delegation in Barcelona, still reminded Franco of a Catalan option. As General Mario Roatta, commander of the Italian *Corpo Truppe Volontarie* in Spain, explained in a telegram sent to Mussolini on January 12, 1937, after having a long interview with Franco in which he would suggest resuming contacts, the leader of the Spanish rebels would affirm the impossibility of recovering that option: "After a long conference with Franco to whom I have exposed the various points indicated on day 4 by Duce. Stop. Franco is grateful, he fully agrees and he insists on following the advice given." However, in face of the Italian proposal, the Generalissimo denied any option to establish any treatment with those circles: "He does not believe it is possible to reach a loyal agreement with Basques and Catalans so that the local elements in favor to negotiations do not count at all [...]."[241]

1937: Contacts for a Separate Peace?

If the second half of 1936 would be the peak time of rumours, a boom of comments, reports and news around a probable Catalan secession, during 1937 these stories and reports did not disappear; bits of news kept coming up in the international press and in diplomats' gossip. In fact, this probability of a Catalan split-off would still be the protagonist of the speculations around a European war on its Mediterranean side. These were partly using arguments similar to those of 1936 but, to a large extent, the talk focussed on alleged contacts of Catalan representatives with the rebels.[242] The fact was, according to some editorials of the French press, that the "Catalan question" was one of the most important issues to be resolved in the Spanish conflict.[243] During and past the fighting of the so-called "Days of May" in Barcelona, the Italian press insisted that while Franco was busy reuniting Spain, in the "red zone" the opposite was happening: "Catalonia does not obey the government of Valencia".[244] There was a consensus that what would happen in Catalonia could determine the fate of the Republic and of the Spanish war in general, and therefore lower a burning, active fire lit in Europe.

A good example of the way interest was maintained was the insistence on Soviet influence in Catalonia. In a symptomatic text that appeared in early January 1937 in the Parisian Catholic daily *La Croix*, it was affirmed that Great Britain would not accept an independent Catalonia under any circumstance. The article also remarked a clear difference between the Catalan and the Basque cases and their possible transaction with the rebels.[245] According to what the author, with the byline J. C., wrote, if in the Basque Country the Franco rebels could respect autonomy based on the right-wing and Catholic predominance of the Basque Nationalist Party (PNV), in Catalonia this was impossible since the country was in the hands of anarchists and communists.[246] The same paper, around the same dates, notes that the highlighted opposition of the Rome–Berlin axis to the creation of an independent Catalonia under Soviet influence persisted in French newspapers, but also in the British press.[247] This circumstance was also noted in *L'Action française* by Jacques Delebecque (a regular contributor) and seemed to satisfy French nationalist right-wing sectors, who saw how the status quo of the Mediterranean appeared guaranteed: nor a Soviet Catalonia nor Italian military bases in the Balearic Islands.[248]

By this point, the "Catalan question" had become quite complex, especially if attention is paid to the statements made by the leader of the PSUC, the Catalan stalinist Joan Comorera, collected by *L'Humanité* in mid-1937. When talking about the separatist danger in Catalonia, Comorera said: "Today there is not, in reality, a separatist danger in Catalonia because the Catalan popular masses feel the Spanish cause more than ever, today they are more willing than ever to help the Spanish people, since they know well that in a fascist Spain there would be no place for an independent Catalonia." And he added, about what he defined as the real Catalan separatist danger: "We affirm this although there are conversations, some projects and some manoeuvres provoked naturally by the Spanish fascists, according to some French capitalist groups and people like Cambó and [Joan] Ventosa [i Calvell] who think that exploiting the noble feelings of the Catalan people, they could create a separatist movement in Catalonia that, in the end, could live under a French protectorate in the same way that Vizcaya could become a British protectorate [...]."[249] These were certainly surprising statements. Lliga leader Francesc Cambó and his close associate Joan Ventosa? The same who collaborated faithfully in favour of the rebel victory? The same ones who allegedly distrusted the Italians? Well, perhaps it was true, and one has to assume the theory widely expressed by all commentators: all the Catalan nationalists were independentists at the bottom of their convictions. This more than extravagant argument would not have continuity. Rather, the accusation give way to the constant press noise that placed the Generalitat about to close an agreement with the Franco side to thus end the war. Apart from a few references to a possible agreement between Franco and the Republic that would respect the autonomy of Catalonia and the Basque Country, rumours would almost never involve the Spanish Republican government, leaving the Catalan government as the sole protagonist of clandestine para-diplomacy.[250]

Following this argument, in mid-February 1937 the correspondent of *Le Figaro* in Republican Spain, Georges Rotvand, quoting British press, suggested that the Generalitat was negotiating with Franco to prevent the war from reaching Catalonia.[251] This information was amplified by the same correspondent a few days later: Rotvand asserted that the only possible way out for Catalan autonomy was to pact its survival with Franco: "Its minimum program would be, in summary, the following: obtain a statute of the widest possible autonomy for Catalonia, which would have the right to elect its Parliament and government. That it would guarantee a favorable situation in the economic and commercial spheres, and, in particular, in all that refers to the use of gold and foreign currencies. To obtain the maintenance of the autonomy in the fields of education and justice."[252] In fact, almost a kind of virtual independence, Irish-style, a British imperial dominion or a free association with Spain that, as Rotvand himself recognized, was difficult to fit in with the Franco positions.

There would be such a proliferation of comments on the matter that, from the beginning of 1937 until the end of the year, the Generalitat was forced to deny them privately and publicly, week in and week out. While at the beginning of February it was the editor-in-chief of the London *Daily Telegraph* who asked in a direct telegram to the President of the Generalitat, Companys, about the alleged negotiations,[253] in March it was the delegate of the Generalitat in London who claimed loyalty to the Republic – on the road, he said, to building an "Iberian Commonwealth".[254] Months later it was the Delegation of the Generalitat in Paris that denied any margin to dealings of this type: "As every time the League of Nations meets, the rebels spread the rumour of a separate peace of Catalonia with Franco. [...] Catalonia, remains loyal to the Republic and peace, and will never initiate conversations with its enemies. Catalonia, that retains its entire territory free of the Franco allies of Italy and Germany, continues its historical tradition as an element of peace and balance in the Mediterranean."[255] This denial was confirmed a few days later personally by President of the Generalitat, Companys.[256] His verbal forcefulness did not convince the French press, and other international newspapers, which continued to persist when *La Croix* stated: "Despite the denials of Barcelona, the rumour of conversations between the delegates of General Franco and emissaries of important Catalan personalities continue to circulate."[257] Or, months later, when the French correspondents insisted to the spokesmen of the Generalitat that they deny or confirm the stories of a separate peace published by the Italian and German press.[258] President Companys would repeat his denial again, with ever more insistence, during the month of November when traveling to Brussels to see his son, suffering from a mental condition.[259] He again repudiated any contacts with the enemy when he stopped in Paris, to meet with the Spanish Republican ambassador, his lawyer and personal friend, Ángel Ossorio y Gallardo.[260] Both in Paris and in the Belgian capital, Companys was obliged insist in his denial that the supposed purpose of his trip might respond to something else than the visit to his hospitalized son.[261]

Companys also had to face the rumours that spoke of a willingness, not only Catalan but Spanish Republican, to reach an agreement with the rebels to end the war or, at least, with the objective of achieving a truce. Proof of this press pressure was the insistence with which the Generalitat would request their delegates in Europe to persist in such a denial.[262] In fact, the president himself firmly denied this possibility in an interview with the correspondent of conservative Parisian daily *Le Petit Parisien*, Henri Delmas, in which the special envoy pointed out to him the will of French public opinion: "I think I can say, Mr. President, that the vast majority of the French would like to see this tragedy finish as quickly as possible. Cannot a formula be found?" This was a question to which Companys answered: "We do not carry out an exasperated militarism. I make war, but I hate war. I do it because I have to fulfill my duty to the country. I do it to prepare for a future and lasting peace. [...] We cannot deal with the rebels."[263]

Catalanist Contacts with French (and British) Political and Diplomatic Sectors. Now Yes?

Long announced by the European and American press, in 1937–38 there would begin to be produced different contacts with with representatives of different powers by Catalan nationalist spokesmen endowed with governmental credentials from the Generalitat, of some or other kind. And this is while the Government of Catalonia was establishing official delegates in Paris and London, respectively Nicolau Maria Rubió Tudurí and Josep Maria Batista Roca. Rubió would organize more or less informal meetings with different French representatives that would be recurrent. This involved some interviews, more or less casual meetings, trips or stays in the neighboring country of Catalan politicians, along with the sending of documentation of the Propaganda Commission of the Generalitat that would try to keep the French attention fixed on the the tradition of Catalan francophilia. The political and cultural proximity of leftist Catalan nationalism and Christian Democracy towards France was more than evident if one follows the existing documentation. For an example, one can see the contacts of the delegate of the Generalitat in Euskadi, Manuel Carrasco Formiguera, a Catalan nationalist

Catholic executed by Franco in 1938, who met with the French Foreign Minister, Yvon Delbos, and the British ambassador to Spain, Henry Chilton, in February 1937.[264] These were conversations that, on the Catalan side, would request mediation of London and Paris to put an end to the war, favoring a future Spain with a federal structure, in which Catalonia and Euskadi would enjoy an almost de facto independence. This proposal was reiterated by the councillor of the Generalitat Ventura Gassol to Delbos himself and to the head of the government, Léon Blum. The idea offered a hypothetical context in which the FAI was crushed by the forces of the Generalitat at the same time that a settlement with General Franco was achieved.[265]

All in all, however, the pieces did not fit together. In this approach, on April 27, 1937, president of the Generalitat Companys, met with the French consul in the Catalan capital, Jacques Pingaud.[266] This encounter produced on the French diplomat a certain messianic impression of Companys, a description repeated by other foreign observers: "Very emotional, sometimes inclined to believe himself a prophet, [who] entertains by lecturing or remembering his revolutionary memories."[267] According to what was said to Pingaud, Companys would develop a discourse very similar to the one that had already been transmitted to the French consul by Josep Tarradellas, the first councillor (until May 5); he had been told much the same by a leader of the FAI a few days before. The message was that things were going well in the military operations on the Madrid front, but that, at the same time, it seemed almost impossible to conciliate and pacify the tension between the different labour sectors and parties in Catalan politics (scarcely surprising insofar as there would be a prolonged shootout between the two sides in Barcelona during the third to seventh of May, with perhaps five hundred killed). But there was no proposal nor request for negotiation.

The tone of Pingaud's reception would be followed a few days later at a new meeting of Companys with a French representative. On this occasion, it was Admiral Richard visiting the port of Barcelona in charge of the deployment of the French Marine Nationale along the coasts of eastern Spain (i.e., control areas of the Spanish coast carried out by the London Non-intervention

Committee). In a brief note sent from Paris to the French embassy in Spain, the military officer transmitted the animosity of Companys towards the FAI, accusing the anarchists of secret contacts with underground Falangist elements: "During a long conversation, the president has expressed his firm intention not to negotiate with the FAI, whom he accuses of having a secret agreement with the Falangists and of controlling [public] order in Catalonia."[268] Certainly this would be an accusation – the alleged FAI–Falangist connection – that would be maintained and extended during the war between different elements of left and right Catalan nationalism, both inside Catalonia and in French exile. But aside from the accusation, again, there was no real request of French intermediation.

The lack of effective requests would not stop the rumour mills. This was manifested again by the French consul, Jacques Pingaud, who, writing along the diplomatic hierarchy, exposed to the ambassador and thence to the ministry in Paris, alleged negotiations between elements of the ERC and Franco representatives. This, wrote Pingaud, was an Esquerra totally "overwhelmed by extremist elements" and that began to see more advantages in the predominance of the conservative and right-wing sectors than in the dictatorship of the proletariat of the revolutionaries. According to Pingaud, Esquerra should look for a space in the future Franco Catalonia. And the ERC should take such a step because it seemed that the events could be precipitated due to the possible collaboration between the FAI and the Falangists, the latter operating underground.[269]

Thus, if direct requests did not exist – yet – it also must be said that the written communications of the left-wing Catalan nationalism through some international organizations and certain press spokespersons would not follow a separatist trend. Rather they identified themselves as autonomists or federalists, contradicting the opportunity that geopolitics of the late 1930s gave them according to all the foreign ministries and military general staffs. As an example, we can see the historial allusion of Jaume Miravitlles, in the editorial to one of the first issues of *Le Journal de Barcelone*, official organ of the Generalitat which appeared in Paris throughout 1937. Remembering other historical scenarios of the past and wrting in a French–Spanish context, the Propaganda Commissioner evoked the figure of: "Napoleon, who came to Spain as heir to the great ideas of the French Revolution, but who implanted them by force and through a constitution written in Bayonne under the sign of royal desertion and of feudalism." To define his point, Miravitlles added: "Napoleon, a great military man and a great politician, would suggest in Catalonia, the way it has always done in the Peninsula when deciding foreign interests, the idea of separation [but] nationalist Catalonia did not accept an independence that would have been a treacherous choice."[270] This same historical analogy already had been made a few months earlier in an inflamed pro-Catalan nationalist article – but not pro-separatist – by the Occitan journalist Pierre-Louis Berthaud. Convinced that Catalonia did not have sufficient strength to be independent, he affirmed in relation to Napoleon: "One after the other, the Convention, then Bonaparte, tried to raise a Catalan Republic. But is independence a gift that is accepted from abroad? No, like assimilation, it is obtained by force . . . [sic]."[271] Perhaps this was the key to everything said so far. Would the outside pressure, the foreign conviction, be powerful enough to provoke movements in Catalonia?

Months later, a curious dichotomy of identites became apparent in the letters sent by the Unió Catalana pro Societat de les Nacions (Pro-League of Nations Catalan Union), both to its European counterparts and to the League of Nations itself: the promotion of simultaneous Spanish and Catalan citizenship. Leading in this direction, in a letter of September 2, 1937 signed by the delegates in Paris and London of the Generalitat, Nicolau Marià Rubió Tudurí and Josep Maria Batista Roca, with the significant addition to the philologist Pompeu Fabra, modern systematizer of the Catalan language, stated: "As citizens of the Spanish Republic, we want nothing more than to impose respect, in Western Europe, to the principle that states that the permanence and the changes of governments must be decided by the votes of the citizenry and not by the force of arms." To this complicated consideration in Europe at those unquiet times, they added: "As Catalans, we refuse to allow ourselves to be included in a Spanish militarist imperialism, preached with a spirit and a language that are not those of

Catalonia. [...] We want to live peacefully and democratically, in the fraternity of the Iberian peoples and those of the S.D.N. [League of Nations]."[272]

1938: Towards Drowning in Defeat, with a French Lifeguard?

The last full year of the war in Catalonia was 1938. In Catalonia, the conflict was over on February 11, 1939, and then, at the very end of March, "National" forces took Madrid, Alicante and Valencia, thus ending the struggle officially on the First of April 1939). Franco had won the Civil War.

During 1938, the Generalitat would intensify its attempts to establish contact with French authorities, at least according to the international press. The Soviet role was marginalized, and Paris again took center stage. Based on the supposedly special proximity of the Catalan president to the figures of the French Republican government, newsprint space would be given to a series of speculations that would not disappear until the end of the war. Nevertheless, the press always was kept in mind that the position of the London–Paris block regarding Catalonia would not change. First, because the British had shifted the policy: on February 20, 1938, the secretary of the Foreign Office, Anthony Eden, who opposed unbridled concessions to Hitler, as well as his undersecretary, Robert Vansittart, resigned, and were replaced by Lord Halifax and Alexander Cadogan, who were much more oriented towards what was then called "appeasement". Halifax and Cadogan, together with the conservative prime minister, Neville Chamberlain, would defend their apparent ability to reach agreements with Hitler and Mussolini to avoid a general conflagration of Europe. Moreover, in London everything seemed to be directed towards the sacrifice of Republican Spain, after concessions in Austria (in mid-March 1938) and Czechoslovakia (the Munich Pact, at the very end of September). Meanwhile, in Paris, the instability of the successive governments of Camille Chautemps (resigned successively on January 15 and March 10) would provoke a new executive chaired by the socialist Léon Blum. The Blum cabinet did not last a month, from mid-March to early April. In the midst of this ominous continental correlation of forces, some Catalan appeals seemed completely desperate.

The eventuality of the rapprochement of Barcelona, now capital of the Spanish Republic, and Paris had already been insistently heard about during the first months of the war. Now, when the end of the war began to approach Catalonia, the subject would not stop reappearing. Or, at least, when its future seemed already decided. In a world where hot spots multiplied – Austria, Spain, Czechoslovakia, not to mention Manchuria – could Catalonia still play some role? Well, every possibility would be explored or valued, from the Franco conviction that the British wished to promote a federal Spain with Catalans and Basques under the protection of Paris and London, to any other option.[273] But nothing was sure, and everything could change in a matter of days. This was the general perception in the spring and early summer of 1938.

In this sense, the Catalan authorities were willing to try anything. There were some contacts for show, like the meeting in Barcelona of President Companys with Jean Longuet, a notable French socialist (and grandson of Karl Marx), but no longer a deputy, among other distinguished visitors, like the U.S. Socialist leader Norman Thomas. The meeting with Longuet was intended to convey information regarding the military situation and Catalan policy, while demanding the help of France.[274] This description was given by Longuet a few days later to the French Foreign Minister, Joseph Paul-Boncour. Longuet transmitted the impression that, if an offensive against Catalonia was launched, the Generalitat would try to "dissociate itself from the governmental cause, proclaiming, in one form or another, its annexation to France and renewing, then, the desperate appeal, currently made by the government of Spain, for French assistance".[275] In any case, Longuet was dead on September 11, killed in a car accident.

But then new possibilities of French intervention were opened, coming from another direction. The French military attaché at the embassy in Barcelona, Henri Morel, backed by the new French government led again by Blum, encouraged similiar initiatives in the Catalan capital. Apparently, on March 15, 1938 – three days after the annexation of Austria by Hitler, the *Anschluss* – Blum convened an extraordinary meeting of the Permanent Committee of National Defense formed by himself, by the Minister of Defense, the radical-socialist Édouard Daladier, and the foreign minister Joseph Paul-Boncour, in addition to the major commanders of the French army. These were the days in which France was assuring Czechoslovakian diplomats – and British ones – that if Hitler took a step in the direction of Prague, Paris would respond by mobilizing its army and attack Germany. These were moments in which the Czechoslovak representatives, pressured by all the international actors in favor of a successful solution to the Czech–German Sudeten dispute, spoke of a French intervention in Spain to cut the Nazi initiative in central Europe, as well as a British one to avoid Italian dominance in the Mediterranean.[276]

In this context, the project proposed at the meeting, regardless of what had to be done with the expansionist voracity of Hitler, was none other than to invade Catalonia – or the Balearic Islands – if Franco responded negatively to a French ultimatum that ordered him to abandon Italian–German foreign aid. This proposed plan obtained the opposition of the army as a whole, against the criterion of of the navy – in particular Admiral François Darlan – who remained firm in his geostrategic analysis of 1936. The reason? According to General Maurice Gamelin, Chief of the General Staff of National Defense, the general military mobilization of France and its resources was indispensable, as was the essential participation of London, which was held to be quite improbable. In addition, it was assured that French military aviation could not endure even fifteen days in the face of the attacks of the German Luftwaffe, given that, in addition to whatever happened on the Rhine, the air arm would have to defend the Pyrenean border, as well as possibly protect the unlikely transfer of Franco-African troops.[277] In the face of these arguments, the favorable position of Blum and Paul-Boncour, and the navy, against the pessimism of Daladier and the armed forces – both land and air – would not be sufficient.[278]

But, in spite of the defeat of the defenders of the intervention in the Permanent Committee, no decisive resolution was taken, since five days later Morel was called to Paris to talk about the issue, which did not have sufficient support from the army. Morel de

Foucaucourt was an aristocrat and career officer, in the line of *L'Action française*, until the Spanish war made him break with Maurras, along with many friends and colleagues. When Blum asked him point-blank for his opinion, Morel de Foucaucourt characteristically answered that invasion was what a king of France would do. Nevertheless, the project was discarded. This was the result of the direct pressure to which the French diplomatic representatives and military attachés in Rome and other capitals of Europe were subjected to by the Germans and Italians. According to what was affirmed in the *Città eterna* and the capital of the Reich, any entry of France into Catalonia unfailingly would unleash a general European war.[279] This, in turn, was explained by the European press, placing once again the immediately upcoming Franco victory as the origin of a "situation that would be thus created on the other side of the Pyrenees and in the western Mediterranean" which should "naturally retain the most serious attention from the cabinets of Paris and London".[280]

In any case, if the press was to be believed, the content of the meeting of the Permanent Committee of National Defense was leaked immediately. By whom? Those in favour or those against intervention? It was very clear that France was at a dead end, when, simultaneously, the country had to decide what to do with Catalonia, Spain in general, and Czechoslovakia as well.[281] This was so obvious, that in a farewell visit to Léon Blum and Joseph Paul-Boncour given by the outgoing ambassador of the Spanish Republic in Paris, Ángel Ossorio y Gallardo, he would ask directly about the possible French assistance to an independent Catalonia.[282] This was a question made by some deputies of the National Assembly, such as the radical-socialist Gaston Riou, secretary of the Foreign Affairs Committee of the Chamber, who made clear his refusal to be involved in the Spanish conflict. In a radio broadcast, Riou would show himself contrary to the incorporation of Catalonia into the French Third Republic under the slogan "Spain for the Spanish".[283]

The pressure, at least that of the media, was such that, days later, some dailies still were insisting that the issue remained pending a decision. This circumstance was explained, perhaps without truth, by the Italian press: "In many circles there is insistence on sustaining that France cannot admit in any case that Catalonia is to be occupied by the troops of general Franco [...]", a situation in the face of which the French government would do nothing but "insist on a mistaken position and that delaying the decision seems extremely suspicious".[284] All this flap, while the Italian press, notably the *Corriere della Sera*, also published another article which picked up the unlikely story of an alleged offer of Catalonia to France, made by Spanish Republican prime minister Juan Negrín.[285] Or the news that, albeit discreetly, would occupy the front page of some newspapers, which reported the removal of Marià Rubió Tudurí as the head of the ERC organ, *La humanitat*, due to his insistent campaign proposing the annexation of Catalonia to France.[286] Despite the large amount of news articles hither and yon reporting intrigues, the delegations of the Generalitat in Europe insisted on denying any separate Catalan peace.[287]

At that point, after March 1938, everything was made public, true or false. Some important diplomats took note of the matter, such as the British ambassador in Paris, Sir Eric Phipps.[288] Those days, the Apostolic Nuncio in France, Valerio Valeri, an archbishop *in partibus*, unsurprisingly well connected to the French right, who cited the Permanent Committee in a report about a conversation with the French foreign minister Paul-Boncour: "A fortnight ago it was discussed, in fact, of an intervention by France in Catalonia and of the occupation of the island of Menorca, a project that would have found favor with some ministers and some members of the general staff."[289] Such was the pressure from the sectors to the left of the new Blum government, that the Italian embassy would worry about a real intervention as expressed in the telegrams sent to Rome by the chargé d'affaires – no new ambassador had been appointed – Renato Prunas, a career diplomat.[290] This means this was not just a fear created expressly by the Italian or German press as propaganda. The possibility was real or perceived as such.[291] In fact, months later – September of 1938 – the new French Foreign Minister himself, Georges Bonnet (an outstanding "appeaser" in the comparatively long-lived Daladier government that replaced Blum), would drop a comment to the influential if unofficial Franco representative in Paris, José María Quiñones de León, that the General Staff of the *Armée* had organized plans to send troops to Catalonia in case of the the outbreak of a general European war.[292] That there were plans was also known by the well-informed among the Spanish Republican political class, such as, for example, the socialist Indalecio Prieto, since early April out of government and now bitterly opposed to Negrín.[293]

The press of the whole world would once again echo the same theme, placing Catalan secession – and sometimes Basque separation as well – as possible elements of the end of the Spanish war derived from the pressures of London and Paris.[294] There was one doubt: what would be the usefulness of Catalonia for one or the other side, a question which the English press emphasized during those weeks. The diplomatic writer of the *Manchester Guardian* remarked in mid-May: "They [the Germans] consider it [Catalonia] as an important basis for a future war against France and for the development of espionage against France and Great Britain. They believe that if they dominate Catalonia they will reinforce strongly the Berlin-Rome axis that will have, so to speak, an extension in the Mediterranean. With Catalonia as a base, the Germans and Italians would thus be able to threaten the Mediterranean communications of France and control the Balearic Islands."[295] This was a possibility that had not been posed for the future of the rest of the territory in Republican hands (the central area of Spain and Valencia), nor for the Basque Country. The important and strategic question was Catalonia and the Balearics in relation to France.

Thus, despite the French government's veto on military action in Catalonia, the issue continued to float in the political and diplomatic environment. While the wife of President Companys moved to Paris, on April 15, 1938, Franco's troops conquered Vinaròs (Vinaroz in Castilian Spanish) on the Valencian coast.[296] Having lost the North in 1937, what remained of the territory of the Republic was now fragmented into two isolated parts: Catalonia, attacked on the west and the south, was disconnected from a "central zone" with Madrid and Valencia. In this context, on April 18, 1938, a long report on the political, military, and even psychological situation in Catalonia was prepared by the consular section and sent by the French embassy in Barcelona to the foreign ministry in Paris. In the report, there reappeared, yet once again, the possible future of a Frenchified Catalonia: "Catalonia, before becoming a Franco state, would prefer to become French. It has been said that a movement, supported indirectly by France, was born and affirmed to be in favor of a plebiscite. Catalonia would be called by its own government of the Generalitat to pronounce itself, by individual and secret ballot, on their union with France."[297] In fact, some European leaders would echo this theme – that hinted at underground diplomatic initiatives coming from Paris, before and after the consular report. Thus, on March 23, the Brussels daily *Le Soir* asked the former Belgian minister, the Socialist leader Émile Vandervelde, President of the IOS or Socialist Workers' International, about the rumours, implying his involvement, actively denied by a minister of the coalition government of Paul-Émile Janson, which included the Parti Ouvrier Belge.[298] Days later, as explained on the cover and in two columns of the Swiss *Journal de Genève*: "A great temptation has been insinuated into the thinking of certain [French] ministers: that of adding Catalonia to the great Republic, before General Franco can manage to conquer the province. This Anschluss, which would be realized by the holy cause of the left [...]."[299] These were rumours or insinuations of operational actions that launched a diplomatic storm between Paris and Rome, with strong threats by Mussolini. French insecurity was such that the following day the Swiss newspaper felt obliged to include – on the front page – a note correcting itself, probably due to the pressure of the French embassy in Berne. As it states: "The intention to add Catalonia into France has not been insinuated in the thoughts of certain ministers, but in certain sectors of the extreme left that have praised the project (aborted) of the sending of two French divisions to Catalonia."[300] Be that as it may, it was not a strictly French allusion. And it is true that a report of the German chargé d'affaires in London a few days later was similar, although clearly milder. In that case, it would have been the deputy assistant secretary of the Foreign Office who would have told the Nazi diplomat that "it would be desirable for a lasting pacification of Spain, that Catalonia, according to tradition, might be endowed with a certain autonomy in the interior of Spain".[301]

The insinuation remained alive in the press. In the month of

June, the idea was still picked up by the Italian press and certain infuential American newspapers like the *The New York Times*, which spoke of the French disposition to help the Catalan autonomists create a new "satellite State on the southern face of the Pyrenees [...]".[302] This was a possibility that the Parisian press itself would contemplate through the different stories of a French military action to avoid the fall of Barcelona.[303] This option, however, would be publicly denied by Léon Blum, by then out of government: "It is made clear that it is a lie that the second government of the Popular Front thought to send three divisions to Catalonia."[304] However, the rumour was asserted – even requested as action – by some commentators on the communist left such as the PCF spokesman Gabriel Péri, who defended military action as necessary to both to defend France and to keep the Pyrenees border open for the arms trade to help safeguard the Spanish Republic.[305] However, such a French entry into the Spanish conflict had limits: it did not have to go as far as separating Catalonia from Republican Spain by turning it into a protectorate of Paris, something Péri claimed that had been tried from the north side of the Pyrenees: "This danger existed, these attempts were taken, and my information allows me to say that among these, the most outrageous were inspired by Paris. I do not I think I go too far ahead, after having questioned Mr. Companys and the men of the Generalitat, saying that this intrigue has no opportunity to end well. Catalonia knows that it is within the Republic and that the Republic that will defend its own freedoms."[306] One State only, the Spanish Republic, perhaps temporarily reduced to Catalonia, plus the so-called "central zone", had to fulfill the function of the Maginot line to the south.

In sum, the possibility of French intervention would be taken seriously everywhere. In some moments, the Catalan idea popped up, as a reminder or alternative, when the various French governments were also evaluating another radically different option with which to neutralize the border of the Pyrenees: to diplomatically recognize Franco. These possibilities were developed in parallel to the activities of the delegate of the Generalitat in London, Josep Maria Batista Roca. Precisely during the months of April, May and June of 1938, Batista would meet with different figures of certain relevance – this is analyzed in more detail by Josep Sánchez Cervelló. On April 22, he spoke with Sir Horace Wilson, influential private adviser to Neville Chamberlain; while on June 22 he talked with Walter Roberts, director of the department of Western Europe. The synthesis of the proposals of Batista on behalf of the President of the Generalitat were the following: (a) Catalonia, with Euskadi, was willing to dissociate itself from the Spanish Republic while defending democratic positions; (b) The war had to be stopped; and (c) Incentives could be offered to Franco, Italy and Germany to facilitate their acceptance of British mediation. Whatever the interest shown by the British authorities, at least in listening to the proposals, was not transformed into any further receptivity, by entering into any sort of collaboration or negotiation with any other power, including their French allies.[307]

With France but through Italy?

The amount of Catalan rumours had for a long time been excessive, but this would continue. And it was not just the press with insinuations of imprecise contacts but also in the newshound detection of very concrete diplomatic manoeuvres. Almost two years after the failed contacts with Italian diplomacy, in 1938 another initiative was developed by Catalan nationalists to achieve a separate peace of Catalonia that would lead to its independence with the eventual collaboration of Rome. On this occasion, Italian diplomacy would not serve merely as a transmitter, but would be directly impelled to work for this objective.

On April 4, 1938, an alleged Italian journalist based in Barcelona but also residing in Paris, a certain G. Ruggiero, wrote a letter to Mussolini's own secretary, Osvaldo Sebastiani (although a copy would be sent to the head of the Cabinet of the *Ministero della Cultura Popolare*). The author requested Italian mediation to obtain peace in Spain, together with the independence of Catalonia. But who was this G. Ruggiero? After much research, the precise answer to the question turned up in a unexpected place: in the archive of the Monastery of Montserrat. In a file there, appears the correspondence of Lluís Nicolau d'Olwer with the Italian antifascist journalist installed in Barcelona, Giuseppe Torre Caprara. In April 1931, Nicolau d'Olwer had been the Minister in the Republican Provisional Government, in representation of the Catalan party Acció Catalana Republicana; later he would be governor of the *Banco de España*, Spain's national bank of issue. In 1931, Torre Caprara had published a book, *El Fascismo al desnudo: revelaciones de un periodista italiano*, and he continued to be more or less well known through his articles on international politics in the Catalan nationalist press, such as the weekly *Mirador* and the newspaper *La Publicitat*, both publications of the ACR, writing under the pseudonym of "Tiggis". Between 1935 and 1939, Torre Caprara would write more than two hundred letters or notes to Nicolau d'Olwer from Paris, in a large number of which he showed interest in all the attempts and possibilities that Catalan nationalism could explore in its own favour during the Spanish conflict. In this roundabout way, a request for a Fascist mediation favorable to Catalonia was sent on April 4, 1938. The idea apparently had already been made manifest in 1937 and created a possible line of contact of "Ruggiero" with the Italian ambassador in Brussels, Gabriele Preziosi, from whom he would wait for instructions before proceeding to consolidate the initial contacts.

On a date very close to the governmental and military debates held in Paris, in mid-March, Torre Caprara wrote a letter to Nicolau d'Olwer in which he claimed to have knowledge of certain British positions regarding Catalonia: "First of all I know from a British government source, that in one of the notes sent from the Foreign Office to Rome mention is made of the question of Catalonia, as one of the conditions for the 'pacification of Spain'." Torre's signed letter continued adding that, of course, the power in Catalonia (which would encompass the Balearic Islands) would pass into the hands of the moderate sectors, thanks to the accord that could be led by Italy, and that would provoke Barcelona: "in the squares [...] would be erected immortal monuments in honor of the Chief [Mussolini]".[308] A Catalonia that, according to "Ruggiero", had always been pro-Italian, even towards the country of Mussolini, in contrast to a supposed dislike of Castilian Spain (both the Republican and Franco side). This assessment led the journalist to affirm that the Catalan authorities would accept an agreement "for an independent Catalonia, under a kind of Italian protectorate". This would be a new State where Italy would have preference and advantages in commercial and industrial matters far superior to those that could be obtained from Franco. The letter ended with a sentence addressed to Sebastiani and Mussolini: "Italy would get much more with a friendly line and from Catalonia would come words of gratitude and not imprecation."[309]

Three days later, Torre Caprara sent a new letter to Sebastiani in which he reiterated the importance of the Italian interests at stake if that negotiation came to fruition. He further insisted in a letter to Sebastiani from May 3, 1938, which included an explanatory note entitled *"Indipendenza della Catalogna"* in which it was said that Torre claimed to know personally the secretary of the Duce and Mussolini himself. He continued to explain fully the different Catalan and Franco positions towards Rome: the former, totally favorable to an understanding with Italy, and the latter, absolutely opposed, despite military pragmatism. This was a supposed reality that he tried to demonstrate with several declarations of Franco thanking the German help but not the Italian one. Apart from these general matters, which called for mediation to achieve peace in Spain, that "would not be quick by use of arms", the letter focused on a Catalonia that could be set up as a counterbalance favorable to Italy in the event of a military victory of Franco. In relation to Catalonia he wrote: "Nothing is as sad as the 'fratricidal' struggle that is taking place between Italians and Catalans." This was a statement that was based on different factors, the first of which was the excellent relationship between the two countries and the magnificent reception that Italian intellectuals and businessmen had always found among "all classes of Catalan society, at all times, without excluding those that immediately preceded the events of July 1936". In the second place, there was a Catalonia "that unfortunately is not well known" in Italy. For this reason, Catalan society did not understand why Italian troops and planes attacked Catalonia instead of building a friendship based on their common characteristics: "The independence of Catalonia, whether in the present or in the future, can be very useful for Italian interests, be they political, commercial, industrial and/or economic, as well as other sectors. Italy must have the interest of attracting, instead of alienating, the spirit of that noble people, which has all the characteristics of Latin civilization." This was a necessary and indispensable Italian aid that was needed if one wanted to pacify the Iberian Peninsula since "everyone, absolutely all the Catalonian people do not want to know anything about a return to their slavery, under Spain, and that the Catalans will never, never and never resign themselves to such a fate".[310] These were very similar arguments to those expressed by Josep Dencàs in 1934 and 1936, or by other similar commentators during the 1930s in the face of France.

The direct strength of the letters of Torre Caprara (or "Ruggiero") should have had some effect on Italian diplomacy if credit is given to the scattered notes on the negotiations that he himself sent to Lluís Nicolau d'Olwer. As he claimed, his letters were getting results, as he had information that Italy was pressing Franco to start negotiations with the Generalitat. According to this information, the Italian Embassy in Franco Spain was influencing to accept an agreement between the Catalan government "and Count Ciano – Incredible!". Apart from this, Torre Caprara would have managed to establish contact with an Italian intermediary to whom he would remind the "pro-Italian feelings of Catalonia [...]" in a supposed beginning of negotiations between "Barcelona and Rome".[311]

The following letters from the Italian journalist to Nicolau d'Olwer would be a pile of rumours and summaries of conversations in which alleged Italian emissaries would value the possibility of helping Catalonia to achieve a separate peace, without reaching any concrete agreement. This was at the same time as the press chronicles of the trips of the President of the Generalitat to Paris in May 1938, as well as those of other Catalan emissaries, or of some conversations held with the direct collaborators of the French Minister of Foreign Affairs, Georges Bonnet. After that, the paper trail of the requests of "Ruggiero" would disappear for a few months, until he dispatched a last letter on the first of October of that same year. This letter was accompanied by a brief summary of the proposals of "Ruggiero", among which one was worth noting: the one that believed impossible the imposition of Bolshevism in Spain, at the same time as the improbable end of the war by armed struggle.

Likewise, he affirmed that the majority of the opposition of Catalan society to Franco and the great benefits that would be accorded Italy if it helped to facilitate a peace that would favor the Republic and propitiate an independent Catalonia.[312] These arguments had to be complemented with the fatigue of Mussolini and Ciano in the face of the increasingly evident slowness of a Franco victory.[313]

In fact, this perspective towards Italy would be defended years after the Civil War by the pro-independence activist and writer Ramon Arrufat when he said: "If, for centuries, the domination of the Mediterranean was a struggle between France and Italy perhaps the time had come for Catalonia to try its luck with a country of the opera [i.e., Italy], and this country [again, Italy], that of the hegemony in the Latin Sea against a strong Spain and an even stronger France, and before an independent Catalonia, which could not be any danger for Italy, since it came to stand between the [respective] strengths of Spain and France."[314] Arrufat kept proposing a hypothetical interpretation of the effects of a Catalan approach to Italy: "The years of 1936–1937, in which the nationalist, political and patriotic Catalonia, could have changed radically the route towards a practical solution for the benefit of Germany and Italy against Spain and France. More a political split neutralized the action of Italy and Germany in favor of national Spain." Always in Arrufat's assessment: this decided approach of the Catalan nationalism towards Mussolini would have completely changed the foreign intervention in the Spanish conflict: "Let us suppose for a moment that the Italy of the Duce and of Ciano had accepted the Catalan proposal; and then Hitler would have opened his eyes to look towards a rebellious Catalonia. The aid that later they gave selflessly to the nationals [Franco] surely would not have been necessary, since the Spanish Republic would have ceased with its resistance, and favored Franco: first, because Catalonia was the bulwark of the Republic and the most visible flag of anti-fascism; and second, because the separatist feeling would have reacted in favor of the nationals."[315] According to this reasoning, Catalonia could have survived separated from Franco's Spain, thanks to the protection of Italy and Germany: "On the part of Italy, one ally more in the western Mediterranean against France, and a future power out of combat because of the excision of Catalonia as it recovered its political personality. Italy remained in a noble position with respect to Spain [...]. In these conditions, nationalist Spain would have had to accept the ruling in the near future. The moment was delicate." And he added in relation to Germany: "They could continue to maintain good diplomatic relations with the victorious Spain of the civil war, while continuing to support the position of Catalonia, as this was a timely opportunity for the dismemberment of decadent France, advocated by the General Staff of the policy directed by Hitler."[316]

However, despite the arguments of Torre Caprara during the war and the analysis of Arrufat afterwards, the Italian route was by then completely discarded. Franco caused the despair of Mussolini, perhaps, and it was not less true that the Italian economy and army were bleeding to death in Spain – shortly after doing so in Ethiopia – but, at this point, a 180-degree turn in Rome's position simply was not credible.

Last Attempts, again with France (1938–1939)

The time was late. Having touched upon the unconvincing, it was the occasion to consider with distress the merely debatable: to return to the side of the French, to the already desperate attempts to provoke a favorable reaction to the Spanish Republic from the Quai d'Orsay with Catalonia as the center of any operation: this position was sustained in Paris – not without multiple conflicts – by Marià Rubió Tudurí, a member of the ERC. Rubió was in clear and direct opposition to the Spanish Republican government. In fact, Rubió would be relieved from the direction of Esquerra's newspaper, *La humanitat*, after publishing a controversial article in which he proposed the incorporation of Catalonia into France.[317] According to several reports of the French embassy in Barcelona, the position of the Republican executive presided by Juan Negrín had hardened, so that in terms of the "Catalan question", his viewpoint did not differ much from that of the Franco side. Nicolau d'Olwer mused in public to that effect.[318]

Precisely for this reason, according to Rubió, France had to intervene and help the Catalan cause. He reiterated this statement several times. For example, Rubió published a public message addressed to French public opinion: *Lettre à un patriote français. Vers la germanisation de la Catalogne;*[319] he also sent a note to the Quai d'Orsay as a result of the ministerial crisis of the Spanish Republican executive in August 1938, that would culminate with the departures of the ministers of the ERC and the PNV. A report was sent from Paris to the French embassy established in Barcelona on August 31, 1938, which tried to underline the alignment of Catalonia and Euskadi (speaking of the nationalist sectors of their autonomous governments) with the democratic European referentials of the moment, France and Great Britain: "The governments of Catalonia and the Basque Country had assumed a strictly liberal and democratic policy in the interior, in accordance with the international policy of Paris and London." This was a position that, according to Rubió Tudurí, was marked by the will of democratic and liberal resistance of the Catalans and Basques and the disagreement, in this sense, with the whole of the Spanish revolutionary forces and, specifically, with the Negrín government, which intended to resist until the end with a recentralizing policy, in clear collision with the Generalitat: "The objectives of the Catalans and the Basques are, more than ever, military resistance, and, therefore, the preservation of democracy, and freedoms in general, as well as those of Basques and Catalans in Spain. These methods are certainly different from those of the current cabinet; but these methods are, in our opinion those from which the Spanish Republic can expect the greatest benefits."[320]

With greater prudence, the French ambassador Eirik [sic] Labonne wrote a report at the end of April 1938 to deny any viability for mediation plans promoted or proposed by France and Great Britain during that year. In a report written in Barcelona that cannot be interpreted as an active proposal of action, it was affirmed that all attempts to propitiate the beginning of a negotiation to end the war or to "humanize" the struggle had failed. None of the opponents, especially the pro-Franco side in positive positions, would accept to stop the offensive in order to mitigate the effects of the war or to negotiate an end to battle, no matter where the proposals of pacification came from. This reality impelled the ambassador to place the neutrality and the non-intervention of France as the only feasible alternative for his country. This position was widely discussed by the denials of certain press articles that appeared in France and in which, once again, there was careful discussion of a possible Catalan secession promoted by the Republican central government installed in Barcelona.[321] This was a possibility that, if true, would respond to a totally defeatist analysis by the Negrín government (in the opposite direction of the official position it insistently manifested). As Ambassador Labonne himself affirmed, none of this corresponded to the facts on the ground in Catalonia. This was a perspective, Labonne believed, perhaps adulterated by two different components: the desire for peace insistently detected in Catalan society – noted by very diverse observers[322] – and, in addition, the important influence that some of the delegates of the Generalitat (and other Catalans living in France) had on certain journalists. In a clear reference to this interaction between Catalan spokesmen and the French press, Labonne wrote in specific relation to the brothers Marià and Nicolau Maria Rubió Tudurí: "These articles clearly reflect the influence of various Catalan personalities installed in France since March and their conversations with several French interlocutors. In this sense, the activity of Mr. [Marià] Rubió Tudurí, Catalan deputy, is especially relevant. Personally, the most sympathetic, too francophile perhaps as he is almost French, [...]. He is interesting, he knows how to persuade, as he persuaded himself, that France will one day have a role to play in Catalonia and that the past Catalan history is not the destiny of tomorrow."[323]

Labonne knew Rubió Tudurí well if the latter's war memoirs are to be trusted. As explained by Marià Rubió, since the arrival of Labonne as the new ambassador in Barcelona, his contacts with the diplomat were constant. These were conversations in which, always according to Rubió, Labonne would show the little consideration that he felt was deserved by the president of the Generalitat of Catalonia, whom he considered "lacks tone".[324] Anyway, Labonne already knew the Rubio's elder brother – the delegate of the Generalitat in Paris, Nicolau Maria, a respected architect – whom he had interviewed in the French capital immediately after being assigned to Barcelona. In an article in which he reviewed the diplomat's career, the elder Rubió praised the proximity of Labonne with Catalonia, in contrast with the later opinions of his brother and of Jaume Miravitlles as can be seen further: "Mr. Labonne has many sympathies for Catalonia, knows Barcelona and admires it. And it must be said that the Catalan correspondent has also felt a great sympathy for the ambassador [...]", and he added, referring to the importance placed in Barcelona: "Well, it is worth noting, it is in Barcelona that this French ambassador will be established. This will be one of the consequences of the transfer of the [Republican] Government. No doubt remains, the Catalan spirit, so close to the French one, will be appreciated by Mr. Labonne; there is no doubt of the sympathy with which he will be received in Barcelona will find in him an effusive response."[325]

These were omens of a good understanding that would not be fulfilled, according to the Catalan testimony. Before reaching the collision with the French ambassador, however, the rumour mill continued on its way. By the late summer of 1938, tension in Europe had moved to the center of the continent. At the end of September, while Czechoslovakia took all the diplomatic prominence, in Spain the secessionist or mediationist options would be – at least for the moment – completely discarded. All the siren songs about a possible international intervention in Catalonia persistently expressed by the diplomatic or journalistic gossip would be totally disappointed by the Munich agreements of September 29, 1938. Czechoslovakia was delivered to Nazi Germany by pieces, starting with the Sudetenland, although that breakup was not necessarily visible at the time. The cession took place in a mediation prompted by a Mussolini, not consulted and worried because of the expansionist attitude of Hitler, contrary to what had been arranged in their respective secret agreements. Accordingly, the Italian dictator would try to stop the outbreak of a general war. And so he did, with the consent of London and Paris, of Neville Chamberlain – sneeringly labelled thereafter by French leftists "Neville J'aime Berlin" – and Edouard Daladier, in exchange for a certain extension of peace.

As everybody now knows, Hitler's promises were worthless. Neither also were those of the democratic powers available to the

Czechs. The West was very critical of Prague for its refusal to grant autonomy to the Sudetenland, to facilitate a plebiscite, or to try to find a solution to German demands. Nor had the Czechoslovak government been able to force its backers to exercise the agreements sealed since 1934. Avoiding the outbreak of a conflict on a continental scale, in an enthusiastic ambient of peace, the Catalan and Spanish Republican options vanished. French acquiescence before the suggestion of the Italian dictator would mean the victory of Hitler and the impossibility of extending the war of Spain to the rest of the continent. This was not an inherently pleasant hope, but perhaps it seemed quite logical from the Catalan and Spanish Republican prism. With France and Britain at the head, perhaps there would be a turnabout favorable to the Republican cause in Spain or it was conceivable that the territories not yet dominated by the Franco side could be saved from conquest. Disappointment was expressed by the French ambassador in Barcelona, Eirik Labonne, in a long report dated October 5, 1938, in which – as it were – he recorded the death of the last lifeguard kept alive with artificial respiration on the Spanish and Catalan shore.[326] Surely this was one of the last reports to go out to Paris, but certainly the last one that Labonne would write before leaving Barcelona to occupy the position of Resident General in the French protectorate of Tunisia.[327]

This was a change of ambassadors that, apparently, would respond to a simple diplomatic reorganization, but that could have another motivation. Putting a practical side on the turn of events, Jaume Miravitlles, the Propaganda Commissioner of the Generalitat and responsible for Foreign Affairs, would explain the replacement of Labonne by Jules Henry at the end of 1938 in a completely different way. And he would do it twice. In the first instance and in an extensive manner in a report dated November 4, 1938 that has been preserved in the archive of Josep Tarradellas, and, secondly, in one of his interesting – at the same time always dubious – volumes of memoirs published years later. Thus, and always according to the version of Miravitlles, that change of ambassador would take place due to an interview – approved by the presidents Companys and Azaña – that he himself would maintain with the French foreign minister at that time, the radical-socialist

Georges Bonnet, a strong partisan of "appeasement", to probe the French position on a possible negotiation that would put an end to the war through international mediation. In this way, at the end of July 1938, just as the fury of the battle of Ebro river was exploding, the Generalitat delegation in Paris would arrange a private and secret interview at Bonnet's personal home, which would take place with complete cordiality, as Miravitlles would later recall. This meeting would discuss the possibility of France and Britain pressing the Spanish contenders in order to force them to sit at a negotiating table so as to end the conflict. This was a possibility that Miravitlles argued from the necessary neutralization of the Soviet influence on the Republican side. Faced with this demand, Bonnet's response was clear: that was precisely his position and the British position, but it seemed impossible to get either side to agree to negotiate. Miravitlles replied: if it were completely true about Franco and Negrín, it was also true that the president of the Republic, Manuel Azaña, or the ex-minister Indalecio Prieto, had publicly declared their willingness to promote a negotiated end to the war. In fact, before his replacement, Labonne had persistently informed Paris of the different points of view in conflict around resistance or mediation.[328]

At this point, Miravitlles expressed his ideas to Bonnet, convinced as he was that they had not been transmitted with enough force to Paris by Labonne: "It is what I supposed and this is the conviction that it has led me, precisely, to see you personally at risk of the dangers in which I could incur." And he added, with regard to the consideration that he felt was deserved by Labonne's diplomatic action: "Since some time ago, Mr. Bonnet, I have closely followed the performance in Barcelona of your ambassador, Mr. Eirik Labonne. High members of the embassy (I did not tell him that it was the air attaché) have contacted me, knowing my political activity, to explain to me the official and private conduct of your representative."[329] The report written in 1938 was even more accentuated: "I took advantage of the occasion, since Labonne was not a man affected by the politics of the Republicans and especially by the politics of the Catalans, in order to emphasize this bad impression even more, that the minister had of his ambassador." As reported by Miravitlles, Labonne's activities were more focussed on his private leisure than on his "diplomatic duties at such grave moments for the history of Spain, of Europe and of the world".[330] To this criticism he added the accusation in which he claimed that the ambassador participated in black market operations and trafficked in works of art.[331] But apart from these personal considerations, what worried Miravitlles most was the excessive confidence and follow-up that Labonne had towards the president of the Republican government, Juan Negrín: "Mr. Labonne is not the ambassador of Georges Bonnet close to the Spanish prime minister, Mr. Negrín, but Negrín's ambassador close to the French Foreign Minister. The French ambassador in Barcelona informs the Government of Paris of everything that suits the political interests of Mr. Negrín. Labonne's vision of Spanish politics is very different from what it really is."[332]

To all this has to be added the lack of communication between Labonne and the Generalitat, as Miravitlles reported in 1938: "[...] Bonnet asked me: 'Is it that Labonne often sees the President of the Generalitat?' I answered no, and then Bonnet said that he would give precise orders to Labonne, so that he would often see the President of the Generalitat."[333] These orders, apparently, would have been received reluctantly in the embassy, according to what the informants of the legation would communicate to Miravitlles, and that they would even get to have an effect on the French consul in Barcelona, René Binet: "He [Labonne] had received orders to visit Lluís Companys often, and in front of some high officials of the embassy he had said he did not want to go. And he had done even more: knowing that Consul General Mr. Binet had friendly relations with councillors Pi Sunyer, Sbert and Bosch Gimpera, he expressly forbade him from maintaining too intimate contact with them."[334] This prohibition would provoke a reaction from Binet, who, contradicting the orders received from his superior, argued that his consular functions forced him to maintain these contacts in a fluid way. These were the factors that, according to Miravitlles, would lead his allies in the embassy to request actions in Paris to obtain the change of ambassador: "Our friends from the embassy begged me to make an effort so that this man was separated from his functions, because he was a declared enemy of Catalonia [...], he did not take literal care of his function. All the reports, for example, that I sent him were stopped at the embassy, without reaching their [ultimate] recipient [...]."[335]

If these comments were not enough to condition Bonnet's position, Miravitlles sent him a long report (also sent to Minister Anatole de Monzie, another well-known "appeaser"), stating in writing his vision of Labonne's mismanagement. Given all these comments from Miravitlles, and always according to this same source, Bonnet would corroborate certain information received from his chief of staff, Jules Henry. Henry was the man that Bonnet would decide to place in the position of Labonne as the French representative in Republican Spain: "It will be as if I had 'my ears in Barcelona'. It is from this moment that we will be able to approach the Spanish problem under more objective bases and through normal diplomatic channels."[336] This change in theory would bring a new context that would still take several months to fully exist. But, far from the opinion expressed by Bonnet, the new ambassador would not modify anything.[337] Rather, and always according to the Propaganda Commissioner of the Generalitat, the attitude and manners of Labonne would be repeated in the figure of a Henry "spellbound" by Juan Negrín.[338]

Within this context, that did not change as a background scenario, by the end of 1938 the rumours pressed hard upon Catalan and Republican desperation. On the one hand, Swiss diplomacy – Ambassador Egger was transferred to Barcelona at that time by the destroyer HMS *Ivanhoe* of the Royal Navy – claimed that Companys and the Generalitat were in open confrontation with Negrín: "The once powerful Generalitat with Companys [...] is in an inferior position in a desperate struggle with the government that has just arrived from Valencia. The last attempt was to eliminate Negrín and bring [Julián] Besteiro and the moderate Socialists to the government. This attempt failed. The result was a brief crisis and the harsh replacement of two Spanish ministers. It is true that the Generalitat made the most desperate efforts to convince the government to move to Albacete [where the International Brigades were headquartered], Murcia [above the naval base at Cartagena] or any other place. [...] It also seems to have been true that Companys was already making a bold move to negotiate with Franco. All his aspirations were frustrated."[339] To a large extent, what was placed on the table was the opposition to Negrín and the hypothetical pact with Franco.

At the same time there circulated, published in the press, certain never-confirmed news stories about petitions to the League of Nations to protect the autonomy of Catalonia.[340] More seriously, by then Italian diplomacy could follow the contacts of certain sectors of Catalan nationalism. Specifically, the Italians were informed about the Catalan contacts with the Norwegian Minister of Foreign Affairs, Halvdan Koht. In this regard, on October 26, 1938 the Italian ambassador in London, Dino Grandi, sent a telegram in which he spoke of the impossibility of confirming or denying the contacts initiated between the government of Burgos and the Catalan government. Thus, the note reported on the initiative of the Norwegian foreign minister to achieve a peace that would mean the maintenance of the Catalan autonomy (understood practically as independence).[341] This alternative should be linked to the efforts of liaison conducted by Companys towards the French government: "Without speaking of a real and public French protectorate, Companys would have given assurances in the sense that, if this project was carried out, the new Catalan State would naturally gravitate in the Paris political orbit."[342] This possibility would receive the approval of a Great Britain that was favorable to intervene to achieve the end of the war in Spain. With this situation, in the following *"telespresso"* sent from Rome to several legations, the contact of Koht with Nicolau Maria Rubió Tudurí was confirmed as an effort to "try to conclude, under the auspices of S.D.N. [the League], an armistice that would precede peace and save the independence of Catalonia".[343] Once again, this initiative would align the diplomatic pressure of France and Great Britain, which would separate the Catalan fate from that of republican Spain, and which in turn would have to go through the formation of a new Catalan government, guaranteed to be free of German and Italian influences.

The first corroboration of this proposed solution was accompanied by the alleged interception by Falangist spies of a summary of the meeting between Koht and Nicolau Maria Rubió Tudurí, who besides Paris was also the Catalan delegate in Geneva; the notes had been sent by him to the Catalan representative in Brussels.

According to this captured document, the Norwegian–Catalan meeting would have been held on September 18, with a draft of the armistice already well advanced, but which lacked some necessary nuances from the Catalan view, "so that it would not be intended to be finished with a political formula that was, by definition, unitary [i.e., centralizing] and anti-Catalan".[344] In addition, the words attributed to the Catalan delegate spoke of a very good predisposition on the part of Koht, and of the conviction of being able to influence both France and Great Britain in the direction of not accepting an authoritarian regime in Spain protected by other powers.

A few weeks later, Italian diplomacy continued its inquiries into those contacts. The embassy in Oslo sent a report confirming the meeting between Koht and the ex-minister and leader of Acció Catalana Republicana, Lluís Nicolau d'Olwer (sent in September 1938 as a delegate of Republican Spain to the League of Nations). There, in Geneva, Koht and Nicolau d'Olwer, both professors of History and old acquaintances from the academic world as well as the circles of the pro-League of Nations Movement of the 1920s, would try to propitiate negotiations, an initiative that promptly would fail.[345] These were contacts that, once confirmed, seemed to fall apart quickly; as the Italian embassy wrote: "I have the honor to communicate that, from the information that has been gathered about the steps taken in Geneva by Minister Koht, the result of these would be in effect upset here with the representatives of Catalonia. Such conversations, as it seems, would not have reached any concrete agreement, because the Catalans would not be prone to reach a separate peace."[346]

Whether a direct failure or a demonstration of Spanish Republican loyalty, the Norwegian-sponsored peace démarche was depressing, seen with Catalan nationalist eyes in Barcelona. A sense of desperation unfailingly had to reach the President of the Generalitat, who – everyone insisted – was bent on selling Catalonia to the French government. As explained by the French consulate in San Sebastian, the press of the Franco zone affirmed: "Companys tries to sell Catalonia but Spain will claim until the last portion of its territory, as Generalissimo Franco recently declared." And added the consul, with respect to a distant possibility, that a "Companys, comfortably installed in France" would try to sell the country at the same time as "making it French".[347] According to what was mentioned by writers in the pro-Franco press, that precisely was the intention: to convert Catalonia into a new Czechoslovakia (as well protected as the original one by the Franco-British surrender of Munich?). Even more, as was gathered by the press notes of the French agency Havas and of the Republican agency Espagne sent to French representatives, in declarations made by the former president of the Catalan Parliament, Joan Casanovas, established in France after an attempt to overthrow Companys in late 1936. What had to be allowed to Catalonia was the right to exercise self-determination. Beyond this demand, beyond any "Byzantine discussions" (i.e., useless complexitites), the only feeling that remained alive was the love of the "homeland" ("*pàtria*") determined by "the concern for remaking peace and shortening the martyrdom of Catalonia". Already well known to all, the nail was hammered in once again with the umpteenth nod to France, in stressing the geostrategic role of an independent Catalonia: "A reconciled and united Catalonia would become, between the Pyrenees and the Mediterranean, a factor of balance and order".[348] This was a public – but very complicated – position, openly and strongly opposed by the Spanish Republican government.[349]

At last? The Weight of the Logic of the Outside Perspective

Everything was nearing the end, but there was still room for a series of manoeuvres and appeals by the Generalitat toward the French government. There was enough wiggling room, a margin to try to whisper an attempt to apply from the Catalan side the logic of European thought – the alleged Catalan push for independence – accrued during years of observation of Barcelona politics. A final sigh where it seemed possible to comply with the external analysis. As a culmination of the conversations held by the Generalitat delegate in Paris, Nicolau Maria Rubió Tudurí would almost attempt a dramatic gesture, then think the better of it. In a "Note, not sent", as can be seen written by hand on a document dated November 21, 1938, Rubió Tudurí affirmed that in the face of the Negrín government, of its clashes with the Generalitat, and of what he described as excessive Communist influence, there was only one proposal to make: "It is clear that if the Government of Catalonia presided by Mr. Companys is led to make a gesture against the Negrín Government – the excesses of power which have created an implacable hostility to Catalan opinion – the war would end immediately. This gesture, Mr. Companys cannot do without the collaboration of the powers directly interested in the rapid restoration of peace in Spain".[350] In short, he intended to provoke the defeat of the Republic through an indefinite gesture, perhaps a coup d'état – but with what forces? – that would overthrow the Negrín government. At the same time, France should protect Catalonia by facilitating its secession. But the note was not sent. It would not be put on the table officially. Perhaps it was a document stillborn, already dead given the incapacity of the Catalan government to act. At least this is what the note seems like, although it did express a route explored individually by Rubió and to some extent or other agreed upon with President Companys. The geopolitics of the western Mediterranean would not be altered. Neither France nor the Generalitat would carry out any disturbing action.

And that was that, despite some reminders from the Italian press. With the Spanish war almost finished in Catalonia, one of the main theoretical magazines of Italian Fascism, *Crítica Fascista*, put on the table the important advantages that the possession of Catalonia would have meant for the French army.[351] This commentary was made at the same time that the General Staff of the French army made plans for a possible occupation of Menorca, still under Spanish Republican control.[352] But that is what military staff work is supposed to be about: planning contingencies. In any case, this option, which together with any French insinuation about Catalonia, was cut short by Italian pressure.

The matter was clearly stated in an article by the journalist Giovanni Ansaldo in the newspaper owned by the family of the Italian foreign minister, Galeazzo Ciano, *Il Telegrafo*, a day after the Franco occupation of Tarragona, on January 15, 1939: "Italy, in relation to Spain, has perfectly contradictory direct interests in relation to the French. Italy is interested because Spain can be reconstituted in unity, and also that it does so through a vigorous State, without the local autonomies that mortally wounded it. Italy is interested in a national Spain dominating Catalonia, without which it would only be a forgotten peripheral state at the tail of Europe. Italy will act in Spain until it recovers its natural limits, firstly in the Pyrenees. [...] Despite French wishes, Spain will not be dismembered; in spite of the last attempts of French imperialism, there will once again be a border of the Pyrenees in the hands of the Spaniards."[353] Forcefulness was necessary, from the Italian point of view, if attention is paid to what the Chief of Cabinet of the Ministry of Foreign Affairs, Filippo Anfuso, wrote in his memoirs: "Until the conquest of Barcelona, Mussolini considered possible a French intervention in Catalonia in order to save the Republic of Madrid [...]."[354] The impression is even stronger if one studies the direct notes of Anfuso's superior, Minister Ciano, who on January 16, 1939 wrote: "The victory now seems certain. Therefore, we do not intend to allow any French intervention. This morning I called Mr. Perth [sic: Lord Perth, the former Sir Eric Drummond, British Ambassador in Rome] and I had the following conversation: 'I assure you that if the French intervene strongly in favor of the reds of Barcelona, we will attack Valencia. Thirty battalions with war material are ready to be embarked on the first alarm'."[355]

Issues linked to the international tensions derived from the last moments of the Spanish war and of the last hopes of a negotiated end would take a new direction at the beginning of February 1939, when the French ambassador asked Negrín to surrender before battle action could reach the French border of the Pyrenees. At a time when most of the embassies had already crossed the border or had settled in Perpignan (only that of Mexico remained in Catalonia), French diplomats tried to prevent the Italian and German troops incorporated in the Franco army from combat within the limits of the territory. This desire was apparently achieved a few days later with the signing of the Bérard–Jordana agreements of February 25, in which France recognized the Franco government in exchange for the promise of neutrality in the event of general war in Europe. With the fighting still going on, the announcement of the pact would make it easier for Britain to imitate the text, considering Franco as the real and effective head of Spain. What remained of the Spanish Republic had its days numbered.[356]

Everything had ended for the Catalan nationalists and the Catalan left, with all their nuances and intrigues, although not for the Spanish Republicans. Negrín maintained the central area where he would return to prolong the war until Franco forces entered Madrid on March 28, the next day finally reaching and seizing Alicante and Valencia. Franco proclaimed the official end of the conflict on April 1. In fact, with Catalonia occupied and while the Belgian representative, Walter Loridan, was installed in the French town of Amélie-les-Bains, he sent to Brussels the following note in reference to the Catalan and Basque vision of nationalism at the end of the conflict: "I have found here different members of the government of the Generalitat of Catalonia, especially the former councillors D. Bosch Gimpera, rector of the University of Barcelona, Sbert [...]. All criticized the attitude of the president of the council Negrín, declaring that they had always been in favor of an agreement." And he added, specifying the position of moderate Catalan nationalism: "Catalonia, I have been told especially by Messrs. Sbert and Bosch Gimpera, could have been saved, a few months ago, its autonomy and some of its freedoms with the help of France and England."[357] In short, what they clearly expressed was their own failure, that of Catalan nationalism, by not forcing the democratic powers to position themselves. Or, seen from another angle, the demonstration of Spanish fidelity inherent to left-wing Catalan nationalism. If an international negotiation of peace or mediation had been proposed by appealing to London and Paris or by proclaiming independence, thereby forcing Rome and Berlin to challenge the French and British again, the whole scenario, perhaps, would have changed radically. Or perhaps not. Because at that time neither Sbert nor Bosch Gimpera speculated on a pact with Franco. On April 1, 1939 the already dictator of the "New Spain" or *Estado español* signed the last military statement of the Spanish conflict: the war was over, he pronounced, and he had prevailed. A long dictatorship began. But, in spite of the many fears expressed over the previous three years, this would not entail either the arrival of the Nazis or the Italian Fascists to the southern French borders with Spain. In fact, it would be on the *north* side of the Pyrenees border where German troops would arrive, after occupying France in June 1940 (their *"zone militaire littorale"* extended to Hendaye, and the *"zone occupée"* would take half the Department of Pyrénées-Atlantiques), and, later, the remainder, all of the *"zone libre"*, when taking control of the collaborationist regime of Vichy led by Marshal Philippe Pétain in November 1942. When the Italians attacked France in June 1940, they too got a small border area to occupy in the armistice agreement, which also grew in late 1942.

Before all this, on March 14, 1939, Hitler facilitated the independence of Slovakia. The "Slovak State" was established as a client entity of Germany; and later, in July, formally constituted as the Slovak Republic – as a preliminary step to the conquest of Prague and the dismantling of the hated Czechoslovakia. Mussolini occupied Albania a month later, overthrew his ally king Zog I, and added an additional crown for Italian king Victor Emmanuel III, while creating a department responsible for spreading irredentist propaganda about Kosovo. Likewise, the Croatian independence movement was subsidized by Italy as a destabilizing element of the Yugoslav monarchy. Meanwhile, the Polish government was alarmed by the possible emergence of an independence movement in the Ukrainian majority areas within its borders. Europe was on the verge of war and everyone used their own or other nationalist claims to achieve their goals. The Romanians, the Hungarians and the Bulgarians aspired to move their respective borders, under German consent. The same could have happened in Catalonia with France or the Soviet Union as the protagonist. The dynamics seemed to bring the Old World closer to General War, the second in a quarter of a century. And everything speeded up.

But nothing was so simple as the Catalan options, because everything was so unpredictable, unstable and fickle that anything could happen. On May 22, the "Pact of Steel" between Italy and Germany was sealed; in the document, mutual military assistance was formalized. Then, just three months later, on August 23, 1939, the impossible became reality: the Soviet–German pact was signed.

Hitler and Stalin agreed on a policy of non-aggression and the partition of Poland. The "two demons" of the western democracies allied? In the midst of this dance of unexpected alliances, France and Great Britain, together with the small nations of Central Europe and the Balkans, and, in addition, the United States, all acted in a disoriented fashion.

Finally, war broke out with the beginning of the attack of the German armed forces against Poland on September 1 of that year. Édouard Daladier and Neville Chamberlain declared war on the Reich two days later. After six years of repeated breaches of the peace treaties of 1919, when the argument for the incorporation of territories of German population was no longer valid, when Central Europe was in the hands of Hitler, and Spain and Catalonia completely in the hands of his ally Francisco Franco, the French and British were engaged in a war they did not want. Treaty after treaty, from the Versailles Pact shattered in March 1936 with the remilitarization of the Rhineland onwards until the Munich Accord of September 1938, Hitler had broken his own promises. Likewise, the alleged anti-German containment block in Locarno, Stresa or Munich had proved incapable of stopping Nazi expansionism. The bloodshed initiated in Manchuria or Ethiopia, in Spain, China, and Austria, by the future Axis partners in the different theatres of World War Two made its way across the whole of Europe and destabilized the planet. The Soviet Union went from being "the threat" to avoid in the Spanish war, to becoming an ally of Hitler in late August 1939, a week before the Polish war, and then – with the German invasion of June 22, 1941 – to becoming an essential part of London's effort to stop Hitler.

Catalonia – like the Basques, like republican Spain, for that matter – was never accorded the right to be a "free" partner in what, in the wake of the Pearl Harbor attack, U.S. President Franklin Delano Roosevelt, in January 1942, called the "United Nations" coalition fighting the Axis – the United Kingdom (with the Commonwealth and the Empire), the Soviet Union, and the United States, together with the "Free Poland", the "Free French", "Free China", and other Allied countries under Axis occupation. Franco dabbled in the world struggle by sending "volunteers" – a "Blue Division" – to fight on the Russian front, but his regime never stopped engaging with the Anglo-American powers. The Catalan illusion of statehood of the interwar years was over, together with the Spanish republican dream, at least as far as outsiders were concerned.

Notes

1 The present text is a more complete version of that published in the volume originally edited in Catalan. The author would like to thank the many persons who have helped in his research, notably among consular staff in Barcelona, as well as in archives of the ministries of foreign affairs of numerous countries. In particular, I would like to thank the Belgian consul general in Barcelona, Paul van den Broeck, for granting me the possibility to consult the consulate archive and for the recommendation addressed to the ministry's archives in Brussels, and the the help that I received there. My thanks to those responsible and archivists of the Ministry of Foreign Affairs of Portugal to the Tapada das Necessidades, since they make returning to research in Lisbon always a privilege. Equally, I would like to emphasize my gratitude to the archivists of the French Foreign Affairs ministry, both in Nantes, for the Consular materials, and in Paris, for embassy records; to those of German ministry; to those of the Swiss ministry in Berne – thank you for letting me practice my French; and, especially, to those of La Farnesina in Rome, that houses the Italian Foreign Affairs ministry, for their intense search work for documents often difficult to find. I add my appreciation for the incredible consultation hours and facilities of the Hemeroteca of the National Library of Argentina, offered by Mariano Moreno, as well as the kindness of Alba Lombardi of the Historical Archive of the Ministry of Foreign Affairs of Argentina. I must also express my special debt to Jean Trémoulet Thienemann, son of the French Consul in Barcelona between 1934 and 1936, for his generosity in the use of the family archive. In Catalonia, my warmest thanks to the Montserrat Tarradellas i Macià Archive, especially to the former director, Montserrat Catalán. Similarly I must recognize the full worth of the facilities for the consultation of so much bibliography at the CRAI-Pavilion of the Republic of the University of Barcelona.

In the translation of this essay, Catalan political terms – words like *"catalanisme"* and *"catalanista"*, or *"independentista"* – with subtle gradations of meaning and which lack easy equivalents in English-language dictionaries, have been simplified in a generic usage: "Catalan nationalism". Both the author and the translator agree that it should be pointed out that current Catalan politics make this expression debatable in local parlance. For the first quote: letter from Vidal i Barraquer to Pacelli: cited in: M. M. Fuentes, J. M. Quijada and N. Sánchez, *Correspondència del Dr. Francesc d'Assís Vidal i Barraquer Cardenal Arquebisbe de Tarragona amb Secretaria d'Estat de la Santa Seu (1936–1939)*, València, Tirant, 2015, p. 87. For Pope Pius XII and Bavaria: J. Cornwell, *El Papa de Hitler. La verdadera historia de Pío XII*, Barcelona: Planeta, 2000; also A. Rhodes, *El Vaticano en la era de los dictadores*, Barcelona, Euros, 1975. For the second quote, Sir Norman King's undated report in French files: CADN, CB, Gces., Dépêches politiques, Correspondance Confidentielle, (1936–1939), *Note*, without date.

2 B. de Jouvenel, "Franco prépare une nouvelle Espagne", *Vu*, n. 451, 4-XI-1936. This interview was reprinted in B. de Jouvenel, "La España que quiere el General Francisco Franco", *El País*, Montevideo, 4-XII-1936.

3 "Azaña annuncia ai catalani l'imminente caduta di Madrid", *Corriere della Sera*, 29-X-1936.

4 F. Tuohy, "All eyes on Catalonia", *The Sphere Magazine*, 14-XI-1936.

5 G. Fioravanzo, *Basi navali nel mondo*, Milan, Istituto per gli Studi di Politica Internazionale, 1936. See also: H. Hummel and W. Siewert, *La Méditerranée*, Paris, Payot, 1937.

6 "Les difficultés de Franco s'accumulent. Et la situation Internationale est de plus en plus confuse", *La Wallonie*, Liège, 23-XI-1936; "Le conseil d'un journal anglais. Une Espagne fédérative, la Catalogne indépendante?", *Journal de Genève*, 23-XI-1936.

7 Politisches Archiv Auswärtiges Amt (PAAA), Barcelona, Rav 66, *Das Problem Katalonien*, without date nor author.

8 Take as an example the different lectures given by the outstanding deputy and left-wing writer, a militant Belgian Wallon federalist, Louis Piérard, about Catalonia in diverse daily sessions organized by the Socialist Federation of Charleroi ("Dans le centre", *Journal de Charleroi*, Belgium, 15-XII-1936). Months later, Piérard published a long description of his trip to Barcelona as a member of a delegation of Belgian deputies ("De Barcelone à Valence par le front d'Aragon", *Regards*, 15-IV-1937).

9 At the end of August, some official Nazi press notes affirmed the existence of a Marxist plan to make Catalonia, Euzkadi and the Balearic Islands independent in the case of the fall of Madrid ("Baskische

Seperatisten unter Zwang der Marxisten", *Deutsches Nachrichtenbüro*, 20-VIII-1936).

10   "Madrid governments flee to coast", *Sunderland Daily Echo and Shipping Gazette*, Great Britain, 7-XI-1936.

11   On this aspect, see: A. Gonzàlez i Vilalta, "La interpretació equívoca del nacionalisme català: la mirada internacional i la distància entre diplomàcia i premsa (1931–1934)", in A. Gonzàlez i Vilalta, M. López Esteve and E. Ucelay-Da Cal, *6 d'octubre. La desfeta de la revolució catalanista de 1934*, Barcelona, Base, 2014, pp. 113–145.

12   I. Saz, *Mussolini contra la II República*, Valencia, Alfons el Magnànim, 1986, p. 56.

13   See: A . Gonzàlez i Vilalta, "The Catalan Nationalist Option: Italian Fascist Intrigues in Barcelona (1931–1943)", *Bulletin for Spanish and Portuguese Historical Studies*, 2011, pp. 1–27.

14   N. Pascazio, *La rivoluzione di Spagna*, Rome, Nuova Europa, 1933, p. 348.

15   I*bid*.

16   E. Faldella, *Venti mesi di guerra in Spagna (luglio 1936–febbraio 1938)*, Florence, Felice Le Monnier, 1938, p. 15.

17   F. Belforte in his book, *La Guerra Civile in Spagna. Gli interventi stranieri nella Spagna rossa*, v. II, Rome, Istituto per gli studi di política internazionale, 1938, p. 303.

18   N. Quilici, *Spagna*, Rome, Istituto Nazionale di Cultura Fascista, 1938, p. 48.

19   M. Rubió i Tudurí, N. Mart [N. M. Rubió i Tudurí], *Catalunya amb Europa. Més enllà del separatisme*, Barcelona, Arc de Berà, 1932, pp. 62–63.

20   For example, in the faraway Australia: "The Part of Catalonia", *The Sydney Morning Herald*, 11-IX-1936.

21   See: A. Gonzàlez i Vilalta, *Cataluña bajo vigilancia. El consulado italiano y el fascio de Barcelona (1930–1943)*, Valencia, PUV, 2009, pp. 233–235.

22   "Carta al General Franco", 24-IX-1934. Taken from J. A. Primo de Rivera, *Textos de doctrina política*, Madrid, Delegación Nacional de la Sección Femenina de F.E.T. y de las J.O.N.S., 1966, p. 297.

23   On this work, which was a part of a project of reconstruction of the conservative Catalanist space during the first Franco period, see the study of E. Ucelay-Da Cal in R. Arrufat, *Macià*, Juneda, Editorial Fonoll, 2007, pp. 51–54.

24   Many years later Jaume Miravitlles dedicated to him some pages in his

work: *Los comunicados secretos de Franco, Hitler y Mussolini*, Barcelona, Plaza & Janés, 1977, pp. 100–103; 127–136.

25   P. Meléndez y Solá, *La unidad hispánica. España y Cataluña (1892–1939)*, Barcelona, without editor, 1946, p. 148.

26   *Ibid.*, p. 152.

27   *Ibid.*, p. 152.

28   *Ibid.*, p. 156.

29   See, in general terms: E. Ucelay-Da Cal, *La Catalunya populista: imatge, cultura i política en l'etapa republicana, 1931–1939*, Barcelona, La Magrana, 1982.

30   K. Pruszyński, *En la España roja*, Barcelona, Alba, 2007, p. 65.

31   P. Meléndez y Solà [R. Arrufat], *Unidad hispánica. España y Cataluña (1892–1939)*, *op. cit.*, pp. 155 and 156.

32   NARA, US Barcelona General Consulate, 1936–1939, entry 3170, telegram sent by the embassy in Valencia to the consulate in Barcelona, 12-X-1936.

33   I. Ehrenburg, *España república de trabajadores*, Barcelona, Crítica, 1976. [1932], p. 168. It should be remembered that in April 1936 Ehrenburg visited Companys: "Elías Ehrenburg está en España y visita en Barcelona al señor Companys", *Mundo Obrero*, 8-IV-1936.

34   Archivo General Militar de Ávila, C.320,3,1/9. See also: M. Caminal, *Joan Comorera. Guerra i Revolució (1936–1939)*, vol. II, Barcelona, Empúries, 1984, p. 33.

35   See how the German or Belgian press wrote already of a Soviet Catalonia just a few days after the start of the war: R. de Marés, "Neutralité et non-intervention", *Le Soir*, 7-VIII-1936.

36   I. Ehrenburg, *España república de trabajadores*, *op. cit.*, p. 168.

37   X. M. Núñez Seixas, *Internacionalitzant el nacionalisme: El catalanisme polític la qüestió de les minories nacionals a Europa (1914–1936)*, Catarroja, Afers, 2010.

38   See, as an example: G. Falanga, *L'avamposto di Mussolini nel Reich di Hitler. La politica italiana a Berlino (1933–1945)*, Milan, Marco Tropea Editore, 2011 [2008].

39   See: J. Coverdale, *La Intervención fascista en la Guerra Civil española*, Madrid, Alianza, 1979 [1975] and I. Saz, *Mussolini contra la II República*, *op. cit.*

40   See a synthesis of the different interpretations in: Á. Viñas, *Franco, Hitler y el estallido de la Guerra Civil. Antecedentes y consecuencias*, Madrid, Alianza, 2001, pp. 384–402.

41   See among others: Y. Denéchère, *La politique espagnole de la France de*

1931 à 1936. Une pratique française de rapports inégaux, Paris, L'Harmattan, 1999 and by J. L. Neila, *La 2ª República española y el mediterráneo. España ante el desarme y la seguridad colectiva*, Madrid, Dilema, 2006; *España y el Mediterráneo en el siglo XX,* Madrid, Sílex, 2011, pp. 167–213.

42 To cite the most influential work: J. B. Duroselle, *La décadence, 1932–1939*, Paris, Imp. Nationalle, 1979.

43 See among others: H. Lagardelle, *Mission à Rome. Mussolini*, Paris, Plon, 1955 and R. Festorazzi, *Laval-Mussolini. L'impossibile Asse*, Milan, Mursia, 2003.

44 For a general description of the Spanish interests and activities in the Mediterranean see: J. L. Neila, *España y el Mediterráneo en el siglo XX*, *op. cit.*, pp. 216–245.

45 R. Sabatier de Lachadenède, *La Marina Francesa y la Guerra Civil de España (1936–1939)*, Madrid, Ministerio de Defensa, 2001, pp. 106–107.

46 F. Nadal, "La cartographie militaire des Pyrénées françaises et la guerre civile espagnole", in *Sud-Ouest Européen*, n. 31, 2011, pp. 169–182.

47 *Les Archives Secrètes de la Wilhelmstrasse, III. L'Allemagne et la Guerre Civile Espagnole (1936–1939)*, Paris, Plon, 1952, p. 16.

48 J. M., "Catalogne contre Espagne?", *Journal de Genève*, 3-IX-1936.

49 C. Graves, "When Franco wins", *The Sphere*, Great Britain, 10-X-1936.

50 *Les Archives Secrètes de la Wilhelmstrasse, III. L'Allemagne et la Guerre Civile Espagnole (1936–1939)*, Paris, Plon, 1952, p. 20.

51 "Princes Risborough. Lecture on Spain", *The Bucks Herald*, Great Britain, 30-X-1936.

52 L. R., "Sons de cloches. L'Espagne", *L'Écho d'Alger*, 31-X-1936.

53 M. H. Hamon, "Beat Napoleon, Can Beat Franco, Catalans Boast", *The Toronto Daily Star*, 24-XI-1936.

54 "L'opinion britannique", *Le Soir*, 31-VII-1936.

55 Radio Club Português, "Entre Burgos e Barcelona", *Diário de Notícias*, Lisboa, 3-VIII-1936. Also in the British press: "Rebel warning to Barcelona", *Larne Times*, Antrim, Northern Ireland. Equally imprecise were other notes: "Catalonia. Move towards complete independence", *The Sydney Morning Herald*, Australia, 21-VIII-1936. The strong reaction on the rebel side in: "¡Cataluña, pagarás tu traición! La declaración de independencia no es más que un disfraz a su situación angustiosa y caótica", *El Diario Palentino*, Palencia, Spain, 3-VIII-1936. On this same day the most open commentary appeared supposedly transmitted by Radio Sevilla in rebel hands, in which it was confirmed that the

difference of opinion in Barcelona was between those who believed the moment had come to declare independence and those, like the CNT, were on the side of not making this decision and would act together with the rebel military ("Un communiqué politique des insurgés", *Le Soir*, 31-VII-1936).

56 Havas, "Ultimas noticias. Espanha. Catalunha está agindo em plena independência", *Diário da Manhã*, 12-VIII-1936; D.N.B, "Confirma-se a proclamação da independência da Catalunha", *Diário da Manhã*, 22-VIII-1936; Havas, "A Catalunha não se tornou independente", *Diário de Noticias*, 23-VIII-1936; "L'indépendance du gouvernement catalan", *Le Soir*, Brussels, 23-VIII-1936.

57 R. G. W., "Kataloniens Schicksal und Zukunft", *Der Morgen. Wiener Montagblatt*, 10-VIII-1936.

58 "Tour du monde", *Journal de Charleroi*, 7-VIII-1936.

59 K. Bourne, D. Cameron Watt (ed.), *British Documents on Foreign Affairs: Reports and papers from the Foreign Office confidential print. Part II, From the First to the Second World War. Series F, Europe, 1919–1939, v. 27, Spain, July 1936-January 1940*, Frederick, Md., University Publications of America, 1990, p. 28. The report is dated 31-VIII-1936.

60 Cited in J. Casanovas, "La Catalunya de Mr. King", in *Perspectiva Social*, n. 35, 1994, pp. 54–55.

61 Havas, "A Catalunha proclamará a sua independência? Continua a ser uma incógnita a atitude que, em tal caso, tomarão os anarquistas", *Diário de Noticias*, 29-VIII-1936.

62 Havas, "Os anarco-sindicalistas são os donos das vidas dos catalães", *Diário de Noticias*, 3-IX-1936; United Press, "Na Catalunha, Companys não representa coisa alguma para as turbas alucinadas", *Diário de Noticias*, 29-VIII-1936. Even within these contradictions, during the entire war, the rumour of an imminent Catalan independence was maintained, taken as real and plausible; such stories would accompany any important decision made by the Generalitat (Havas, "Na Catalunha. Os catalães desinteressam-se totalmente do Governo de Madrid", *Diário de Noticias*, 3-X-1936 or Havas, "A confusão das bandeiras e dos hinos catalães", *Diário de Noticias*, 7-X-1936).

63 K. Bourne, D. Cameron Watt (ed.), *British Documents on Foreign Affairs: Reports and papers from the Foreign Office confidential print. Part II, From the First to the Second World War. Series F, Europe, 1919–1939, v. 27, Spain, July 1936–January 1940, op. cit.*, p. 28. The report was dated 31-VIII-1936.

64 J. Casanovas, "La Catalunya de Mr. King", in *Perspectiva Social, op. cit.*, p. 56.

65 "Future of the Catalans *(The Times)*", *The Palestine Post*, 3-IX-1936.

66 "Los rebeldes anuncian para hoy la caída de Madrid", *La Tribuna Popular*, Montevideo, 25-VII-1936; "Los rebeles piensan entrar en Madrid el miércoles o el jueves", *La Tribuna Popular*, Montevideo, 28-VII-1936.

67 Archivio Storico Ministero Affari Esteri, (ASMAE), Gabinetto del Ministro e Segretaria Generale (GMSG), 1923–1943, n. 773, Corrispondeza relativa alla Guerra Civile Spagnola, Luglio–Dicembre 1936, V, Barcellona, Telegrammi di Barcellona, *Situazione Catalogna (17 agosto)*, Telegrama n. 8080 del 17-VIII-1936. A few days previously, a first reference can be found (which is not followed up in the documentation) relative to the fear of French intervention in Catalonia and to the possible reaction of Nazi Germany, when the Italian consul in Barcelona, Carlo Bossi, transmitted a declaration of the German consul of Barcelona: "This consul . . . tells me today that he has been informed by his government that in Rome it has been considered and the ambassador Von Hassel will have considered the future need to intervene in Catalonia if the situation worsens and if the French government gives too evident support to the Spanish leftists." (ASMAE, GMSG, 1923–1943, n. 1103, Informazione da Ambasciate, leg. e consolati, *Nuovo Governo Catalano. Notizie della guerra civile*, Telegram n. 7555 of 2-VIII-1936).

68 ASMAE, GMSG, 1923–1943, n. 775, Telegrammi da St. Jean-de-Luz, *Proclamazione independenza Catalogna*, Telegram n. 8263 of 21-VIII-1936. The telegram of the ambassador Pedrazzi would be transmitted to a long list of Italian legations throughout Europe and the north of Africa: London, Paris, Berlin, Moscow, Warsaw, Brussels, Lisbon, the Vatican and the International City of Tangiers. Some correspondents believed to see the same situation: H. E. Knoblaugh (for the Associated Press), "Catalonia's Secession Spurs Other Independence Move", *The Akron Beacon Journal*, Akron (Ohio), US, 20-VIII-1936.

69 "Independence of Catalonia", *Daily Advertiser*, Waga Waga, Australia, 10-IX-1936.

70 Archives du Consulat de la Belgique à Barcelone (ACBB), Barcelona, expedient "Minas de Súria", without date.

71 "The New Gouverning Council in Catalonia. Socialist, but not a Separatist or Soviet Administration", *The Manchester Guardian*, 29-X-1936.

72   F. Kuhn, "Catalonia Sets Up a Virtually Independent State", *The New York Times*, 20-VIII-1936 and AP, "Catalonia Moves Toward Secession", *The New York Times*, 20-VIII-1936.

73   "Le candide dichiarazioni di Casanova", *L'Osservatore Romano*, 28-VIII-1936.

74   "La 'Generalità' di Barcellona avrebbe deciso si staccare la Catalogna della Spagna", *La Stampa*, 21-VIII-1936.

75   J. Miravitlles [R. Batalla, ed.], *Veritats sobre la Guerra Civil Espanyola*, Barcelona, Editorial Base, 2015, p. 174.

76   See, for example: D. Abad de Santillán, *Por qué perdimos la guerra*, Barcelona, Plaza & Janés, 1977, pp. 158–191.

77   "The part of Catalonia", *The Sydney Morning Herald*, 11-IX-1936.

78   See among others concerning the assurance of the fall of Madrid and the following offensive in Catalonia: J. Guiraud, "M. Blum entre deux feux", *La Croix*, 3-XI-1936

79   G. Rotvand, "Le Cabinet de Madrid partagerait le pouvoir avec les syndicats et les extrémistes de gauche", *Le Figaro*, 5-VIII-1936.

80   G. Rotvand, "Les appréhensions de Madrid. Les gouvernementaux tenteraient une démarche à Genève", *Le Figaro*, 18-VIII-1936. Months later once again there would be speculation about the reaction of the SDN in the face of a demand for recognition of the hypothetical Catalan state in relation to the international organization (G. Rotvand, "Le recours espagnol a la S.D.N. Le gouvernement nationaliste de Burgos voit dans l'initiative de Valence une manœuvre qui doit rester sans effet", *Le Figaro*, 29-XI-1936).

81   The French preoccupation that tied the possible independence of Catalonia with the potential creation of a similar movement to take over the Catalan-French regions – as of those zones of the Basque and the Basque-French – only would be contemplated by the very extremist leader of French nationalism, Charles Maurras, "La politique. IV L'affaire catalane", *L'Action française*, 28-X-1936. This was a possibility that some rumours seem to offer, as possessing certain advantages for France. In this sense, as was reported in *Le Temps*, the British press commented the possible offer of the Balearic Islands to France made by the Generalitat in the same manner that general Franco did to Italy; *Le Temps*, "Le problème de la non-intervention en Espagne", 10-IX-1936.

82   *Journal officiel de la République française. Débats parlementaires. Chambre des députés*, 1er Séance, 5-XII-1936, p. 3342.

83   L. Romer, "L'unité espagnole", *Le Figaro*, 20-VIII-1936.

84 J. Allen, "Catalonia eyes Portugal as aid for new empire", *Chicago Tribune*, 8-XI-1936.

85 Archivo Histórico Ministerio de Relaciones Exteriores y Culto de Argentina, Leg. 5, España, Revolución, Informaciones recibidas del Consulado General en Barcelona, 2-VIII-1936, p. 3.

86 D*ez anos de Política Externa (1936–1947), a nação portuguesa e a segunda guerra mundial*, Lisbon, Ministério dos Negócios Estrangeiros, Imprensa Nacional, 1961, p. 71, report of Casanova of 3-VIII-1936 sent day 15 of that month.

87 *Ibid.*, p. 367; the report was dated 28-IX-1936.

88 USMMI, OMS, 270, fascicolo n. 1535, *Relazioni sulla permanenza a Barcellona*, report of Goiran from the ship "Alberto di Giussano", *Permanenza a Barcellona*, of 28-VIII-1936.

89 USMMI, OMS 27, fascicolo n. 160, Archivio segreto Colleoni, *Permanenza a Barcellona*, report of the admiral Goiran from the ship *Colleoni* of 11-IX-1936.

90 USMMI, OMS 268, fascicolo n. 1522, *Notizie politiche*, report of the admiral Tur sent from the ship *Eugenio di Savoia* on 16-X-1936.

91 V. Tur, *Plancia Ammiraglio*, v. 3, Rome, Canesi, 1963, pp. 231–232.

92 *Ibid.*, p. 234.

93 It appears that the national flag of each respective ship was raised in addition to the Catalan and Spanish ensigns, while playing the national anthems (W. Cortada, *A City in War: American Views on Barcelona and the Spanish Civil War, 1936–1939,* Wilmington, Scholarly Resources, 1985, p. 27).

94 M. Portela Valladares, *Memorias*, Madrid, Alianza Editorial, 1988, p. 79. The argument in question had already been published during the war in different headlines of the rebel zone: "Unas breves memorias del señor Portela", *Imperio*, Toledo, 9-X-1937 and *Heraldo de Zamora*, 8-X-1937.

95 F. De Ninno, *Fascisti sul mare. La Marina e gli ammiragli di Mussolini*, Bari, Laterza, 2017, pp. 171–172.

96 J. Massot i Muntaner, *Menorca dins del dominó mediterrani (1936–1939)*, Barcelona, Publicacions de l'Abadia de Montserrat (PAMSA), 2008, pp. 19–20.

97 On the diplomatic play concerning the Balearics, see, among others, the works of: J. Massot i Muntaner: *Vida i miracles del "Conde Rossi". Mallorca, juliol–desembre 1936/Màlaga, gener–febrer 1937,* Barcelona, Pamsa, 1988; *El cònsol Alan Hillgarth i les Illes Balears (1936–1939)*, Barcelona, Pamsa, 1995; *Menorca dins del dominó mediterrani (1936–*

1939), op. cit.; Arconovaldo Bonacorsi, el conde Rossi, Barcelona, Pamsa 2017. Evidently, the contemporary classics of the war: C. Bernieri, *Mussolini alla conquista delle Baleari,* Barcelona, CNT-FAI, 1937 (published in Spanish the same year and reedited by Malatesta, Madrid, 2012).

 98 R. Sabatier de Lachadenède, *La Marina Francesa y la Guerra Civil de España (1936–1939), op. cit.,* p. 108.

 99 *Les Archives Secrètes de la Wilhelmstrasse, III. L'Allemagne et la Guerre Civile Espagnole (1936–1939), op. cit.,* pp. 102, 107.

100 F. L. Kluckhohn, "Catalonia Offers base for Spanish Leftists", *The New York Times,* 8-XI-1936.

101 Augur, "Paris sees victory by Franco Forces", *The New York Times,* 26-VIII-1936.

102 Ch. Capus, "Séparatismes", *L'Express du Midi,* Toulouse, 8-V-1937.

103 Some newspapers would refer to this historical dynamic: "Catalan tragedy", *The Scotsman,* 6-I-1938.

104 See: J. Avilés Farré, "Un país enemigo: Franco frente a Francia, 1939–1944", in *Espacio, Tiempo y Forma,* Serie V, "H. Contemporánea", t. 7, 1994, p. 110.

105 J. Vázquez Sans, *España y Francia. Meditaciones de actualidad,* Barcelona, Imp. Ángel Ortega, Barcelona, 1939, pp. 141–142.

106 C. Reber, "La faute de l'Abbé M . . . ou de la Phalange à la Gestapo", *Ce Soir,* 28-III-1937.

107 ASPFAE, P. n. 11163, Comunicat de premsa. Le rôle de la Catalogne dans l'équilibre européen, 14-X-1937.

108 F. Pauser, *Spaniens Tor Zum Mittelmeer Und Die Katalanische Frage,* Lepizig-Berlin, Teubner, 1938, pp. 23–29. In the same line were other German authors such as Hermann Gackenholz or H. Hummel and W. Siewert, *Il Mediterraneo,* Valentino Bompiani, Milan, 1938, pp. 161–162.

109 *Axis plans in the Mediterranean: an analysis of German geopolitical ideas on Italy, France, Balearic Islands, Gibraltar, Catalonia and Spain,* London, London General Press, 1939 (also in: <http://contentdm.warwick.ac.uk/cdm/ref/collection/scw/id/16648>, consulted on 28-XI-2017).

110 F. De Ninno, *Fascisti sul mare. La Marina e gli ammiragli di Mussolini, op. cit.,* pp. 193–194.

111 E. Monroe, *Les enjeux politiques en Méditerranée,* Paris, Armand Colin, 1939, p. 129.

112 *Les Archives Secrètes de la Wilhelmstrasse, III. L'Allemagne et la Guerre Civile Espagnole (1936–1939)*, Paris, Plon, 1952, p. 13.

113 P. Gretton, *El factor olvidado. La Marina Británica y la Guerra Civil Española*, Madrid, Editorial San Martín, 1984, pp. 124–126.

114 L. Pratt, *East of Malta, West of Suez: Britain's Mediterranean Crisis, 1936–1939*, Cambridge, Cambridge University Press, 1975, p. 43.

115 ASMAE, GMSG, 1923–1943, n. 1103, Corrispondenza provinente da R. Ambasciata in Spagna, *Segreto (situazione militare franchisti. Colloquio Ferrarin-Mola)*, Telegram n. 8285 of 21-VIII-1936.

116 A. Vangraefschepe, "Une visite au front de Majorque dans les iles Baléares ou les rebelles bombardentun navire-hopital. L'audacieuse expédition de Majorque constituera une des belles pages de l'histoire du peuple catalan", *Le Peuple*, Brussels, 9-IX-1936. This article would form a part of a series – all reflected on the cover pages – on different aspects commented positively about Catalonia in war: "Un entretien avec Garcia Oliver, chef du quartier général de défense catalane", 13-IX-1936; "La justice en Catalogne. A borde de l'*Uruguay*", 26-IX-1936. A year later another series was started, in this case signed by H. Dubois, also extraordinarily positive: "Randonée en Catalogne. Force, organisation", 5-VIII-1937; "Randonée en Catalogne. À vint-cinq mètres sous terre, dans Barcelone bombardée en pleine nuit", 6-VIII-1937.

117 K. Bourne, D. Cameron Watt (ed.), *British Documents on Foreign Affairs:Reports and papers from the Foreign Office confidential print. Part II, From the First to the Second World War. Series F, Europe, 1919–1939, v. 27, Spain, July 1936–January 1940*, Frederick, Md., University Publications of America, 1990, p. 25. The report was dated 28-VIII-1936.

118 J. Casanovas, "La Catalunya de Mr. King", in *Perspectiva Social, op. cit.*, p. 55.

119 *Documenti Diplomatici Italiani*, Ottava serie, 1935–1939, v. 5, 29-IX-1936, pp. 142–143. Other sources affirmed that Catalonia would enter the SDN in the same fashion as the British Dominions ("Catalonia's intentions. Independance if Franco Wins", *West Australian*, Perth, Australia, 16-XI-1936).

120 ASPFAE, P. n. 11163-I, 1935–1936, Espagne Politique 1936, report of the ambassador Everts sent to Brussels, 22-X-1936.

121 NARA, US Barcelona General Consulate, 1936–1939, entry 3170, *President Manuel Azaña in Barcelona*, 6-XI-1936. The interview took place 24 October.

122 C. Rivas Cherif, *Retrato de un desconocido. Vida de Manuel Azaña*, II, Barcelona, Grijalbo, 1979, p. 359.

123 ASPFAE, P. n. 11059, 1936, Espagne 1936, report of the ambassador Everts sent to Brussels, 9-XI-1936.

124 In reference to Antonov-Ovseyenko and the role of Soviet diplomacy in relation to Catalonia, see: J. Puigsech, *Falsa leyenda del Kremlin. El consulado y la URSS en la Guerra Civil española*, Madrid, Biblioteca Nueva, 2014. For an example of the vision transmitted to the public opinion, see: "Il doppio gioco francese di fronte alla situazione spagnola", *Corriere della Sera*, 16-XII1-1936.

125 "No Armistice", *The Evening News*, Great Britain, 3-XI-1936. A few days earlier similar information had been published: "Bruits de tractations", *L'œuvre*, 25-X-1936.

126 "New Catalan currency", *The Manchester Guardian*, 22-XII-1936; *La Stampa*, Turin, 21-XII-1936.

127 AFS, Madrid, Politische Berichte und Briefe, Militärberichte, Band 8, 1935–1938 (Dossier), Madrid, Rapport Politique n. 29, 27-X-1936.

128 "Catalonia and Franco. Alleged Peace Offer". [*Daily Telegraph*, London], *Kalgoorlie Miner*, Australia, 17-XII-1936; "Catalonia seeks Republic", *The Courier-Mail*, Brisbane, Australia, 6-I-1937.

129 "Paris, le 26 octobre. Bulletin du jour. Les événements d'Espagne", *Le Temps*, 27-X-1936. Azaña's arrival to Barcelona had been announced several days previously ("Acharnée et féroce la lutte se poursuit en Espagne", *Le Petit Parisien*, 22-X-1936; "M. Azaña s'installe à Barcelone", *La Croix*, 23-X-1936; "Une grande tournée d'inspection du Président de la République sur les fronts de combat", *L'Humanité*, 23-X-1936, according to this article Azaña moved into the "Palau" (Palace) of the Generalitat, or L. Daudet, "Avant la prise de Madrid. Fuite d'Azaña à Barcelone", *L'Action française*, 23-X-1936, an article that discussed the danger to France implicit in the fall of Madrid and the subsequent one of Barcelona, which would provoke a wave of "Hispanic-Moscow" refugees to the north of the Pyrenees). On the other hand, concerning the desire of the Republican government to retire to Catalonia so as to convert itself into the "Bastion of the Republic" in the same fashion of the Spanish left between 1934 and 1936; see: "Lendemains espagnols", *La Croix*, 10-XI-1936. Azaña's movements in Catalonia and the relation of the Catalan authorities with the Republican government would be the object of some articles as, for example: "Déclarations du Président Azaña", *Le Petit Parisien*, 12-XI-1936.

130 "La Catalogne demande l'armistice", *L'Avenir du Luxembourg*, Belgium, 27-X-1936.

131 M. Azaña, *Causas de la guerra de España*, Madrid, Diario Público, 2011, p. 90.

132 "La journée" and "La politique étrangère et les affaires d'Espagne. Moscou s'apprêterait à coopérer activement avec les rouges pour faire de la Catalogne un Etat communiste", *La Croix*, 22-X-1936.

133 "Sowjetstaat Katalonien?", *Salzburger Volksblatt*, 22-X-1936.

134 "L'accordo tra Caballero e l'ambasciatore Rosenberg", *Corriere della Sera*, 9-VII-1937.

135 "Les visées italo-hitlériennes sur la Catalogne", *L'Humanité*, 27-X-1936. Also in: M. R. Anglès, "La presse italienne, à propos des affaires d'Espagne, attaque la Russie soviétique. Est-ce prélude d'une action diplomatique?", *Le Figaro*, 30-X-1936.

136 "La Catalogne citadelle d'imperialisme rouge", *L'Avenir de Luxembourg*, Belgium, 25-XI-1936.

137 "Antonov-Ovsejenko Kataloonia valitsuse juhi juures", *Edasi*, Estonia, 6-X-1936 or "Moscou abandonnant Madrid veut créer la République rouge de Catalogne", *L'Avenir du Luxembourg*, Belgium, 23-X-1936.

138 "Le oscure mene di Mosca per sovietizzare la Catalogna", *Corriere della Sera*, 21-X-1936. Also see, among others: "Il piano comunista per la sovietizzazione della Catalogna", *La Stampa*, 23-X-1936 and "Le disposizioni del Cominterm per l'intervento diretto in Spagna", *La Stampa*, 24-X-1936. In this last article, taken from the French press, the reference is made explicitly to the assumed approval by the Komintern of a detailed plan of action in Catalonia that would force the creation of a Catalan Soviet Republic. Halfway to such "news": D. Davidson, "Los Revolucionarios Creen Que el Viaje de M. Azaña Responde al Traslado del Gobierno", *El País*, Montevideo, 21-X-1936. And even more outstanding as the cover headline: "M. Azaña estudia en Barcelona el traslado del gobierno central de España para aquella ciudad", *El País*, Montevideo, 25-X-1936.

139 "Dopo Madrid le forze di Franco punteranno sulla Catalogna", *La Stampa*, 21-X-1936.

140 J. Miravitlles [R. Batalla, ed.], *Veritats sobre la Guerra Civil Espanyola*, *op. cit.*, p. 175.

141 J. Puigsech, "Catalunya, una nació particular des del punt de vista soviètic", in A. Gonzàlez i Vilalta, *Une Catalogne indépendante? Geopolítica europea i Guerra Civil Espanyola (1936–1939)*, Barcelona, Memorial Democràtic, 2017, pp. 242–244.

142 J. Puigsech, "Catalunya, una nació particular des del punt de vista soviètic", *op. cit.*, p. 245.

143 *Ibid.*, p. 246.

144 "Spagna. I nazionali dominano la concadi S. Sebastiano. Madrid e Barcellona sarebbero d'accordo circa la indipendenza catalana", *La Stampa*, 8-IX-1936.

145 ASPFAE, P. n. 11163-I, 1935–1936, Espagne Politique 1936, Légation à Berne (Baró Pierre van Zuylen), 8-IX-1936.

146 In fact and after the closing of the German consulate of Barcelona in November 1936, the Belgian embassy in Berlin informed their government of the nervousness existing in the top staff of the Nazi regime referring to the future "of Spain especially in reference to Catalonia" (ASPFAE, P. n. 11059, 1936, Espagne 1936, Ambassade de Berlín, 26-XI-1936).

147 ASMAE, GMSG, 1923–1943, n. 775, Telegrams from Paris, *Avvenimenti di Spagna-Catalogna*, Telegram n. 8583 of 28-VIII-1936.

148 DDI, Ottava serie, 1935–1939, v. 5, telegram from the embassy in Berlin of 2-X-1936, p. 160. The British element was given as very firm just a week later in a telegram sent by Bossi in which he affirmed that London would play the role of support of Catalan separatism, recognizing the new state in the Mediterranean picture (*ibid.*, p. 131).

149 ASMAE, GMSG, 1923–1943, n. 775, Telegrams from Paris, *Situazione in Spagna (colloquio con Ambasciatore di Germania)*, Telegram n. 11166 of 12-XI-1936. After the Italian consulate was closed in Barcelona, and in a new conversation of the Italian ambassador in Paris with Alexis Léger, the latter expressed the French assurance that Catalonia would not resist the rebel offensive any important time.

150 ASMAE, GMSG, 1923–1943, n. 775, Telegrams from Paris, *Colloquio con Leger*, Telegram n. 10408 of 19-X-1936 (published in DDI, Ottava serie, 1935–1939, v. 5, pp. 272–273). On 28-X-1936 the Italian consulate in Toulouse discussed the visit of Ventura Gassol to the French prime minister, Léon Blum, in an attempt to request aid from the French authorities (ASMAE, GMSG, 1923–1943, n. 777, Regio Consolato Tolosa, *Aiuti a Madrid*, Telegram n. 10672 of 28-X-1936).

151 ASMAE, GMSG, 1923–1943, n. 775, Telegrams from Paris, *Colloquio Leger-Cerruti su situazione in Spagna*, Telegram n. 11328 of 17-XI-1936.

152 *Archives secrètes de la Wilhelmstrasse III. L'Allemagne et la Guerre Civile Espagnole (1936–1939), op. cit.*, p. 79. The report is from 22-X-1936. For the original document: PAAA, RAV Barcelona 66, *Frage der Anerkennung der neuen spanischen regierung und gegebenenfalle einer selbatändigen katalanischen regierung durch Frankreich*, Paris, 22-X-1936.

153 G. Peri, "Les gouvernements de Rome et de Berlín préparent une démonstration navale dans les eaux espagnoles", *L'Humanité*, 5-XI-1936 and M-R. Anglès, "Comment la solidarité italo-allemande se dessine peu à peu contre la France", *Le Figaro*, 6-XI-1936. In fact, French newspapers collected some commentaries from their Nazi press that claimed that Catalonia was completely "sovietized" ("Un traité secret a-t-il été conclu entre Madrid et Moscou?", *Le Figaro*, 3-XII-1936). The French press also collected certain information, some of it critical, with the help of French (and also British) military intelligence in the Republic through the French–Catalan border: "Trois avions britanniques se rendent à Barcelone" and "Un etrange trafic aurait lieu à la frontière des Pyrénées", *Le Figaro*, 16-VIII-1936.

154 W. d'Ormesson, "La France devant le guêpier catalan", *Le Figaro*, 21-XI-1936.

155 Y. Denéchère, *Jean Herbette (1878–1960). Journaliste et ambassadeur*, Paris, Ministère des Affaires étrangères, 2003, pp. 257–315.

156 "Le débat de politique extérieure devant la Chambre", *L'Humanité*, 6-XII-1936. Also on this intervention in the National Assembly but without commentary of the newspaper ("Une demande d'interpellation de M. Henri de Kerillis", *Le Petit Parisien*, 28-XI-1936). See also in the British press the commentaries concerning the diverse interventions of Kerillis about this: "France's alleged intervention in Spain", *The Manchester Guardian*, 30-I-1937. "Manifestation à Barcelone en l'honneur de l'U.R.S.S.", *Le Petit Parisien*, 9-XI-1936; "Le 19e anniversaire de la révolution russe à Barcelone", *Le Figaro*, 9-XI-1936. The figure of the Sovietic consul would receive certain attention up to the end of his life after returning to the URSS and being arrested ("Actualités internationales", *Le Figaro*, 19-X-1937).

157 G. G. Krivitsky, *Yo, Jefe del Servicio Secreto Militar Soviético*, Guadalajara (Mexico), Nos editorial, 1945, p. 139.

158 "The Catalan Workers. An interview with the Russian Consul", *The Manchester Guardian*, 22-XII-1936.

159 ASMAE, GMSG, 1923–1943, n. 773, Corrispondeza relativa alla Guerra Civile Spagnola, Luglio–Dicembre 1936, V, Telegrammi da Barcellona, *Istituz. Consolato Gen. Sovietico con 7 funzionari*, telegram n. 9757 of 1-X-1936.

160 PAAA, RAV Barcelona, 66, *Sowjietische Lieferungen nach*, report sent from Moscow on 26-X-1936.

161 ASMAE, GMSG, 1923–1943, n. 773, Corrispondeza relativa alla Guerra Civile Spagnola, Luglio–Dicembre 1936, V, Telegrammi da Barcellona, *Rifornimenti ai "rossi"*, Telegram n. 10332 of 17-X-1936.

A day later there was insistence on the Sovietic military and diplomatic great activity in Catalonia (Archivio Centrale dello Stato, ACS, Ministero Marina, Gabinetto 1934–1950, busta n. 240, *Segreto. Rivoluzione in Spagna. Telegrammi. Volume VII*, Telegram sent from the "Eugenio di Savoia" on 18-X-1936).

162 T. Pàmies, *Quan érem Capitans (Memòries d'aquella guerra)*, Barcelona, Dopesa, 1974, p. 51. According to what can be documented, the Sovietic diplomat only received a few lessons of Catalan from the translator Francesc Payarols (P. Estelrich, "Francesc Payarols, traductor", in *Quaderns. Revista de traducció*, n. 1, 1998, p. 145).

163 ASMAE, GMSG, 1923–1943, n. 773, Corrispondeza relativa alla Guerra Civile Spagnola, Luglio–Dicembre 1936, V, Telegrammi da Barcellona, *Situazione in Spagna*, Telegram n. 11117 of 10-XI-1936. It should be stated that the Italian diplomacy also was worried about the establishment of relations between the USSR and the government of Euzkadi before the fall of the Basque area into the hands of the rebel troops.

164 Cited in J. Casanovas, "La Catalunya de Mr. King", in *Perspectiva Social*, *op. cit.*, p. 55.

165 ASMAE, GMSG, 1923–1943, n. 772, Partenza agosto 1936, *S.S. e la situazione in Spagna*, Telegram n. 4741 of 29-X-1936. On the other hand, it should be said that the Vatican press published very few references to the subject: "Il Reich contro la formazione di una repubblica comunista catalana", *L'Osservatore Romano*, 13-XII-1936.

166 USSME, OMS F6, n. 327 A, Ottobre 1936, n. 31, *Intervento russo a favore dei rossi*, Salamanca, 31-X-1936.

167 "Catalonian Republic Project", *The Scotsman*, Great Britain, 24-X-1936. Also in: "Les conversations de Berchtesgaden", *Paris-Soir*, 25-X-1936.

168 "Pact with Soviet. French Foreign Minister and Obligations", *The Scotsman*, Great Britain, 22-X-1936. Also in: "M. Delbos enlightens the Chamber", *The Irish Times*, 22-X-1936.

169 "'Anti-Red' Pact", *The Scotsman*, 4-XII-1936.

170 "Germany & Japan. A Pact Explained", *Portsmouth Evening News*, 3-XII-1936.

171 "The Spanish Danger", *Yorkshire Post*, 19-X-1936. Collected also, among others, in the "Bulletin périodique de la presse anglaise du 5 au 28 octobre 1936", p. 2 of the French Foreign Ministry.

172 Diplomaticus, "La guerre d'Espagne et l'équilibre méditerranéen", *L'Écho d'Alger*, 21-XI-1936.

173 "La Guerre Civile en Espagne. Roma et Berlín reconnaissent le gouver-
    nement du général Franco", *La Croix*, 20-XI-1936. This opinion was
    maintained the following day (J. Caret, "L'inquiétude européenne",
    La Croix, 21-XI-1936 and also in: "L'U.R.S.S. va-t-elle reconnaitre la
    République Catalane?", *Le Figaro*, 19-XI-1936.

174 "L'Italie et les affaires d'Espagne", *Le Temps*, 2-XI-1936. Also in
    "Manœuvre du Kominterm dit-on à Rome", *Le Petit Parisien*, 29-XI-
    1936.

175 M-R. Anglès, "L'Italie contre l'attitude des soviets", *Le Figaro*, 14-
    XI-1936 and M-R. Anglès, "L'Italie déclare que son action restera
    dans le cadre de l'accord de non intervention", *Le Figaro*, 24-XI-
    1936. Previously, "La bataille reprend sur les fronts de Madrid. Le
    général Queipo de Llano menace la Catalogne d'une intervention des
    puissances fascistes", *L'Humanité*, 3-XI-1936. In the same way that
    the powers allied with Franco were opposed to any and all Soviet
    influence, they were also against all plan of peace that contemplated
    any kind of independence referendum for Catalonia which, as
    believed by Berlin, Rome and Lisbon, would end up with a new
    Soviet republic in the western Mediterranean ("La Guerre Civile en
    Espagne. Le Vatican faite des réserves sur le projet de médiation", *Le
    Figaro*, 14-XII-1936).

176 ASMAE, GMSG, 1923–1943, n. 773, Corrispondeza relativa alla
    Guerra Civile Spagnola, Luglio–Dicembre 1936, V, Barcellona,
    Telegrammi di Barcellona, *Rivoluzione spagnuola*, Telegram n. 8660 of
    4-IX-1936.

177 ASMAE, GMSG, 1923–1943, n. 773, Corrispondeza relativa alla
    Guerra Civile Spagnola, Luglio–Dicembre 1936, V, Telegrammi in
    arrivo da Berlino, *Visita S.E. Ciano (Protocollo analogo questione cata-
    lana)*, Telegram n. 10308 of 16-X-1936 (published in the DDI,
    Ottava serie, 1935–1939, v. 5, p. 253). Weeks later there would be
    insistence on the possible aid, now combined between Great Britain
    and France, for the pro-independence hopes of certain political sectors
    of the Catalan and Basque areas. This possibility was refused once again
    by Léger from Paris: "Léger has answered me that the British interest
    in the Spanish Basque region is comprensible because there the largest
    number of British citizens live, who have considerable interests. Léger
    excludes nevertheless that there is any British intention of help the
    Basque nationalist movement, nor the Catalan one [...]." (ASMAE,
    GMSG, 1923–1943, n. 775, Telegrammi da Parigi, *Governo inglese e
    governo separatista basco*, Telegram n. 11731 of 27-XI-1936). Already

weeks before the consul Bossi had informed of the assumed petition of protection of some elements of the Generalitat in Great Britain (ACS, Ministero Marina, Gabinetto 1934–1950, busta n. 240, *Segreto. Rivoluzione in Spagna. Telegrammi. Volume V*, Telegram sent from the "Colleoni" on 11-IX-1936).

178 "La Guerra Civile en Espagne. Un avertissement à la Catalogne", *Le Figaro*, 2-XI-1936 or "Recognition Question", *The Yorkshire Post and Leeds Intelligencer*, Great Britain, 2-XI-1936. In a similar sense and referring to the Nazi inclination to recognize Franco and attack Catalonia also, "La réunion de Vienne et l'opinion italienne. Les protocoles de Rome et l'accord austro-allemand", *Le Figaro*, 11-XI-1936. Days later, the press speculated about the Italian-German recognition of the Franco government and the degree of control sustained by the Republican government of the socialist Largo Caballero over Catalonia ("Rome et Berlín reconnaissent le gouvernement Franco", *Le Petit Parisien*, 19-XI-1936, also in *Le Figaro*).

179 "Auch Katalonien wird befreit", *Berliner Taglebatt*, 26-XI-1936.

180 G. Ciano, *L'Europa verso la catastrofe*, Milan, Mondadori, 1948, p. 89 (in the Spanish version, *Europa hacía la catastrofe*, p. 50). It should be pointed out that in the pacts signed by Fascist Italy and "National" Spain, the will to maintain the integrity of the Spanish territory was made explicit. See, for example, the first point of the protocol signed by Franco and Ciano on 28-XI-1936 (ASMAE, Gabinetto del Ministro e Segretaria Generale 1923–1943, from here on GMSG, 1923–1943), b. 1160, *Spagna. Documenti segreti. 6. – Protocollo del 28-XI-1936*) or that the German press denied any intention of taking over any territory by Rome or Berlin (*Berliner Börsen-Zeitung*, 27-X-1936, collected in the "Bulletin périodique de la presse allemande du 12 octobre au 8 novembre 1936", p. 7 of the French Foreign Ministry).

181 "Ciano atvyksta i Berlyna", *Vakarai*, Lithuania, 21-X-1936; United Press, "Se dará un comunicado acerca de la visita del Conde Ciano a Alemania", *El País*, Montevideo, 23-X-1936.

182 R. de Marès, "L'Europe et la crise espagnole", *Le Soir*, Brussels, 1-XII-1936. See many other editorials, for example, the cover article of M. Reymond, "Politique Étrangère. Les deliberations de Berlin", *Tribune de Lausanne*, Switzerland, 29-X-1936. The fear of a Catalan Bolschevik nucleus lasted in the articles of Reymond, as for example: "Politique Étrangère. Situation confuse", 26-XI-1936.

183 G. Gonella, "Acta diurna. Dall Mediterraneo all'Estremo Oriente", *L'Osservatore Romano*, 20-XI-1936.

184 *Le Soir*, 2-XII-1936.

185 "Hear Nazi Subs Ready to Raid Barcelona", *The Toronto Daily Star*, 27-X-1936.

186 "Moskauer borbereitungen fur eine 'Sowjetrepublik Katalonien'", *Völkischer Beobachter*, Berlin, 23-X-1936.

187 "Offizielle Sowjetisierung Kataloniens", *Berliner Taglebatt*, 23-X-1936; "Sowjet Barcelona", *Berliner Taglebatt*, 24-XI-1936.

188 "Was Wird Moskau tun?", *Berliner Taglebatt*, 24-X-1936.

189 *Foreign relations of the United States diplomatic papers, 1936. Europe*, Spain, p. 544, report of 29-X-1936, accessible at: <http://digicoll.library.wisc.edu/cgi-bin/FRUS/FRUS-idx?id=FRUS.FRUS1936v02> [consulted on 31-I-2017].

190 A few days after the Italian–German diplomatic recognition of Franco, the German consulate in Barcelona sent various press articles (from *Las Notícias* and *La humanitat*) that denounced the intervention of Rome and Berlin in the war, as well as the aid given to the rebels (PAAA, Rav Barcelona, 66, *Berichttsdurchschlaege*, without specific dates in November of 1936).

191 *Foreign relations of the United States diplomatic papers, 1936. Europe*, Spain, p. 548, the report was of the ambassador Dodd in Berlin dated 3-XI-1936, accessible at: <http://digicoll.library.wisc.edu/cgi-bin/FRUS/FRUS-idx?id=FRUS.FRUS1936v02> [consulted on 31-I-2017].

192 *Foreign relations of the United States diplomatic papers, 1936. Europe, Spain*, p. 544, the report is from 29-X-1936, accessible at: <http://digicoll.library.wisc.edu/cgi-bin/FRUS/FRUS-idx?id=FRUS.FRUS1936v02> [consulted on 31-I-2017].

193 *Foreign relations of the United States diplomatic papers, 1936. Europe, Spain*, p. 560, the report is from 19-XI-1936, accessible at: <http://digicoll.library.wisc.edu/cgi-bin/FRUS/FRUS-idx?> [consulted on 31-I-2017].

194 K. Bourne, D. Cameron Watt (ed.), *British Documents on Foreign Affairs: Reports and papers from the Foreign Office confidential print. Part II, From the First to the Second World War. Series F, Europe, 1919–1939, v. 27, Spain, July 1936–January 1940*, Frederick, Md., University Publications of America, 1990, p. 69. The report is from 3-I-1937. Also the same information is repeated in the British press: "Independence of Catalonia position in federal Spain", *The Times*, London, 5-I-1937.

195 PRO, Foreign Office 371/20545-W 14590/62/41. For the Catalan

version: G. Mir, *Aturar la guerra. Les gestions secretes de Lluís Companys davant del govern britànic*, Barcelona, Proa, 2006, pp. 362–365.

196 PRO Foreign Office 371/20545-W 14590/62/41, Ibid., 30-X-1936.

197 "I resultati dei colloqui di Berlino. L'integrità della Spagna", *La Stampa*, 26-X-1936. For the conversations and the Italian-German position in relation of the Spanish civil war and those of elements of European politics, see for example the exhaustive detailed descriptions done by *Il Popolo d'Italia* between 20 and 28-X-1936.

198 "Visit of Count Ciano to Berlin", *Dundee Evening Telegraph*, Great Britain, 20-X-1936.

199 G. Rotvand, "La Guerre Civile en Espagne. La prise de Navalcarnero ouvre aux nationaux la route de la capitale", *Le Figaro*, 23-X-1936 and "L'Allemagne et l'Italie sont d'accord pour établir un front antisovié-tique", *Le Figaro*, 24-X-1936; "Le séjour du comte Ciano en Allemagne", *Le Temps*, 25-X-1936. Weeks later, G. Rotvand would insist on an Italian-German agreement to avoid the creation of an inde-pendent Catalonia ("La Guerre Civile en Espagne. Rome et Berlín se préparent-ils à aider ouvertement le gouvernement de Franco?", *Le Figaro*, 18-XI-1936). *L'Action française* of 24-X-1936 was the only paper that published the points of the Ciano–Neurath agreement clearly. The fourth point explicitly indicated the opposition to the creation of an independent and communist Catalan Republic.

200 J. Jolinon, "Chantage au feu", *L'Humanité*, 29-X-1936.

201 G. Tabouis, "Après la visite du Comte Ciano. Une alliance italo-alle-mande serait conclue contre l'U.R.S.S.", *L'Œuvre*, 24-X-1936.

202 G. Guêze, "Les idees et les faits. Espagne et Catalogne", *L'Express du Midi*, Toulouse, 24-X-1936.

203 "Vingt-trois navires soviétiques chargés d'armes pour l'Espagne auraient franchi les Dardanelles", *Le Figaro*, 28-X-1936.

204 J. L., "Le separatisme catalan", *L'Express du Midi*, Toulouse, 21-X-1936. Previously he had published, with the same title, a first part on 17-X-1936.

205 ASMAE, GMSG, 1923–1943, n. 773, Corrispondeza relativa alla Guerra Civile Spagnola, Luglio–Dicembre 1936, V, Telegrammi da Barcellona, *Discorso del Duce a Milano e situazione a Barcellona*, Telegram n. 10955 of 4-XI-1936. The Soviet press reflected the agreement and the accusations of control against Moscow: "Um jornalista de Moscou nega que o governo da Catalunha seja soviético e acusa a Itália e a Alemanha de conspiração para o destruir", *Diário de Noticias*, New Jersey, United States, 28-X-1936.

206 ASMAE, GMSG, 1923–1943, b. 1432, (US 226), *Guerra Civile spagnola atteggiamento della Germania. Collaborazione italo-tedesca negli aiuti al generale Franco*, 29-XII-1936. Report sent from Salamanca to the Foreign Affairs Minister Galeazzo Ciano.

207 Instrucción del Ministerio de Exteriores Alemán a Legación alemana ante el Cuartel General franquista en Salamanca, Berlín, 21.1.1937 (PAAA, R 60533), in: X.M. Núñez Seixas, "Nacionalismos periféricos y fascismo: Acerca de un memorándum catalanista a la Alemania nazi (1936)" in *Historia Contemporánea* (Universidad del País Vasco), n. 7, 1992, pp. 311–333.

208 *Ibid.* Letter of Werner Hasselblatt to General Wilhelm Faupel, Berlín, 15.1.1937 (PAAA, R 60533).

209 "Italia insinúa que no tolerará una base comunista en España", *El País*, Montevideo, 2-I-1937. And, in the same newspaper and on the same day, a note from the United Press, "Italia no acepta en Cataluña una base comunista".

210 P. Gretton, *El factor olvidado. La Marina Británica y la Guerra Civil Española*, Madrid, Editorial San Martín, 1984, p. 286.

211 *Ibid.*, pp. 279–288.

212 "Un'altra realizzazzione della política del Duce", *Corriere della Sera*, 3-I-1937; "Britain and Italy Sign Accord for Mediterranean Harmany", *The New York Times*, 3-I-1937. The same news will be sent around the world, as for example: "Italy Will Not Allow Soviet in Catalonia", *The Jerusalem Post*, 6-I-1937.

213 "L'eco mondiale dell'intesa italo-britannica. Documenti", *Corriere della Sera*, 5-I-1937; see also: "Accordo mediterraneo e incognita spagnola", *Corriere della Sera*, 6-I-1937. La claredat de la premsa italiana era recollida per la britànica: "Mediterranean Pact. Italian 'Reservations' About Catalonia. 'No 'Red' Republic'", *The Scotsman*", 5-I-1937.

214 "Tension in Europe Graver", *Western Daily Press*, Great Britain, 5-I-1937.

215 Cited in web: <http://www.adamoli.org/benito-mussolini/pag0644-.htm> [consulted 28-IV-2017].

216 "News of the week. Mr. Eden on Spain", *The Spectator*, Great Britain, 22-I-1937.

217 A. Eden, *Memorias, 1923–1938. Frente a los dictadores*, Barcelona, Noguer, 1962, p. 566; and the original: *Facing the Dictators*, Boston, Houghton Mifflin, 1962, p. 487. On the pact, among other sources: P. Nello, *Dino Grandi*, Bologna, Il Mulino, 2003, pp. 167–185; R. Lamb, *Mussolini e gli inglesi*, Milan, Tea, 2002, pp. 249–255.

218 "Lo que nos interesa del pacto italo-inglés", *Lucha*, 8-I-1937.

219 "En virtud del Pacto de Roma, Inglaterra no consentirá una Cataluña independiente", *Labor*, 11-I-1937.

220 A. Cortesi, "Italians Hope Mediterranean Pact Will Be Barrier to Soviets in Catalonia", *The New York Times*, 10-I-1937. This was what was believed by readers of the British press: A. Berriedale, "The Spanish Situation", *The Scotsman*, 6-I-1937.

221 R. Quartararo, *Roma tra Londra e Berlino. La politica estera fascista dal 1930 al 1940*, Rome, Jouvence, 2001 [1980] v. I., pp. 434–446; E. Moradiellos, *La perfidia de Albión. El Gobierno británico y la guerra civil española*, Madrid, Siglo XXI, 1996, pp. 125–131.

222 *Archives secrètes de la Wilhelmstrasse III. L'Allemagne et la Guerre Civile Espagnole (1936–1939)*, Paris, Librairie Plon, 1952, p. 127.

223 "Un accordo di enorme valore per la stabilità europea", *Corriere della Sera*, 4-I-1937.

224 J. Rabassa Massons, *Josep Dencàs i Puigdollers. El nacionalisme radical a la Generalitat*, Barcelona, Rafael Dalmau editor, 2006, p. 126.

225 USMM, OMS, n. 29, fascicolo 175, telegram from Admiral Goiran from the "Fiume" to the Navy Headquarters of 2-VIII-1936. An incomplete summary of this telegram in: ASMAE, GMSG, 1923–1943, n. 777, Naval Ministry, Telegram of 2-VIII-1936.

226 The arrest of Dencàs, which was made public by the international press ("Italy Arrests Fugitive", *Chicago Daily Tribune*, 14-VIII-1936 or "Exministro catalano incarcerato a Genova", *L'Osservatore Romano*, 15-VIII-1936) would provoke some reactions that attempted to alliviate his situation, such as that of the Montserrat monk Pere Damià Garriga who arriving in Italy attempted to realize some initiatives in his favor (H. Raguer, *Arxiu de la l'Església catalana durant la guerra civil. I. Juliol-desembre 1936*, Barcelona, PAMSA, 2003, pp. 242–243).

227 ASMAE, GMSG, 1923–1943, n. 777, Naval Ministry, Telegram of 13-VIII-1936. It should be stated that in no case was reference made to the political antecedents of Dencàs and to his contacts with the consulate in 1934. The information concerning Dencàs' arrest arrived very quickly to Catalonia. For example: "Josep Dencàs, expulsat d'Estat Català pel delicte de deserció. El fugitiu del 6 d'octubre no ha parat fins a Gènova", *La humanitat*, 16-VIII-1936 or "Josep Dencàs detingut a Itàlia i expulsat d'Estat Català", *Diari de Tarragona*, 16-VIII-1936. The spokesman of his former party did not want to hear of him nor to know about any relation with Fascist Italy: "From a telegram we found yesterday Dencàs [was] under the domination of

Mussolini. The news has been confirmed. The fact of his confinement or imprisonment in Marassi does not interest us. It has the same value if he has been persecuted by Mussolini, or if he has been protected by Mussolini [...]." ("El senyor Dencàs", *La humanitat*, 18-VIII-1936). The information was public at the European level: "En Catalogne. Un ex-ministre catalan, réfugié en Italie, est interné", *Le Soir*, Brussels, 15-VIII-1936.

228 The documentation concerning Dencàs and Glanadell Torras which should exist in the Italian Foreign Affairs, if not in the daily inventory of 1936, has disappeared; one can see the empty folder with his name. The *sotofascicolo*, despite all the remarkable work by the archivists of the Farnesina, has not appeared in any archive.

229 Archivio di Stato di Genova, Prefettura di Genova, Profughi della Spagna, series of three telegrams without date and a last one dated 23-VIII-1936.

230 See: E. Ucelay-Da Cal, A. Gonzàlez i Vilalta, X. M. Núñez Seixas (ed.), *El catalanisme davant del feixisme (1919–2018)*, Maçanet de la Selva, Gregal, 2018.

231 See: E. Ucelay-Da Cal, A. Gonzàlez i Vilalta (ed.), *Contra Companys, 1936. La frustración nacionalista ante la Revolución*, Valencia, PUV, 2012.

232 "Separatisten von Anarchisten erschossen", *Deutsches Nachrichtenbüro*, 12-XII-1936; Reuter, "Alleged Plot in Catalonia", *Yorkshire Post and Leeds Intelligencer*, Great Britain, 1-XII-1936; "Companys door anarchisten gearresteerd?", *De Indische Courant*, Netherlands, 1-XII-1936.

233 According to what is affirmed in the memoirs of the ERC deputy, Miquel Guinart, *Memòries d'un militant catalanista*, Barcelona, PAMSA, 1988, pp. 6 and 67, he saved Maspons i Anglasell (Barcelona, 1872; Bigues, 1966) from the revolutionary violence in Lleida during the first days of the war.

234 A very similar request, perhaps the same one, was insinuated about the cousin of the mayor of Barcelona, Carles Pi i Sunyer, who in the name of this second individual requested from Bossi an Italian intervention from Franco. The proposal was the surrender of Catalonia in exchange for the maintenance of autonomy, so as to avoid the destruction of the country (USMMI, OMS 268, fascicolo n. 1522, *Relazione sulla situazione politico-militare in Catalogna {Avvenimenti dal 16 ottobre al 10 novembre}*, report of the Admiral Vittorio Tur written from the ship *Eugenio di Savoia* on 10-XI-1936).

235 "Katalonia peab läbirää kimisi mässajatega", *Päevaleht*, 17-VIII-1936.

236 ASMAE, GMSG, 1923–1943, 1923–1943, b. 775, *Proposta trattativa fra Governo catalano e nazionalista di Burgos*, 16-XI-1936, p. 1 (reproduced in the *Documenti Diplomatici Italiani*, Ottava Serie 1935–1939, Volume 5, pp. 465–466). The telegram was sent afterwards to Budapest where the minister Ciano had to make an official visit. Also, his bureau head sent a note to Mussolini in which the plan was announced, albeit with prudence. As De Peppo in the Italian foreign ministry argued at the time, the parties that proposed the pact were the same as those responsible for the situation of lack of order existing in Catalonia, even if, on the other hand, such a reality could change rapidly.

237 ASMAE, GMSG, 1923–1943, b. 775, *Proposta trattativa fra Governo catalano e nazionalista di Burgos*, 16-XI-1936, p. 4.

238 ASMAE, GMSG, 1923–1943, b. 1102, *Spagna, Anfuso (Comm.) Misione in Spagna*, 23-XI-1936. An almost identical reply would be given to the representatives of the Basque Nationalist Party (PNV) a few days later (Archivo del Nacionalismo vasco, Fondos del PNV, BBB-280-2, *Nota reservada para el Sr. Ajuriaguerra presidente del Bizkai Buru Batzar*, December 1936).

239 In a telegram dated 26-XI-1936, Rome informed his delegate to Franco that Bossi leaving Barcelona would eliminate the possibility of contacting with Maspons i Anglasell (ASMAE, GMSG, 1923–1943, b. 1102, *Spagna, Anfuso {Comm.} Misione in Spagna.*)

240 Diplomaticus, "La guerre d'Espagne et l'équilibre méditerranéen", *L'Écho d'Alger*, 21-XI-1936.

241 Uficcio Storico dello Stato Maggiore dell'Esercito (USSME), F 18 OMS, fascicolo n. 14, telegram of 12-I-1937.

242 G. Péri, "Les nuages de l'invasion fasciste. Méditerranée . . . ", *L'Humanité*, 10-X-1937.

243 "La Crise Catalane", *Le Temps*, 2-VII-1937.

244 A. Benedetti, "Un anno di guerra in Spagna", *Corriere della Sera*, 17-VII-1937.

245 In reference to the relations between Catalans and Basques, it is curious to point out that I can only locate a short note describing the arrival of the Lehendakari Aguirre to Barcelona ("La guerre civile en Espagne. Le président du gouvernement basque M. Aguirre se rend à Barcelone", *Le Temps*, 5-XII-1937).

246 J. C., "La question de la Catalogne", *La Croix*, 8-I-1937. One should be very aware of the vocabulary used by certain part of the press in relation to Euzkadi, for example, at the moment of the approval of the

Basque Statute: United Press, "La Nación Vasca juró lealtad al gobierno español", *El País*, Montevideo, 9-X-1936.

247 "L'Angleterre opposée à l'établissement d'un Etat soviétique en Espagne", *La Croix*, 5-I-1937 and also in "L'Allemagne répondrait demain à la note franco-anglaise", *Le Petit Parisien*, 5-I-1937. In the same sense, M-R. Anglés, "L'accord anglo-italien", *Le Figaro*, 4-I-1937. Some days later *Le Temps* and *Le Figaro* reproduced an interview of Benito Mussolini that had appeared in the German press in which he emphasized that he would not permit any kind of Soviet installation in Spain or in a concrete territory such as Catalonia ("Une interview du Duce", *Le Temps*, 18-I-1937 or "M. Mussolini affirme que le bloc germano-italien est intangible", *Le Figaro*, 19-I-1937).

248 J. Delebecque, "Nouveaux dangers de l'affaire espagnole", *L'Action française*, 4-I-1937. A few days later and on the cover, the same author insisted that if one day a so-feared independent and Soviet Catalonia was created, the "eternal" Spain would not permit ir to live long ("L'Espagne eternelle", *L'Action française*, 9-I-1937).

249 "La Pasionaria met le peuple espagnol en garde contre les ennemis de l'arrière", *L'Humanité*, 12-VIII-1937.

250 "La Guerre Civile en Espagne. Attaques nationalistes, contre-attaques gouvernementales sur le front de Madrid", *La Croix*, 15-I-1937.

251 G. Rotvand, "La Catalogne négocierait avec Franco", *Le Figaro*, 10-II-1937.

252 G. Rotvand, "La résistance rouge va-t-elle s'effondrer?", *Le Figaro*, 15-II-1937.

253 Companys' reply, through Martí Rouret, was more than firm about the impossibility of establishing any negotiation of these characteristics (cited in J. Sánchez Cervelló, *¿Por qué hemos sido derrotados? Las divergències republicanes y otras cuestiones*, Barcelona, Flor del Viento, 2006, pp. 199–200).

254 J. M. Batista i Roca, "Letters to the Editor. Catalonia's part in the Spanish Civil War. Loyal Solidarity with the Republican Forces", *The Manchester Guardian*, Great Britain, 29-III-1937.

255 "Pas de paix séparée entre la Catalogne et le général Franco", *La Croix*, 12-IX-1937. Months before the Catalan delegation in Paris had had to claim as false an assumed Franco plot in Barcelona ("Il n'y a pas eu de complot à Barcelone", *L'Humanité*, 17-I-1937). Between one question and another, the US consulate in Barcelona received another note of the same nature (NARA, US Barcelona General Consulate, 1936–1939, entry 3170, box 31, 14-VII-1937). Much before, a few weeks

after the start of the war, the official Nazi news agency, the DNB, collected rumours of supposed offers of contact from the Generalitat ("Katalanische Regierung sucht Fühlung mit Burgos?", *Deutsches Nachrichtenbüro*, 17-VIII-1936).

256 "La Catalogne ne pactisera 'jamais avec l'ennemi', déclare M. Companys", *La Croix*, 19-IX-1937.

257 "En Espagne", *La Croix*, 21-IX-1937. Before, for example, on the cover: "Grave Peril Faces Madrid in Catalonia", *St. Petersburg Times*, Florida (US), 27-VIII-1937.

258 "Une mise au point à Barcelone", *Le Petit Parisien*, 12-XI-1937.

259 "M. Companys regagne Barcelone", *La Croix*, 16-XI-1937; "M. Companys a quitté Bruxelles", *Le Petit Parisien*, 16-XI-1937 or "Il n'est pas question d'armistice entre Salamanque et Barcelone", *Ce Soir*, 15-XI-1937.

260 M. Chaves Nogales, "M. Ossorio y Gallardo prend possession de son poste", *Ce Soir*, 2-VI-1937.

261 Stopping in Paris, see: "Le président Companys a traversé la capitale", *Le Petit Parisien*, 13-XI-1937. In reference to his stay in Brussels, the Delegation of the Generalitat in the Belgian capital had to declare as false that the Catalan President had met with any diplomat to negotiate anything with the Franco side: "M. Companys entend garder l'incognit en Belgique" and "L'arrivée du Président catalan", *Le Petit Parisien*, 15-XI-1937. See also the French diplomatic sources: CADN, AM, Série B, n. 554, 17-XI-1937. It should be remarked that when Companys' son left Catalonia there was a press note in which *The Times*, indicated he had left with the French vessel *Commandant Teste* ("Le fils du général [sic] Companys débarque à Toulon", *Le Soir*, Brussels, 23-VIII-1936).

262 See the report of the Propaganda Comissary and its section of Foreign Affairs of 18-IX-1937 on this question, in:
< http://www.memoria.cat/lluis-companys-avila/1891937-carta-de-josep-maria-batista-i-roca-a-lluis-companys-i-diversos-documents-que-li-adjunta-en> [consulted on 13-IV-2018].

263 H. Delmas, "Une trêve des armes est-elle possible en Espagne? Déclarations du président Companys à notre envoyé spécial Henri Delmas", *Le Petit Parisien*, 22-V-1937.

264 K. Bourne, D. Cameron Watt (ed.), *British Documents on Foreign Affairs: Reports and papers from the Foreign Office confidential print. Part II, From the First to the Second World War. Series F, Europe, 1919–1939, v. 27, Spain, July 1936–January 1940*, Frederick, Md., University

Publications of America, 1990, pp. 90–91. The report is from 23-II-1937.

265 J. Avilés Farré, *Pasión y farsa. Franceses y británicos ante la Guerra Civil Española*, Madrid, Eudema, 1994, p. 86. The meeting therefore with the supposed intentions of Gassol would be announced in the press (*Northern Daily Mail*, Great Britain, 7-XI-1936). Days before he had passed through Geneva and Brussels ("Autour du conflit. M. Ventura Gassol en Belgique?", *Le Soir*, Brussels, 29-X-1936).

266 I have not been able to find any report concerning the meeting of Pingaud with Companys on 25 January ("Generalidad de Cataluña. Aclaraciones", *La Vanguardia*, 24-I-1937).

267 CADN, AM, Série B, n. 554, Conversation avec le Président de la Généralité, 27-IV-1937. Report sent by the Barcelona consulate to the Ministry of Foreign Affairs and, from there, to the French embassy in Spain on 11-V-1937.

268 CADN, AM, Série B, n. 554, Telegram sent from Paris on 12-V-1937.

269 CADN, CB, Gces., Dépêches politiques, Correspondance Confidentielle (1936–1939), Tractations entre nationalistes et Catalans, sent by the Barcelona consul to the Quai d'Orsay, 18-II-1937.

270 J. Miravitlles, "Parallélisme", *Le Journal de Barcelone*, Paris, 27-I-1937.

271 P-L. Berhaud, "La Catalogne et l'Espagne de demain", *La Revue hebdo madaire*, 31-X-1936, p. 585.

272 Archives de la Société des Nations (ASDN), Ginebra, R. 3659, 1933–1937, dossier 17950, Political situation in Spain, Various correpondance, 2-IX-1937.

273 J. Avilés Farré, *Pasión y farsa*, *op. cit.*, p. 128.

274 Companys would received many visits of international well-known figures. Each consulate would study what was important to its own internal policy. For example, in July 1937, the US representation would comment the presence of the leader of the Socialist Party of the United States, Norman Thomas, in Barcelona (NARA, US Barcelona General Consulate, 1936–1939, entry 3170, box 31, Norman Thomas in Barcelona, 25-V-1937).

275 *Documents Diplomatiques Français* (DDF), 1932–1939, 2ª Série (1936–1939), Tome VIII (17 Janvier–20 Mars 1938), Imprimerie Nationale, 1973, Paris, Note du Cabinet du Ministre, 18-III-1938, pp. 936–937.

276 See in general the telegrams of Checoslavakian diplomacy, but especially those of 1938, as reordered by the Nazis, in F. Berber, *La política europea desde 1933 a 1938 reflejada en los documentos de Praga*, Berlin,

Publicaciones del Instituto Alemán para Investigaciones de Política Exterior, [1940?], pp. 83–96.

277 R. Sabatier de Lachadenède, *La Marina Francesa y la Guerra Civil de España (1936–1939)*, *op. cit.*, p. 303.

278 An abbreviated explanation of this incident in: J.M. Reverte, "Cuando Francia quiso invadir España. El Gobierno frente populista de Léon Blum debatió sobre la intervención militar el 15 de marzo de 1938", *El País*, 10-XII-2006. Also in: Michel Catala, "L'attitude de la France face à la Guerre d'Espagne: l'échec des négociations pour la reconnaissance du gouvernement franquiste en 1938", in *Mélanges de la Casa de Velázquez*, tome 29-3, 1993, pp. 243–262 or E. Moradiellos, *Negrín. Una biografía de la figura más difamada de la España del siglo XX*, Barcelona, Península, 2006, pp. 135–138.

279 A-A. Inquimbert, *Un officier français dans la guerre d'Espagne. Carrière et écrits d'Henri Morel (1919–1944)*, Rennes, Presses Universitaires de Rennes-Service Historique de la Défense, 2009, pp. 218–220. For a short summary of Morel and his position, see by the same author: "Monsieur Blum . . . un roi de France ferait la guerre", a *P.U.F.*, 2004/3, pp. 35–45.

280 R. de Marès, "L'autre danger", *Le Soir*, 17-III-1938. The following day there was insistence on the danger of the Italian–Franco advance up to the border in Catalonia: R. de Marès, "De l'Autriche à l'Espagne", *Le Soir*, 18-III-1938.

281 "Spain's Crisis", *Gloucestershire Echo*, Great Britain, 16-III-1938; "France's difficulties", *The Yorkshire Post and Leeds Intelligencer*, West Yorkshire, Great Britain, 16-III-1938.

282 "Government may armistice", *Yorkshire Post and Leeds Intelligencer*, *op. cit.*, 16-III-1938.

283 *L'Écho d'Alger*, 18-III-1938.

284 Stefani, "La pressione dei rossi su Blum per l'intervento in Spagna", *Corriere della Sera*, 23-III-1938. The Flemish Belgian press used much more prudence: "De oorlog in Spanje. De tweede phase van het Franco-offensief op Catalonië", *Ht Handelsblad van Antwerpen*, Antwerp, 23-III-1938. Although a few days later everything would change and the central part of the front page would headline the rumours of the Catalan incorporation into France: Taxander, "Catalonië", *Het Handelsblad van Antwerpen*, Antwerp, 4-IV-1938.

285 "Negrín ha offerto allà Francia il protettorato della Catalogna", *Corriere della Sera*, 23-III-1938.

286 "Il a tout de même question de céder la Catalogne à la France", *L'Avenir du Luxembourg*, Belgium, 31-III-1938.

287 For example, the Brussels delegation indicating false information: "Un démenti de la Généralité de Catalogne", *L'Avenir de Luxembourg*, Belgium, 24-III-1938.

288 K. Bourne, D. Cameron Watt (ed.), *British Documents on Foreign affairs: Reports and papers from the Foreign Office confidential print. Part II, From the First to the Second World War. Series F, Europe, 1919–1939, v. 27, Spain, July 1936–January 1940, op. cit.*, p. 184, Paris, report of 7-IV-1938.

289 ASV, Sacra Congregazione degli Affari Ecclesiastici Straordinari (SCAES), Spagna, 1936–1939, Pos. 899 P.O., Fasc, 303, Visita del Sig. Paul-Boncour, letter of the "Nunciatura Apostòlica" of France to the Secretary of State of 28-III-1938, p. 33.

290 G. Borzoni, *Renato Prunas diplomatico (1892–1951)*, Catanzaro, Rubbettino, 2004, pp. 96–97.

291 "L'unione allà Francia della Catalogna progettata a Barcellona?", *La Stampa*, 22/23-V-1938.

292 Cited in R. Miralles, "Georges Bonnet y la política española del Quai d'Orsay: 1938–1939", in *Mélanges de la Casa de Velázquez*, Tome 30–3, 1994, p. 129.

293 Precisely in reference to former Defense minister Indalecio Prieto, the Swiss legation in Madrid affirmed at this time that the Generalitat and its president Lluís Companys were compromised more than ever with the stability of the Republican government and with the leadership of Prieto (AFS, Madrid, Politische Berichte und Briefe, Militärberichte, Band 8, 1935–1938 (Dossier), Madrid, 5-III-1938).

294 During these days there was speculation on a supposed negotiation of the Spanish Republican government in Paris concerning the independence of Catalonia ("Catalonia's Status", *The West Australian*, Perth, Australia, 17-III-1938); "Armistice in Spain urged. Independance For Catalonia", *The Courier-Mail*, Brisbane, Australia, 29-III-1938.

295 This was news that appeared in the *Manchester Guardian* of 19-V-1938 collected in the "Bulletin périodique de la presse anglaise du 13 avril à 22 mai 1938"", p. 14 of the French Ministry of Foreign Affairs.

296 The arrival of Carme Ballester to Paris was reported in the graphic pages of the French press: *Ce Soir*, 8-IV-1938. Previous trips by Ballester had also been reported in the press ("Nouvelles diverses. Mme

Companys est partie pour Paris", *Tribune de Lausanne*, Switzerland, 1-XI-1936).

297 CADN, AM, Série B, n. 585, Guerre Civil d'Espagne, Avril 1938, Situation politique et militaire, La Catalogne et la résistance. – Eventualités., 19-IV-1938.

298 "À propos d'un faux bruit. Un deménti catalan" and "Ce que dit M. Vandervelde", *Le Soir*, Brussels, 23-III-1938.

299 "À l'Occident", *Journal de Genève*, 2-IV-1938.

300 "Rectification", *Journal de Genève*, 3-IV-1938.

301 *Archives secrètes de la Wilhelmstrasse III. L'Allemagne et la Guerre Civile Espagnole (1936–1939)*, *op. cit.*, p. 529. The report is from 25-IV-1938.

302 A. Cortesi, "Press hints Italy balk on Spain", *The New York Times*, 8-VI-1938.

303 "Les conversations franco-italiennes. Une note officieuse du 'Corriere Padano'", *Le Petit Parisien*, 18-V-1938. Days later references would return concerning the rumours that had appeared in the Italian press about a possible French military intervention in Catalonia ("La presse italienne s'en prend à la France", *Le Figaro*, 8-VI-1938.

304 "Au Congrès socialiste de Royan. Un exposé de politique générale de M. Léon Blum", *La Croix*, 8-VI-1938.

305 G. Cogniot, "Ouvrez la frontière de Catalogne!", *L'Humanité*, 5-II-1938 or G. Péri, "Aider l'Espagne est une condition de la défense nationale française", *L'Humanité*, 17-III-1938.

306 G. Péri, "II. La nouvelle Espagne", *L'Humanité*, 30-VII-1938.

307 See: E. Moradiellos, "El gobierno británico y Cataluña durante la República y la Guerra Civil: del "oasis catalán" al infierno de la revolución social", in *El Basilisco,* n. 27, January–June 2000, pp. 21-36; G. Mir, *Aturar la guerra. Les gestions secretes de Lluís Companys davant del govern britànic, op. cit.*

308 ASMAE, R. P. 1931–1945, Spagna, busta n. 32 (1938), 5-IV-1938 (Paris). See: G. Torre, *El Fascismo al desnudo: revelaciones de un periodista italiano*, Barcelona, Mentora, 1931.

309 ASMAE, R. P. 1931–1945, Spagna, busta n. 32 (1938), 5-IV-1938 (Paris).

310 ASMAE, R. P. 1931–1945, Spagna, busta n. 32 (1938), 28-IV-1938 (Paris).

311 AAM-Fons Lluís Nicolau d'Olwer, Correspondència amb Giuseppe Torre Caprara, 10-V-1938.

312 ASMAE, R. P. 1931–1945, Spagna, busta n. 32 (1938), 1-X-1938 (Paris). The document summarizes the letter of Ruggiero done by the *Ministero degli Affari Esteri*.

313 To observe this question, one needs only to study the diary of the Italian Foreign Minister (*Diario, 1937–1943*, Milan, Bur, 2005) which, in multiple passages, expresses the boredom in his government with Franco's military tactics, the long time it took to end the conflict and economic expenses created.

314 P. Menéndez y Solá [R. Arrufat], *Unidad Hispánica. España y Cataluña (1892–1939)*, *op. cit.*, p. 158.

315 *Ibid.*, pp. 168–169.

316 *Ibid.*, p. 169.

317 "La Catalogne et la France", *Le Soir*, Brussels, 30-III-1938.

318 CADN, AM (Barcelone), Série B, n. 585, Guerre Civil d'Espagne, Avril 1938, Situation politique et militaire, La Catalogne et la résistance. – Eventualités., 19-IV-1938.

319 N. M. Rubió i Tudurí, *Lettre à un patriote français. Vers la germanisation de la Catalogne*, Paris, impr. de Lecoeur, 1938

320 CADN, AM, Série B, n. 585, Guerre Civil d'Espagne, Février 1938, Situation politique et militaire, Note remise au Département par M. Rubió, le 27 août 1938, au sujet de la crise ministérielle du 16 août, 31-VIII-1938.

321 Concretely, the Labonne report referred to the interim articles: "La solution du conflit espagnol viendra-t-elle de Catalogne?", *L'Indépendant*, 16-VII-1938 and by P. Dominique, "Pour la paix en Espagne. Barcelone est-elle toujours du même avis que Madrid?", *La République*, 13-VII-1938.

322 See, for example, the article of I. Ehrenbourg, "Sur le front d'Aragon", *Regards*, 14-VII-1937.

323 *Documents Diplomatiques Français*, 2a serie, IX, Paris, 1974, p. 420. Translated into Catalan by J. Massot i Muntaner in the critical edition of the memoirs of M. Rubió i Tudurí, *Barcelona 1936–1939*, Barcelona, PAMSA, 2002, p. 239. In fact these movements in Paris were followed intensely by the French authorities – the Interior Ministry – which in a report of 28-IV-1938 reviewed the meetings and contacts of the Rubió brothers in the French capital. According to what they affirmed, both one and the other were in favor to annexing Catalonia to France or leaving it under French protection. This intention led to carrying out different contacts with French businessmen with industrial and economic interests in Catalonia so as to check out their opinions (Archives Nationales, seu de Pierrefitte-sur-Seine, F/7/14737, Réfugiés catalans 1938–1940, Mouvement autonomiste catalan en vue de rattechement à la France). Some days before, another

report in Catalan clarified the wishes of these sectors in the following questions: "La independència de Catalunya; règim d'un protectorat francès; unió duanera; autonomia respecte a la llengua i els costums; ocupació per les tropes franceses." (AN, Pierrefitte-sur-Seine, F/7/14737, Réfugiés catalans 1938–1940, Mouvement autonomiste catalan en vue de rattechement à la France, 5-IV-1938). In fact, all this activity of the Rubió brothers also was tied to the contacts maintained with the French Minister of Public Works, Anatole de Monzie, and certain French business groups working in the same direction to pressure so as to achieve Catalan independence under a French "umbrella" and a later economic exploitation of the country (see A. Gonzàlez i Vilalta, *Cataluña bajo vigilancia*, *op. cit.*, pp. 257–263).

324 M. Rubió i Tudurí, *Barcelona 1936–1939*, *op. cit.*, p. 238.

325 N. M. Rubió i Tudurí, "L'ambaixador de França a Barcelona", *El Poble*, Tortosa, 23-X-1937.

326 CADN, AM, Série B, n. 585, October 1938, 5-X-1938.

327 "M. Henry Labonne marcha a Túnez", *La Vanguardia*, 10-XI-1938. The decision had been taken a few weeks previously ("La evolución de la política colonial francesa", *La Vanguardia*, 23-X-1938), even though the rumours situated Labonne at the head of the French embassy in Moscow ("Dice la señora Tabouis", *Front*, Girona, 13-X-1938).

328 See: E. Moradiellos, *Negrín*, *op. cit.,* 6, pp. 329, 332, 337, 345, 404, 413, 422.

329 J. Miravitlles, *Veritats sobre la Guerra Civil Espanyola*, *op. cit.*, p. 289.

330 J. Miravitlles, *ibid.*, pp. 289–290.

331 The report of 1938 made much more concrete these accusations: usage of gasoline received from the Spanish Republican authorities, of food sent from France and of the "traffic of influences", among others. (AMTM, 7.1 Comerç Exterior, report without a title by J. Miravitlles dated 4-XI-1938, p. 2).

332 J. Miravitlles, *ibid.*, p. 290.

333 Arxiu Montserrat Taradellas i Macià (AMTM), 7.1 Comerç Exterior, report without a title by J. Miravitlles del 4-XI-1938, *ibid.*, p. 1.

334 AMTM, *ibid.*, p. 1.

335 AMTM, *ibid.*, pp. 2–3.

336 J. Miravitlles, *Veritats*, *op. cit.*, p. 290.

337 The French embassy requested the acceptance of the Spanish Republican authorities to the nomination of Henry on 27-X-1938 with a note of J. Fouques Duparc (AMAE, Madrid, Personal, PG 331, Exp. 24552, Labonne, Pierre Eirik).

338 J. Miravitlles, *op. cit.*, p. 292.

339 AFS, Madrid, Politische Berichte und Briefe, Militärberichte, Band 8, 1935–1938 (Dossier), Politische Berichte, 1938, Die Lage in Barcelona, 14-IX-1938.

340 "Le problème reste entier", *La Croix*, 23-IX-1938.

341 These contacts also had to be related with some of the previous activities of Koht. Thus, in 1916, he had formed part of a committee for the study of the national question in the "Organisation Centrale pour une Paix Durable", which published in 1917 a project of dealing with the rights of national minorities (for this question, see X. M. Núñez Seixas, *Entre Ginebra y Berlín, op. cit.*, pp. 108–9). Koht was Minister for Foreign Affairs for the Norwegian Labour Party between 1935 and 1941. Within the Norwegian academic world he was (and is still) considered an outstanding intellectual, although a very weak minister. This opinion of his political career is based on his own "frankness", for example, during the Russian invasion of Finland in 1940.

342 ASMAE, R. P. 1931–1945, Spagna, busta n. 34, Koht-contatti con separatisti catalani, "Separatismo catalano" (London Ambassador, T. 6020 R.).

343 ASMAE, R. P. 1931–1945, Spagna, busta n. 34, Koht-contatti con separatisti catalani, (Ministero degli Affari Esteri, 26-X-1938, T. 236532).

344 ASMAE, R. P. 1931–1945, Spagna, busta n. 34, Koht-contatti con separatisti catalani, (Comando Truppe Volontarie, 1-X-1938, Num. di protocollo 7369-25/66).

345 ASMAE, R. P. 1931–1945, Spagna, busta n. 34, Koht-contatti con separatisti catalani (Oslo, 11-XI-1938, T. 1117/403).

346 ASMAE, R. P. 1931–1945, Spagna, busta n. 34, Koht-contatti con separatisti catalani (Geneva, 17-XI-1938, T. 5329/152). This note was sent to the legations of Sant Sebastian, Berlin, Paris and Oslo.

347 CADN, AM, Série B, n. 585, GC 1-A 2-etc, Situation Politique, telegram signed by Lasmartres in Sant Sebastià, 4-XI-1938.

348 CADN, AM, Série B, n. 585, GC 1-A 2-etc, Situation Politique, Déclarations de l'ancien Président de la Généralité de Catalogne, 11-XI-1938. Evidently the telegram from the Havas Agency confused, even if it was clarified in the text, the head of the Catalan government or the *"Conseller Primer"* with the President of the Generalitat of Catalonia. Four days afterwards, French diplomacy received a new note, in this case sent by the "l'Agence Espagne", in which were

collected the publications of the declarations of Casanovas to *La Vanguardia,* Barcelona, 15-XI-1938.

349 Ribécourt, "L'Espagne luttera jusqu'au bout pour son indépendance et n'acceptera aucune mediation", *Ce Soir*, 21-XI-1938.

350 ANC, Fons Nicolau Maria Rubió i Tudurí, note of 21-XI-1938.

351 "Roma 1° Febbraio XVII", *Critica Fascista*, 1-II-1939, pp. 97–98.

352 J. Massot i Muntaner, *Menorca dins del dominó mediterrani (1936–1939), op. cit.*, pp. 56–57.

353 Cited in J. Miravitlles [R. Batalla, ed.], *Veritats sobre la Guerra Civil Espanyola, op. cit.*, pp. 176–177. The article is from 16-I-1939.

354 F. Anfuso, *Roma, Berlino, Salò (1936–1945)*, Milan, Garzanti, 1950, p. 110.

355 G. Ciano, *Diario 1937–1943*, consulted at: <http://www.liberliber.it/mediateca/libri/c/ciano/diario _1937_1943/pdf/ciano_diario_1937_1943.pdf> [consulted on 1-V-2017] p. 381.

356 G. Bonnet, *Fin d'une Europe. De Munich à la guerre*, Geneva, Cheval Ailé, 1948, pp. 84–92.

357 ASPFAE, P. n. 11163, 1938–1939, Guerre Civile Espagne 1939, Amélie-les-Bains (France), 17-II-1939. Some weeks before different councillors of the Generalitat had requested the British embassy for help in ending the war in Catalonia, with negotiations (E. Moradiellos, *Negrín, op. cit.*, p. 413).

Chapter 4

Catalonia, a Very Particular Nation from the Soviet Point of View

Josep Puigsech Farràs

"Barcelona is close to the border, and local pedants do not get tired of boasting: 'We are not Spanish, we are almost French.' Here, there are many cars and few donkeys. [...] In a word, Barcelona is already Europe. [...] Catalan nationalists are content with very little. [...] The Catalan nationalists like to be proud in all forms of their cultural and social progres of their region. 'This is not Spain!'"

> From the unfavourable chapter concerning the bourgeoisie and Catalan nationalism of I. Ehrenburg, *España, república de trabajadores*, Barcelona: Crítica, 1976 [1932], pp. 167, 168, 169.

On October 1st of 1936, the consulate general of the Union of Soviet Socialist Republics (USSR) was established in Barcelona. Its first location in the Catalan capital was situated, provisionally, at the Majestic Hotel, on the city's central boulevard. A few weeks later, it was set up in the upper part of Barcelona, specifically on Tibidabo avenue, number 15, in one of the houses owned by the wealthy Andreu family. And this is where it remained permanently located until Republican forces began their retreat into exile, across the Pyrenees in January 1939. However, from the end of 1937 onwards, consular space would be shared with the Soviet embassy, as the latter would arrive in Barcelona together with the whole of the Republican Spanish State apparatus, when the city was designated the new capital of the Spanish Republic, replacing Valencia.[1]

Knowledge in the USSR relative to Catalonia, and specifically concerning the reality of Catalan national feeling, was practically non-existent when the Spanish Civil War began. After the Bolshevik triumph of 1917 and the configuration of the Third International in 1919 as an instrument to export the Communist revolution from Russia to the rest of the world, the direct contacts of the Soviet context with Catalonia had been practically non-existent. This ignorance was especially striking given that the so-called "Third Period" of Soviet Communism, from the end of 1927 to the Spring of 1934, had in principle defended the seccession of "oppressed peoples" from their subjection to "bourgeois States". On the Soviet side, the existence of Catalonia and its national particularities had only been noted in 1932, by the influential Soviet author and journalist Ilya Ehrenburg in a way that was sharply critical. Later, once the Civil War had begun, during the month of September 1936, he informed again on the subject, once more without sympathy.

It is true that a few individual Catalans achieved some visibility in the Soviet system. Andreu Nin, the Catalan figure that attained most relevance, became known in party circles in the USSR insofar as he became a member of the directorate of the Red International of Labour Unions in the 1920s. But at no time did he mark as a priority the spreading of knowledge regarding the existence of Catalonia and Catalan national sentiment (of which he had been an enthusiast when young) among his communist co-believers. Nin was a staunch trotskyite, and left the Soviet Union in 1930, to reestablish himself in Barcelona as a partisan of his cause.

But there were others. Ramon Casanelles, a former anarcho-syndicalist who became a faithful stalinist, could be considered the second Catalan figure who occupied political positions of relevance in the Soviet context, in his case tied to the sphere of the official Communist Party of Spain (PCE), and who followed a similar behavior to that of Nin, when in the Soviet Union, only to change when he returned to Catalonia in 1932, and founded the PCE's Catalan regional subsidiary (the PCdeC, the Communist Party of Catalonia), before being killed in a motorocycle crash in 1933. And if to this is added all the centralist mentality of most militants of the official "Spanish Section of the Third International", the means to promote any awareness the existence of Catalonia and its national substance were practically non-existent.

It is also true that, after the the mid-1920s, Catalan travelers visited the USSR in increasing numbers. By the early 1930s, figures as ideologically varied as the writer Josep Pla, the journalist Eugeni Xammar, the medical doctor Jaume Pi i Sunyer or his cousin, the economist and politician Carles Pi i Sunyer, the conservative jurist Ferran Valls i Taberner, the industrialist and philathropist Francesc Blasi, among others, visited Russia to learn about the social transformations of the USSR. But their purpose was not to discuss and debate with the locals about Catalonia and what Marxists called "the Catalan national question".

In fact, only the separatist leader Francesc Macià would break this circle of silence. His trip to the "country of the Soviets" in 1925 confronted the leadership of the Third International with the existence of Catalonia and the most extreme expression of Catalan nationalism. But it would be a passing moment, not taken too seriously. In fact, the leadership of the International, despite having approved the financing of Macià's plan to overthrow the military dictatorship of general Miguel Primo de Rivera, finally did not execute this decision, and left Macià to his own resources.[2] Primo de Rivera governed from September 1923 to January 1930, when a transition was begun. Nevertheless, in mid-April 1931, Macià, having returned to Barcelona, was able to proclaim the Spanish Republic and agree upon an autonomy for Catalonia. This feat, however, was criticized by the then leadership of Spanish stalinists.

In short, when in October 1936 the Soviet consulate showed empathy towards Catalan society, while recognizing Catalonia as a nation, it carried out a remarkable qualitative leap.

Antonov-Ovseyenko, Old Bolshevik Hero with Catalan Rapport

The new consul general who arrived in Barcelona in October 1936 – not even four months into the Civil War in Spain – was Vladimir Antonov-Ovseyenko. He was a figure of mythic proportions in the Bolshevik narrative of the Russian Revolution of 1917, since he had headed the forces of the Revolutionary Military Committee in Petrograd that stormed the Winter Palace, overthrew the Kerensky government, and gave rise to the beginning of Lenin's rule. His reputation became a source of enthusiasm in revolutionary Barcelona.

Antonov-Ovseyenko would command the consular mission in the Catalan capital until September 1937.[3] He then would be retired and returned to Russia by order of Josif Stalin, to face the height of the Soviet purges. From that moment on, his post would remain vacant. Alexei Strakhov, the consular secretary in Barcelona, henceforth would assume the public representation of the Soviet diplomatic entity and accordingly would become the relevant figure of the consulate.

But, while he was active, Antonov-Ovseyenko entranced the revolutionary press in Barcelona. He was the physical representative of the great working-class power, struggling toward world revolution. He seemed to show sympathy for the Catalan context and for the president of Generalitat, Lluís Companys. And he even indulged the anarcho-syndicalists. Antonov-Ovseyenko, as a personality, incarnated a stunning public relation success. But he was just consul general. The consulate general of the USSR was a more complex entity than its titular head. The consulate depended on the embassy, which in turn was under the control of the Soviet People's Commission on Foreign Affairs (NKID), the equivalent of the Ministry of Foreign Affairs in Western European states, which, at the same time, was under the control of the Political Bureau – or Politburo, in Soviet acronyms – of the Communist Party of the USSR.

Antonov-Ovseyenko managed his post with ability, communicating a fellow sympathy to Catalan nationalists (who attributed his feelings to his Ukrainian background), but adhering carefully to the Soviet party line on Catalan obligations to the Spanish Republic and to the common war effort. Catalan republican leaders had a long list of grievances in relation to Spanish behavior towards Catalonia and Catalan institutions. This was evidenced on October 21, 1936, when Antonov-Ovseyenko met with the president of the Spanish Republic, Manuel Azaña (shortly after he fled Madrid and installed himself in Barcelona), and Catalan president Companys.[4]

The consul, starting off from an explicit rejection of any separatist position, conveyed to President Azaña the list of grievances which Companys had sent the Soviet envoy from his first meetings in the Palace of the Generalitat. Azaña denied them all, from the first to the last. Instead, what he could not deny was the existence of a separatist tendency that was gaining strength in Catalonia but, at the same time, Azaña was convinced that the trend would never get enough political and social support to be able to actually bring to fruition any kind of process of detachment. This list of Catalan grievances was not new, and existed long before the figure of Antonov-Ovseyenko appeared on the scene. Ilya Ehrenburg, in all likelihood the first unofficial representative of the Soviet authorities sent to Catalonia once the Civil War had begun, in a Barcelona that he had described years before, was the first recipient of the grievances evinced by Companys.[5]

The establishment of the Soviet embassy in Madrid at the end of August 1936 had allowed Moscow representatives to the Spanish Republic to have immediate and direct news, however limited and vague, of the special situation that was being lived in Catalonia after the beginning of the Civil War. And, and from the ambassadorial point of view, none of this news was positive, given that it was a territory of vital strategic and economic importance in the face of the military interests of the Republic. The embassy was concerned about the hegemony of the anarcho-syndicalist movement in the Catalan rearguard, together with the existence of an actively autonomous government in Catalonia – the Generalitat – that had assumed the attributions of the Central government, and, in addition, the complex presence of a national factor that questioned the current model of state unity of the Spanish Republic.[6]

Ilya Ehrenburg had met with Companys in mid-September 1936, and the Catalan president had presented him with complaints and criticisms, of which Ehrenburg notified the leadership of the NKID, and this passed on to the Political Bureau of the Communist Party of the USSR. The list was very clear: it detailed the centralist, authoritarian and inflexible attitude of the Government of the Republic towards the Catalans, which in turn generated an insensitive and contemptuous treatment towards Catalonia and its institutions of self-government. Catalonia was treated like just another region of the Republic, when it was distinct and different, with a Statute of Autonomy, approved by the Parliament of the Spanish Republic in 1932.

But, in July 1936, the failure of a right-wing military coup d'état and the outbreak of a generalized Civil War had brought about the collapse of the central Republican control in Catalonia, so that it obtained, de facto, the status of autonomous republic. Such a status should be maintained, insisted Companys. But there were also many other detailed objections: Companys also denounced the refusal of the Government of the Republic to give the Generalitat full management of the Catalan educational centers when the Republican State did not have effective capacity to influence them. The central government had shown itself unwilling to send arms, airplanes and war material to Catalonia. It had ignored or boycotted the economic measures proposed by the Government of the Generalitat to obtain financing and management of resources available in the rearguard, as well as acquiring new ones abroad. More concretely, and especially significant from the Russian point of view, the Spanish Republican government even had exhibited its reluctance that a Soviet diplomatic delegation – the consulate – be established in Barcelona.[7]

The public sympathy of Antonov-Ovseyenko with Catalan protestations showed a sensitivity for Catalan republican autonomy, and perhaps even for what Soviet sources called Catalan "revolutionary nationalism", but was balanced against the will to curb the increasing dynamics of what was termed "separatism" in Catalonia. This was the Soviet position to which he adhered.

An immediate answer was needed to help solve problems arising from the ongoing Civil War in Spain, and a solution might be to reverse the disregard with which the central Republican State treated Catalonia. This led the consul to a new meeting at the end of November 1936. Antonov-Ovseyenko met face-to-face with the President of the Republic, Manuel Azaña, by then installed in the abbey of Montserrat, but also with – since September 4 – the prime minister of the Republic, Francisco Largo Caballero, who had abandoned Madrid for Valencia at the beginning month of November.[8] The Soviet consul demanded concessions from the central Republican State, specifically a real recognition of the national diversity of the Republic. Both authorities were accused of not effectively recognizing Catalonia – nor, also, the Basque Country – as the epicenter of the national question in the Spanish Republic. The main reason – thought Antonov-Ovseyenko, with his Catalan contacts and sources – for the centralist and regressive politics applied by the Government of the Republic was the short-sighted vision with which figures like Azaña and Largo Caballero analyzed Spain's national diversity. Both did so from a centralist and regressive "Castilian" mentality, that was incapable of valuing the benefits of a possible increase of the degree of autonomy of the historical nations of Spain.

The consular positions regarding Catalan separatism and the grievances that Catalonia suffered were much more realistic than those of the President of the Spanish Republic, Manuel Azaña, precisely because they were free from the prejudices with which Catalonia was looked at from the central Republican State. At the same time, they were based on the Soviets' own experience dating back to the Russian civil war that, between 1918–1922, had shown that without the support of the different nationalities of a revolutionary State, a military victory over the enemy was not feasible. The Soviet consul, therefore, was ultimately much more realistic and pragmatic than the president of the Spanish Republic.

Both factors were combined by the consul in a perception that considered necessary to carry out some type of warm response that might help curb what was feared as the ascending secessionist dynamic of separatism in Catalonia. Concessions of symbolic importance were useful. For this reason, Antonov-Ovseyenko had no hesitation in proposing the presence of official representatives of the Government of the Generalitat within the institutional representation of the Spanish Republic in foreign affairs. There were also requests that the Republic assume a more fundamental recognition of the national sentiment of the Catalans.

Antonov-Ovseyenko, in fact, had already begun to move further in this direction. A few days before he had an interview with Nicolau Maria Rubió Tudurí, delegate of the Generalitat whom Antonov-Ovseyenko had helped with his accreditation in relation to the Soviet representation to the League of Nations, and whom he hoped the Government of the Spanish Republic would include as one of the members of the its official delegation to the League at Geneva. Both Rubió and the Soviet consul coincided in their assessment that the Spanish Republic had to reorient the national question in the Catalan case.

Rubió Tudurí, with whom Antonov-Ovseyenko had been dealing, was in favor of applying a broader autonomy for Catalonia, which required surpassing the then current statutory framework. In fact, Rubió proposed to take advantage of the context of the move of the capital of the Republic from Madrid to Valencia as a starting point in the basic transformation of the national model of the Spanish Republican State. Rubió's hopes came from the war measures and territorial initiatives of the new Largo Caballero cabinet, with the Basque autonomy Statue accepted on October 6, and, on the same day, the Defense Council of Aragon. On December 23, President of the Republic Azaña approved a decree which proposed the reorganization of the Republican State through provincial defense councils, thus transforming the old provincial deputations or civil administration executives. In some cases like Asturias-León, the new entities would become inter-provincial defense councils, which would be recognized as the maximum republican authority in each zone. However, there was no possibility to make the changes go further because of the negative predisposition of the Government of the Republic.[9]

The consul, in addition, argued that the Catalans had not pressed for increasing autonomy in governmental functions, but rather that the tendency had been precipitated by the context of the Civil War, and, with its onset, the weakness that the central Republican State had shown since July 1936. The central State had been overcome by the outbreak of war. Its effective collapse had forced territories that had a strong national configuration, such as Catalonia, to look out unilaterally for their own survival. The measures taken by the Generalitat were based on those elements that defined the national strengths of Catalan society because they allowed Catalonia to better articulate the management of its own territory. In addition, this practice did not imply a selfish attitude of Catalonia towards the rest of the Republic, as critical voices asserted. In fact, the consul said it was clearly the opposite. From Antonov-Ovseyenko's point of view, Catalonia fully contributed to the armed efforts of the Republic, both in terms of military and human resources, with the best energy and quality possible. The central Republican State, for its part, was the one that did not comply with the agreements fixed with the Generalitat. It did not provide the agreed sums of economic financing, or the supplies of raw materials for the Catalan industries, nor did it treat correctly the Catalan authorities that were fully involved in the war effort for the sake of the whole of the Republic.

Thus, from the consul's viewpoint, the tendency to downgrade Catalonia had to be overcome if the desired objective was to achieve a better internal balance within the Republic and, with it, to generate a unity of efforts and feelings in the republican rearguard so as to manage matériel in a coordinated and efficient way for the battle front. For this reason a qualified leap was proposed. The consulate claimed a real recognition of what was supposed to be the Catalan autonomy and, even more, to extend its content. For this, there was the proposal of the definition of the Republic as a federal State, following the model of the USSR, since it was considered the best possible instrument to guarantee the real recognition of a fuller autonomy – given that the autonomous institutional variant developed since 1932 had proved unable to achieve a common effort – at the same time which would also allow improving the economic and military treatment that was offered in Catalonia.

The proposal made by the consul was not a mere gesture. The consul had documented himself extensively, reviewing the country's most recent history, and had no doubt that the nationalism was inseparable from the past and the present of Catalonia. Antonov-Ovseyenko was convinced that one of the most important successes attained "nationally", although with nuances, had been the achievement of the Statute of Autonomy. But, at the same time, he detected that this Statute had been the result of a partial amputation of the Statute of Núria – written up by Catalans and voted on in a referendum in 1931 – and, therefore, that Catalans had been partially mutilated in their national aspirations. The consul was convinced that the Catalans wanted to articulate themselves as an autonomous state within a Spanish Federal Republic. But Madrid's response had been to place them as an autonomous region within a unitary or "integral" Spanish Republic. The grievances did not end there. The Catalans voiced their frustration toward their aspirations to control the educational, judicial, social, military and economic apparatus in Catalonia. And if to this were added the grievances regarding the measures that the Government of the Republic had carried out already in Catalonia since the beginning of the Civil War – and that Ehrenburg had already gathered and made explicit. The final result could not be any other than the discontent towards the central Republican State and, as a final result, an increase of pro-separatist positions.[10]

Thus, the consulate was not only understanding, but also realistic, towards those motives that provoked the growth of institutional breakaway tensions in Catalonia. In fact, the consulate situated in the leading sectors of Catalonia and the middle class the core where this increase was located and this, from the Soviet point of view, explained the rumours in which President Companys said he was considering proclaiming Spain as a Federal Republic and Catalonia as a state member of the same, as he already had done once unsuccessfully, on October 6, 1934. However, Companys finally did not opt for the ideal creation of an independent State but remained loyal to the idea of an integrated state within the framework of a Spanish federation. However, the consulate at no time would show itself to be in favor of anything resembling Catalan institutional separation. First, there was communist discipline: that position had been communicated from the management of the NKID, and therefore, for Antonov-Ovseyenko, it was unthinkable not to abide by orders coming from his more senior hierarchy. But, second, and even more importantly, because the consul himself was not in favor of separation. In the first instance, for ideological reasons, because the political formation of the consul had taken place within a Soviet world that was distant from such theses. In the second instance, for pragmatism, since in the current situation of internal but internationalized conflict a hypothetical Catalonia broken off from the rest of the Republic would fail, with irremediable impact added to its failure. The separation would lead to the configuration of a new and small State deeply weakened from its inception, since it would not have outside support. Worse still, this would also evidently debilitate the Spanish Republican State. From Antonov-Ovseyenko's point of view only a united State, great and cohesive, was in a position to achieve international recognition in the context of the 1930s, and also would be able to face the fight against the rebel forces to win the Civil War.

That said, the consulate – and the consul general personally – showed a much more open and flexible attitude than that seen from the presidency of the Republic or from the Spanish Republican Government, but also from the management of the NKID. In fact, it was no surprise that Maxim Litvinov and Nikolai Krestinski, leading figures of the NKID, ordered the consulate to move away from the maximalist positions that had been proposed in favor of the establishment of a federal system for the Spanish Republic. The leadership of the NKID was aligned with a Republic defined as a State, first of all, indivisible, and, in the second instance, effectively synonymous with the Castilian Spanish idea of nation. Therefore, if from the consulate of Antonov-Ovseyenko there was an option for the recognition of other nations besides that of "Castilian" Spain, the leadership of the NKID demanded that this sympathy should be shown in a diffuse way, since this other nation – Catalonia – was not in a condition to modify the current national structure of the Spanish Republic nor question Spanish Republican unity. This notification would bring the consulate to abandon the theses in favor of a federal model for the Spanish Republic. However, there was no instruction to stop recognizing Catalonia as a "nation" rather than a mere region, and, at the same time, requests and suggestions were permitted for a substantial improvement in the treatment received in Catalonia by the central Republican State.

Antonov-Ovseyenko was recalled to Moscow at the end of the summer of 1937. His removal accentuated an atmosphere of suspicion. All in all, the withdrawal of the consul, and, shortly thereafter, the establishment of the Soviet embassy in Barcelona, as the representatives followed to shift of Dr. Negrín's central government from Valencia to the Catalan port, left the Soviet consular office in Catalonia in a semi-comatose state from which it never recovered. The consulate general as such would continue to exist, but its powers were assumed directly by the embassy.[11] The mentality and pro-centralist behaviour that characterized the

Soviet embassy in the Spanish Republic, as well as that of the little known figure of Alexei Strakhov, left the Soviet diplomatic representation in Barcelona without the specific instrument of interpellation that it had had with Catalan society since October 1936. Of this reality, both Lluís Companys and the different members of the government of the Generalitat were perfectly conscious. The best proof of this was the constant insistence of Companys to the consular secretary about the lack of a replacement of the figure of the Soviet general consul in Barcelona and the effects that this created. Strakhov transmitted this clearly to the leadership of the NKID. This last organization, however, paid little to no attention to the constant petitions made in September 1937 of a "[...] Catalan Government [that] is very interested in knowing if a consul of the URSS is to be established in Barcelona or not; and, if so, if it will be soon".[12]

Strakhov, the Centralist *Appartchik*

The removal of Antonov-Ovseyenko accentuated an atmosphere of suspicion. Thus, the lack of a ranking Soviet consul general in Barcelona and the subsequent arrival of the embassy in Barcelona annuled any Soviet public sympathy for the nationalist positions in the Generalitat. "Catalan national reality" would be uniformly interpreted from a centralist perspective, from the autumn of 1937 onwards. Catalonia was considered a simple region of the Spanish Republic, with peculiar institutions. Its autonomy was recognized in administrative terms by Soviet diplomats, but not its specificity and national sentiment. The Soviet vision was that of a Catalonia seen as an autonomy in simple administrative terms, that is, as a delegation resulting from a transfer of power dictated by the Spanish Parlament and executed by the Government of the Republic. In other words, Catalonia was no more than an autonomous region, a minor entity for anyone used to Russian territorial forms. The recognition of its national identity was strongly dimished.

As of this change, a vision was consolidated which already had been present, although in minority, in a sector of the consulate since the end of July of 1937. Strakhov had denounced the nature of Catalan autonomy in general, and more specifically the Government of the Generalitat, as its executor, as responsible for the tense relations of Catalonia with the Government of the Republic.[13] Soviet perspective and tone was completely switched around from the days of Antonov-Ovseyenko. Strakhov acknowledged the existence of a long list of grievances made by President Companys, among which stood out the indifference with which the Government of the Republic viewed Catalonia, the arrogance and humiliation which the Generalitat felt in many ways: politically, to the point that sometimes its members were not recognized as members of a government but simply as members of a lesser parliament; financially, as the debt of the central State with the Catalan autonomy kept increasing; and, last but not least, nationally, insofar as the central government qualified Catalan as a dialect and not a language, and refused to accept its use as a working medium through which to carry on correspondence, communications and contacts between the Generalitat and the Government of the Republic.

However, consular secretary Strakhov was convinced that these much-denounced Catalan grievances were a misrepresentation of reality. In fact, he considered them to be instruments in the service of the interests of certain political forces and Catalan labour unions that wanted to create a climate of opinion of rebuff and even hostility towards the Government of the Republic and the whole of the central Republican State, as well as towards the USSR. In Strakhov's perspective, some Catalan parties did so to legitimize their own particular separatist projects, as was the case of of the governing Esquerra Republicana of Catalonia (ERC). Others, such as the revolutionary socialist Labour Party of Marxist Unification (POUM), and the anarcho-syndicalist National Confederation of Labor (CNT), did so to discredit the position of the Soviet Union, and its political representatives in the Republic, specifically the Communist Party of Spain (PCE), which whole-heartedly participated in the Negrín cabinet, and the Unified Socialist Party of Catalunya (PSUC), which, by August 1938, had a presence in the Government of the Republic. Anti-communists in general declared themselves in favor of the liberal democratic model for the

Catalan rearguard and for the whole of the Republic, against the alleged predominance of communist influence.

In fact, the political battle against this double separatist and anti-communist component would become the main concern of the last months of consular activity in Catalonia.[14] The supposed political maneuvers of the anarchist and "poumist" sectors against the PCE and the PSUC were united to the purported clandestine manoeuvres of ERC and Acció Catalana Republicana (ACR), willing to carry out separatist initiatives and accordingly bring Catalonia to chaos. The fears of "Catalan separatism" were increasingly noticeable within the consular apparatus. Strakhov denounced the ERC and ACR as organizations that had betrayed republican legality and committed treason against the Spanish Republic. The motive of such accusations were the professed negotiations that some members of these formations were carrying out with Franco's representatives to achieve a separate peace for Catalonia. Specifically, Strakhov accused two advisers of the Esquerra, Josep Maria Espanya and Bonaventura Gassol. These conversations would have taken place in France and, what was worse, without the approval of Companys. Strakhov denounced not only the existence of these movements, but also the fact that they were clandestine actions carried out by a part of Catalan separatism which did not obey the orders of their leadership. The conversations would therefore have taken place against the will of President Companys, who, nevertheless, and always according to the version of Strakhov and the consulate, had known about them and had disavowed them. That would explain why Companys had proposed renouncing the position of president of the Generalitat, a rumour that circulated intensely in the Catalan political circles since the arrival of the Madrid/Valencia central Government in Barcelona in November 1937, and as tensions increased in the summer of 1938. Thus, the consular secretary showed concern for the activism of a sector of "Catalan separatism" that was beyond the control of the leadership of the Generalitat. This, in fact, was much more serious than the existence of the separatist impulses and secret contacts abroad. The consulate was aware that the existence of these connections among Catalans in France could not be avoided. But what was demanded was that this sector stopped acting as a "fifth column" against the survival of the Republican State.

As can be seen, for Strakhov the only positive part of this situation had been Companys' behavior. The Catalan president was clearly worth the term of *our friend*, an expression which, in fact, had been used from the first day in 1936, for the special relationship of Companys with the representatives of the Soviet consulate in Barcelona.[15] The consulate valued the fact that the Catalan president had totally disavowed the alleged conversations with Franco representatives. In fact, that Companys, to make himself clear, had convoked a press conference to dissociate himself publicly from both his councillors, Josep Maria Espanya and Ventura Gassol, emphasizing that neither one nor the other had acted as members, much less as representatives, of the Government of the Generalitat. This attitude was considered by the consulate as a proof of firmness regarding the separatist sector that attempted to act unilaterally. The Catalan president had behaved integrally and had maintained his political honor intact, since the highest political authority of the Catalan autonomy had remained faithful to the Republican State. In fact, Companys had done so to the point of showing himself willing to go into exile, rather than agree to a separate peace between Catalonia and the pro-Franco representatives. For the consulate, it was the best possible information that could be said about what it considered the threat of "Catalan separatism". Even more so when Companys closed this episode asking for the celebration of an institutional meeting between representatives of the Government of the Generalitat, the Government of the Republic and the President of the Republic, Manuel Azaña, in order to redirect relations that could have been seriously damaged as a result of the episode of the self-exiled councillors Espanya and Gassol.

The opposition to what the Russian – and the Spaniards – called "Catalan separatism" had been, in fact, a common denominator of the trajectory of the Consulate General from its first day installed in Barcelona. However, in the case of the consul general, Antonov-Ovseyenko, there was no doubt about conceding Catalonia all the attributes of a "nation". Nor did Antonov-Ovseyenko hestitate in acknowledging the clumsiness often exercised by the government of the Spanish Republic either in national and political matters, as well as military and economic questions in regard to Catalonia. The time between summer of 1936 and that of 1937 was characterized by the Soviet consular recognition of the reality and specificity of Catalonia as a nation, easy for Catalan nationalists to idealize in retrospect. Catalonia was considered by the Soviet representative as a nation with a unique language, a specific culture and history, along with its own traditions, different from the rest of the territories that formed the Spanish Republic. Unquestionably, it was a symbolic recognition always within certain insurmountable limits: the adamant opposition to separation. In private meetings, Antonov-Ovseyenko might defend federalism, but not as a fully official posture. In the substantive sense, Antonov-Ovseyenko's stance was not different from the positions made evident by Strakhov, and assumed by the embassy. The Soviet diplomatic representation – installed in Barcelona in November 1937 – was not willing at any time to question the existing legal framework of the Republic, nor to propose a modification of the actual national structure of the Spanish Republican State, much less, border modifications which could imply the breakaway of Catalonia from the rest of Spain. But, unlike his successor Strakhov, a grey functionary, an *appartchik*, "Old Bolshevik" Antonov-Ovseyenko had a sense of style, of public empathy, that won him much favour in Catalonia.

A Broad Set of Conclusions

Any evaluation about Soviet diplomatic actions in Catalonia must start with the initial Russian lack of knowledge, nuanced and in detail with respect to Barcelona and Catalonia, and its divergences from a generic perception of Spain. To best reconstruct the Soviet consulate's position regarding the Catalan situation from a Catalan nationalist viewpoint, it is necessary to analyse the general background of Russian diplomacy.

The starting point would be what at first the Soviets grasped about the existence of Catalonia as a historical territory, and, from this, what understanding could be had in Moscow about nationalist perspectives, and what, to nationalist opinion, was the depth of the

Catalan national feeling? Furthermore, to what extent was the discourse of national liberation – a defended *posture* from the Soviet world viewpoint – applied to the case of Catalonia and, on the other hand, with what limitations? And, finally, to what extent did the needs of the foreign policy of the USSR condition the consular position towards Catalonia?

To answer these questions, it becomes necessary to evaluate Soviet theorizing about national liberation. It was a discourse already generated during the "October Revolution" of 1917, and then passed through the filter of the Communist International, founded in 1919, that supported the liberation of the oppressed nations and peoples. However, when the Soviets spoke of these nations, they did so thinking of key nationalities within the great European empires before the Great War, peoples of which they expected that the fight for their national liberation would be joined together with the struggle for social liberation in the form of a communist revolution. In this way, therefore, the minority nations within Western European states that were not the empires that disintegrated in 1918, and that, in addition, had their borders consolidated, as was the case of Spain, were not really a part of this project.

Were this ideological reticence not enough, it should not be forgotten that if the "Catalan national question" had any reference in the Soviet world, it had tended to be seen from a very unfavorable point of view, that did not imply or include the recognition of Catalan national interests. On the one hand, the democratic liberalism represented by Macià in 1931–33 was far from the communist political project. On the other, the different Catalan regional organizations in the sphere of the Third International had given more problems than benefits to the configuration of the communist movement in Spain: such as the case of the Catalan-Balearic Communist Federation (later the BOC, or Workers' and Peasants' Block) or the creation of the Communist Party of Catalonia (PCdeC). The first – the BOC – constituted the best possible example of what, seen from the Soviet world, was considered a simple regional federation of the "Spanish Section of the Communist International" that broke organically with the PCE to then define itself as an alternative formation, and therefore became an enemy. In the case of the PCdeC, its experience showed how a communist formation was developed on the edge of the strict sphere of the Third International, but which could be recognized as a legitimate offspring of the "October Revolution".[16] It is therefore understandable that from the consular personnel there existed an unwavering reluctance to grant the status of "oppressed nation" that was to be encouraged to carry out its national liberation and so achieve the fullness of what Catalan nationalists called a "Catalan national reality". Neither the theoretical corpus of the Third International and the Soviet model, nor the experience lived with the Catalan political communist organizations, favoured that the Soviet consulate might place Catalonia in such standing, whatever Catalans might expect.

Another aspect that also must be valued are the effects of Soviet foreign policy on the Catalan situation. The "Collective Security" policy defined Soviet foreign attitudes during much of the decade of the 1930s, especially after 1933–34. This was characterized by the willingness to reach some kind of an agreement with the European liberal powers, basically the United Kingdom and France, in order to knit an anti-fascist alliance in Europe. In theory, the alliance would have avoided the expansion of fascism in Europe, and, thus, minimized any increase in the possibility of a territorial attack by any of the fascist powers on the USSR, insofar as the Soviet Union was considered the main ideological enemy of fascism. The best way to try to achieve this accord passed through the defense of the liberal democratic model in Western European States, or, more precisely, the Soviet commitment to avoid the development of a disruptive and subversive communist model in those same democratic countries.[17] The Spanish Republic was part of this group of European states. And Catalonia, as a Spanish autonomous region, was one of its components. As a result, there were no options for which the Soviet diplomacy in Catalonia, as first representative of Soviet foreign policy, counted on a destabilization of the political borders of the Spanish Republic for the benefit of a hypothetical configuration of an independent Catalonia. Such an attitude was non-existent. Such a breakup was in contradiction to the logic and practice of "Collective Security" that the Soviets were developing on the Spanish Republic, first through their embassy in Madrid – and later Valencia – and, as to be expected, not through their consular delegation in Barcelona. The praxis of the consul in Catalan territory would be very explicit in this sense: full support to the Government of the Generalitat as a legitimate authority of the Spanish republican State, considering it as the stronghold of institutional power and of the defense of the liberal democratic model of the Republic; as well as unconditional support to the re-establishment of cordial relations between Madrid/Valencia and Barcelona or, in other words, between the Government of the Republic and the Government of the Generalitat, so as to consolidate the political stability of the republican rearguard based on the democratic-liberal values with which the Spanish Republic had been born and with which this young State in the extreme European west had been developed.[18] Thus, it would be no surprise that the Soviet consular delegation in Barcelona distanced itself from any approach to any "separatist" theses, even of the mildest sort. Doing so would imply contradicting the entire Soviet approach to foreign relations before August 1939. The mere image of a hypothetically independent Catalonia, that could be accused by Great Britain and France of being under Soviet control, generated absolute reluctance on part of the Soviets.

Finally, a last element must be taken into account. Vladimir Antonov-Ovseyenko, Soviet citizen but of Ukrainian nationality, was a figure that potentially had to have a great empathy and even an apparent show of harmony with the what nationalists termed "Catalan national reality". After all, he was a member of a national minority – the Ukrainians – that formed part of a large Soviet State within the USSR, identified, de facto, with the Russian nation. This would explain, of course, how he realized from the first moment that Catalonia was something different from the rest of the Spanish Republic. Not only for its own language, massively used by the population, but also for its political autonomy, for its own particular way of doing things, with the presence of specific and unique political and syndical forces. Catalonia had its own government and, a not unimportant detail, its own history, with a closeness to the French border (and French Catalonia), which gave the country its own very particular European touch. In fact, it should not be forgotten that Antonov-Ovseyenko learned the Catalan language and used it on some occasions in public. Obviously, this was an operation of political propaganda, both on the part of the Government of the Generalitat, as well as on the part of the consul general.[19] But, by way of contrast, it can be compared to the fact that Marcel Rosenberg, the Soviet ambassador sent to Madrid, not only did not even speak Spanish, and at no time did he even show any interest in learning that language. Antonov-Ovseyenko, on the other hand, did achieve a working knowledge of Catalan. This was one proof that the consul had understood the importance of the language in the configuration of the Catalan national perception of collective reality.

In any case, and going further, it is also true that the Soviet citizenship and the Ukrainian nationality of the consul general at the same time played against maximalist positions, such as the separatist one. The russification that historically the Ukraine had received during the Tsarist era had diluted deeply Ukrainian national peculiarities. The "October Revolution" and the later configuration of the Soviet State had helped to partially recover some elements of Ukrainian identity, but at the same time, they had done so by clearly marking its limits. The possibility of pushing towards a separation from the "Workers' State" of which they were a part was the main limit not to be crossed. The logic, articulated under the discourse of the social liberation that the USSR was developing, automatically, also implied national liberation. Therefore, if one idea was united with the other, what need could there be to get separated? The Finnish case had been the only one of the former territories of the Czarist Empire that had carried out, and had been allowed to carry out, the right of self-determination defended by the Bolsheviks.[20] So, then, the imagination of Antonov-Ovseyenko was what it was: a commitment for the recognition of national diversity in the configuration of each State, even to the point of verbally accepting the remote possibility of separation (or greater disconnection), but as something not to be acted upon in reality. A scheme that, as has been seen, was applied in the case of Catalonia.

In short, and given the consular position on the "Catalan national question", the result makes improbable affirmations such as those made by the Propaganda Commissar of the Generalitat of Catalonia, Jaume Miravitlles, when he stated that the establishment of the Soviet consulate in the Catalan capital had as its objective attracting, fighting or neutralizing nationalist political forces, with ERC at the head.[21] The consular gamble between October 1936 and July 1937 went together with the recognition of Catalonia as a nation and, moreover, with an awareness of its poor handling by the central State, the Spanish Republic. It was, then, a relevant jump from the Soviet viewpoint, if one is aware of the prior knowledge the Soviets had of Catalonia, and, by extension, of the importance of its national sentiment before the beginning of the Spanish Civil War; if taken into account, the logic of the Soviet discourse in favor of the liberation of oppressed peoples and how, in principle, Catalonia did not form part of such a category; and if valued, also, what were the interests of the Collective Security policy, as assumed by the Soviets, which in no case accepted a position in favor of an independent Catalonia. However, it is equally true that as of July 1937 and, especially, September 1937, such flexibility was dampened, so as to end up being definitely swallowed up by a centralist and emphatically pro-Spanish State vision, that diluted the specificity with which Catalonia had been previously recognized. Certainly, the consular positions until the summer of 1937 had been the result of a mixture of pragmatism and sincere identification towards the Catalan reality and had collected an explanation of a situation that, on the other hand, seems that had not been exclusive in the years of the Civil War, nor much less from the vision developed by the Soviets in relation to the national situation of Catalonia.

Without any doubt, Catalonia had been a particular nation for the Soviets. Quite particular, in fact. The description portrayed here, with the turning point between the summer and autumn of 1937, is perhaps the most obvious proof.

Notes

1 This essay has been restructured – without other significant changes – from its original Catalan essay version to facilitate its access to English-language readers. In general terms, see: J. Puigsech, "Un consolat

significatiu per a un búnquer especial». *L'Espill*, n. 53, Autumn 2016, pp. 193–196.

2   J. Puigsech, *La Revolució Russa i Catalunya*, Vic: Eumo, 2017, pp. 107–133 and 140–177.

3   The role of Antonov-Ovseyenko, in matters not centered on the Catalan nationalist matters, is fully covered in the bibliography referring to the Sovietic participation in the Spanish Civil War. See, among others: R. Radosh, R.; M. R. Habeck; and G. Sevostianov, *Spain Betrayed: The Soviet Union in the Spanish Civil War*, London/New Haven: Yale University Press, 2001; D. Kowalsky, *La Unión Soviética y la Guerra Civil Española,* Barcelona: Crítica, 2003; F. Schauff, *La victoria frustrada. La Unión Soviética, la Internacional comunista y la Guerra Civil Española*, Barcelona: Debate, 2008.

4   J. Puigsech, "An intimate diplomatic view. The Spanish Civil War according to the personal diaries of the Soviet Consul Vladimir Antonov-Ovseyenko", *International Journal of Iberian Studies*, vol. 29, n. 1, 2016, p. 32.

5   I. Ehrenburg, *España república de trabajadores*, Barcelona: Crítica, 1976 [1932], pp. 167–173.

6   I. Ehrenburg, *Gentes, años, vidas. Memorias*, Barcelona: Planeta, 1985, p. 189.

7   J. Puigsech, "Los pasos de la diplomacia soviética para establecer el consulado de la URSS en Barcelona". *Ayer*, n. 86, 2012, pp. 187–194.

8   This meeting with Largo Caballero was not the first. There had been a previous one, on September 4, 1936, in which the Soviet consul had situated himself in a line that would connect with that discussed here, as can be seen in: J. Puigsech, "An intimate diplomatic view . . . ", *op. cit.*, p. 26.

9   J. Puigsech, *Falsa leyenda del Kremlin. El consulado y la URSS en la Guerra Civil española,* Madrid: Biblioteca Nueva, 2014, pp. 111–112.

10 *Ibid.*, pp. 148–154.

11 *Ibid.*, pp. 277–289.

12 A letter by Strakhov to the NKID published in *ibid.*, p. 277.

13 *Ibid.*, pp. 260–261.

14 *Ibid.*, pp. 289–293.

15 J. Puigsech, "El nostre amic Companys. La sintonia de la diplomàcia soviètica envers el president republicà", *Afers. Fulls de recerca i pensament*, n. 77, 2014, pp. 195–215.

16 J. Puigsech, *La Revolució Russa . . . op. cit.*, pp. 126–127 and 181–188.

17 R. Donaldson and J. L.Nogee, *The Foreign Policy of Russia: Changing*

Systems, Enduring Interests, New York/London: M. E. Sharpe, 2005, pp. 37–74.

18   J. Puigsech, "An intimate diplomatic view . . . ", *ibid.*, p. 33.

19   J. Miravitlles, *Més gent que he conegut*, Barcelona: Destino, 1981, p. 196.

20   R. Service, *Historia de Rusia en el siglo XX,* Barcelona: Crítica, 2000, pp. 36–38 and 94–137.

21   J. Miravitlles, *Episodis de la Guerra Civil Espanyola*, Barcelona: Pòrtic, 1972, p. 196.

Chapter 5

A Catalan Separate Peace During the Civil War? Catalan Nationalist Fantasy and Spanish Republican Criticisms Regarding the Role of Catalonia, 1936–1939

Josep Sánchez Cervelló

The purpose of this study is to clarify the accusations launched by the central government of the Spanish Republic against the Catalan and Basque autonomous authorities during the Civil War of 1936–1939.[1] Specifically, the intention is to see whether the criticisms that alleged an effective desire of Catalan and Basque nationalists to achieve a separate peace behind the back of the Republic had a real basis in fact. Such an investigatory effort cannot escape the Basque–Catalan conjunction, since both regional governments coordinated their strategies during the war years, in this and other aspects. As is well known, the institutional collapse of the Republican State after the military coup of July 17, 1936, in the Protectorate of Morocco, allowed that both Catalonia and, later, Euskadi, to fill the vacuum left by the central administration in their territories. Clearly, both regions assumed powers that were not foreseen in their respective autonomy statutes of 1932 and 1936. In the Catalan case, a Central Committee of Antifascist Militias was immediately established in the summer, then a specific ministry of Defense was created as well, along with a

Catalan war industry, among with other improvised institutions. In the Basque case, after the establishment of the Bilbao government in October 1936, a regular army of Euskadi was formed, led by the *Lehendakari* – Basque head of government – José Antonio Aguirre. Further measures were taken: currency was emitted, passports were issued, at the same time as justice was also reorganized and a Basque university was created.

In fact, such regional initiatives against State authority were nothing more than another chapter in an established tradition of political tension. The back-and-forth between the Catalan or Basque "periphery" and the Spanish centre was already apparent at the very beginning of the twentieth century. It would become a constant in Spanish politics with the loss of Cuba, the Philippines and Puerto Rico in 1898. Dispossessed of what had remained of the Empire in the "Disaster" of 1898, Spanish nationalists accused Catalan nationalism of treason to Spain. For example, in 1901, a pro-militarist newspaper bitterly pointed out: "Nothing more has been done than lifting the suspension of constitutional guarantees and the Catalanists [Catalan nationalists], taking advantage of the freedom offered to them by our laws, continue their suicidal labor against national unity and in favor of the loss of prestige and the dishonor of the name of Spain. *La Veu de Catalunya* has reappeared to continue its separatist campaigns. *La Renaixença* once again places in preferred columns the Bases of Manresa, the separatist program of the Catalans. The choral groups are preparing to sing everywhere [the Catalan nationalist anthem] *Els Segadors*, and the preparations for broad and powerful Catalanist propaganda are activated, the objective of which must not be other than the dismemberment of the Fatherland. [...] Yes, if it depends on us, as soon as the Parliament were opened, the first proposed bill that would be presented would be very brief and complete, to extend the action of the Criminal Code, imposing a death penalty on all Spaniards who shout against the unity of the Fatherland or who are shown to be full conspirators against such a sacred and immaculate ideal. Let us repeat ourselves, today what has been said so many times: bad seed is that of Catalanism; it is not enough to prune it; it has to be totally destroyed."[2]

This is one eloquent example, among hundreds of others, of the traditional distrust of political Madrid against Catalan nationalist political leaders, President Lluís Companys of the Generalitat, the Catalan autonomous government, and the heretofore dominant political party, Esquerra Republicana de Catalunya (ERC, Republican Left of Catalonia). The wartime situation in Spain in the late 1930s made these feelings much worse. Accepting that such misgivings were exacerbated during the Civil War by the relative Catalan ability to act freely, it must be added that, from the beginning of the Spanish conflict, both the president of the Generalitat and his government, as well as the Basque *Lehendakari* and his executive, had shown the desire to widen autonomy beyond their respective statutory limits. The project to act – for example, in international affairs – appears to have been initially designed by the Basque nationalists, and it would seem that the Catalan nationalists entered the game later.

Certainly, the realities between Barcelona and Bilbao were divergent. In fact, in Euskadi nothing was the same as in Catalonia. In Bilbao, the Government was controlled by the christian democrats of the Basque Nationalist Party (PNV-EAJ); the revolutionary forces were few, and did not carry the weight they possessed in Catalonia. Nevertheless, the will to redirect the constitutional order towards goals of more self-government were similar between the Basque and Catalan governments. A clear sign of this trend can be seen in the activities of the Basque nationalist Manuel de Irujo. Between September 1936 and May 1937, he served as minister without a portfolio in the Spanish Republic's government led by left socialist Francisco Largo Caballero; de Irujo was chosen to cover the new Basque Statute of Autonomy, proclaimed on October 6, not quite three months after the outbreak of the fighting. He was retained as Minister of Justice when the central government of Juan Negrín replaced Largo in May 1937. Using his position, Irujo discreetly proposed coordinated action between the Basque government and the Generalitat with the objective that both attempt to attain international representation.

The Informal Diplomatic Delegations of Catalans and Basques Abroad

In December 1936, Irujo wrote to the president of the leadership of the Basque Nationalist Party saying: "Spain has no solution", and therefore, "Euskadi and Catalonia ought to aspire to have, in [Spanish Republican] embassies and consulates, an aide attached to the consul or ambassador, who would permit a coordinated representation but with its own personality, distinct. If we do not take these measures we will not advance in the confederal route [...]. The Generalitat approves and knows this policy, which I have commented with Tarradellas and Companys. The army, the currency, foreign trade, the [right of] pardon, the exchange [of prisoners], the policies regarding ports and borders, ecclesiastical relations, [freedom to control] delegations, inside and outside the Republic, international aviation lines, must be conquests guaranteed to prevail over [*superación*] the services [of the State]."[3]

In practice, since the approval of self-government, the Basque *Euzko Jaurlaritza* (or Basque Government) maintained delegations abroad. The two most important were the office in London, directed by José Ignacio de Lizaso and Ángel de Gondra, and the one in Paris, run by Rafael Picavea Leguía and José María Izaurieta Echevarría. Their initial purpose was to purchase war materials and food, but they would also undertake political negotiations whenever possible, even carry out important conversations, after the fall of Euskadi to the pro-Franco forces in July 1937, with the direct participation of Irujo himself and of the *Lehendakari* Aguirre.

Irujo's influence on the Spanish Republic's connections with the Western democracies was, of course, fundamental, as he was Minister of Justice, and initially in charge of prisoner exchanges with the Franco authorities. He kept in close contact with Britain's commercial chargé-d'affaires, John Leche, with the Swiss doctor Marcel Junod, the official representative of the International Red Cross in Spain, and with the British consul in Bilbao, Ralph Stevenson. These contacts would continue after the transfer of the Basque Government to Barcelona in the summer of 1937, where Irujo expanded his relations, now with the French ambassador to the Republic, Eirik Labonne, also present in Barcelona.[4]

From the viewpoint of the Basque nationalists, everything was different in Catalonia. In Barcelona, the Catalan nationalist element was definitely not in control. The anarchist revolution forced many thousands of conservatives to flee, many of whom were nonetheless Catalan nationalists. Once in exile, in their majority, they opted for the Franco cause. Right-wing Catalan leader Francesc Cambó was the paradigm of this option, and he financed the Information Service of the Border of the Northeast of Spain (SIFNE, the acronym in Spanish): most SIFNE agents were from his party, the *Lliga Catalana* (Catalan League). Cambó was, in addition, the author of a manifesto made public in October 1936, in support of the insurrection; although his declaration was not as "lame and servile"[5] as ardent Franco supporters would have wished, his commitment to the new Spanish "national cause" was absolute.[6] Therefore, the Catalan nationalist and reknowned academic Pere Bosch Gimpera noted bitterly that Cambó "advised all the Catalans who left Barcelona [to go into exile] to go to the national area [i.e., pro-Franco held zone]".[7]

The truth was that, in France, Catalan exiles of both sides were mixed up together: while while some had pledged themselves to the military insurgency begun in mid-July 1936, others fought initially to defeat the revolt, although, later in the summer, many had to flee as anarcho-syndicalists and anarchists of the CNT-FAI seized the streets and even some of the levers of power that the ERC had previously controlled. To a certain extent, both groups of exiles were united in their Catalan national sentiment and class hatred against the working-class leaders that had taken control in Catalonia. In this environment the need arose to look for what was called "civil peace" (as an antonym to "civil war"), an agreement which had to be sealed between Catalans, with no attention paid to ideological sides and having as a basic objective the answer to the "national question", a feeling which supposedly they all shared.[8]

According to the "Special Information Brigade" organized by anarcho-syndicalist and anarchist spies and observers in France,[9] these groups of Catalan exiles from both sides acted "inspired by factional elements or even in accordance with the disturbing guidelines emanating from the fascist camp. Therefore, we consider it necessary to take immediately all the preventive measures so as to disrupt the plans of these individuals". The reports of the Special Information Brigade indicated that the search for a separate peace by Catalans also implied the desire to end the revolution.[10]

The infiltration of the confused Catalan émigré milieu by pro-Franco espionage is well documented.[11] In this environment, many of rumors that assured that a separate peace would be possible in Catalonia were cooked up and circulated, an effort to which the SIFNE and the *Lliga Catalana* contributed.[12] In fact, Cambó, who financially backed the espionage organization and had led the Lliga for almost two decades, revealed an exact knowledge of this supposed secessionist maneuver in his own diaries.[13] All this rumor-mongering, both outside and inside of Spain, would weaken Republican cohesion, and, very specifically, increase the lack of trust of the central Republican Government regarding Catalan politics.

Parallel to the convergence that was propitiated outside of Spain by this demand of Catalan exiles for "civil peace", in October 1936 a Propaganda Commissariat was created under the direct authority of the president of the Generalitat, of which the imaginative publicist Jaume "Met" Miravitlles would be the main individual responsible. Within this organism, an annex was created for tasks of foreign propaganda, which acted as an informal sort of "Catalan Ministry of Foreign Affairs". An office representing the Generalitat was established in Paris, under the orders of the Menorcan Nicolau M. Rubió Tudurí, and another similar agency in London with the conservative independentist Josep Maria Batista Roca at the head. From 1937 to 1939, their task would consist of looking for the ways to make understandable the messages and initiatives of the Generalitat to the diplomatic chancelleries of the European democracies.[14]

The Unsuccessful Attempts to Reach a Separate Peace

The first hints of the parallel diplomacy of the Catalan Government appeared in the press on February 9, 1937, when the chief editor of the *Daily Telegraph* in London sent a telegram to Lluís Companys indicating the following: "According to afternoon British press: A section of the Catalan Government has established contact with Franco so as to avoid direct conflict with the rebels, in the event of overcoming the Government of Valencia. STOP. We would very much appreciate authorized information from Your Excellency on this subject. Thank you in advance."[15] The official response was issued by Martí Rouret, undersecretary of the Catalan Presidency, with a straightforward negation: "Received telegram. His Excellency asks me to tell you that the information is absurd and the mere supposition will hurt us. Autonomous Catalonia within the democratic Republic will fight and defeat the rebels, who are the instrument of international fascism."[16]

Despite the official denial, the British press was not far off from the facts. Just two weeks later, the leader of the Catalan nationalist Christian democrats, the *Unió Democràtica de Catalunya* (Democratic Union of Catalonia), Manuel Carrasco Formiguera, had met with the British ambassador, when His Britannic Majesty's embassy, like some other foreign representations, had retired from the shambles in Madrid to a safer location across the French Basque border in Hendaye. Carrasco's purpose was to convince the British Government to initiate a mediation with Basque and Catalan approval.[17] Republican Spanish police circles working in Paris confirmed the news that there were peace contacts between the Basque Government, with the participation of the Vatican, of Italy and with the full knowledge of the Burgos Junta, Franco's executive.[18] The information also referred to the mediating role of the British and the approaches that they had maintained with the Valencia Government and with the Generalitat.[19]

During 1937 there were other initiatives aimed at seeking a peace with Catalonia and the Basque Country. One of the steps of the parallel diplomacy was that as cultural emissaries. Thus Ventura Gassol, formerly Catalan councillor of Culture of the Generalitat, but in exile since October 1936, now became the president of a commission in charge of the "Medieval Catalan Art Exhibition in Paris" that was open to the public from March to May 1937. In the course of the art show, the prestigious Catalan prehistorian Pere Bosch i Gimpera visited Paris and discreetly established multiple contacts. In the course of the war, Bosch would carry out numerous confidential diplomatic activities, in favour of the Generalitat and, also, at the request of the President of the Republic, Manuel Azaña himself. In fact, to strengthen his authority abroad and take advantage of the special relationship that Bosch had with Azaña, Companys made him Councillor of Justice in the Generalitat government remodeling of July 1937. The Barcelona daily, *La Vanguardia*, having become unofficially the newspaper that reflected Spanish prime minister Negrín's views, always gave detailed information about the trips of Bosch Gimpera, because in the governamental circles his movements were known and reported on.[20] On July 3, Azaña, after one audience granted to Bosch Gimpera, wrote in his private notebook: "I have used him for sending some messages to the ambassadors in Brussels and London".[21] It was obvious that there was an extraordinary diversity of foreign policies coming out of Republican Spain: not only did official letters and communiqués issue from the Foreign Ministry of the Government of the Republic, but also there was informal policy intelligence being unofficially passed on by the presidency of the Republic, the Government of Catalonia, and the Basque Government.

Already in early April of 1937, a document from the anarchist Special Information Brigade in Perpignan indicated the growing convergence of interests between the exiled Catalans and the representatives of the Generalitat. The following was noted: "Casanovas [the president of the Catalan Parliament][22] telephoned [...] because they warned [Batista] Roca and Gisbert, representatives of Palestra [a Catalan nationalist youth group headed by Batista], to move to Paris and there, all together, with another representative of Euskadi, to go to London to get in contact with a delegation of the British government. It is unknown to what purpose [...]. I see that behind this comedy is a sinister design: the desire, if they see the matter of the war badly, to negotiate an arrangement with the fascists, to avoid in Catalonia the horrors of an invasion."[23]

Republican Criticisms of Catalan and Basque Intiatives

The knowledge of the external contacts of Catalan and Basque nationalists, together with a constant media attention concerning these actions, managed to make angry both President Azaña and prime minister Negrín, despite their considerable differences. Azaña wrote in his diary on July 29, 1937: "The defection of Catalonia (because it is nothing less) has become palpable."[24]

But the external contacts increased as of October 18 when the Basque Government decided to establish its headquarters in Barcelona. Previously, in August, the PNV had negotiated in secret with the Italians, and *Lehendakari* Aguirre had rejected the invitation of the head of the Government, Negrín, to move the headquarters of the Basque executive to Valencia, where the Republican central government was established since it fled Madrid in November 1936.[25] Also in this period, there was an exchange of messages between the Catalan Generalitat and the French government through the ex-Catalan councillor of the Interior Josep Maria Espanya.[26] On the 11th of November 1937 Companys had an interview in Paris with the Minister of War, Edouard Daladier, and the Foreign Minister, Ybon Delbos.[27] The coordinated policy of the Generalitat and the Basque Government made relations between Negrín, Companys and Aguirre definitively worse.

During this period, the Generalitat was trying to consolidate its political space in the face of the Republican government, which was moving from Valencia to Barcelona in November 1937. As an expression of this need for national affirmation, Catalan authorities had began to distribute among Catalan soldiers an emblem with the Generalitat crest and the word *Catalunya* (Catalonia). The campaign was carried out by the Propaganda Commissioner of the Generalitat, with the aim of addressing "the spiritual needs of the Catalan soldiers who fight against the *fascio* and in consideration that the four bars are found everywhere where there are Catalans, [the Propaganda Commissioner] offers an emblem with the coat of arms of Catalonia. The first emblems – 30,000 – have been distributed, at the request of the interested parties, to our compatriots fighting in the front of Madrid. Catalan fighters! When you go to fight do it on behalf of Catalonia, when you go to fight do it thinking of Catalonia. It must also be seen that the fighting is in the name of Catalonia. Nothing more appropriate than the emblem that the Propaganda Commissioner will give you for free".[28]

On November 1, 1937, the Government of the Republic was resettled in Barcelona. This fact did not please the Catalan Government which complained, acidly, to Negrín. With this decision, according to Palmiro Togliatti, the delegate of the Komintern in Spain, it became dangerous for Catalonia to imitate the actions of Euskadi. The Basque government had worked on the fringes of the Government of the Republic and would give "a certain guarantee against the possibility of developing and triumphing in Catalonia a movement tending to break the front of the resistance to fascism and to reach a separate peace".[29]

The criticisms that Togliatti made of the Basque nationalists were very harsh. He pointed out that the nationalist minister Manuel Irujo should be considered a traitor, and that he worked for a Republican defeat. Togliatti added: "The fact that the [Republican] Government has not removed him is serious. The least that can be said is that Negrín fears the Basques, who are about to organize themselves as a small state within the State, with its own Government, its own administration, and the claim to have its 'own' army, its 'own' navy, etc. Through Basque nationalist behaviour the worst influences are carried out in the area of the Government and including the masses."[30]

In this context, the presence of the Republican central Government in Catalonia produced considerable tension. The Catalan press controlled by the Generalitat required the recognition of Catalan national idiosyncrasy, forcing the Interior minister to request his officials the maximum respect for Catalan as the language of the territory.[31] At that moment, Mariano Ansó, undersecretary of Justice, was present at a conversation between Negrín and Companys in which the first urged the Catalan leader to "abstain from any intervention in international politics and complained that the names of Catalonia and Spain appear on occasions as different entities [...]. Here began the back-and-forth of a situation that was to last until the end of the war".[32] Really, it was a negative interaction that started from the exact moment that the war began in July 1936.

Furthermore, in January of 1938 Companys wrote to Negrín complaining that although he had been assured that the desire was to reach an effective cooperation between both governments, such an objective had not been reached. In the retelling by Mariano Ansó, Companys related that: "I warned him [Negrín] that the [central] Government's stay in Barcelona, which satisfied us so much, could be very beneficial for the whole unity [all of Republican Spain], but it could also, if exquisite care was not taken in the procedure, create confrontations" [...]. "'The Catalan president added, quoting his own words to Negrín: 'The Government moved to Barcelona almost three months ago and because of the experience lived so far, it is almost necessary to say, Mr. President, that what has happened is that which was wished to be avoided'." Companys listed a series of measures that eroded the power of the Generalitat and in particular "one decree on press and another on censorship, the regulation of which, he said, corresponded to the Generalitat, which the State, using paper cuotas, access to hard currencies or other resources, could submerge".[33]

Antonio Cordón, analyzing the relations between Companys, who was a friend, and Negrín, of whom he was undersecretary of Defense, said that "they could not be more tense. I do not know if this is the influence of Negrín's suspicion that the authority of Companys could be utilized for the achieving a separate peace [...], as some supposed that Companys had already tried, or because Negrín was also rooted in the centralist sentiment, in spite of the Statute, or by a draft of defense of his authority as governing the Republic, in which the president and minister of Defense always showed excessive intransigence or, as I think the most likely, for the combined action of all these factors and, moreover, that of a personal antipathy. Practically, Negrín avoided any relationship with Companys. I do not remember any act or ceremony which they attended together".[34]

This struggle between the central Republican Government and the Generalitat led to a greater cooperation between Basque and Catalan authorities. Joint action was agreed upon in different meetings, such as, for example, that of 16 November, at the Basque

Delegation in Paris, between the Basque and Catalan presidents. Or later, they would meet again in the French capital, where Companys would also hold interviews on several occasions with the French Finance minister, Vincent Auriol.[35]

Once the battle of the Ebro began – on July 25, 1938 – the Republican Minister of Interior, the Basque socialist Julián Zugazagoitia, had a conversation with Negrín in which the latter said: "I'm not fighting the war against Franco so we can relive in Barcelona a stupid and small-town [*pueblerino*] separatism [...]. There is only one nation: Spain! This noiseless and persistent separatist campaign cannot be allowed, and it must be cut off at the roots if you want me to continue being minister of Defense and directing Government policy, which is national policy."[36] And, in fact, the reaction against the nationalists to the political crisis that exploded in August was conditioned by this thinking. Azaña himself, on August 6, met with Jaume Miravitlles, Propaganda Commissioner of the Generalitat, to whom reported the Catalan unofficial "ambassadors", when he himself had just returned from France. Miravitlles had held an interview with the French Foreign Minister, and Azaña alluded to cynical "*numanti-nos*". Thus was a well-known reference to the opponents of Rome in the Hispanic city of Numantia in the second century BCE, who preferred suicide to surrender; by extension, a reference to those who upheld the struggle against Franco at all cost; But, more pointedly, Azaña was mocking such defenders of all-out resistance to the death as being cynical, as such spokespersons had an escape plan "with a plane [waiting] and with c/c [checking acounts] in Switzerland."[37] Surely Azaña was referring to the selfsame Miravitlles, who traveled abroad with frequency. His epithet of "numantinism" referred to the official version of the Generalitat of "resisting at any sacrifice", without specifying the clandestine negotiations that were carried out in coordination with the Basques.

As a result, the Government of the Republic closely followed the movements of the peripheral nationalisms and their representative institutions. This is why Negrín's Foreign Minister, Julio Álvarez del Vayo, would send instructions to the ambassador in Paris, telling him that he could only resist, and added, in an explicit reference to what the Catalans and Basques advocated, "any more or less masked solution of an outcome of a 'federative type' [sic]. Any arrangement that presupposes the yielding of any part of the country, including its islands, is to be rejected with firmness and outrage".[38] On November 17, Azaña – despite his own manoeuvres – wrote in his diary: "I call the Government's attention about the 'official' friends that carry out diplomatic efforts in Paris and London, sowing confusion and reducing authority of the Government. They do damage. Need to put an end to that. Unauthorize it."[39]

The poor institutional relationship between the autonomous governments and the central Republican authority was evident on the eve of the fall of Catalonia at the end of January 1939. The *Lehendakari*, Aguirre, and the president of the Generalitat, Companys, moved to the Perxers farmhouse, located near the town of La Vajol, just before the Catalan and Spanish border with France. They had agreed to leave for exile on February 5, together with Azaña and the top authorities of the Republic. That day, when there was still no sunlight, an entourage with several cars departed for the meeting point agreed upon with Azaña, but, when they arrived, they had the disagreeable surprise of verifying that the president of the Republic and his retinue had entered France two hours previously. This lack of courtesy would be clarified by Azaña's brother-in-law, Cipriano Rivas Cherif, who accompanied him, explaining that the Republican head of State did not want that his representation and category to be judged as equal to those of Aguirre and Companys.[40] Such lack of consideration by Azaña, who seemed in the midst of the disaster to only worry about protocol, can be better understood if the precedents and existing tensions in the Republican political center can be perceived. This has been clear in other similar initiatives, such as the failed negotiations for the evacuation of non-combatants led by the International Red Cross between late 1936 and early 1937.

Documents and Commitments of the Catalan and Basque Negotiators

Before the disastrous end of the war took place, in late 1938 when faced with the inexorable defeat of Republican arms, the Catalan and Basque governments made a more determined effort to end the whole conflict. They left a significant trail of documents describing their activities. As has been explained, the PNV had long-term relations with diverse British authorities, links which were reinforced during the Spanish war. These contacts were centralized by José Ignacio Lizaso who, after the fall of Bilbao in 1937, was installed in the Republican embassy of Spain in London. On the other hand, with the establishment of the central Government of the Republic in Barcelona, the acting British ambassador, now John H. Leche, moved to the resort town of Caldes d'Estrach, popularly known as "Caldetes", together with Dennis Cowan, offical liaison agent of the commission for the exchange of prisoners and a member of MI5. It was then that Manuel de Irujo, Minister of Justice of the Republic and responsible for the exchanges with the Franco side,[41] and Bosch Gimpera, responsible for the portfolio of Justice in the Catalan Government, came together into direct relations with the British diplomats. These were interested in the fate of the detainees held by the Republican side, and both Irujo and Bosch allowed them to visit the prisons of the State and of the Generalitat, verifying the difference between these two, and the centres that were under military control of the SIM, the Republic's Military Information Service. They also could verify that both the PNV and the Catalan left forces, the ERC and ACR, were moderate parties favorable to the Western democratic model, a position that contrasted with a significant part of the supporters of the Spanish Popular Front. And when, given his pro-Republican bias, Leche was replaced by Ralph Stevenson, former British consul in Bilbao, Catalan and Basque leaders continued maintaining cordial relations with Leche, links that would extend after the fall of the Republic.

On March 28, 1938, Manuel de Irujo wrote Companys a note pointing out to him the telegram he had received from *Lehendakari* Aguirre. He said: "Given the interesting moments in the perspective of Catalonia and Euskadi, I consider it urgently needed that Batista Roca leave London, and {with} another delegate in Paris, meet with me in Paris, if I still find myself here {at that time}. Irujo added for Companys: 'You'll see if you think it is appropriate that Mr. Batista Roca leave straight away. I will try to meet with him to receive your orders'."[42]

All this was doubtlessly the continuation of the work that Irujo had been doing since April 1937. It concerned polling the British and French governments on the possibility of negotiating a "just peace" that would guarantee the survival of both the Catalan and Basque autonomies.[43] This labour, carried out separately from the Government of the Republic and official diplomacy, had the support of the Catalan nationalist and republican parties. Significantly, the Catalan–Basque initiative coincided with the crisis of the central Executive – in early April 1938 – after the resignation of socialist Indalecio Prieto from the Ministry of Defense, the consequent rupture between his followers and those of Negrín in socialist ranks, together the recent breakthrough of the Aragon front, and the demoralization visible in the Republic's rearguard which was subject to the continuous bombings of Franco's aviation. The arrival of Batista Roca in London was secret, coordinated with the Basques. Batista did not have any contact with the Republican diplomatic legation, because the Basques, so as to have more room for manoeuvre, were no longer installed there, as of January of 1938, when Irujo was substituted as Minister of Justice, replaced by the staunch follower of Negrín, Mariano Ansó.[44] The influence of the Basques in the English circles was great "because they had achieved, by means of the collaboration of a British information centre {i.e., public relations}, to maintain a certain presence, even publishing articles that were favorable to their cause in the press, advocating federalism as a solution to the Spanish problem".[45] Batista Roca would attempt that the Catalan Government contract the same publicity company so to be able to influence British public opinion in the same way, but, from Barcelona; he was assured that it was not possible, given reasons of budget.

Furthermore, the main "friends" of the PNV were the British conservatives and especially Joseph Ball, advisor to prime minister Neville Chamberlain and tied to the interior espionage service,

MI5. Ball met with Batista for the first time on April 22, 1938 when Franco, having conquered the Northern areas in republican hands in the previous year, abolished the Basque Statute, and had split the remaining territory of the Republic in two, reached the town of Vinarós (Vinaroz in Castilian Spanish) on the 15th of April. By then, in seizing Lleida, Franco on the April 5 had also abolished the Catalan autonomy statute. Almost everybody believed that the war was lost, and for this reason precisely Negrín eliminated Prieto in those same days.

In international terms, British and Italians had just signed a pact, six days before. The only "news" that concerned the Republic was that Fascist Italy committed itself to withdraw its troops and war matériel when the war ended, evidencing that Britain awaited Franco's victory. Batista Roca spoke with Ball on the commitment of the British Government to peace, about the possibility of organizing an armistice in Spain, believing that, after the pact with Italy, Britain was ready to press Mussolini to oblige Franco to negotiate. It was believed identical pressure could be realized in Paris, an effort that, in turn, could influence the central Government of the Republic. Ball replied that Franco would not enter into any pact because he was convinced of his own victory. Batista Roca pointed out that he could attract Franco in exchange for some sort of immediate peace. And when Ball asked him about the compensations to be given to the Italians and the Germans, Batista said that Mussolini would have to be heavily paid, perhaps in gold, for the efforts made during the war, while he considered that the Germans could be compensated with the Spanish African colony of Rio de Oro, in the south of the Western Sahara. Ball replied strongly that this proposal would compromise the communication lines between the British Isles and Africa, and by extension the entirety of the Empire. Then Batista Roca answered that such a territorial cession was better than offering commercial and mining advantages in Spain. Ball, regarding this conversation, concluded that the objective of Batista Roca was to save a Catalonia that "was interested in its own national development and to maintain itself as distant as possible from the rest of Spain".[46]

The document with the proposals of Batista Roca arrived at the desk of the Prime Minister Neville Chamberlain. The proof that the British and French authorities took seriously the Catalan and Basque attempt to get an armistice in Spain comes from an encrypted telegram which Leche sent to London on May 30, indicating that Companys had contacted Georges Bonnet, French Foreign Minister. Companys acted in coordination with the Basque president to try to pressure Negrín to allow efforts to find an exit from the war. Leche concluded by indicating that soon a Basque delegation presided over by Aguirre would go to Paris.[47]

Then, José Ignacio de Lizaso, of the PNV, put his circle of political connections in the British capital at the disposal of Batista as the representative of the Catalan Government. And, together, Batista and Lizaso, under the advice of Alexander Cadogan, undersecretary of Foreign Affairs, handed a document to Edward Lindley Wood, Viscount Halifax, secretary of the Foreign Office, on June 23, 1938. Halifax was one of the most senior figures in the Conservative Party, and considered the architect of "appeasement". In parallel to this diplomatic *pourparler* in London, Rubió Tudurí and Picavea sent the same document to the French government.[48]

The text indicated: "The military revolt, after two years of undecided struggle, has turned into a war of attrition, for which a decisive end is still not in sight and in which the western half of the country, with foreign aid, struggles to conquer and subdue the eastern half. On the Mediterranean coast, the Catalan-speaking countries, including Catalonia, are perhaps the decisive factor behind the prolonged resistance of the Republican Government, and, under the current circumstances, are determined to continue this resistance [...]. Direct attacks against the Catalan border by rebel and foreign armies, the bombing of our cities and open towns – a cause of death or mutilation of thousands of non-combatants – and the subsequent attitude taken by the rebel authorities by have abolishing the Statute of Autonomy of Catalonia: these factors, together with the demand made by the rebels of 'an unconditional surrender', has pushed us to follow the only possible policy: to continue, with all our efforts, to oppose the aggressor [...]. Keep in mind that neither a military victory, if produced, would mean peace nor the final settlement of this conflict. A much more serious problem than the war itself is the restoration of friendly relations between peoples, after the brutalities and destruction caused by this conflict. The rebel military victory would represent simply a repetition of the previous conquest by Castile, with foreign aid, of the other nations of the Peninsula, a conquest to which partially can be attributed to the present struggle."

The text went on to add: "For the Catalans there is no doubt that a continuation of the war can only further complicate the issues that need to be resolved before a lasting peace and, if the Government of His Britannic Majesty believes it can be useful, we would be willing to use our influence in the Republican Government to open the way to an armistice, first, and, later, once peace is obtained in the Peninsula, we would contribute to the general security of Europe."

The memorandum continued by highlighting the contribution that Catalans and Basques could give to peace, intervening "between the two opposing Spanish sides", and convincing the Government of the Republic to accept the following points: the plan of the Committee of Non-Intervention for the withdrawal of foreign forces; any plan that would lead to an end of hostilities; conciliatory steps on all fronts; the appointment of international arbitrators to collaborate in exchanges of prisoners, and return of refugees; prohibition of executions and prohibition of reprisals, and so forth. The note added that the Catalan and Basque governments would carry out these efforts if "the proposing parties and supervisors of the armistice guarantee respect for the Statute of Autonomy of Catalonia". In addition, they wanted Catalonia to be represented directly at the peace conference, to help "intrapeninsular peace". It was also indicated that "the future Government of the Peninsula" should be decided through a referendum subject to international supervision.

According to the proposal, the referendum in Catalonia, "which is already an autonomous country", should be celebrated separately from the rest of Spain and the voters had to be asked about the political nature of the autonomous government, and if they considered it necessary to expand its powers. Besides Catalonia, the authors also wanted to put the Balearic Islands and Valencia under international protection, which would convert them into demilitarized zones. And to further sweeten the pill for the British, "guarantees would be offered to British interests in Catalonia, excluding all foreign competitors, of a political or economic nature". The document concludes that, for the interest of European security, the recognition of Catalan autonomy was a necessity, an affirmation that was justified by stating the following six points:

"1. Between the diverse nations of the Iberian Peninsula, the countries of Catalan language, including Catalonia and Valencia, are absolutely identified in their political institutions and in their social and economic organization with the Western European countries. Catalonia and Valencia are the extension of Western Europe to the south, along the Mediterranean coast of the Peninsula. 2. In the case of military action against France or the United Kingdom, a free and demilitarized Catalan country would make it impossible for attacking forces to use the western sector of the Pyrenees or the Mediterranean coast [...]. 3. In the same way, the basic resources of the Catalan country, as well as its own industrial production that, in some cases, represents 90% of the total Spanish figure, would be in the service of France or of the United Kingdom in case of war. 4. Peace in the Peninsula in itself cannot be guaranteed without a Catalan people [being] nationally satisfied, since it is the will of the Catalans to maintain, or recover, their freedom that has always caused internal disturbances. 5. [...] Catalonia, Valencia and the Balearic Islands represent a natural national unity and it is the desire of these three regions to join in a democratic and autonomous regime. The autonomous Catalan nation, in close cooperation with the Basques and, eventually, with an autonomous Galicia, could form a group of powers in the Peninsula, the strongest economically and they could act as mediators between the opposing parts of Spain, in close intelligence with the western European countries. 6. The Catalans are sympathetic to the idea of recognizing the autonomy of Galicia."[49]

On July 21, almost a month later, Alexander Cadogan presented the proposal made by the Non-Intervention Committee regarding the withdrawal of foreign volunteers to Lizaso and Batista Roca, trying thus to verify the real capacity of influence of his interlocutors with the central Republican Government. Catalans and Basques accepted the challenge and the two nationalist representatives in the Executive asked the members of the Spanish Republican Council of Ministers for their opinion. They had the support of four "non Marxist" ministers (three had to be the affiliates of Izquierda Republicana, the Republican Left loyal to president Azaña, whereas the fourth is not clear) so they managed to obtain the majority of the cabinet, not counting the prime minister. They let Halifax know on July 28, in a new memorandum in which they underlined their decisive influence in the Government of the Republic. Nevertheless, they also pointed out that the Executive considered that there were difficulties in the British proposal, and conditioned acceptance to details regarding the control system to be instituted, both in the air and by sea, like the supervision of only four rebel ports, considered insufficient.[50] These problems had much to do with the opinion of the military, as with the criteria of Negrín and Azaña. After all, given the questions made, however privately, to the ministers, everybody in authority knew the steps that Catalans and Basques representatives were taking.

After a month, on August 29, 1938, Batista Roca delivered a new memorandum to Halifax, in which he gave his personal version of the August crisis in the Spanish cabinet. In mid-August, the Catalan minister Aiguader, of the ERC, and Irujo, of the PNV, were replaced respectively, by Josep Moix of the PSUC, and Tomás Bilbao, of the left-wing Acción Nacionalista Vasca. The ministerial change – according to Batista – indicated that the resignations of the Basque and Catalan ministers were due to the intransigence and radicalism of Negrín, while they (the ERC and the PNV) were the main moderate liberal and democratic forces that existed in Spain. For this reason, they continued to put themselves under the jurisdiction of His Britannic Majesty to seek peace.[51]

Months later, in October, the line of action remained the same. In Paris, thanks to the governmental, political and press contacts established by Ventura Gassol, his sucessor in the position as Councillor of Culture of the Generalitat, Carles Pi Sunyer would undertake a series of interviews that nontheless did not produce any positive results.[52] Meanwhile, in London, on October, 12, a new memorandum by the Catalans and Basques was sent to the British Government, with the backdrop of the Czechoslovakian crisis and the subsequent Munich Agreements. Both delegations agreed with the dismemberment of Czechoslovakia, pointing out that the solution found for the Sudetenland could serve as an example for the Spanish conflict, based on the principle of self-determination of nationalities. And after reiterating their commitment to mediation, peace and European security reflected in the first joint memorandum, they pointed out that the Castilian project to create Spain had failed and they attached a map of the Spanish nationalities that had to be considered when negotiating peace.[53] They also insisted on the fact that Catalonia and the Basque Country represented a third force between the two extremist Spains.

The new document added few new features. After referring to the principles defined in the Memorandum of June 23, 1938, it drew attention to the following four-point program:

"1. The Basques/Catalans realized that the national problems and the question of self-determination had a decisive influence in the Czechoslovakian crisis, having been recognized that these two factors were essential for peace in Europe. This would confirm the thesis of the non-Castilian people of the Spanish State that neither the consolidation of a regime that could be established in the peninsula nor a lasting peace will be possible without the recognition due to the national problems of the Basques and Catalans and their rights to self-determination.

2. These two countries represent a third force in the war, where their participation has been, to a large extent, due to the desire to preserve their national rights, but their influence on all aspects of Spanish public life and their own democratic constitutions, equidistant from both extremist elements now at war, represent a basis for the future.

3. The Basques and the Catalans have taken note of the procedure adopted by the British Government for the problem of the Sudeten Germans, with the sending of a mission of experts to Czechoslovakia. If considered useful, we would welcome a similar method of investigation for the study and the resolution of the problems of the nationalities of the Peninsula, always

under the assumption that the desires of the 250,000 Basque people who are in exile or imprisoned and arrested in concentration camps, in the hands of the rebel authorities, are completely taken into account. We want to emphasize that the national Basque/Catalan problem is much less complicated than that of the Sudeten Germans, since under the constitution of the Spanish Republic an autonomous government was established in Catalonia and another in Euskadi, in accordance with the wills of the Basque and Catalan peoples, freely established in a plebiscite [...]. Although we have to remember that the Basque and Catalan autonomy statutes approved by the Parliament of the Republic were less broad than the Plan of Autonomy voted by the Basque and Catalan people in their plebiscite.

4. We believe that no new expression of self-determination is necessary to confirm the Basque and Catalan autonomies in accordance with the present status quo, but if it were considered necessary for an internal or international agreement in Spain, we would not have objections to accept a new plebiscite with international guarantees, as described in the Memorandum of 23-VI-1938."

The memorandum continued: "The non-recognition of Basques and Catalans to self-determination already legally expressed, would result not only in the breakdown of the agreement by which the Basques and Catalans consider themselves linked to the Spanish State, but also in the establishment of a constitutional Government that would become an illegal organ, forcing the Basques and Catalans to believe that no peaceful and legal coexistence would be possible with the Spaniards; and as a result, it would push them to oppose the consolidation of a Spanish state contrary to their national will – this way it would introduce an element of taking apart any future agreement plans. This perspective is consistent with the Republic's government policy expressed in the 4th section of the 13 points enunciated by Negrín."

Were all the above not sufficient, the Catalan and Basque proposal further underlined their agreement with the principle of self-determination and the verified plebiscite in the crisis of

Czechoslovakia, with the Munich Agreement, with the appointment of an international commission and the occupation of certain areas by international armed forces, which they considered a beneficial precedent for the Peninsula.[54]

The Catalan and Basque authorities were convinced that all European policy was ultimately decided in London; they then thought of reinforcing their respective delegations with people of greater political weight. For this reason, the Basque delegation was increased with the former minister Irujo and the Catalan one with the ex-councillor and famed prehistorian Bosch Gimpera. Then they prepared for another meeting with Sir Alexander Cadogan at the Foreign Office for November 26. The Basques were in charge of preparing the agenda, but on the scheduled day Cadogan had to leave for Paris, and he was substituted by Frederic Moncey, head of the Western European Department.[55] The interlocutors had the impression that "the Republican cause is considered lost by the English Government and that the Munich Pact represented abandoning all interventions even in the moment of peace". The nationalist delegation insisted that "a Spain in which the Catalan and Basque problems were not taken into account, would never achieve stability, and they delivered a note reinforcing the conversation".[56]

The new note stated, rather optimistically, that the post-Munich circumstance was the ideal moment to act, because conditions existed to impose a cessation of hostilities, a suggestion that evidently was naive given that Franco had just won the battle of the Ebro. Their analysis was based on the following postulates:

1. The two sides had sufficient military power to continue the war indefinitely, and Franco knew he had no capacity to defeat the Republic.
2. The operative stagnation at which both armies had arrived.
3. The renewal of hostilities should be avoided.
4. Leaving the situation of stalemate could lengthen suffering and hinder a future reconciliation.

Furthermore, given the international situation, it was thought that, after the Munich Pact and the effect of appeasement politics in the Mediterranean, it would be easy to pacify one of the centers of greatest conflict in Europe. To this purpose, the Western powers could attempt the following three objectives:

1. To assign a prominent role to Mussolini, who had already "had an important role in the resolution of the problems of Central Europe", along with France and Great Britain.
2. The reorganization of Spain, due to its international impact, would have to be carried out in accordance with the interested powers, but leaving the solely to the Spaniards the solution of their domestic problem.
3. "The liberties [sic] of the Basque and Catalan demilitarized countries, placed under international control, would be the best solution to ensure the security of the French borders and its lines of communication with North Africa".[57]

Bosch Gimpera's mission was frustrated by the distrust that his trip engendered with the Negrín government; the misgivings meant that, after two days in London, he was called back urgently to Barcelona.[58]

After the hasty return of Bosch Gimpera, Irujo remained in London, insisting on the need for the British to commit themselves to peace in Spain. To this end, Irujo sent Cadogan, on December 7, 1938, yet another memorandum, with explicit support of the Catalan Government, in which it was said that the solution of the Spanish war was the convocation of a peace conference, which should be held in London, with the presence of all the parties that had intervened in the conflict. And in order to set it up, it was suggested that the initiative should be started by Great Britain with the same method that had been used at the Balkan Conference of 1932. The suspension of hostilities should be discussed; a general amnesty proffered, with the exception of criminal offences; the way in which public order and the maintenance of the status quo would be guaranteed on all fronts at the time of the cessation of hostilities; and international sanctions to be applied against those who did not attend the peace conference.

The peace plan was to begin with the demilitarization of the Pyrenean border, which could be placed under the control of an international police force. The memorandum pointed out: "To all extents and purposes, the border zone is understood to be the territory of Catalonia and the Basque Country (Alava, Guipúzcoa, Vizcaya and Navarre)." Irujo's plan thereby called for establishing an international protectorate in Catalonia, the Basque country and Navarre. It also indicated that "once this control has been established, the conference will deliberate on the proposal to celebrate popular voting in the two autonomous countries". In this plebiscite, the population would be asked what regime it wanted: democratic or totalitarian, autonomous or unitary.

Previously, the general amnesty had to be granted, as well as the demobbing of all Catalan and Basque soldiers, "so they can exercise the suffrage", and the transfer to Catalonia and Euskadi of all emigrants outside the territories. There would be freedom of propaganda. The conference would also discuss the need to carry out a plebiscite "in the rest of the territory in the status quo, adopting for this all the securities that had been put into practice in Catalonia and the Basque Country. The celebration of this referendum, excluding Catalonia, Euskadi and, if need be, Galicia, would take place the same day, on the date that was set by the Peace Conference." It was added that "the formula for the Spanish plebiscite may be the same as that adopted in the Basque and Catalan plebiscites or any other [...] as long as it does not ignore or denaturalize the results of previous plebiscite consultations made in Euskadi, in Catalonia and, if the case be so, in Galicia". The representatives that were elected after the various plebiscites would deliberate "on the constitution of central or confederal power [...]. The procedure outlined redesigns the history of Spain with a regime made up of free peoples who self-govern. The fair play of free will will give the project a permanent solution". This plan furthermore showed an alternative formula that would pass through the convocation of a plebiscite accessible to everyone in the State. The referendum would ask for a vote on: "Democratic or totalitarian regime; monarchy or republic, leaving the autonomous problems subject to particular plebiscites of the respective peoples. This guarantee is essential for the success of any solution". However, it was pointed out that the Catalan and Basque Governments preferred the first model over the second, because "by organizing the peninsular peoples according to their will, it will facilitate the constitution of the confederal organ or a joint connection".[59]

In February 1939, when Catalonia had already been completely occupied by Franco's forces, Batista Roca and Lizaso still sent a final memorandum to Halifax in which they pointed out that the Republic would continue to resist despite the fall of Catalonia, and that mediation by the British was necessary to end the war.

In this final effort it was reiterated that "Basques and Catalans, as long as the fundamental rights of their peoples were safe", would unconditionally place themselves under the orders of the British Government, noting that both nations had always been democratic and sympathized with this form of government. It was said that "the current situation can only be considered by Basques and Catalans [...] a military conquest and the administration of General Franco cannot be considered ever as a legitimate Government of their peoples who inevitably, if there were no conversations, would lead to continuous disorders and revolts".[60]

Once in exile, with the Civil War over, Irujo and Lizaso, as delegates of the Basque Government, and Batista Roca, Bosch Gimpera and Pi Sunyer, of the Catalan Generalitat, continued maintaining excellent relations with the British, and would persist in preparing reports and memoranda claiming the right of self-determination for their peoples.[61]

Conclusions

The perception that in Catalonia there were sectors who wanted a separate peace was not really clear until 1937; it became visible when the Aragon front collapsed in the Spring of 1938. At that time, the demoralization was general and contacts and talks were accelerated by representatives of the Generalitat and the Government of the Basque Country with the Vatican, the United Kingdom, and France.

Nevertheless, Catalan and Basque activities in foreign policy were coordinated since the end of 1936, as evidenced by the letter from Minister Irujo to PNV leader Doroteo de Ziarritz. Forcibly this policy, on the part of the two peripheral nations under an autonomous regime, had to come into conflict with the general diplomacy carried out by the central government of the Republic. This latent tension was, to a great degree, due to knowledge about such relations that was in some manner well known, be it through the republican government's information services, through the agents of the CNT-FAI who were in France, and, also, through facts gathered by the Soviet NKVD and GRU as is shown by Togliatti, in his description of the causes why the Central Government was established in Catalonia.

The separate peace project was far more wishful than realistic. From the Catalan side, initiatives included the hope that the Catalan Countries project (*Països catalans*) might be brought about, although Mallorca was already in the hands of Franco from the beginning of the conflict, and Valencia, which had mostly voted the PSOE,[62] had not been consulted about its future in national terms. But, disregarding this question, what appears to be singularly naïve and stunningly ingenuous was the belief that Franco would accept "interposition" forces at the borders of Catalonia and the Basque Country, when he had already repealed the "Economic concert" of Vizcaya and Guipúzcoa June 23, 1937, and abolished the Statute of Catalonia, on April 5, 1938, after the conquest of Lleida.

The ultimate irony was that the fact that Catalan autonomy and the alleged "scandal of Catalan separatism" had been one of the reasons put forward by the coup participants in the summer of 1936 to unleash the Civil War in the first place.

Notes

1 This chapter with some minimal adaptation and modification is a translation into English of the Catalan version, of: J. Sánchez Cervelló, *¿Por qué hemos sido derrotados? Las divergencias republicanas y otras cuestiones*, Barcelona: Flor del Viento, 2006, pp. 196–220.

2 *La Correspondencia militar*, n. 7.048, 13-III-1901, p. 2.

3 "Carta de Manuel Irujo a Doroteo de Ziarritz, del Euzkadi Buru Batzar, Barcelona, 24-XII-1936". Cited in Arrien, G., Goiogana, I. *El primer exili dels bascos. Catalunya 1936–1939,* Barcelona–Bilbao: Fundació Trias Fargas/Fundación Sabino Arana, 2001, pp. 705–706.

4   A. Amezaga, *Manuel Irujo. Un hombre vasco,* Bilbao: Fundación Sabino Arana, 1999, p. 278.

5   B. de Riquer, *L'últim Cambó (1936–1947). La dreta catalanista durant la guerra civil i el franquisme,* Vic: Eumo, 1996, p. 64.

6   J. A. Parpal and J. M. Lladó, *Ferran Valls Taberner, un polític per a la cultura catalana,* Barcelona: Ariel, 1972, p. 262.

7   P. Bosch Gimpera, *Memòries,* Barcelona: Ed. 62, 1980, p. 274.

8   On the civil peace movement, see: A. Gonzàlez i Vilalta, *La tercera Catalunya (1936–1940),* Barcelona: Edicions del 1984, 2014.

9   Made responsible for confronting the information received from abroad, it was composed by seven agents of the third class and five auxiliaries directed by Mariano Gómez Emperador who depended on the "Servei de Seguretat Interior" under the authority of Dionisio Eroles of the CNT-FAI.

10 Archivo Histórico Nacional-Madrid (AHN). "Informe confidencial del Servei Informatiu de l'BEI", n.d., 15-I-1937, 2 pp. typed. Leg. 1791. Caixa 1. "Causa General".

11 In addition of the agents of Burgos, there were also those of the anarchists as well as Soviet espionage. See: S. Minev, *Las causas de la derrota de la República española,* Madrid: Miraguano, 2003, p. 259; also, to show the ease of infiltration: R. Doll Petit, *Els 'catalans de Gènova': Història de l'èxode i l'adhesió d'una classe dirigent en temps de Guerra,* Barcelona: Abadia de Montserrat, 2003, p. 176.

12 See: M. Heiberg and M. Ros Aguado, *La trama oculta de la guerra civil. Los servicios secretos de Franco, 1936–1945.* Barcelona: Crítica, 2006, pp. 101–140, and M. García Venero, *Historia del Nacionalismo Catalán.* Madrid: Ed. Nacional, 1966, vol. II, p. 42.

13 F. Cambó, *Meditacions,* Barcelona: Alpha, 1982, vol. I, p. 25.

14 Next to this institutional initiative, there was another, more or less official: the *"Comité Catalan pour la paix civile"*, created in Paris in February of 1937, promoted by Alfredo Mendizábal, full professor of the University of Oviedo, and by Joan B. Roca Caball, leader of UDC. From this starting point, various more peace committes arose: Spanish, French, British and Swiss. These entities had the support of an important nucleus of christian democrats like Georges Bernanos, Emmanuel Mounier, Jacques Maritain, Luigi Sturzo, François Mauriac, Elie Baussart, who not only did not give support to the Franco cause, but denounced his barbaric repression and brutal assassinations. See: Gonzàlez i Vilalta, A., *La tercera Catalunya, op. cit.*

15 AMTM, "Excmo. Sr. Lluís Companys", London, 9-II-1937, 1 p. typed.

16 AMTM, "Redactor jefe", s. l. [Barcelona], n.d. [11-II-1937], 1 p. typed.

17 G. Mir, *Aturar la guerra. Les Gestions secretes de Lluís Companys davant el govern britànic,* Barcelona: Proa, 2006, pp. 369–372.

18 For a vision of the whole of the contacts between Basque nationalists and the Franco authorities, see: C. M. Olazábal Estecha, *Negociaciones del PNV con Franco durante la Guerra Civil,* Bilbao: Fundación Popular de Estudios Vascos, 2014.

19 International Institut voor Sociale Geschiedenis, Amsterdam, "Informe acerca de las gestiones llevadas a cabo por determinados elementos con objeto de concretar un armisticio . . . ", Paris, 19-II-1937, 2 pp. typed. 005E.

20 "El Dr. Bosch i Gimpera en Praga". *La Vanguardia*, 21-V-1937, *La Vanguardia*, 11-VII-1937.

21 M. Azaña, *Memorias de guerra 1936–1939*, Barcelona: Grijalbo-Mondadori, 1996, vol. II, p. 121.

22 This refers to Joan Casanovas i Maristany, president of the Catalan Parliament. See J. Casanovas i Cuberta, *Joan Casanovas i Maristany, president del Parlament de Catalunya*, Barcelona: Publicacions de l'Abadia de Montserrat, 1996.

23 AHN-Madrid, "BI", Perpiñan, 4-IV-1937. 1 p. typed. "Causa General", Caixa 1791, Exp. 5.

24 M. Azaña, *Memorias de guerra, op. cit.*, vol. II, p. 176.

25 L. Mees, "Tan lejos, tan cerca. El Gobierno Vasco en Barcelona y las complejas relaciones entre el nacionalismo vasco y el catalán", *Historia Contemporánea*, n. 37, pp. 557–591.

26 A. Manent, *Josep Mª Espanya. Conseller de la Mancomunitat i de la Generalitat de Catalunya*, Barcelona: Dalmau, 1998, p. 73.

27 F. Soldevila, *Dietari de l'exili i del retorn*, Valencia: Ed. 3 i 4, 1995, p. 59.

28 *La Vanguardia*, 25-VII-1937.

29 L. Colomer, "La preparació de la independencia de Catalunya durant la guerra civil", *L'Avenç*, n. 73, (July–August 1984), pp. 36–44.

30 L. Mees, *op. cit.*, p. 565.

31 *La Vanguardia*, 6-XI-1937.

32 M. Ansó, *Yo fui ministro de Negrín,* Barcelona: Planeta, 1976, p. 207.

33 AMTM, "Excmo. Sr. Negrín", Barcelona, 21-I-1938, 5 pp. typed.

34 A. Cordón, *op. cit.*, pp. 339–340.

35 The information comes from Enric Roig, who was the delegate responsible for payments of the Generalitat de Catalunya in París. See:

L. Crusell, "Lluís Companys i Carme Ballester a França". *Avui*, 14-I-1979.

36 J. Zugazagoitia, *Guerra y vicisitudes de los españoles,* Barcelona: Tusquets, 2001, p. 470.

37 M. Azaña, *Memorias de guerra, op. cit.*, p. 399.

38 AHN-Madrid. "Excmo. Sr. Marcelino Pascua", Barcelona, 18-X-1938, 3 pp. typed. Fons M. Pascua, Caixa 1, Leg. 21.

39 M. Azaña, *Memorias de guerra, op. cit.*, p. 408.

40 C. Rivas Cherif, *Retrato de un desconocido. Vida de Manuel Azaña,* Mèxic D. F.: Oasis, 1961, p. 309.

41 Together with José Giral. Giral wrote *Año y medio de gestiones de canjes,* s. l. [Barcelona], n.d. [1938], explaining their activities.

42 AMTM, "Ministro de la República". Barcelona, 28-III-1938, 1 p. typed.

43 F. Mascarell, "Conversa amb Josep Mª Batista i Roca", *L' Avenç,* n. 7/8 (August–September 1978), p. 16.

44 Arxiu Nacional de Catalunya (ANC). "La tasca realitzada per la delegació catalana de London", Fons Josep Andreu Abelló, 22 pp. typed. Inventari 408, R 1396.

45 "La tasca realitzada per la delegació catalana de London", *op. cit.*

46 G. Mir, *op. cit.*, pp. 242–245.

47 G. Mir, *op. cit.*, p. 278.

48 The Basques presented a document that spoke of the requests in common but in name of the Basque people, and the Catalans did the same in the name of Catalan, even though the text and articles were identical. Therefore, the source used is Catalan, if it only cites Catalonia and, if it is the Basque text, it cites Euzkadi.

49 The Catalan memorandum can be consulted in L. Crusellas, "Franco no va voler la pau. Gestions de Batista i Roca a London". *Serra d'Or,* n. 232 (January 1979), pp. 15–18. And the Basque in the "Archivo del Nacionalismo Vasco – Fundación Sabino Arana" (ANV-FSA), GE-493-1.

50 ANV-FSA. "Memorandum", London, 28th July 1938, 4 pp. typed. GE – 493-1.

51 ANV-FSA. "As a consequence . . . ", s. l., 29th August 1938, 2 pp. typed. GE-493-1.

52 C. Pi i Sunyer, *La guerra 1936–1939. Memòries,* Barcelona: Pòrtic, 1986, pp. 170–173.

53 The map divided Spain into four groups: the regions of Castilian language, those of Catalan, including the capital, Valencia and Mallorca, the Basque area that included Navarre, and Galicia.

54 "Memorandum Presented to . . . ", London, 12-X-1938, 52 pp. typed.

55 P. Bosch i Gimpera, *op. cit.*, pp. 270–277.

56 ANC, Fons Josep Andreu Abelló, "La tasca realitzada per la delegació catalana de London", *op. cit.*.

57 "Suggestions brought to the consideration", London, 22 XI-1938, 4 pp. typed.

58 "La tasca realitzada per la delegació catalana de London", *op. cit.*

59 The memorandum concluded with an annex that was to serve as the base of discussions of the Peace Conference. The steps were divided into those that had to be accepted previously to the convocation and those that were of immediate application (suspension of hostilities, amnesty, organization of the police and public order); those referring to the provisional regime based on the constitution of tribunals, demilitariza-tion, the behavior of the army, the return of refugees, constitution of the civil government, and transitory periods in diverse areas of the Administration: municipal, autonomous and of the state, and in the establishment of basic liberties. In the definitive regime were to be established the bases of the future constitution that would be subject to a plebiscite. ANV-FSA. "As a contribution to the task . . . ", s. l., n.d. [7.XII.1938], 14 pp. typed.

60 ANV-FSA. "Memorandum", London, 14-II-1939, 3 pp. typed.

61 F. Vilanova, F. (ed.), *Viure el primer exili: cartes britàniques de Pere Bosch Gimpera i Carles Pi i Sunyer (1939–1940)*, 2 ed., Barcelona: Fundació Pi i Sunyer, 2004, and Arxiu Carlos Esplá, "El futuro de Cataluña y Euzkadi". London, 18-I-1941, 2 pp. typed.

62 A. Checa Godoy, *Prensa y partidos políticos durante la II República*, Salamanca: Universidad de Salamanca, 1989, p. 92.

Bibliography

A., Zondergeld, *De Friese beweging in het tijdvak der beide Wereldoorlogen*, Leeuwarden, De Tille, 1978.

Abad de Santillán, D., *Por qué perdimos la guerra*, Barcelona, Plaza & Janés, 1977.

Almirall, V. and Pich i Mitjana, J. (ed.), *Antologia de textos*, Barcelona, Generalitat de Catalunya, Institut d'Estudis Autonòmics, 2011.

Alvarez Junco, J., *La Comuna en España*, Madrid: Siglo XXI, 1971.

Amezaga, A., *Manuel Irujo. Un hombre vasco*, Bilbao: Fundación Sabino Arana, 1999.

Anfuso, F., *Roma, Berlino, Salò (1936–1945)*, Milan, Garzanti, 1950.

Ansó, M., *Yo fui ministro de Negrín*, Barcelona: Planeta, 1976.

Armstrong, H. C., *Grey Wolf: Mustafa Kemal: An Intimate Study of a Dictator*, Harmondsworth (UK): Penguin, 1940.

Arrien, G., Goiogana, I., *El primer exili dels bascos. Catalunya 1936–1939*, Barcelona-Bilbao: Fundació Trias Fargas/Fundación Sabino Arana, 2001.

Arzalier, R., *Les perdants. La dérive fasciste des mouvements autonomistes et indé-pendantistes au XXe siècle*, Paris: La Découverte, 1990.

Axis plans in the Mediterranean: An analysis of German geopolitical ideas on Italy, France, Balearic Islands, Gibraltar, Catalonia and Spain, London, London General Press, 1939.

Azaña, M., *Causas de la guerra de España*, Madrid, Diario Público, 2011.

Bachstein, M. K., *Wenzel Jacksch und die sudetendeutsche Sozialdemokratie*, Munich/Viena: Oldenbourg, 1974.

Bagehot, W., *The English Constitution* (1867), Brighton, Chicago, Toronto: Sussex Academic Press, 1997.

Batail, J.-F., *Les destinées de la Norvège moderne (1814–2005)*. Paris: Michel de Maule, 2005.

Beer, M. and Dyroff, S. (ed.), *Politische Strategien nationaler Minderheiten in der Zwischenkriegszeit*, Munich: Oldenbourg, 2014.

Belforte, F., *La Guerra Civile in Spagna. Gli interventi stranieri nella Spagna russa*, v. II, Rome, Istituto per gli studi di politica internazionale, 1938.

Benoist-Méchin, J., *Mustapha Kemal ou la mort d'un empire*, Paris, Albin Michel, 1954.

Beramendi, J.G. and Máiz, R. (ed.)., *Los nacionalismos en la España de la II República*, Madrid: Siglo XXI/Consello da Cultura Galega, 1991.

Berber, F., *La política europea desde 1933 a 1938 reflejada en los documentos de Praga*, Berlin, Publicaciones del Instituto Alemán para Investigaciones de Política Exterior, [1940?].

Bethell, L. (ed.), *Central America since Independence*, New York: Cambridge University Press, 1992.

Bernieri, C., *Mussolini alla conquista delle Baleari*, Barcelona, CNT-FAI, 1937.

Biagini, A. Motta, G. (eds), *Empires and Nations from the Eighteenth to the Twentieth Century,* Newcastle-upon-Tyne (UK), Cambridge Scholars Publishing, 2014.

Bonnet, G., *Fin d'une Europe. De Munich à la guerre*, Geneva, Cheval Ailé, 1948.

Borzoni, G., *Renato Prunas diplomatico (1892–1951)*, Catanzaro, Rubbettino, 2004.

Bosch Gimpera, P., *Memòries*, Barcelona: Ed. 62, 1980.

Bourne, K., Cameron Watt, D. (ed.), *British Documents on Foreign Affairs: Reports and papers from the Foreign Office confidential print. Part II, From the First to the Second World War. Series F, Europe, 1919–1939, v. 27, Spain, July 1936–January 1940*, Frederick, Md., University Publications of America, 1990.

Brand, J., *The National Movement in Scotland*, London: Routledge & Kegan Paul, 1978.

Brissa, J., *La guerra de los Balcanes*, Barcelona, Maucci, 1913.

Broué, P., *Révolution en Allemagne (1917–1923),* Paris: Éditions de Minuit, 1971; Paschen, J., «*Wenn Hamburg brennt, brent die Welt*». *Der kommunistische Griff nach der Macht mi October 1923,* Frankfurt am Main: Peter Lang, 2010.

Brubaker, *Nationalism Reframed. Nationhood and the National Question in the New Europe*, Cambridge: Cambridge UP, 1996.

Cambó, F., *Meditacions*, Barcelona: Alpha, 1982.

Campos Matos, S. and Bogotte Chorão, L. (coords.), *Península Ibérica. Nações e transnacionalidade entre dois séculos (XIX e XX)*, Vila Nova de Famalicão, Edições Humus, 2017.

Cardini, F. and Valzania, S., *La scintilla: Quando l'Italia, con la guerra di Libia, fece scoppiare il primo conflitto mondiale,* Milan: Mondadori, 2014.

Carney, S., *Breiz Atao! Mordrel, Delaporte, Lainé, Fouéré: Une mystique nationale (1901–1948)*, Rennes: Presses Universitaires de Rennes, 2015.

Carrère d'Encausse, H., *Le Grand Défi: bolcheviks et nations, 1917–1930*, Paris: Flammarion, 1987.

Carrère d'Encausse, H., *Réforme et Révolution chez les musulmans de l'empire russe,* Paris: Presses de la Fondation nationale des sciences politiques, 1966.

Casanovas i Cuberta, J., *Joan Casanovas i Maristany, president del Parlament de Catalunya*, Barcelona : Publicacions de l'Abadia de Montserrat, 1996.

Castelao, A. R., *Sempre en Galiza*, Buenos Aires: Ed. As Burgas, 1944.

Cataruzza, M., Dyroff, S. and Langewiesche, D. (eds.), *Territorial Revisionism and the Allies of Germany in the Second World War: Goals, Expectations, Practices*, Oxford/New York: Berghahn, 2012.

Checa Godoy, A., *Prensa y partidos políticos durante la II República*, Salamanca: Universidad de Salamanca, 1989.

Church, C. H. and Head, R. C., *A Concise History of Switzerland,* Cambridge (UK): Cambridge University Press, 2013.

Ciano, G., *L'Europa verso la catastrofe*, Milan, Mondadori, 1948.

Clarke, C., *The Sleepwalkers: How Europe Went to War in 1914*, New York: Harper Perennial, 2012.

Cornwell, J., *El Papa de Hitler. La verdadera historia de Pío XII*, Barcelona: Planeta, 2000.

Corsini, U. and Zaffi, D. (ed.), *Die Minderheiten zwischen den beiden Weltkriegen*, Berlin: Duncker & Humblot, 1997.

Cortada, W., *A City in War: American Views on Barcelona and the Spanish Civil War, 1936–1939*, Wilmington, Scholarly Resources, 1985.

Coverdale, J., *La Intervención fascista en la Guerra Civil española*, Madrid, Alianza, 1979.

Crankshaw, E., *Bismarck,* London, Macmillan (1981). pp. 181–183.

Cross, M. F. and Williams, D. (eds.), *The French Experience from Republic to Monarchy, 1792–1814, New Dawns in Politics, Knowledge and Culture*, Basingstoke (UK), Palgrave-Macmillan, 2000.

Davies, H. D., *The Welsh Nationalist Party 1925–1945: A Call to Nationhood*, Cardiff: University of Wales Press, 1983.

Davies, N., *White Eagle, Red Star: The Polish–Soviet War, 1919–20*, London: Pimlico, 2003.

De La Villa, A. and Vivero, A. (prologue of Rodrigo Soriano), *Cómo cae un trono (la revolución en Portugal)*, Madrid: Renacimiento, 1910.

Dedijer, V., *The Road to Sarajevo,* New York: Simon & Schuster, 1966.

Denéchère, Y., *Jean Herbette (1878–1960). Journaliste et ambassadeur*, Paris, Ministère des Affaires étrangères, 2003.

Denéchère, Y., *La politique espagnole de la France de 1931 à 1936. Une pratique française de rapports inégaux*, Paris, L'Harmattan, 1999.

Derry, T. K., *A Short History of Norway*. London: Allen & Unwin, 1968.

Dez anos de Política Externa (1936–1947), a nação portuguesa e a segunda guerra mundial, Lisbon, Ministério dos Negócios Estrangeiros, Imprensa Nacional, 1961.

Documents Diplomatiques Français (DDF), 1932–1939, 2ª Série (1936–1939), Tome VIII (17 Janvier–20 Mars 1938), Imprimerie Nationale, 1973, Paris.

Doll Petit, R., *Els 'catalans de Gènova': Història de l'èxode i l'adhesió d'una classe dirigent en temps de Guerra*, Barcelona: Abadia de Montserrat, 2003.

Donaldson, R. and Nogee, J. L., *The Foreign Policy of Russia. Changing Systems, Enduring Interests*, New York/London: M. E. Sharpe, 2005.

Duroselle, J. B., *La décadence, 1932–1939*, Paris, Imp. Nationalle, 1979.

Dyer, P., *Citizen Emperor: Napoleon in Power, 1799–1815*, London, Bloomsbury, 2014.

Eden, A., *Facing the Dictators*, Boston, Houghton Mifflin, 1962, p. 487.

Ehrenburg, I., *España república de trabajadores*, Barcelona, Crítica, 1976 [1932].

Ehrenburg, I., *Gentes, años, vidas. Memorias*, Barcelona: Planeta, 1985.

Elton, Lord, *Imperial Commonwealth*, London: Collins, 1945.

Estat Català, *La Catalogne rebelle,* Paris: Agence Mondiale de Librairie, 1927.

Estelrich, J., *La qüestió de les minories nacionals i les vies del Dret*, Barcelona: Catalònia, 1929.

Falanga, G., *L'avamposto di Mussolini nel Reich di Hitler. La politica italiana a Berlino (1933–1945)*, Milan, Marco Tropea Editore, 2011 [2008].

Faldella, E., *Venti mesi di guerra in Spagna (luglio 1936-febbraio 1938),* Florence, Felice Le Monnier, 1938.

Festorazzi, R., *Laval-Mussolini. L'impossibile Asse*, Milan, Mursia, 2003.

Fink, C., *Defending the Rights of Others: The Great Powers, the Jews, and International Minority Protection, 1878–1938*, Cambridge: Cambridge UP, 2004.

Fioravanzo, G., *Basi navali nel mondo*, Milan, Istituto per gli Studi di Politica Internazionale, 1936.

Fischer, F., *Germany's Aims in the First World War,* New York: W. W. Norton, 1961.

Fontana, S. (ed.), *Il fascismo e le autonomie locali*, Bologna: Il Mulino, 1973 Trencsényi, B. and Kopecek, M. (eds.), *Discourses of collective identity in Central and Southeast Europe (1770–1945): Texts and commentaries*, Budapest: CEU Press, 2010, vol. 3.

Friend, J. W., *Stateless Nations: Western European Regional Nationalisms and the Old Nations*, Basingstok: Palgrave-Macmillan, 2012.

Fuentes, M. M., Quijada, J. M. and Sánchez, N., *Correspondència del Dr. Francesc d'Assís Vidal i Barraquer Cardenal Arquebisbe de Tarragona amb Secretaria d'Estat de la Santa Seu (1936–1939)*, València, Tirant, 2015.

García Venero, M., *Historia del Nacionalismo Catalán*, Madrid: Ed. Nacional, 1966, vol. II.

Glenny, M., *The Balkans: Nationalism, War, and the Great Powers, 1804–2011*, New York: Penguin, 2012.

González Calleja, E., *La España de Primo de Rivera: La modernización autoritaria, 1923–1930*, Madrid: Alianza, 2005.

Gonzàlez i Vilalta, A., *Cataluña bajo vigilancia. El Consulado italiano y el Fascio de Barcelona (1930–1943)*, Valencia: PUV, 2008.

Gonzàlez i Vilalta, A., *Cataluña y Barcelona en la crisis europea (1931–1939). ¿Irlanda española, peón francés o URSS mediterránea?*, Maçanet de la Selva, Gregal, 2019, pending publication.

Gonzàlez i Vilalta, A., *La tercera Catalunya (1936–1940),* Barcelona: Edicions del 1984, 2014.

Gonzàlez i Vilalta, A., López Esteve, M. and Ucelay-Da Cal, E. (ed.), *6 d'octubre. La desfeta de la revolució catalanista de 1934*, Barcelona: Base, 2014.

Graham, M. T. Jr., *New Governments of Central Europe*, New York: Holt, 1924.

Graham, M. T. Jr., *New Governments of Eastern Europe*, New York: Holt, 1927.

Gretton, P., *El factor olvidado. La Marina Británica y la Guerra Civil Española*, Madrid, Editorial San Martín, 1984.

Griffith, A., *The Resurrection of Hungary* [1904], Dublin, UCD Press, 2003.

Guinart, M., *Memòries d'un militant catalanista*, Barcelona, PAMSA, 1988.

Heiberg, M., and Ros Aguado, M., *La trama oculta de la guerra civil. Los servicios secretos de Franco. 1936–1945*, Barcelona: Crítica, 2006.

Hermannsson, B., *Understanding Nationalism: Studies in Icelandic Nationalism, 1800–2000*, Stockholm: University of Stockholm, 2005.

Hermans, T., Vos, L. and Wils, L. (ed.), *The Flemish Movement. A Documentary History, 1780–1990*, London: Bloomsbury, 2015.

Hiden, J., *Defender of Minorities. Paul Schiemann, 1876–1944*, Londron: Hurst, 2004.

Holt, E., *Protest in Arms. The Irish Troubles, 1916–1923,* New York: Coward-McCann, 1961.

Hopkinson, M., *Green Against Green: The Irish Civil War*, Dublin, Gill, 2004.

Hopkinson, M., *The War of Independence*, Dublin, McGill–Queen's University Press, 2004.

Horrabin, J. F., *Atlas of Current Affairs*, London: Gollancz, 1934.

Hroch, M., *Das Europa der Nationen. Die moderne Nationsbildung im europäischen Vergleich*, Göttingen: Vandenhoeck & Ruprecht, 2005.

Hroch, M., *On the National Interest. Demands and Goals of European National*

Movements of the Nineteenth Century: A Comparative Perspective, Prague: Art Faculty, Charles University, 2000.

Hummel, H. and Siewert, W., *La Méditerranée*, Paris, Payot, 1937.

Jacob, J. E., *Hills of Conflict. Basque Nationalism in France*, Reno: Univ. of Nevada Press, 1994.

Kee, R., *The Bold Fenian Men: The Green Flag*, vol. 2. Northhampton (MA): Interlink Publishing, 1983.

Keogh, D., *Ireland and Europe, 1919–1948*, Dublin, Gill & Macmillan, Limited, 1988.

Kinross, P., *Ataturk: A Biography of Mustafa Kemal, Father of Modern Turkey,* New York, William Morrow, 1964.

Kitromilides, P. M. (ed.), *Eleftherios Venizelos: The Trials of Statesmanship,* Edinburgh (UK): Edinburgh University Press, 2008.

Kowalsky, D., *La Unión Soviética y la Guerra Civil Española,* Barcelona: Crítica, 2003.

Kreins, J.-M., *Histoire du Luxembourg*, Paris, PUF, 1996.

Krivitsky, G. G., *Yo, Jefe del Servicio Secreto Militar Soviético*, Guadalajara (Mexico), Nos editorial, 1945.

Lagardelle, H., *Mission à Rome. Mussolini*, Paris, Plon, 1955.

Lamb, R., *Mussolini e gli inglesi*, Milan, Tea, 2002.

Leach, D., *Fugitive Ireland. European Minority Nationalists and Irish Political Asylum, 1937–2008*, Dublin: Four Courts Press, 2009.

Les Archives Secrètes de la Wilhelmstrasse, III. L'Allemagne et la Guerre Civile Espagnole (1936–1939), Paris, Plon, 1952.

Llorens i Vila, J., *Catalanisme i moviments nacionalistes contemporanis, 1885–1901: missatges a Irlanda, Creta i Finlàndia,* Barcelona, Dalmau, 1988.

Lynch, J., *Las revoluciones hispanoamericanas, 1808–1826*, Barcelona: Editorial Ariel, 2008; also, by the same author: J. Lynch, *Caudillos en Hispanoamérica 1800–1850,* Madrid: Editorial Mapfre, 1994.

Lyttelton, A., *The Seizure of Power: Fascism in Italy 1919–1929*, London: Weidenfeld & Nicolson, 1973.

Máiz, R. and Requejo, F. (eds.), *Democracy, Nationalism and Multiculturalism*, London: Frank Cass, 2005.

Malcolm, N., *Bosnia: A Short History,* London: Pan, 1994.

Mallinson, W., *Cyprus: A Modern History,* London: I. B. Tauris, 2009.

Manela, E., *The Wilsonian Moment: Self-determination and the International Origins of Anticolonial Nationalism*, Oxford: Oxford UP, 2007.

Manent, A., *Josep Mª Espanya. Conseller de la Mancomunitat i de la Generalitat de Cataluny*a, Barcelona: Dalmau, 1998.

Mango, A., *Ataturk: The Biography of the Founder of Modern Turkey,* New York: The Overlook Press, 2002.

Maspons i Anglasell, *Els Drets de ciutadania i la Societat de Nacions*, Reus: Gràfics Navas, 1927.

Massot i Muntaner, J., *Arconovaldo Bonacorsi, el conde Rossi*, Barcelona, Pamsa 2017.

Massot i Muntaner, J., *El cònsol Alan Hillgarth i les Illes Balears (1936–1939)*, Barcelona, Pamsa, 1995.

Massot i Muntaner, J., *Menorca dins del dominó mediterrani (1936–1939)*, Barcelona, Publicacions de l'Abadia de Montserrat, 2008.

Massot i Muntaner, J., *Vida i miracles del "Conde Rossi". Mallorca, juliol-desembre 1936/Màlaga, gener-febrer 1937*, Barcelona, Pamsa, 1988.

Mayer, J., *The Persistence of the Old Regime: Europe to the Great War*, New York, Pantheon, 1981.

Médioni, M-A., *El Cantón de Cartagena*, Madrid: Siglo XXI, 1979.

Meléndez y Solá, P., *La unidad hispánica. España y Cataluña (1892–1939)*, Barcelona, without publisher, 1946.

Mevius, M. (ed.), *The Communist Quest for National Legitimacy in Europe, 1918–1989*, London: Routledge, 2010.

Minev, S., *Las causas de la derrota de la República española*, Madrid: Miraguano, 2003.

Mir, G., *Aturar la guerra. Les gestions secretes de Lluís Companys davant del govern britànic*, Barcelona, Proa, 2006.

Miravitlles, J. [R. Batalla, ed.], *Veritats sobre la Guerra Civil Espanyola*, Barcelona, Editorial Base, 2015.

Miravitlles, J., *Episodis de la Guerra Civil Espanyola*, Barcelona: Pòrtic, 1972.

Miravitlles, J., *Los comunicados secretos de Franco, Hitler y Mussolini*, Barcelona, Plaza & Janés, 1977.

Moradiellos, E., *La perfidia de Albión. El Gobierno británico y la guerra civil española*, Madrid, Siglo XXI, 1996.

Moradiellos, E., *Negrín. Una biografía de la figura más difamada de la España del siglo XX,* Barcelona, Península, 2006.

Napo, F., *1907, la révolte des vignerons*, Tolouse: Privat, 1971.

Neila, J. L., *España y el Mediterráneo en el siglo XX,* Madrid, Sílex, 2011.

Neila, J. L., *La 2ª República española y el mediterráneo. España ante el desarme y la seguridad colectiva*, Madrid, Dilema, 2006.

Nello, P., *Dino Grandi*, Bologna, Il Mulino, 2003.

Nordstrom, B. J., *The History of Sweden,* Westport (CT): Greenwood 2002.

Núñez Seixas, X. M. & Storm, E. (eds.), *Regionalism and Modern Europe. Identity Construction and Movements from 1890 to the Present Day*, London et al.: Bloomsbury, 2019.

Núñez Seixas, X. M. (ed.), *From Empires to Nations: Nationality Questions during the First World War and its Aftermath*, Leiden: Brill, 2019 (pending publication).

nales y la política internacional en Europa, 1914–1939, Madrid: Akal, 2001.

Núñez Seixas, X. M., *Internacionalitzant el nacionalisme. El catalanisme polític i la qüestió de les minories nacionals a Europa (1914–1936)*, Catarroja/València: Afers/ Universitat de València, 2010.

Núñez Seixas, X. M., *Movimientos nacionalistas en Europa. Siglo XX*, Madrid: Síntesis, 2004 [2nd ed.].

Olazábal Estecha, C. M., *Negociaciones del PNV con Franco durante la Guerra Civil*, Bilbao: Fundación Popular de Estudios Vascos, 2014.

Ortmann, H., *Rheinischer Separatismus und Westdeutsche Republik: zu den politischen Zielen im Rheinland in den Jahren von 1918 bis 1923*, Hildesheim: Universitätsverlag Hildesheim, 2016.

Page, S. W., *The Formation of the Baltic States. A Study of the Effects of Great Power Politics upon the Emergence of Lithuania, Latvia, and Estonia*, Cambridge (MA): Harvard University Press, 1959.

Pàmies, T., *Quan érem Capitans (Memòries d'aquella guerra)*, Barcelona, Dopesa, 1974.

Parpal, J. A. and Lladó, J. M., *Ferran Valls Taberner, un polític per a la cultura catalana*, Barcelona: Ariel, 1972.

Pauser, F., *Spaniens Tor Zum Mittelmeer Und Die Katalanische Frage*, Lepizig-Berlin, Teubner, 1938.

Perkins, K., *A History of Modern Tunisia*, Cambridge (UK): Cambridge University Press, 2004.

Pocock, J. G. A., *The Ancient Constitution and the Feudal Law: a study of English Historical Thought in the Seventeenth Century*, Cambridge: Cambridge University Press, 1987 (2nd ed.).

Portela Valladares, M., *Memorias*, Madrid, Alianza Editorial, 1988.

Prat de la Riba, E., *La nacionalitat catalana*, Barcelona, Tip. L'Anuari de l'Exportació, 1906.

Primo de Rivera, J. A., *Textos de doctrina política*, Madrid, Delegación Nacional de la Sección Femenina de F.E.T. y de las J.O.N.S., 1966.

Pruszyński, K., *En la España roja*, Barcelona, Alba, 2007.

Puig Campillo, A., *El Cantón Murciano*, Murcia: Editora Regional de Murcia, 1986.

Puigsech, J., *Falsa leyenda del Kremlin. El consulado y la URSS en la Guerra Civil española*, Madrid, Biblioteca Nueva, 2014.

Puigsech, J., *La Revolució Russa i Catalunya*, Vic: Eumo, 2017.

Quartararo, R., *Roma tra Londra e Berlino. La politica estera fascista dal 1930 al 1940*, Rome, Jouvence, 2001 [1980] v. I..

Quilici, N., *Spagna*, Rome, Istituto Nazionale di Cultura Fascista, 1938.

Rabassa Massons, J., *Josep Dencàs i Puigdollers. El nacionalisme radical a la Generalitat*, Barcelona, Rafael Dalmau editor, 2006.

Radosh, R., Habeck, M. R. and Sevostianov, G., *Spain Betrayed: The Soviet Union in the Spanish Civil War*, London/New Haven: Yale University Press, 2001.

Raguer, H., *Arxiu de la l'Església catalana durant la guerra civil. I. Juliol-desembre 1936*, Barcelona, PAMSA, 2003.

Rhodes, A., *El Vaticano en la era de los dictadores*, Barcelona, Euros, 1975.

Riquer, B. de, *L'últim Cambó (1936–1947). La dreta catalanista durant la guerra civil i el franquisme*, Vic: Eumo, 1996.

Rivas Cherif, C., *Retrato de un desconocido. Vida de Manuel Azaña*, II, Barcelona, Grijalbo, 1979.

Roosevelt, T., *The Naval War of 1812*, New York, G.P. Putnam & Sons, 1900.

Roseman, M., *The Villa, The Lake, The Meeting: Wannsee and the Final Solution*, London: Allen Lane, 2002.

Rothschild, J., *East-Central Europe between the Two World Wars*, Seattle/London: Univ. of Washington Press, 1992.

Rothschild, J., *Pilsudski's Coup d'Etat*, New York: Columbia University Press, 1966.

Rougerie, J., *La Commune de 1871*, Paris: PUF, 2014.

Rovira i Virgili, A., *Catalunya i la República*, Barcelona: Undarius, 1977 [1931].

Rubió i Tudurí, M., N. Mart [N. M. Rubió i Tudurí], *Catalunya amb Europa. Més enllà del separatisme*, Barcelona, Arc de Berà, 1932.

Rubió i Tudurí, N. M., *Barcelona 1936–1939*, Barcelona, PAMSA, 2002.

Rubió i Tudurí, N. M., *Lettre à un patriote français. Vers la germanisation de la Catalogne*, Paris, impr. de Lecoeur, 1938.

Ryle Dwyer, T., *The Squad and the Intelligence Operations of Michael Collins*, Douglas Village (Cork), Mercier Press, 2005.

Sabatier de Lachadenède, R., *La Marina Francesa y la Guerra Civil de España (1936–1939)*, Madrid, Ministerio de Defensa, 2001.

Sánchez Cervelló, J., *¿Por qué hemos sido derrotados? Las divergències republicanes y otras cuestiones*, Barcelona, Flor del Viento, 2006.

Saz, I., *Mussolini contra la II República*, Valencia, Alfons el Magnànim, 1986.

Schauff, F., *La victoria frustrada. La Unión Soviética, la Internacional comunista y la Guerra Civil Española*, Barcelona: Debate, 2008.

Seignobos, C., *Les aspirations autonomistes en Europe. Albanie, Alsace-Lorraine, Catalogne, Finlande, Iles Grecques, Irlande, Macedoine, Pologne, Serbo-Croatie*, Paris: Librairie Félix Alcan, 1913.

Service, R., *Historia de Rusia en el siglo XX,* Barcelona: Crítica, 2000.

Seton-Watson, H., *Eastern Europe between the Wars, 1918–1941,* New York: Harper & Brothers, 1948.

Soldevila, F., *Dietari de l'exili i del retorn,* Valencia: Ed. Climent, 1995.

Stewart, A. T. Q., *The Ulster Crisis, Resistance to Home Rule, 1912–14,* London: Faber & Faber, 1967.

Taylor, A. J. P., *The Struggle for Mastery in Europe 1848–1918.* Oxford (UK): Oxford University Press, 1971.

Ther, P. and Sundhaussen, H. (eds.), *Regionale Bewegungen und Regionalismen in europäischen Zwischenräumen seit der Mitte des 19 Jahrhunderts,* Marburg: Herder-Institut, 2003.

Timmermann, H. (ed.), *Nationalismus und Nationalbewegung in Europa, 1914–1945,* Berlín: Duncker & Humblot, 1999.

Tökés, R. L., *Béla Kun and the Hungarian Soviet Republic: The Origins and Role of the Communist Party of Hungary in the Revolutions of 1918–1919,* New York: Praeger, 1967.

Tuchman, B., *Los cañones de agosto,* Barcelona: Península, 2004.

Tur, V., *Plancia Ammiraglio,* v. 3, Rome, Canesi, 1963.

Ucelay-Da Cal, E., *Breve historia del separatismo catalán: del apego a lo catalán al anhelo de la secesion,* Barcelona Ediciones B-Penguin Random House, 2018.

Ucelay-Da Cal, E., *El imperialismo catalán. Prat de la Riba, Cambó, D'Ors y la conquista moral de España,* Barcelona, Edhasa, 2003.

Ucelay-Da Cal, E., Gonzàlez i Vilalta, A., (ed.), *Contra Companys, 1936. La frustración nacionalista ante la Revolución,* Valencia, PUV, 2012.

Ucelay-Da Cal, E., Gonzàlez Vilalta, A., Núñez Seixas, X. M., (eds.), *El catalanisme davant del feixisme (1919–2018),* Maçanet de la Selva, Gregal, 2018.

Ucelay-Da Cal, E., *La Catalunya populista: imatge, cultura i política en l'etapa republicana, 1931–1939,* Barcelona: La Magrana, 1982.

Upton, A. F., *The Finnish Revolution 1917–1918,* Minneapolis (MI): University of Minnesota Press, 1980.

Vatikiotis, P. J., *The History of Modern Egypt: From Muhammad Ali to Mubarak,* London: Weidenfeld & Nicolson, 1991.

Vázquez Sans, J., *España y Francia. Meditaciones de actualidad,* Barcelona, Imp. Ángel Ortega, Barcelona, 1939.

Veiter, T., *Nationale Autonomie. Rechtstheorie und Verwirklichung mi positiven Recht,* Viena/Leipzig: Braumüller, 1938.

Vilanova, F. (ed.), *Viure el primer exili: cartes britàniques de Pere Bosch Gimpera i Carles Pi i Sunyer (1939–1940),* 2 ed., Barcelona: Fundació Pi i Sunyer, 2004.

Viñas, Á., *Franco, Hitler y el estallido de la Guerra Civil. Antecedentes y conse-cuencias*, Madrid, Alianza, 2001.

Walder, D., *The Chanak Affair,* London, Hutchinson, 1969.

Wheeler, D., *A Ditadura Militar Portuguesa (1926–1933)*, Lisboa: Europa-América, 1986.

Wheeler-Bennett, J., *The Nemesis of Power: German Army in Politics, 1918–1945.* New York: Palgrave-Macmillan, 2005.

Yvia-Croce, Y., *Vingt années de corsisme, 1920–1939. Chronique corse de l'entre-deux guerres*, Ajaccio: Editions Cyrnos et Méditerranée, 1979.

Zamoyski, A., *Warsaw 1920: Lenin's Failed Conquest of Europe,* London: HarperCollins, 2008.

The Editor and Contributors

Arnau Gonzàlez i Vilalta, editor of this volume, was born in Barcelona in 1980. He is tenured professor at the Universitat Autònoma de Barcelona, specializing in the history of Catalan nationalism, with a particular interest in the detailed interworking of backdoor political and media channels: how to use journalistic campaigns as tools of influence, how to take advantage of opportunities offered by consular relations, how to make and sustain contacts implied in informal diplomacy by Catalan figures of influence. And indeed, how to take advantage of rare access to international policy-making debate among the powers. Gonzàlez i Vilalta is the author author of fifteen books, including several studies of Catalan president Companys in the 1930s. One of his early works was *Cataluña bajo vigilancia: El consulado italiano y el fascio de Barcelona, 1930–1943* (in Castilian Spanish, 2009), which detailed Italian consular and community activity in the Catalan port city. Among his latest works in Catalan, his pioneering study *Amb ulls estrangers. Quan Catalunya es preocupa per Europa. Diplomàcia i premsa durant la Guerra Civil* (in Catalan, 2014) was devoted to press coverage of Catalan issues in a crisis period. His *Cataluña y Barcelona en la crisis europea (1931–1939). ¿Irlanda española, URSS mediterránea o peón francés?* is forthcoming in 2020. His current work is the study of French and Argentine diplomacy during the 1930s.

Future research plans include an analysis of the French view of Franco's regime and the implications there of to the Basque terrorist phenomenon (ETA). Arnau Gonzàlez i Vilalta and Professor Ucelay-Da Cal have worked in collaboration on matters such as the failed 1936 coup attempt against Catalan President Companys in November 1936 (*Contra Companys 1936*, 2012, in Castilian Spanish). Together, they wrote a key study of the relevant Catalan politician, *Joan Lluhí i Vallescà* (in Catalan, 2017). And in collaboration with Nuñez Seixas, in 2018 together they published a contributory study in Catalan on the failed role of Fascism in Catalan political nationalism, *El Catalanisme davant del feixisme (1919–2018)*.

Enric Ucelay-Da Cal, translator of this volume, was born in 1948 in New York City, the son of Spanish Republican exiles. His father's political evolution from Galician-style communism, his later adaptation to U.S. anti-communism, and his pioneering enthusiasm for "reintegrationism" (the use of Portuguese-style vocabulary and grammar in written Galician), with an eye to the dream of incorporating Galicia into Portugal, as well as his right-wing supports in Conservative Portuguese society, left Ucelay-Da Cal with a lifetime fascination for the vagaries of nationalism. Ucelay-Da Cal studied at Bard College in New York State and did his doctorate at Columbia University. For many years he taught History at the Universitat Autònoma de Barcelona, and later was invited to join the Humanities department of the Universitat Pompeu Fabra, of which he still remains Emeritus Professor. He is the author of infuential works, such as *La Catalunya populista* (1982) and *El imperialismo catalán* (2003, in Castilian), as well as numerous academic articles in these and other languages (a large number of which which may be accessed in pdf format at <enricucelaydacal.weebly.com>). He has taught outside Spain, notably at Duke University, and Venice International University. He lives with his wife in Barcelona.

Xosé M. Núñez Seixas, born in Ourense in 1966, obtained his PhD from the European University Institute in Florence and is currently Professor of Modern History at the University of Santiago de Compostela, in Galicia, where he resides, together with his family. Between 2012 and 2017 he taught at the Ludwig Maximilian University in Munich. He has published books and articles on the comparative history of nationalist movements and national and regional identities, on the influence of overseas migration from Spain and Galicia to Latin America, and on the social impact of modern war and the experiences of armed conflict in the twentieth century, in particular of Spaniards. His most recent books are *Patriotas transnacionales* (in Castilian Spanish, 2019) and

Die bewegte Nation. Der spanische Nationalgedanke 1808–2019 (in German, 2019).

Josep Puigsech, born in 1972, is professor of Contemporary History at the Universitat Autònoma de Barcelona. His speciality is the study of the relation between Spain – and especially Catalonia - with Russia during the Soviet period, especially during the period 1917 to 1949. The international dimension of Spanish and especially Catalan communismn is a prime focus of his research work. Professor Puigsech is the author of numerous books, including *Falsa leyenda del Kremlin: El consulado y la URSS en la Guerra Civil española* (in Spanish, 2014), and most recently, *La revolució russa i Catalunya* (2017). He has written many articles devoted to the Partit Socialista Unificat de Catalunya (the United Socialist Party, or PSUC, which was related to the Communist International), and its complex relation to the Komintern. His current research involves British responses to Spanish–Soviet relations in the twentieth century.

Josep Sánchez Cervelló, born in Flix, on the Ebro River in 1958, is a student of Spanish Contemporary History and is Dean of the Faculty of Humanities at the Universitat Rovira i Virgili in Tarragona. Unusually for a Spanish-trained historian, Professor Sánchez Cervelló began by being specializng in the History of Portugal, where he prepared his PhD thesis on the Portuguese revolution of 1974 and the influence of Portuguese events on the Spanish Transition from, in his terms, 1961 to 1976. Professor Sánchez Cervelló has retained his formative curiosity in Lusitanian matters and has published on the Contemporary History of Africa and the Portuguese colonies, including Mozambique. On the Spanish field he has written about the Second Republic of 1931-1936, the Civil War and Republican Exile. His scholarly investigations include the secret negotiations to end the conflict in a manner favourable to Catalan nationalist interests, which came to naught. Interested in the *longue durée* of popular politics he has worked on the nineteeth-century resistance to the restoration of the Bourbons in 1874. And given his birthplace, his research has led him to the civic implications of local strife resulting from the momentuous battle of the Ebro in 1938. A particular research interest relates to the presence of foreign volunteers of the International Brigades in the abundant common graves that still remain on Catalan waysides some eighty years after the Spanish Civil War was formally closed.

Index